NEW YORK RE

CLASSICS

# CLASSIC CRIMES

WILLIAM ROUGHEAD (1870–1952) was born in Edinburgh, where he studied law and became an expert on criminology. Between 1889 and 1949 he attended every murder trial of significance that was held in the High Court of Justiciary in Edinburgh and published accounts of them in a series of best-selling books. He held the legal title of Writer to His Majesty's Signet and was an editor of the Notable British Trials Series.

LUC SANTE is the author of *Low Life*, *Evidence*, and *The Factory of Facts*.

# CLASSIC CRIMES

## A SELECTION FROM THE WORKS OF WILLIAM ROUGHEAD

Made by W. N. Roughead

■

*Introduction by*

LUC SANTE

NEW YORK REVIEW BOOKS

*New York*

THIS IS A NEW YORK REVIEW BOOK
PUBLISHED BY THE NEW YORK REVIEW OF BOOKS

Introduction copyright © 2000 by Luc Sante
All rights reserved.
Deacon Brodie, The West Port Murders, The Sandyford Mystery,
The Slater Case, and The Merret Mystery were originally published
in *Knaves' Looking-Glass*; Katharine Nairn and The Arran Murder,
in Twelve Scots Trials; To Meet Miss Madeleine Smith, in *Mainly
Murder*; Constance Kent's Conscience, in The Rebel Earl; The Balham
Mystery and Dr. Pritchard Revisited, in *Malice Domestic*; The
Ardlamont Mystery, in *Rogues Walk Here*.

This edition published in 2000 in the United States of America by
The New York Review of Books, 1755 Broadway New York, NY 10019

Library of Congress Cataloging-in-Publication Data
Roughead, William, 1870–1952.
   Classic crimes : a selection from the works of William Roughead /
   introduction by Luc Sante
      p.    cm.
      ISBN 0-940322-46-3 (pbk.: alk. paper)
      1. Murder—Great Britain—Case Studies.  2. Crime—Great Britain—
   Case studies. I. Sante, Luc.  II. Title.
   HV6535.G4  R56  2000
   364.15'23'0941—dc 21                          00-009225

ISBN 0-940322-46-3

Book design by Red Canoe, Deer Lodge, Tennessee
Caroline Kavanagh, Deb Koch
Printed in the United States of America on acid-free paper.
10  9  8  7  6  5  4  3  2  1

September 2000
www.nybooks.com

# CONTENTS

# INTRODUCTION

THE GENRE WE call "true crime," obviously one of the very oldest in literature, has, despite a biblical pedigree, spent much of its career in the literary slums. The genre from which it is adjectivally distinguished—although seldom referred to as "false crime"—has produced classics as well as potboilers, but the nonfictional narrative of crime has chiefly been associated with such raffish vehicles as the ballad broadside, the penny-dreadful, the tabloid extra, the pulp detective magazine, and the current pestilence of paperbacks uniform in their one-sentence paragraphs, two-word titles, and covers with black backgrounds, white letters, and obligatory splash of blood. There's really nothing wrong with any of these—even the current paperbacks are bound to seem more charming as time passes. Still, you might wonder: Where is the Homer of true crime, its Cervantes, its Dostoevsky?

William Roughead might at least be its Henry James. The two were friends and correspondents, and they shared a variety of interests and inclinations: complex characters, hopelessly tangled motives, labyrinths of nuance, arcane language, byzantine sentence structure. Roughead was a Scotsman who was born in 1870 and died in 1952, although the unknowing reader would be forgiven for ascribing to him a set of dates several decades earlier, so resolutely unmodern is his prose—not that it is in any way stiff, cold, musty, or particularly quaint. He began his career at twenty-three as a Writer to the Signet, a term that has no literary implication, referring rather to an elite body of Scottish attorneys. His passion for the law extended well beyond his actual duties. As he notes in passing several times herein, he was from his youth both a frequent spectator at major trials and an indefatigable collector of newspaper clippings on criminal cases that interested him, and he went on to edit a number of the volumes in the celebrated Notable British Trials series, then to collect his commentaries in books issued by a small press in Edinburgh. His works were taken up by a commercial publisher only when he was in his sixties.

So mercantile calculation clearly played no part in determining his choice of pursuits. His was one of those astoundingly ambitious Edwardian hobbies that differed from professions only in their lack of financial compensation—it was a time when every retired general seemed to be translating Hesiod and every diplomat apparently had a sideline in paleontology. In Roughead we can observe the most sophisticated and refined expression of the British middle-class armchair fascination with crime. When, in "The West Port Murders," Roughead invites us to look over his shoulder at "an inch-square bit of brown leather" that is in fact a fragment of the tanned skin of the murderer and ghoul William Burke, handed down by the author's grandfather, the scene—we imagine Roughead wearing a dressing gown and a velvet cap, examining the grisly relic with a bone-handled magnifying glass—contains in full that collision, of placid, well-furnished, and obsessively well-organized pedantry with savage howling atavism, that is the keynote of that fascination.

Virtually all the hallmarks of the classic British mystery appear here, the apparent originals of those overly clever poisonings, those horrors in sleepy priories and dramas set against majestic Highland backdrops, those appallingly unlikely suspects and convenient foreign scapegoats, those algebra-problem alibi timetables, those ever-present watchful servants, those pathetically mundane overlooked clues. These cases have an advantage over their fictional descendants, however, by virtue of their mess, complication, frequent lack of satisfactory closure, and of course their psychological depth. They are anything but cozy. Roughead is not especially interested in clever paradoxes and neat resolutions; in fact he is not nearly as fascinated by the clue-hunting and deductive cogitation aspects of his cases as he is by their elaboration in the courtroom. A murder for him is of interest chiefly insofar as it provides the premise for a rich, complex trial at which personalities can clash, unfold, reveal their wrinkles.

Personality is the tie that binds together these twelve otherwise relatively disparate cases, which are mostly murders but not all, and are mostly but not all set in Scotland. Roughead writes about cases he observed himself, but he also delves into the archived transcripts and writes vividly of cases that took place a century or more before his birth. The protagonist can be obviously guilty, or obviously guilty but nevertheless released or acquitted, or falsely accused, or even, as in "Katharine Nairn," not accused at all, as the slippery Anne Clark steals every scene of that particular show, despite its title. At their best, trial transcripts combine theatrical movement, interplay, and suspense with the voyeuristic fascination presented by someone else's open trunk. They can supply all the ingredients for a sophisticated and modernistically jagged portrait, but it takes someone like Roughead to know how to extract and display those ingredients without losing momentum to procedural detours and longueurs—courtroom scenes have, after all, produced some of the most deadly boring stretches in movie history.

Roughead, with his jeweler's eye for extravagantly serpentine characters, his taste for unresolvable conflicts, self-devouring schemes, and barely decipherable motives, his pleasure in stories that disdain such conventions as a clear-cut beginning, middle, and end, is something of a cubist posing as a fogey. His own personality, vivid at every moment even when he is not actually an actor in the scene, is fundamental to his strategy, and to his charm. He is certainly no shrinking violet, and neither is he one of those rigorously deadpan journalists who insist on letting the facts speak for themselves. He is at once stage manager, color commentator, handicapper, gossip, and final-appeals judge. He is relentlessly discursive, his asides convincingly sounding as if they are being whispered along a bench, and digressive too. But his sense of timing is superb: though he'll take the reader on a walk through the past or through the neighborhood, he will always be back in time for the crucial next question. There are, to be sure, thickets of local reference and forgotten allusion, and he seldom fails to introduce a barrister without summarizing the now obscure highlights of his illustrious later career, but the reader can simply file these under "atmosphere."

His prose represents the full range of the English language, circa 1880, as played on a cathedral organ with the largest possible number of manuals, pedals, and stops. He traffics in rare words, disused expressions, abstruse variants, and strictly local idioms, deploying them for reasons that are sometimes historical, sometimes psychological, often shamelessly musical. You can open the book anywhere and light on a random sentence— for instance, "The secret marauder came and went without a trace, save for the empty till, the rifled scrutoire, or the displenished plate-chest that testified to his visitation." Numerous ways exist of expressing this thought that would convey all the essential information in fewer and more austere terms, but that "scrutoire," that "displenished" have a majesty about them that at once relates to the magnificence of the marauder's character—the flamboyant Deacon Brodie—and gives a glimpse of his times, the 1780s. And anyway, the sentence gives pleasure, well beyond any question of utility. The usages herein may often send the reader to the dictionary, sometimes even to the OED. The word does not even have to be unusual in itself; I was baffled by his use of "ghostly" (as in "Constance Kent . . . was admitted an inmate of St. Mary's Home . . . under the ghostly ward of the Rev. Arthur Wagner . . .") until I realized that Roughead invariably employs it as a synonym for "spiritual."

These are twelve strong stories. One of them, the tale of the ghouls Burke and Hare, will be familiar to most readers, at least in outline, from Robert Louis Stevenson's *The Body Snatcher* (and its superb 1945 Val Lewton film adaptation). The rest are discoveries: "Katharine Nairn" discloses the chaos and squalor of the eighteenth-century Scottish gentry. Madeleine Smith might be the template of the lethal film noir heroine. The belowstairs drama of "The Sandyford Mystery" all but calls for a floor plan and a stopwatch. "Dr. Pritchard" deserves a stage performance and "The Arran Murder" suggests a great lost Hitchcock movie. If the Balham mystery is something of a black hole, the Ardlamont and Merrett mysteries are black comedies, their defendants' respective tissues of lies so thin and apparently permeable that the wonder is how they thought they could fool anyone—but they did. And finally there is the bizarre, protracted miscarriage of justice that is the case of Oscar Slater, one that invites the usual misuse of the adjective "Kafkaesque." Here, as in a number of the cases, Roughead's barely controlled outrage in the face of injustice—

to the point where he becomes an actor in his own story—reveals that he was no mere vicarious bloodshed buff but an idealist and even a crusader. Such a combination of gifts and attributes as Roughead possessed is seldom found in writers of any description, and it is probably safe to say that they have never otherwise been brought together in the practice of that unfairly déclassé genre, true crime.

—LUC SANTE

CLASSIC
CRIMES

## KATHARINE NAIRN

*Paolo and Francesca in Angus.*

—ANDREW LANG

WHEN DOUCE MR. Thomas Ogilvy brought his young bride home to Glenisla his mother doubtless hailed the event as of happy augury for the house of Eastmiln. Hitherto fortune had frowned upon her family. Her eldest son "grew delirious and hanged himself in '48 in a sheepcot." As the length of the drop was insufficient, "he came down and delved below his feet to make it proper for him," which showed considerable force of character. His brother William "went on board a man-of-war carpenter, and was crushed to death 'twixt two ships." Her husband, who under his chief, Lord Ogilvy, had been out in the Forty-five as a captain of the Prince's army, after the defeat of Culloden was confined in Edinburgh Castle, and, having lain a prisoner in that fortress until 1751, fractured his skull in attempting to escape over the walls "by a net tied to an iron ring." Thomas, the third son, prudently eschewing politics, became by virtue of these calamities laird of the paternal acres. Of her remaining sons, Patrick, sometime lieutenant of the 89th Regiment of Foot, was but newly invalided home from the East Indies, his career eclipsed, while the youngest, Alexander, then prosecuting at Edinburgh his studies in depravity and physic, had just redeemed a nominal celibacy by marriage with a woman of the lowest rank. When therefore Thomas, at the responsible age of forty, wooed and won Miss Katharine Nairn, a damsel of nineteen, the beautiful daughter of Sir Thomas Nairn of Dunsinnan, old Mrs. Ogilvy (by Scots courtesy Lady Eastmiln) may have believed herself entitled to sing the Song of Simeon. How far she was justified in the event the following tale will show.

The marriage, which took place on 30th January 1765, would seem to have been on both sides one of affection. The bride, of a family more rich in ancestry than in money, was better born than her husband, who was but a "bonnet laird." Marrying against the wish of her relatives she brought him at least youth and beauty, whereas Eastmiln (so named by Scottish custom) was a man of small means who had, moreover, anticipated the modern malady—too old at forty. His health, as we shall see, was bad; he was somewhat of a valetudinarian. Mr. Spalding of Glenkilry, the husband of Katharine's sister Bethia, at whose house Thomas Ogilvy probably met his future bride, quaintly described him as wearing "a plaiden jacket and a belt round his middle, much broader than ever he saw another wear, with lappets of leather hanging down his haunches, and a striped woollen nightcap upon his breast, the lower end of which reached near his breeches." His change of state must have proved beneficial, for Mr. Spalding adds, "upon his marriage he took off these happings."

At this time the inmates of the house of Eastmiln were the dowager, her son and his young wife, Patrick the lieutenant, and three female servants. From the date of the marriage until the first of March ensuing all was apparently well with the family. But on that day—ominously enough a Friday—there arrived upon the scene one who was to prove the evil genius of the house and the harbinger of dishonor and death. This was Anne Clark, "aged thirty and upwards," a cousin of the laird. Her private character and professional pursuits, if known, would necessarily have excluded her from decent society, while as a guest she labored under the further disadvantage of being "a notorious liar and dissembler, a disturber of the peace of families, and sower of dissension." Her relatives in Angus, however, knew nothing of all this, and she was received by them "without suspicion, and treated as an equal and a gentle-woman." Miss Clark came ostensibly upon a visit of reconcili-ation from Edinburgh, where she had been associated with her cousin, Alexander Ogilvy, in the sowing of his wild oats. Jealousy was not among her numerous failings, for after his marriage she had lived with his wife's father. By his alliance with "the daughter of a common porter" Alexander had given great offense to his family, and Katharine in particular had not concealed her opinion of his conduct. Hence the appear-ance of Anne in her maiden role of peacemaker. But it was later alleged that she was actuated by a motive less lovely. Both Eastmiln and Patrick, his heir-presumptive, were in ill-health; on their death, should the marriage of the elder prove childless, Alexander the needy would reign in their stead. The first step towards the attainment of this end was to effect an estrangement between the newly-married pair. If such was in-deed her scheme, Anne had no time to lose. Her mission, gen-uine or not, had failed. Alexander's entry in the family black books was indelible.

Miss Clark must have had a winning way with her, inviting to confidence. She and young Mrs. Ogilvy had never met be-fore, yet within a fortnight of her coming Katharine told her she disliked her husband, "and said if she had a dose she would give it him." Nor was this a mere isolated indiscretion, for Miss Clark states that thereafter "Mrs. Ogilvy did frequently signify she was resolved to poison her husband." She even consulted Anne as to the best means of procuring the requisite drug—whether "from Mr. Robertson, a merchant in Perth, or Mrs. Eagle, who keeps a seed shop in Edinburgh, upon pretense of poisoning rats." Anne considered this classic formula open to objection, as being apt to bring the purchaser "to an untimely end," but she generously offered to go herself to Edinburgh "and get her brother, who lived there, to buy the poison." Although a woman with many pasts, Anne, as the cousin of the proposed victim, seems at first sight an unsuitable confidante, but such is her own version of the facts. There for the time the matter rested.

Anne Clark had not been long established beneath that hospitable roof when an ugly rumor concerning Mrs. Ogilvy and her young brother-in-law began to trouble the house of Eastmiln. Anne charitably warned her hostess "to be upon her guard as to her conduct and to abstain from the lieutenant's company." Her well-meant hint, however, proved ineffectual, for on Sunday, 19th May, according to her own account, she obtained indisputable proof of a liaison between them. Katharine, although at once apprised of the discovery by her considerate kinswoman, continued in her evil course with cynical, nay lunatic, effrontery. Anne would fain have supported her story by the testimony of her aunt, but old Lady Eastmiln, who enjoyed the same facilities for seeing and hearing what Anne alleged to have occurred, noticed nothing, despite the fact that her attention was specially called to the matter by her niece at the time. She consented, however, to communicate Anne's "suspicions" to Eastmiln.

It happened that at this time a dispute arose between the brothers "about the balance of a bond of provision resting owing to Patrick Ogilvy," as to which the latter considered himself aggrieved. On Thursday, 23rd May, in the course of a discussion of this vexed question, the laird lost his temper, referred to Anne's allegations, and ordered his brother out of the house. Patrick, indignantly denying the charge, left that afternoon and went to stay with a friend at Little Forter, about three miles distant. That Katharine, whether innocent or guilty, was in the circumstances considerably upset is not surprising. Eastmiln warned his wife that she would injure her reputation "by intermeddling in the differences betwixt him and his brother," which hardly looks as if he took the matter seriously; but the servants swore that they overheard him tell her "that she was too great with Lieutenant Ogilvy, and that they were as frequent together as the bell was to ring on Sunday." Anne says that the laird proposed to leave his own house so as to give the young people a clear field, and that she urged Mrs. Ogilvy to agree, "as she saw little prospect of harmony between them," which, so long as she remained their guest, was no doubt likely enough. Be that as it may, Katharine, with singular imprudence, wrote to the lieutenant begging him to return, which he wisely declined to do. According to Anne's story Mrs. Ogilvy, who had become impatient at her delay in procuring the poison from Edinburgh as promised, told her, after the lieutenant's departure, that "with much difficulty" she had prevailed upon him to furnish it. That same day Anne had an unexplained conversation with a surgeon of Kirriemuir as to the properties and effects of laudanum and the amount of a fatal dose. Whether she shared Rosa Dartle's passion for information or made the inquiry on behalf of Katharine, does not appear.

It is admitted that by the following day husband and wife were so far reconciled that Eastmiln himself wrote to his brother asking him to come back. He sent the letter by a neighbor, to whom he first read it, telling him of Anne Clark's reports, "but that for his [Eastmiln's] part he did not believe them." Patrick, however, still refused to return. He visited various friends in the neighborhood, and while at Glenkilry, the house of Mr. Spalding, Katharine's brother-in-law, he received from her another letter, the contents of which we do not know, unless it be the one produced later at the trial.

On Friday, 31st May, Patrick entertained his brother officer, Lieutenant Campbell, and a friend, Dr. Carnegie, to dinner at an inn in Brechin. He afterwards stated that before he left Eastmiln, Katharine asked him to send her for her own use some salts and laudanum, of which he told her he had a quantity in his sea-chest, then at Dundee. Unfortunately for him, Dr. Carnegie proved that at this dinner he delivered to Patrick at his request "a small phial glass of laudanum and betwixt half an ounce and an ounce of arsenic," which latter "he wrapt up in the form of a penny worth of snuff under three covers." Patrick's reason for wanting the arsenic was, he said, "in order to destroy some dogs that spoiled the game"—which was open to the objection previously taken by Anne to Katharine's hypothetical rats. After paying Dr. Carnegie a shilling for these commodities, Patrick accompanied Lieutenant Campbell to Finhaven as his guest for the week-end.

On Monday, 3rd June, Patrick rode to Alyth to visit his kinsman, Andrew Stewart, who had recently married his sister, Martha Ogilvy. Mr. Stewart had brought the lieutenant's sea-chest from Dundee to his own house, and on this occasion he saw Patrick "working among some salts" in the chest. Next day Elizabeth Sturrock, one of the servants at Eastmiln, came to Alyth upon some household matter, and delivered to Patrick a letter from Katharine, to which he returned an answer by her. Mr. Stewart having announced his intention of visiting Eastmiln the following day, Patrick gave him "a small phial glass, containing something liquid which he said was laudanum, and also a small paper packet, which he said contained salts," together with a letter for Mrs. Ogilvy, all of which he requested his brother-in-law to put into her own hands.

Meanwhile Miss Clark states that Katharine told her she had heard from Patrick, who had "got the poison the length of Alyth," and would send it by Andrew Stewart next day. Anne, ever zealous for the family honor, very properly exhorted her to abandon her nefarious purpose, dwelt upon the consequences likely to ensue "both in this world and the next," and asked her reasons for "this strange resolution." These were that Mrs. Ogilvy did not love her husband, and that he had used the lieutenant ill upon her account. "How happy," said she, "could they live at Eastmiln, if there were none there but the lieutenant, she, and the deponent [Anne]!" That experienced spinster at once pointed out that in no circumstances could Katharine marry her brother-in-law, but was met by the suggestion that they might live abroad. Still, Anne thought it "a dreadful thing to crown all with murder." Mrs. Ogilvy desired "to be let alone, for the conversation was disagreeable to her." Now all this could have been no news to Anne Clark in June, for on her own showing she had known since the middle of March both the nature of Katharine's feelings towards her husband and her fell design.

In the forenoon of Wednesday, 5th June, a chapman (hawker) called and demanded from Eastmiln the price of some cambric, of which Anne was then making ruffles for the lieutenant. As he had been told that Patrick himself supplied the material, the laird was justifiably annoyed, and repudiated liability for the account. Later in the day Andrew Stewart arrived at the house of Eastmiln and privately handed to Katharine the lieutenant's parcel, which she placed unopened in a drawer in the spare bedroom. But Anne was on the alert, and waylaying him, asked if he had brought anything from Patrick. Mr. Stewart, "because he considered Miss Clark as a person given to raise dissension in families," at first denied that he had done so; but, being persistently pressed by her, he finally admitted the fact. Whereupon Anne said "they were black drugs," and that Mrs. Ogilvy meant to poison her husband. Stewart, shocked at the suggestion, was "very much displeased" with her, the more so that she proposed to her aunt to warn Eastmiln of his danger. But "the old lady said it would be improper," being, as appears, a stickler for etiquette.

That night the four relatives supped together—a strange company—at a public-house in the Kirkton of Glenisla. Eastmiln told his brother-in-law, Andrew Stewart, that he had not been well for some time past, and was thinking of consulting Dr. Ogilvy of Forfar. He further said that he was seized with illness the day before, and "had swarfed [fainted] on the hill," for which reason he could drink no ale. So he called for a dram, "which he took, and thereafter seemed hearty and in good spirits." But Miss Clark's conscience, a tender plant, still troubled her, and she unobtrusively left the board in quest of ghostly aid, or, in her own words, "with a view of being advised by the minister what was fit to be done in such a case." The minister of Glenisla was from home, so she rejoined the supper-party without the benefit of clerical counsel, the nature of which, in a situation so delicate, one would like to have known. On the way home Stewart escorted his sister-in-law, the laird following with Anne, who, availing herself of the opportunity, warned him that his life was threatened by his own wife, and begged him to leave home. Eastmiln said he was then too busy to do so, but promised to take nothing from Katharine's hands. It is probable that he was not much impressed by his cousin's solicitude; that he disliked and distrusted her is certain. Apparently the hour was favorable for confidences; Katharine at the same time was telling her companion that she lived a most unhappy life with her husband, and "wished him dead, or, if that could not be, she wished herself dead." This statement, chiming as it did with Anne's suspicions, somewhat startled Mr. Stewart.

When they reached the house, and after Eastmiln and his wife had gone to bed, he proposed to Anne Clark and the old lady that they should either take Mrs. Ogilvy's keys out of her pocket or break open her drawers at the back, so as to see what were the actual contents of the packet. To neither of these practical suggestions could Anne by any means be brought to agree, which is the more remarkable in view of the urgent anxiety expressed by her earlier in the evening. But when Lady Eastmiln, who had gone up to listen at the door of the connubial chamber, reported "that there was then more kindness between them than usual," Mr. Stewart was confirmed in his opinion "that there was no foundation for Miss Clark's fears."

Next morning, Thursday, 6th June, breakfast was earlier than common—"betwixt eight and nine"—as Mr. Stewart was returning that day to Alyth. All the members of the family were present except the laird, who, having been unwell in the night, was still in bed. Katharine poured out a bowl of tea from the teapot, put sugar and milk in it, and, telling the old lady and Stewart that she was taking it up to Eastmiln, left the room. While she was upstairs the party was completed by the appearance of Anne, to whom Katharine, on re-entering the parlor, remarked "that the laird and Elizabeth Sturrock were well off that morning, for they had got the first of the tea." Upon which, Anne says she exclaimed in alarm, " 'What! has the laird got tea?' and on Mrs. Ogilvy answering that he had, the deponent said nothing"—like the parrot in the tale. An hour and a half afterwards, according to Mr. Stewart— Anne says half an hour—Katharine announced that the laird "was taken very ill." Anne ran upstairs to the bedroom, and on returning significantly reported that "Eastmiln had got a bad breakfast." Stewart then went up himself to see what was the matter, and found his brother-in-law suffering from sickness and other distressing symptoms. The laird expressively said that "he was all wrong within." Mr. Stewart proposed to Mrs.

Ogilvy to send for Dr. Meik of Alyth, but she would not consent, saying that "he [Eastmiln] would be better; and she would not for any money that a surgeon should be called, as the consequences would be to give her a bad name from what Miss Clark had said of her." Later, Mr. Stewart persuaded her to let him summon Dr. Meik, "a discreet person," and thereafter set out for Alyth.

Katharine's forecast was so far justified that Eastmiln presently rose "and went first to the stables to see his horses fed, and then to the Shillinghill, where he conversed with some of his tenants." On returning to the house he became violently sick in the kitchen, and had to be helped upstairs to bed. Katharine attended to her husband during the forenoon, but from midday until his death Anne Clark was in possession of the sickroom. She states that Mrs. Ogilvy refused to remain there unless she (Anne) was dismissed, to which the laird would not agree. Anne and some of the servants represent that Katharine tried to exclude people from the room, but it is proved that, apart from those in the house, Eastmiln was visited by at least five persons, including his brother-in-law, Mr. Spalding, and the local precentor, who was summoned by Katharine to pray with him. The symptoms exhibited by the dying man were admittedly vomiting, purging, "a burning at his heart," pains in his legs, restlessness, and persistent thirst. Anne gave him repeated draughts of water and of ale, none of which he could retain; but on her trying him with "a glass of wine and a piece of sugar in it," the sickness ceased for about an hour. On cross-examination, she had to admit that she got the wine from Mrs. Ogilvy. That the laird had become convinced that his wife had poisoned him is clear. When Anne Sampson, one of the maids, brought him a drink of water in the same bowl in which Katharine had given him the tea, he cried out, "Damn that bowl! for I have got my death in it already." He said in the hearing of Elizabeth Sturrock, another servant, "that he was poisoned, and that woman [his wife] had done it." Lady East-miln reproved him for saying so, to which he answered "that it was very true, and his death lay at her [Katharine's] door." Anne, on the other hand, says that the old lady blamed him for taking anything from his wife, when he replied, "It is too late now, Mother; but she forced it on me." He told Andrew Stewart that "he had what would do his turn"; to his friend and neighbor, Mr. Millam, he remarked, "I am gone, James, with no less than rank poison!" At midnight the unhappy man was dead. It was but four months since his wedding-day.

Dr. Meik arrived from Alyth two hours later; it does not appear when he received the summons. He had an interview with the widow, who was apparently "in great grief and concern." She made the remarkable request "that whatever he might think to be the cause of her husband's death, he would conceal it from the world." Patrick Ogilvy, sent for by Mr. Spalding from Glenkilry, where he had been that gentleman's guest, was then in the house, and conducted the doctor to the death-chamber. He struck Dr. Meik as being, like Mrs. Ogilvy, "in great grief and concern." After a brief examination the doctor departed, having, as it appears, come to no conclusion regarding the cause of death.

That morning (Friday, 7th June) the servants, probably at the instigation of the thoughtful Anne, applied certain scientific tests to the fatal bowl, in which they said they had noticed "something greasy in the bottom." The results were negative. They filled the bowl with broth, which was given to a dog, "who eat it up, but was nothing the worse of it." Anne Clark recounts a curious conversation had by her with the lieutenant on his coming from Glenkilry. She told him "she knew the whole affair of the poison," whereupon Patrick admitted sending it to Katharine, but said "he did not think she had so barbarous a heart as to give it."

The funeral was fixed to take place on Tuesday, 11th June,

the lieutenant, as his brother's heir, remaining at Eastmiln to make the requisite arrangements. Mr. Millam, the late laird's friend, tells us that when "the mournings came home" Miss Clark complained to him "for want of a mourning apron, adding that she would make it as dear to them [Katharine and Patrick] as if it was a gown!" This was short-sighted parsimony indeed; Anne's silence was worth many aprons' purchase. On Monday, the 10th, Mrs. Ogilvy dismissed her dangerous kinswoman, giving her money in presence of Mr. Millam, both of which facts Anne afterwards denied on oath. Anne further swore that before she left the house she did not communicate to anyone, "by letters or otherways," her belief that Eastmiln had been poisoned. Yet early in the forenoon of Tuesday, the 11th, her old flame Alexander Ogilvy arrived from Edinburgh, and dramatically stopped the burial on the ground that his brother had not died a natural death. The widow resented her brother-in-law's action—reasonably enough in any view of her conduct—and "behaved very ill, weeping and crying, and wringing her hands and tearing herself." Mr. Millam, hearing what had happened, strangely advised Patrick "to make his escape, if guilty"; to which the lieutenant replied "that God and his own conscience knew that he was innocent." Next morning, at the request of Alexander Ogilvy, Dr. Meik of Alyth and Dr. Ramsay of Coupar-Angus arrived to make a postmortem examination of the corpse, Katharine and Patrick offering no objection. Alexander, however, refused to allow the body to be opened until Dr. Ogilvy of Forfar, who had been desired by the Sheriff to attend, was also present. The two surgeons, therefore, merely inspected the corpse and left, refusing to wait for Dr. Ogilvy. After they had gone the latter arrived, but declined to open the body in the absence of the other surgeons, on the ground that the autopsy might be attended with personal danger. He, in his turn, made an inspection and departed. We shall see later the result of their several observations.

On Friday, 14th June, Katharine and Patrick were apprehended upon the signed information of Alexander Ogilvy, and, having been examined before Mr. George Campbell, Sheriff-Substitute of the county, were consigned to Forfar Jail. That day Miss Clark returned in triumph to Eastmiln, to assist her old friend Alexander in taking possession. On the 17th, the erstwhile medical student, confident in the assumption of his lairdship, "rouped the stocking upon the farm," *i.e.* sold by auction the cattle, etc., on the false pretense of an authority from Patrick, and appropriated the proceeds of the sale.

On 21st June the prisoners, having been removed to Edinburgh, were examined there before Mr. Balfour of Pilrig, Sheriff-Substitute of Edinburgh—the kinsman of Stevenson's David Balfour—and were committed to the Tolbooth to await their trial. It is said that when they landed at Leith, Katharine was with difficulty rescued from the fury of the populace, so strong was the feeling against her by reason of the rumor of her misdeeds.

It may be convenient here briefly to consider the purport of the prisoners' judicial examinations, so far as these relate to the question of the poison. In her first declaration at Forfar Mrs. Ogilvy deponed, "That before Patrick Ogilvy left his brother's house she asked him, any time he was at Alyth, to buy for her and send to Eastmiln two doses of salts and a little laudanum, as she slept very ill. . . . That she took one of the doses of salts on the Friday after her husband's death and the other on the Saturday; and on the Sunday and the Monday nights she took the laudanum each night, and as she did not use the whole laudanum she delivered back the glass and the remainder of laudanum to the said Patrick Ogilvy on his return to Eastmiln after his brother's death"—which, as regards the laudanum, was afterwards proved to be true. She admitted giving her husband the bowl of tea, which "she carried straight from the low room, where they were at breakfast, upstairs to her husband's room." She further declared that Elizabeth Sturrock got the remainder of the bowl of tea, as Eastmiln "did not drink it out." Patrick Ogilvy the same day declared, "That the said laudanum and salts he brought from the East Indies with him, as a remainder of what he used when his health was bad there and on his passage home. . . . That within these two weeks he was at the town of Brechin, and in company with James Carnegie, surgeon, of that place, *but that he received from him no laudanum or any other medicine whatever.*" He corroborated Katharine's account of her request for the drugs.

While in Forfar Jail, Patrick learned from a friend that Dr. Carnegie had disclosed the purchase of the laudanum and arsenic, "upon which the lieutenant seemed to be under some concern," and expressed a desire to see the Sheriff and amend his declaration upon that point; but this could not be done.

When examined before Sheriff Balfour at Edinburgh upon lengthy interrogatories both prisoners, by advice of their counsel, declined to answer the various leading questions put to them, Katharine refusing even to sign her declaration.

On 1st July, Sheriff Campbell of Forfar proceeded to the house of Eastmiln to search the repositories (which since the laird's death had been locked up by the scrupulous Alexander), and found two letters obviously written by Katharine to Eastmiln before their marriage, and later so described in the indictment. These were produced at the trial as proof of her handwriting, with reference to an unsigned, unaddressed letter alleged to have been written by her to Patrick on an unknown date, in the following terms:—

> Dr Captin,—I was sorrie I missed you this day. I sat at the water side a long time this forenoon; I thought you would have comed up here. If you had as much mind of me as I have of you, you would have comed up, tho' you

had but stayed out-by, as there was no use for that; there is more rooms in the house then one. God knows the heart that I have this day, and instead of being better its worse, and not in my power to help it. You are not minding the thing that I said to you or [before] you went out here, and what I wrote for. Meat I have not tasted since yesterday dinner, nor wont or you come here; tho' I should never eat any, it lyes at your door. Your brother would give anything you would come, for God's sake come.

This letter was not recovered by Sheriff Campbell on his search of the premises, but was sent to him later by Alexander Ogilvy. How it came into that gentleman's doubtful hands does not appear. By a curious oversight, Hill Burton, in his narrative of the case, assumes that all three letters were written by Katharine "to her alleged paramour," and even quotes from the two former as such.

The trial commenced before the High Court of Justiciary at Edinburgh upon the 5th of August 1765. The Judges present were the Lord Justice-Clerk (Sir Gilbert Elliot of Minto), Lords Auchinleck (Alexander Boswell, father of the immortal Bozzy), Alemore (Andrew Pringle), Kames (Henry Home), Pitfour (James Ferguson), and Coalston (George Brown). The Lord Advocate (Thomas Miller of Barskimming, the pawky Sheriff Miller of *Catriona*), the Solicitor-General (James Montgomery), Sir David Dalrymple (the future Lord Hailes), and two juniors conducted the prosecution. Alexander Lockhart (afterwards Lord Covington) and the great Henry Dundas appeared for Mrs. Ogilvy; David Rae (later the eccentric Lord Eskgrove) and Andrew Crosbie (Scott's Counselor Pleydell) represented Lieutenant Patrick Ogilvy. The first day was occupied in the usual debate upon the relevancy of the indictment, which was duly found relevant to infer the pains of law. On the following day there was presented to the Court a petition in the name of the pannels regarding Anne Clark, then in custody in the Castle. The movements of this exemplary female since we left her reinstated at Eastmiln are uncertain. Although in her private capacity of friend and relative of the prisoners she had told extra-judicially everything she could against them, and made a formal statement before the Sheriff, she is said to have shrunk from the painful necessity of swearing to her story in the witness-box. She therefore disappeared from the ken of the Lord Advocate until the eve of the trial, when she communicated with his Lordship as follows:—

> Lord Advocat,—Upon my coming to town, I am informed that you have been searching for me. It would never bread in my breest to keept out of the way had it not been for terror of imprisonment; but houping you will be more favorable to me I shall weat upon you tomorrow morning at eight of the clock.

> Anne Clark.

> Sunday evening, eight of the clock.

Despite her "houp," Miss Clark was lodged in the Castle, along with the three women servants from Eastmiln who were to be witnesses in the case. The petition stated that "as she was in a combination to ruin the pannels and, as far as she could, to deprive them of their lives as well as their reputations," it was obviously unfair to them that she should have an opportunity of tampering with the other witnesses. It was accordingly craved that she should be separated from them. This was granted by the Court; but it afterwards appeared that Anne was only removed for one night, and was then replaced in the same room with them as before, by order of Lord George Beauclerk, Commander-in-Chief of the forces in Scotland, who considered "that the room in the gunner's house she was by desire put into, was by no means a place to keep a prisoner in safety."

At seven o'clock in the morning of Monday, 12th August, a jury was empanelled, and the examination of witnesses began. It was the practice of those times that after a jury was once charged with a pannel the Court could not be adjourned until the jury was inclosed, *i.e.* till they withdrew to consider their verdict. The hardships thus entailed upon all concerned where the case was of any length are evident. In the present trial the proceedings up to that stage lasted for forty-three consecutive hours, the jury not being inclosed until two o'clock in the morning of Wednesday, 14th August.

The purport of most of the evidence adduced for the Crown has been given in the foregoing narration, but certain points remain to be considered. With regard to the proof of a criminal intrigue between the pannels, the prosecution relied mainly upon the testimony of Anne Clark—"whose evidence," as Hill Burton well observes, "is always suspicious"—corroborated to some extent by that of the servants, Katharine Campbell, Elizabeth Sturrock, and Anne Sampson. No doubt their memories had been much refreshed by Anne's reminiscences while in the Castle. To Campbell, the most damaging witness of the three, it was objected that she had been dismissed by her mistress for theft, which she practically admitted, and had sworn revenge. The Court, however, allowed her to be examined. When Anne Clark was called, Dundas, for the defense, strongly objected to her admission on the grounds of her infamous character and lurid past; that, in confederacy with Alexander Ogilvy, she herself had propagated the false reports which led to the pannels' arrest; and that she had expressed deadly malice against them, and threatened to bereave them of their lives. Sir David Dalrymple, in reply, did not attempt to whitewash his fair witness, but contended that general proof of character was incompetent; that the crimes charged were occult crimes, only provable by witnesses who lived in the family, "be their character what it will"; that until the evidence was closed it could not be said whether the reports spread by Miss Clark were false or not; and that the pannels must prove the cause of her alleged ill-will. The Court admitted the witness, reserving the question of malice. Anne Clark's examination occupied eight hours. We cannot here discuss the infragrant details of her evidence, though these present many singular and suggestive features—the case was heard with closed doors, from which let the gentle reader, like the stranger admonished by Mrs. Sapsea's epitaph, "with a blush retire"; but in reference to the proof upon this part of the case it be generally remarked that the behavior of the prisoners, as described by Anne Clark and her attesting nymphs, exhibits a reckless disregard of consequences which well-nigh passes belief, while the corroborative evidence of undue intimacy is to a large extent discounted by what we know of the coarseness of speech and manners pervading Scottish society in those days. The acts of familiarity upon which the prosecutor relied to support Anne's tale were said to have occurred in public and before third parties, some even in presence of the husband himself. The very limited capacity of the house of Eastmiln has also to be borne in mind. It appears from an unpublished sketch-plan, prepared for the use of Crown counsel, that the house consisted of two stories; upon the ground floor there were but two rooms, kitchen and parlor, one on either side of the entrance hall or passage; on the flat above were two bedrooms corresponding to the rooms below, with a small closet between them over the lobby. A garret in the roof was used as a store-room. We learn from the evidence that the servants slept in the kitchen, beneath the west bedroom occupied by the laird and his wife; that the east bedroom above the parlor was assigned to the lieutenant; and that Anne Clark and old Lady Eastmiln shared a "box-bed" in the parlor. So homely and primitive were then the habits of the

Scots gentry that a family of five persons and three servants were thus "accommodated" in four small rooms. It is also in evidence that the kitchen ceiling was unplastered, and that the conversation of the laird and his wife in their bed in the room above was clearly audible in the kitchen below. The partition walls, too, were of lath and plaster, which enabled Anne Clark to overhear from the staircase all that went on in the lieutenant's room. Verily the house of Eastmiln was ill adapted to purposes of stealthy intrigue. If Anne Clark's astonishing tale be true, the guilt of the pannels on this count must be accepted; but one hesitates at which the more to marvel—the baseness of Anne if forsworn, or Katharine's unblushing impudence if guilty.

The proof of the murder is in a different case. The ground of the prosecution was that Eastmiln died of poison. This, strange as it may seem, looking to the subsequent verdict, the medical evidence entirely failed to establish. Dr. Meik, who first saw the body, found "the nails and a part of the breast discolored and his tongue swelled beyond its natural size and cleaving to the roof of his mouth." He was "unacquainted with the effects of poison," but having been told by Alexander Ogilvy that poison had been administered in this case, he "conjectured" it to have caused the death. Dr. Ramsay concurred as to the postmortem appearances, with this addition, that the lips were "more discolored than by a natural death," and, upon the same information, agreed with Dr. Meik. Both admitted having seen similar symptoms in cases of death from natural causes. Dr. Ogilvy, who had inspected the corpse at the request of the Sheriff, deponed "That the breast was white and the lips pretty much of a natural color.... That the face, the arms, and several other parts of the body were black and livid, and that the nails were remarkably black." Manifestly the condition of the corpse, which when seen by the surgeons had lain unburied for six summer days, was due to putrefaction. This

Dr. Ogilvy practically admitted, by stating that "he could draw no conclusion as to the cause of the defunct's death." The only appearance that struck him as peculiar was the condition of the tongue, which was "such as occurs from convulsions or other strong causes."

In view of the negative testimony of these experts as to the cause of death, the evidence regarding Eastmiln's general health becomes important. Anne Clark and the three servants represent him as a strong man, sound and hearty until the last day of his life. His mother, a valuable witness on this as upon many other points, was called by neither party—which affords matter for reflection. Mr. Spalding, his brother-in-law, swore that for some years past Eastmiln had been in bad health, "complaining often of a heart-colic or pain in his stomach, attended with a short cough which was not continual but seldom left him." That some years before he had suffered from an "ulcerous fever" (as was otherwise proved to be the fact), and was never the same man again; also that on one occasion, being seized with illness at the house of Glenkilry, Eastmiln "got hot ale and whisky with a scrape of nutmeg in it, and was put to bed without any supper"—a curious remedy for gastric inflammation. Mr. Spalding further stated that in February, the month after the marriage, he wrote to Katharine's mother, Lady Nairn, advising "that infeftment be taken in favor of Mrs. Ogilvy upon her marriage contract," owing to the unsatisfactory state of her husband's health. His brother-in-law, Andrew Stewart, deponed that Eastmiln was "a tender man," whose sister, Martha Ogilvy (Stewart's wife), used to say that he would not be a long liver. He repeated what Eastmiln had told him, as already mentioned, about "swarfing on the hill." James Millam, his friend and neighbor, said that four days before Eastmiln died he complained to him "of a gravel and a colic, and that he could not live if he got not the better of it." On the Tuesday before his death he became unwell at the deponent's house. He had a fire lit to warm him, though the night was not cold, and got heated chaff applied to ease his suffering. He remarked to the witness "that he was fading as fast as dew off the grass; that he could not get peaceable possession of his house for Anne Clark; that he wished her away; and he got from the deponent a ten-shilling note for the expense of her journey." But that faithful spinster was not so easily disposed of. Five witnesses from Glenisla proved that the day before his death Eastmiln had been attacked by severe internal pain while visiting his tenants; that he had to lie down upon the ground; that he said he had not been so ill for six years; and that "he behoved to get Dr. Ogilvy to give him something to do him good." It should be remembered that at this time there is no suggestion of his having been poisoned by his wife, who, if she had the will, had not then the means to do so, and it is difficult to reconcile the evidence of these relatives and friends with the laird's rude health, as sworn to by Anne and the accusing maids. To poison a person in such a condition seems, to the lay mind, a superfluity of naughtiness.

What told most heavily against the lieutenant undoubtedly was his deal in arsenic with Dr. Carnegie at Brechin, of the purchase and disposal of which no satisfactory explanation was offered. But, curiously, it was not even proved that the substance sold was in fact arsenic; all that Dr. Carnegie could say was that he had bought it as such long before, and had "heard from those he sold it to that it had killed rats." So much for scientific testimony in 1765! With regard to Katharine, Anne Sampson, one of the maids, swore that on the morning of the day of Eastmiln's death, having followed her mistress upstairs on some domestic errand, she saw her in a closet adjoining the bedroom, "stirring about the tea with her face to the door," but did not see her put anything in the tea. Mrs. Ogilvy made no attempt to conceal what she was doing, and spoke both to the servant and to a lad employed in the house, who was also present at the time. Elizabeth Sturrock deponed that her mistress had tried to induce her to say she (Sturrock) had drunk the remainder of the tea. She admitted that Mrs. Ogilvy brought her tea that morning, when she was ill in bed, but she denied it was what had been left by Eastmiln. That Katharine did take salts—she being then in a delicate state of health—Anne Clark admits, and is corroborated by Elizabeth Sturrock, who says she "got a part of them." The incriminating letter from Katharine to Patrick produced by Alexander, if genuine, leaves little doubt as to their intimacy. One sentence only can be held to refer to the poison: "You are not minding the thing that I said to you or [before] you went out here, and what I wrote for." This might equally be referable to the salts which she says she had asked him to send her. As already pointed out, this letter was without either date or signature, but the indefatigable Anne, presumably an expert in handwriting, swore that it was written by Mrs. Ogilvy. Yet when shown an undoubted letter of Katharine, addressed to Eastmiln, "she did not know whose handwriting it was."

The case for the prosecution was closed at three o'clock on Tuesday afternoon, and the exculpatory proof and addresses to the jury occupied till two o'clock on Wednesday morning. Of the sixty-four witnesses cited for the Crown twenty-four were examined; a hundred and eight witnesses had been summoned for the defense, but for reasons that will presently appear, only ten of these were called. The contemporary report of the trial unfortunately does not include the speeches of counsel, but we read in the *Scots Magazine* that "the evidence was summed up by the Lord Advocate for the King, by Mr. Rae for Lieutenant Ogilvy, and by Mr. Lockhart for Mrs. Ogilvy." Ramsay of Ochtertyre, who was then at the Scots Bar, says of Lockhart's performance on this occasion: "He never failed to shine exceedingly in a very long trial, when defending criminals whose case appeared to be desperate. Mr. Crosbie told me soon after, that in the trial of the Ogilvies, which lasted forty-eight hours, he stood the fatigue better than the youngest of them. He took down every deposition with his own hands, but no short ones, when he went out to take a little air. In answering Lord Advocate Miller, who was perfectly worn out, he displayed such powers of eloquence and ingenuity as astonished everybody. To save the life of his unhappy client he gave up, with great art, her character; but contended there was no legal proof of her guilt, though enough to damn her fame."

At four o'clock on the afternoon of Wednesday, 14th August, the jury, "by a great plurality of voices," found both pannels guilty as libeled. Lockhart at once entered a plea in arrest of judgment in respect of certain irregularities in the proceedings. We cannot here deal fully with this interesting debate, which throws an extraordinary light upon the judicial procedure of the day—how in the course of the trial the jury repeatedly "dispersed into different corners of the house," eating and drinking as they pleased, and talking to the Crown witnesses and the counsel for the prosecution; how between three and five o'clock on the Tuesday morning only one of the Judges remained upon the Bench, "the rest retiring and conversing in private with sundry of the jury and others"; how, "when the evidence on the part of the pannels began to be adduced, several of the jury showed a very great impatience and insisted that that evidence which the pannels thought material for them should be cut short, and some of them particularly disputed the relevancy and propriety of the questions put by the counsel for the pannels with great heat, insomuch that some of the Judges and other jurymen were obliged to interpose, in order that the exculpatory proof might go on; and the counsel for the pannels were obliged to pass from many witnesses, in order to procure attention from those assizers. Hence, though thirty-three hours were spent in hearing calmly the proof adduced for the prosecutors, yet the proof for the pannels, after being heard by those jurymen with great impatience, was put an end to in about three hours." Finally, how, contrary to an Act of Charles II, whereby the prisoner's advocate was to have the last word, Lord Kames, one of the Judges, addressed the jury upon the whole case after counsel had done so for the defense. This is the first recorded instance in Scots criminal practice of the familiar charge to the jury by the presiding Judge. The Court, in respect of the "regularity and accuracy" with which the trial had been conducted, repelled the plea. But Lockhart had still another card to play; he alleged that his client was pregnant, and in her case judgment was superseded until her condition should be reported upon by five professional ladies. Sentence of death was then pronounced against Patrick Ogilvy, to be executed on 25th September, and the Court rose, doubtless with much relief.

Next day the jury of matrons, which included Mrs. Shiells, a local practitioner eminent in her art, of whom we shall hear again, reported that they could give no positive opinion on the subject of the remit. The Court therefore delayed pronouncing sentence against Mrs. Ogilvy till 18th November, to give the five ladies the opportunity of arriving at a definite conclusion.

Meanwhile the friends of the prisoners were not idle in their interests. Application was made to the King in Council for a respite to Patrick Ogilvy, not of favor but of right, until certain points of law should be determined:—(1) Whether in a capital case an appeal was competent from the High Court of Justiciary to the House of Lords? (2) Whether the proceedings at the trial were fair and legal according to the law of Scotland? and (3) Whether, if the first point were doubtful, the execution of the convict should be respited till that question was judged by Parliament, which was not then sitting? Prior to the determination of these questions, which were remitted to the decision of the Attorney-General for England and the Lord Advocate, Patrick received four reprieves—the three first for fourteen days each, the last for seven days only. He is said to have been a great player on the violin, and the interval between his condemnation and execution was, we are told, "exclusively devoted to his performance on that instrument."

While the young lieutenant's fate yet hung in the balance, the judicial dovecot of the Parliament House was fluttered by the publication in certain Edinburgh journals of an "opinion" by an English counsel, one Mr. M'Carty, upon the points at issue. This gentleman, writing from London on 14th September, animadverted upon the conduct of the trial, holding that the prisoners were prejudiced by being tried for two entirely different crimes upon one indictment. He was of opinion that if the crimes charged were considered separately and the evidence produced to support one crime taken singly, without the assistance of the other, no jury in England would have found the prisoners guilty. "The intrigue was supposed to be certain, because the husband was supposed to have been poisoned; and, on the other hand, the man was believed to be poisoned, because there was a supposed proof of intrigue." After criticizing the peculiar features of the evidence with some freedom and to excellent purpose, Mr. M'Carty saw neither law nor reason why the proceedings of the Court of Justiciary might not be subject, as well as those of the Court of Session, to review by the Supreme Court. These views on the subject of criminal appeal gave great offense to the College of Justice. The publication of the opinion was held to be contempt of Court, and, upon the complaint of the Lord Advocate, the publishers of the *Edinburgh Weekly Journal*, where it first appeared, and of the *Courant, Caledonian Mercury*, and *Scots Magazine*, in which it was reprinted, were haled before the Court of Justiciary to answer for their offense. They severally expressed sorrow for the wrong they had done, and the Court, while dwelling on the "high indignity" which it had thereby sustained, dismissed them with a rebuke.

The law officers of the Crown having reported in the negative upon the questions submitted to them, Patrick Ogilvy was executed in the Grassmarket on 13th November, pursuant to his sentence. Chambers states, so popular was the lieutenant with his regiment, which was then quartered in the Castle, that it was judged necessary "to shut them up in that fortress till the execution was over, lest they might attempt a rescue." A letter from his colonel, giving him an excellent character, is printed in the report of the trial. In "An Authentick Copy" of his dying speech, published at the time, we read, "As to the crimes I am accused of, the trial itself will show the propensity of the witnesses, where civility and possibly folly are explained into actual guilt; and of both crimes for which I am now doomed to suffer I declare my innocence, and that no persuasion could ever have made me condescend to them. I freely forgive every person concerned in this melancholy affair, and wherein any of them have been faulty to me I pray God to forgive them." The newspapers of the day record a shocking incident at the execution. After he was "turned over," the noose slipped and he fell to the ground. The wretched man, "making what resistance he could," was again dragged up the ladder by the hangman and others, "who turned him over a second time, and he continued hanging till dead." For assisting the law on this occasion, a member of the Society of Tron-Men (chimney-sweeps) was expelled from that association and banished to Leith for five years—a grievous punishment for an Edinburgh citizen.

On 18th November the professional ladies were at length enabled to report that Mrs. Ogilvy could not in humanity be hanged for several months, and the Court further delayed sentence until 10th March. Upon 21st November Katharine presented a petition to the Court, praying that a judicial factor should be appointed to administer the estates of the deceased laird in the interests of her unborn child. Alexander Ogilvy, his brother's heir-presumptive, did not meantime oppose the application, but in his answers he indicated that if occasion arose he meant to contest the succession. A factor was duly appointed.

On 27th January 1766, in the Tolbooth of Edinburgh, Mrs. Ogilvy gave birth to a daughter. When the Court met on 10th March to pronounce sentence of death, a physician and two nurses deponed that she was not yet strong enough to be brought up for judgment. The diet was therefore continued for a week. At seven o'clock on the night of Saturday the 15th, however, the interesting invalid summoned sufficient energy to burst her bonds. Her escape, which is said not to have been discovered till the Sunday afternoon, was, as we shall see, probably collusive. The contemporary accounts are suspicious. It is said that, being indulged with "the quiet and privacy which the nature of her illness required," she dressed herself in man's clothes, and, the door of her room having been at her request "left open for the benefit of the air," she naturally walked out. Perhaps the turnkeys and sentries were still celebrating the New Year, old style. On Monday the 17th the Lord Justice-Clerk granted a warrant for her arrest, and the magistrates of Edinburgh issued a notice offering a reward of one hundred guineas for her apprehension. She is described as "middle sized and strong made; has a high nose, black eyebrows, and of a pale complexion"—a description which seems willfully at variance with the received accounts of her beauty. She "went off on Saturday night in a post-chaise for England by the way of Berwick; and had on an officer's habit and a hat slouched in the cocks, with a cockade in it." On the 22nd the Government announced in the *London Gazette* an additional hundred guineas reward for her recapture. It is therein stated that Mrs. Ogilvy, disguised as a young gentleman, very thin and sickly, muffled up in a greatcoat, and attended by a servant, had passed through Haddington on Saturday at midnight, and had pushed on with four horses, day and night, from stage to stage, towards London. The *Gentleman's Magazine* records "that information was received at Mr. Fielding, the magistrate's, office, that on the Wednesday following she was at Dover in the dress of an officer, endeavoring to procure a passage to France"; and in a later report, that having failed to do so, she "returned from Dover to London, took a hackney coach to Billingsgate, got on board a Gravesend boat, with a gentleman to accompany her, agreed with a tilt boat there to take them over to France for eight guineas and a guinea a day for waiting for them four days in order to bring them back; which tilt boat landed them at Calais, but is since returned without them." This, of course, was a device to gain time and baffle her pursuers.

But tradition gives a more probable account of Katharine's escape from the prison. Her uncle, Mr. William Nairn, a well-known and respected member of the Scots Bar, was at that time Commissary Clerk of Edinburgh. He was raised to the Bench in 1786 with the judicial title of Lord Dunsinnan, and in 1790 succeeded to the baronetcy, which, on his death in 1811, became extinct. His Lordship is said to have contrived his niece's freedom. Sir Daniel Wilson, in his *Memorials*, states, upon the authority of Charles Kirkpatrick Sharpe, that Katharine walked out of the Tolbooth "disguised in the garments of Mrs. Shiells, the midwife who had been in attendance on her and added to her other favors this extra-professional delivery." James Maidment, in *Kay's Portraits*, tells the same story, with the additional particular that Mrs. Shiells had feigned toothache for some days before, and muffled her head in a shawl. The doorkeeper, according to Chambers's *Traditions*, knowing what was afoot, gave the fictitious nurse a slap on the back as she left the prison, and bade her begone for "a howling old

Jezebel." Sharpe owed his own introduction to the world to the good offices of this benevolent dame, who, as Chambers notes, was still practicing in Edinburgh so late as 1805.

There are various accounts of Katharine's adventures after she had successfully "broke prison." Sharpe says that in her confusion she "risped" at Lord Alva's door in James's Court, mistaking the house for that of her father's agent, when the footboy who opened the door recognized her, having been present at the trial, and immediately raised an alarm. As the case was heard *in camera*, this lad must have been exceptionally privileged. Her uncle's house was in a tenement at the head of the Parliament Stairs, the site of which is now occupied by the Justiciary Court-room. Thither, says Sharpe, Katharine fled, and was concealed in a cellar by Mr. Nairn till the hue and cry was over, when his clerk, Mr. James Bremner, afterwards Solicitor of Stamps, accompanied her to the Continent. Maidment, on the other hand, states that on the night of her escape a carriage was in waiting at the foot of the Horse Wynd, in which she and Mr. Bremner at once left the city. In view of the contemporary evidence there is little doubt that this is the correct version of her flight. She probably assumed the officer's dress *en route*. Chambers says that the coachman had orders, if the pursuit waxed hot, to drive into the sea so that she might drown herself. The contingency, fortunately for her fellow-traveler, did not arise. Thus Katharine vanished from the ken of her contemporaries, and history knows nothing certain of her fate.

"Was she guilty, was she innocent, and, if innocent, why did Lieutenant Patrick Ogilvy buy arsenic at Brechin?" asks Mr. Andrew Lang; and indeed these are "puzzling questions," which every reader must answer for himself.

Wilson states that Mrs. Ogilvy went from France to America, married again, "and died at an advanced age, surrounded by a numerous family." Maidment says she was afterwards "very fortunate, having been married to a Dutch gentleman," with satisfactory results, as above. Alternatively, she took the veil, and, surviving the French Revolution, died in England in the nineteenth century. Chambers marries her happily to "a French gentleman," and credits her with the usual large family. Similar vague surmises are still current regarding the aftermath of Madeleine Smith.

The only fresh light which the present writer has been able to discover is derived from the following sources:—a paragraph in the *Westminster Magazine* of 1777—"Mrs. Ogilvie, who escaped out of Edinburgh Jail for the murder of her husband, is now in a convent at Lisle, a sincere penitent"; and an unpublished MS. note in a contemporary copy of the trial—"Catherine Ogilvie or Nairn did not marry a French nobleman as was at one time reported. She entered a convent and remained there until the troubles consequent upon the French Revolution compelled herself and the other inmates to fly to England, where she died. My informant, Mr. Irvine, lawyer of Dunse, tells me that a friend of his saw her tomb, with the name 'Catherine Ogilvie' upon it; and that upon inquiry the superior mentioned that of all the females in the convent she was the most exemplary in every respect."

Of the others concerned in the tragedy, the unconscious infant died in the Tolbooth within two months of her birth. She is said to have been "overlaid," but by whom is not recorded. The mother was then in France. It is satisfactory to learn that Alexander Ogilvy took no benefit from the child's death, for on 1st March 1766, the anniversary of Anne Clark's arrival at Eastmiln, that bold spirit was arrested for bigamy, and was in his turn committed to the Tolbooth. One might have expected that Anne would be the redundant bride, but from his indictment it appears that the favored lady was a Miss Margaret Dow, daughter of an officer of the Royal Highlanders, unlawfully espoused by him so lately as 24th February. Upon his trial on 4th August, Alexander pleaded guilty to the charge, and was banished for seven years. He was allowed, however, to remain two months in Scotland to settle his affairs, which he effectually did in the following manner: while leaning over the window of a house in one of Auld Reekie's towering *lands*, he lost his balance, fell out, and was killed on the spot. Thus only Anne Clark and old Lady Eastmiln withstood the changes of that eventful year. "Their conversation must have been rich in curious reminiscences," like that of Lady Bothwell and her first love, Ogilvy of Boyne, when they came together at the end of the chapter.

The case of Katharine Nairn is one of the most attractive in our criminal annals, and should this imperfect summary be the means of sending a stray reader to the report of the trial itself, he will not go unrewarded.

### POSTSCRIPT

The matter of this chapter was collected so long ago as 1913. The seed fell on good ground: see *The Laird*, by Winifred Duke (London: John Long, 1925), in which that well-known Scots novelist has clothed agreeably the dry bones of fact with the living garments of fiction.

Since the above essay was written a full report of the case was made by me in *The Trial of Katharine Nairn*: Notable British Trials series (Edinburgh: 1926), containing the official record of the evidence and many illustrative documents from original sources.

# DEACON BRODIE

*The famous Deacon Brodie—him that was hanged in his sword and cocked hat like a great gentleman, at the drappin' o' his ain scented cambric handkerchief.*

—S.R. CROCKET: *Kid M'Ghie*

IN THE HALL of my home stands a piece of furniture of which I am justly proud. It is an old *aumrie* or cabinet of fair mahogany curiously inlaid, such as in former days it was the wont of douce Scots matrons to store with the family *napery* or household linen. The workmanship is wonderful, and proclaims itself the production of a master-craftsman; and sure enough, upon an inside panel of its double doors is cut in quaint script this legend—it looks like *vers libre*—

Made by William Brodie
for Jean Wilson spouse to
John Carfrae, coachmaker
in the Canongate, 1786.

John Carfrae of Craigend in Liberton, whose town house and coachworks were in Carfrae's Entry in the Canongate, was my great-grandfather. Of his wife I have often heard her daughter, my grandmother—who was herself a very personable dame —complacently relate that she was famed in the Edinburgh of her day as "Bonnie Jean Wilson." Although these well-favored forebears of mine have regrettably failed to transmit their physical charms, from them at least I derive this beautiful heirloom, which since "Bonnie Jean" presided over its snowy contents and lovingly polished its shining surfaces, has remained continuously in the custody of her descendants.

But apart from such feelings of sentiment, the *aumrie* is dear to me by reason of its historic interest and for the sake of him to whose skill it owes its comeliness. William Brodie, or ever he became a celebrated criminal, was a notable artificer; no cabinetmaker of his time could touch him. His father before him, Francis Brodie, was likewise of high repute in the business which he founded in the Lawnmarket and to which his son in due season succeeded. I have a tradesman's account of his, discharged by the old gentleman himself, for furniture supplied by him in 1749 to one Mistress Betty Gordon, with an engraved heading whereon are displayed divers examples of his art, together with this intimation: "AT BRODIE'S LOOKING-GLASS and CABINET-WAREHOUSE the 2d. closs above the Old Bank, Lawn Mercat, south side of the Street, is ready made and to be sold Variety of Furniture in the neatest and most fashionable Manner, with PICTURE and GLASS FRAMES carved and Gilded, as also HOUSE, CARPENTER and JOINER work done by the best work men. FUNERALS, BLACK CLOTH, & SCONCES for hanging Rooms furnished at the lowest Rates. COACH, & CHAIR GLASSES Sold. N.B.—The LOOKING-GLASSES, being Manufactured by my Self will be sold with a reasonable discount for ready Money." And of a truth Francis Brodie dealt generously by his fair customer, seeing that the account includes such items as: "To a Mahogany Desk, £4.10; To an Amboina wood Tea Chist, £1; To a Mahogany Dining Table 3 foot 6 Inch long, £1.16." I wonder what his son charged my great-grandmother for the *aumrie*?

Over and above this patrimonial interest, I regard Deacon Brodie with affection as being the subject of my second book, to wit, the volume devoted to his life and work in the Notable British Trials series, first published in 1906. It is my claim to be his best, at any rate his fullest biographer, and I had lately the pleasure to listen to a broadcast play about him, founded on my report of his trial. As the Deacon was in his day an ardent playgoer I wish he could have heard it, for it was very well done. I doubt whether he would have approved the melodrama: *Deacon Brodie, or The Double Life*: written by Henley and Stevenson, which ought to be so much more effective than it is. Stevenson, however, has touched his hero to better purpose in other of his writings. A further attraction of the subject for me is the fact that the trial was presided over by Lord Braxfield, immortalized as the Justice-Clerk in *Weir of Hermiston*, that puissant judge, on whose memorial I have elsewhere ventured to lay my modest wreath,[1] and also that my great-granduncle, James Carfrae, was a member of the jury.

I

If after the flesh Francis begat William, the Deacon's spiritual father was surely John Gay, for whose delightful work, *The Beggar's Opera*, he professed a profound admiration. The opera was first performed in Scotland in 1728, the year of its original production in London, and at once secured the popular favor. Thenceforth the Edinburgh public had many opportunities to

---

1. "The Bi-Centenary of Lord Braxfield," in *Glengarry's Way*, 1922.

hear its charming strains and revel in its quaint conceits—
opportunities of which Deacon Brodie took full advantage.
Throughout the contemporary accounts of his trial we find
him humming snatches of his favorite airs; and the day before
his death he sang—we are told, "with the greatest cheerfulness"
—Macheath's famous song, beginning:

'Tis woman that seduces all mankind. . . .

The bold Macheath was for him the perfect hero, the em-
bodiment of high romance. Upon that glorious and engaging
rogue, so far as his own inadequate inches, slight physique,
and nervous temperament would permit, he formed his walk
and conversation: the swaggering jollity, the easy good humor,
the dignity upon occasion, the reckless contempt for consequences, the indefatigable service of the fair. And at the end of
the day he fulfilled his exemplar's chief requirement of dying
as a gentleman. Like Macheath, the Deacon had his gang: his
Matt o' the Mint, his Crook-fingered Jack, his Jemmy Twitcher;
and grievously did they give their leader away. Like him, too,
he had his Polly Peachum and his Lucy Lockit, though, more
fortunate than Macheath, he contrived to keep each ignorant
of the other's existence.

How happy could I be with either,
Were t'other dear charmer away!

Thus the Captain, distracted by the rival claims of his competing spouses. Here the Deacon bettered his model: with Anne
Grant and Jean Watt his relations remained co-equal, placid,
amicable, and mutually unknown. Anne bore him two girls
and a boy; Jean, two boys. It takes a man of genius to maintain
for years so nice an equilibrium. And Jean even went the length
of perjury to save his neck.

II

In the Scotland of our pious forebears the family Bible was the domestic ark. Within its hallowed pages was preserved a register of every birth, marriage, and death affecting the home circle, records to which a peculiar solemnity attached. The Brodie Bible, having survived all its respective owners, now rests in peace among the relics of Auld Reekie's past, buried in the Edinburgh Municipal Museum.

The marriage of Francis Brodie with Cecil Grant was blessed by eleven children, of whom, under the abominable hygienic conditions of the time and place, three only struggled to maturity. Francis came of good Scots stock, the Brodies of Milton-Brodie in Elgin; his grandfather, Ludovick Brodie, was a Writer to the Signet. Cecil was the daughter of William Grant, writer (solicitor) in Edinburgh. So the Deacon had enough legal blood in his veins to have kept him in the straight path. It is significant that the entry relating to his birth is neatly cut out of the page: the Brodies, decent folk, had no desire to perpetuate his memory. The two other children who lived to grow up were Jean, after their parents' death her brother's housekeeper, and Jacobina, who married Matthew Sheriff, upholsterer in Edinburgh, of whom we shall hear again. William, the eldest child, was born on 28th September 1741. The house in which he saw the light, where the eight little martyrs lived their brief day, whence Francis and his spouse, full of years and fair repute, set out for their long home, sheltered the Deacon throughout his adventurous career and until his shameful death for well-nigh half a century. Of Brodie's Close, the alley in which it stood, a fragment may still be seen in the Lawnmarket; but the mansion itself was swept away when the ugly Victoria Street was ruthlessly driven slantwise through the adjacent *lands*. From the description of the house given by Chambers in 1825 it must have been a handsome and commodious dwelling. The site of Brodie's workshops and woodyard is now occupied by the foundations of the Free Library in the Cowgate.

## III

We know nothing of Master Brodie's boyhood and youth; but he must have received a good education, for he wrote a fine hand and an excellent letter, could quote appropriately a French phrase, had a pretty taste in harmony, was a member of "The Cape"—the most aristocratic of the Edinburgh social clubs, and held an important place in the government of his native city. Following dutifully in his father's ways, he was apprenticed to the business, and in course of time succeeded him as a Burgess and Guildbrother of Edinburgh. He became, as Deacon of the Incorporation of Wrights (joiners),[2] a member of the Town Council, a distinction which he continued to enjoy until his public downfall seven years later. This position secured for him the bulk of the municipal work connected with his trade, and his private business was the best in the city. When old Brodie died in 1782, the Deacon fell heir to a fortune of £10,000, together with considerable house property in and about the High Street. He ought, therefore, to have been exceptionally comfortable and well-to-do.

But, alas, behind this busy and honorable life there lay hidden a dangerous, and, as it proved, a fatal weakness. The Deacon was an inveterate gambler—not with his social equals at "The Cape," but with crooks and sharpers in the shady purlieus of the town. His principal resort was a disreputable

---

2. It were well, perhaps, to warn the English reader that the title "Deacon" has here no ecclesiastical significance. It denotes the headship of that particular branch of Trade Unionism concerned with the affairs of artisans in woodwork.

tavern, kept by one James Clark, vintner (publican), at the head of the Fleshmarket Close in the High Street, which from the habits of its patrons might have been known by the sign of "The Dice-Box." The company of scoundrels who frequented the house acknowledged the Deacon as their chief, and it is painful to record that the methods of play there employed were something less than fair. A further source of gratification for his ruling passion was furnished by what was then termed the "gentlemanly vice" of cock-fighting, a diversion in which the Deacon was an enthusiastic partaker. He kept his own game-cocks in a pen in his woodyard and was a constant attender of the *mains* held in the cock-pit of his friend Michael Henderson, stabler in the Grassmarket, an eminent "cocker," of whom more anon. At this barbarous pastime he is said to have lost large sums in backing his favorite but fallacious birds. To these sporting losses fell to be added the expense of maintaining no less than three households: his legitimate *ménage* in Brodie's Close and his two mistresses, Anne Grant and Jean Watt, with their respective broods in the several establishments in Cant's Close and in Libberton's Wynd for both of which the Deacon was responsible. All this, of course, began long before his father's death placed him in possession of affluence—his eldest child was twelve years old at the time of the trial—and some means had to be contrived whereby he could refill his exhausted coffers.

It was then that the Macheath complex became acute and operative. He had ever envied the raffish Captain his ability to make others pay the piper for his private pleasures; and to one of the Deacon's whimsical and histrionic tastes there was a piquancy in the contrast between the sober-living, respected Town Councilor and the man behind the mask: the gambler and the roué. Such minor rascalities as he had been wont to practice proving insufficiently remunerative, he decided to take a leaf out of his hero's book and become a robber on a grander scale. Better sport, too, than cheating a chimney-sweep of six guineas by means of loaded dice! To this course he was beckoned as well by the peculiar facilities which his trade afforded as by an ingenuous custom of the Edinburgh tradesmen. It was the habit of these guileless merchants during business hours to hang the keys of their premises upon a nail at the back of the shop door. Deacon Brodie, having concealed in the palm of his hand a lump of putty, would drop in for a crack with a friend over the counter, and so soon as the man's attention was otherwise engaged, a moment sufficed for taking an impression of the key. The fashioning of a new one from the mold thus obtained was an easy job, and thenceforth the friend's warehouse was as free to his visitor as to himself. So simple was the Deacon's "*Open Sesame*." Edinburgh was then an honest town, as witness this confiding custom of its indwellers, of which none had hitherto been base enough to take advantage. Wherefore did surprise, fear, and wrath accompany the swelling list of mysterious midnight burglaries. The secret marauder came and went without a trace, save for the empty till, the rifled scrutoire, or the displenished plate-chest that testified to his visitation. There was much speculating as to his means of ingress and possible identity; but Deacon Brodie was as far beyond suspicion as the Provost of the city or the minister of the High Kirk. There are few things better worth having in this world than a good reputation.

Stevenson has by the magic of his art given us in a single paragraph—which I cannot deny myself the pleasure of quoting—a perfect picture of the man and his methods:—

> A great man in his day was the Deacon; well seen in good society, crafty with his hands as a cabinet-maker, and one who could sing a song with taste. Many a citizen was proud to welcome the Deacon to supper, and dismissed him with regret at a timeous hour, who would

have been vastly disconcerted had he known how soon, and in what guise, his visitor returned. Many stories are told of this redoubtable Edinburgh burglar, but the one I have in my mind most vividly gives the key of all the rest. A friend of Brodie's, nested some way towards heaven in one of these great *lands*, had told him of a projected visit to the country, and afterwards, detained by some affairs, put it off and stayed the night in town. The good man had lain some time awake; it was far on in the small hours by the Tron bell; when suddenly there came a creak, a jar, a faint light. Softly he clambered out of bed and up to a false window which looked upon another room, and there, by the glimmer of a thieves' lantern, was his good friend the Deacon in a mask. It is characteristic of the town and the town's manners that this little episode should have been quietly tided over, and quite a good time elapsed before a great robbery, and escape, a Bow Street runner, a cock-fight, an apprehension in a cupboard in Amsterdam, and a last step into the air off his own greatly-improved gallows drop, brought the career of Deacon William Brodie to an end. But still, by the mind's eye, he may be seen, a man harassed below a mountain of duplicity, slinking from a magistrate's supper-room to a thieves' ken, and pickeering among the closes by the flicker of a dark lamp.[3]

Although Stevenson has told us that the original idea of his *Strange Story of Dr. Jekyll and Mr. Hyde*—"a fine bogey tale," as he describes it—came to him in a dream, there can be little doubt that his subconscious mind was influenced by his old acquaintance with Deacon Brodie. For years he had been

---

3. *Edinburgh: Picturesque Notes.*

writing and re-writing plays about that admirable double-dealer, whose character supplies so striking an example of the duality of man's nature and the alternation of good and evil —or as he himself succinctly has it: "that damned old business of the war in the members." He gives all credit for the plot to his sleeping partners, the Little People; but I am persuaded that in fact he was more indebted to a Brodie than to a Brownie.

## IV

July 1786 marked a turning-point in the Deacon's criminous career. Hitherto he had worked alone, and it was mainly his private friends whom he favored with an exhibition of his skill. That month came to Edinburgh a wandering Englishman named George Smith, traveling the country with a horse and cart. He put up at the inn of Michael Henderson, the sporting publican, in the Grassmarket. There presently he fell sick, sent for his wife to nurse him, and had to sell his hawker's outfit to meet the expenses of his illness. His convalescence was cheered by the companionship of two frequenters of the house, Andrew Ainslie and John Brown *alias* Humphry Moore. All that is known of Ainslie is that he designated himself "sometime shoemaker in Edinburgh," but as to his subsequent means of livelihood he was discreetly silent. Concerning the antecedents of Mr. Brown we are better informed. In April 1784 he was, after trial for robbery, sentenced at the Old Bailey to be transported beyond the seas for the term of seven years.[4] How he came to be still practicing his profession in Edinburgh two years later, a free man, does not appear; for the King's pardon,

---

4. *Select Criminal Trials at Justice-Hall in the Old Bailey.* Vol. I, Appendix No. XII, p. 46. Edinburgh: 1803.

obtained for him to enable him to bear witness against Brodie at the Deacon's trial, was dated only one month before that event. Be that as it may, with these two congenial spirits the invalid was enabled to beguile the time in various games of hazard, wherein, owing to the skill of the players, little was left to chance. His acquaintance was further extended by his introduction to the Deacon, a patron of the house, who recognized the possibilities which Mr. Smith's character presented. He had been bred a locksmith, and as such would prove a useful associate for one of Mr. Brodie's unconventional pursuits. It was soon arranged that they should work together; and when Smith was sufficiently recovered, the bad companions, "in consequence of this concert, were in use to go about together in order to find out proper places where business could be done with success." The fruits of their alliance are fully set forth in my report of the trial, and may here be mentioned briefly. One night in October a gold-smith's shop near the Council Chambers—where by day the Deacon gravely administered the town's affairs—was broken into and many valuable articles were carried off. In November two visits were paid to the premises of one M'Kain, a merchant in the South Bridge. Among the goods removed was a red pocket-book, which Smith bestowed upon the daughter of his host, Michael Henderson, as a mark of his regard.

Through the good offices of his new friend, Smith was now established as a householder in the city, his wife keeping ostensibly a grocery shop in the Cowgate. Messrs. Ainslie and Brown lodged together at their own charges in Burnet's Close, waiting, like Mr. Micawber, for something to turn up. W. S. Gilbert, with that profound knowledge of human nature which distinguishes all his work, has acutely observed:—

> When the enterprising burglar's not a-burgling,
> When the cut-throat isn't occupied in crime,

He loves to hear the little brook a-gurgling,
And listen to the merry village chime.

In the Auld Reekie of the eighteenth century no gurgling fluid
was to be heard save the perennial pouring out of liquor, and
the lugubrious jangle of the Tron Kirk bell—anathematized
of the poet Fergusson—was the only available chime. These
amenities, such as they were, did Brown and Ainslie enjoy to
the full in the chosen place of their recreation: Clark's tavern
in the Fleshmarket Close, where most of their leisure hours
were spent. Not unprofitably; for there was generally an odd
guinea to be won by means of marked cards and loaded dice—
provided always that they played with strangers, unaware of
their peculiar practices. Smith and Brodie, too, were regular in
their attendance, but knowing their men, refrained personally
from putting the skill of these experts to the proof.

December was a quiet month, excepting for some £12 obtained without permission from a tobacconist's shop in the
Exchange; but it was decided that something better should be
done on Christmas Eve. The Deacon had lately been professionally employed in altering the door of the jewelers' shop in
Bridge Street belonging to Messrs. Bruce. This, he pointed out
to his partner, "would be a very proper shop for breaking into."
Smith agreed, and it was arranged that they should meet that
night at Clark's in pursuance of their laudable design. They be-
guiled the time by playing hazard; Smith was speedily cleaned
out, but Brodie's hand was in—or his opponent more amenable
to treatment; he was winning steadily and refused to let business interfere with pleasure. So at four of the morning Mr.
Smith set forth alone upon the enterprise. The lock, to a person of his acquirements, proved a simple matter; and as the result of his perquisitions, the whole contents of the show-cases,
including ten watches and many gold rings, lockets, and other
valuables, changed hands—or rather, feet, for Mr. Smith had

provided an old pair of stockings to which he transferred the spoil. These he concealed in a manger at Michael Henderson's stable, and with a contented mind sought the family bosom in the Cowgate.

Next day the Deacon called to inspect the proceeds, which were valued at £350 sterling. Smith pointed out that as he had taken no part in the risk, Brodie could not expect a full share of the profits. This the Deacon deemed only fair, and contented himself, as a Christmas present, with a gold seal, a gold watch-key set with garnets, and two gold rings, all for his proper use. The residue was taken by Smith to England, where he disposed of it for £105 to one Mr. John Tasker *alias* Murray, who resided at the Bird-in-Hand, Chesterfield, a broad-minded gentleman lately banished from Scotland for theft. This sum, less the expenses of the journey, Smith asked Brodie to keep for him and give him as and when required; but the Deacon "gained a great part of it at play" and thus, after all, had the best of the bargain.

V

In 1787 there were two additions to the cast of The Deacon's Opera. Mr. Brown was on holiday in Stirlingshire, but Mr. Ainslie was co-opted a member of the band. Their first performance was for behoof of a grocer in Leith, whose premises they broke into, filling two wallets with 350 pounds of fine black tea—then a valuable haul. "Ainslie being ill at this time and Brodie being weakly," one of the heavy wallets had to be abandoned on their way back to town in a field at Bonnington, whence it was afterwards recovered by the owner. The 350 pounds of tea seems a poor "bag" after the £350 sterling in Smith's stockings.

Mr. Brown's holiday having been abridged by his banishment

from the county for theft, he returned to Edinburgh, and was promoted by Brodie a person of the drama. For some time the Deacon had been considering the propriety of appropriating the silver mace of Edinburgh University. It was kept in the College library, where it had caught his eye on the occasion of his visiting with Mr. Smith that seat of learning. So on the night of 29th October 1787 the four partners proceeded to business. "Having got access at the under gate, they opened the under door leading to the Library with a false key, which broke in the lock; and thereafter they broke open the door of the Library with an iron crow, and carried away the College mace." The Town Council forthwith offered in vain a reward for the discovery of the "wicked persons" who had done the deed, and Deacon Brodie was officially shocked at the effrontery of the outrage. The mace was forwarded to Mr. Tasker at the Bird-in-Hand, and the macer thereafter knew it no more.

Their next victim was an Edinburgh shopkeeper named John Tapp. Here the usual formula of the Deacon was followed. An impression of the key was taken, Smith made a false one, and Brown dropped in for a chat with Tapp, with whom, being Christmastide, he had a friendly dram. Meanwhile the others let themselves into the house and secured some nineteen pounds, a watch, divers rings, "and a miniature picture of a gentleman belonging to Tapp's wife, which picture they broke for the sake of the gold with which it was backed." The jewelry, like the mace, disappeared into Derbyshire, and Mrs. Tapp never saw her "gentleman" again.

The ensuing robbery—that of Inglis & Horner's shop at the Cross in the High Street—had, as we shall find, far-reaching results. After an abortive attempt by Brodie upon the padlock of the silk mercers' door, Smith made a satisfactory key, and goods to the value of between £300 and £400 were secured. A reward of £100 failed, as usual, to lead to the detection of the perpetrators; but Inglis & Horner were not content tamely to submit to their loss. They petitioned the Government, and so effective were their representations, that on 25th January 1788 there was issued from Whitehall a notice, promising £150 to any person who within six months should give such information as would lead to the apprehension and conviction of the robbers; "Twenty Guineas, whether the offenders are convicted or not"; and if an accomplice in the crime, "*His Majesty's most gracious pardon and the informer's name, if required, concealed.*" This seed, as we shall see, fell on good ground and in due season brought forth abundantly. Meanwhile the spoil of the silk mercers was sent by two separate routes—by the Berwick and the Newcastle carries—to Mr. Tasker at the Bird-in-Hand, and Smith's wife was to go South later to count and reckon with that receptive agent.

## VI

The year 1788, which saw the last of Deacon Brodie's exploits and the close of his earthly activities, opened with two incidents eminently characteristic of his double life as robber and reputable citizen. The first of these occurred on 17th January. At eventide the three confederates, Brodie, Smith, and Ainslie, were fortifying themselves against the fatigues of their nightly labors with a comfortable bowl of punch at their favorite *howff* in the Fleshmarket Close. To them entered one John Hamilton, a master chimney-sweep, who practiced his art in Portsburgh, a neighborhood in after years distinguished as the hunting-ground of Burke and Hare. He was invited to join in a friendly game at hazard, in the course of which he was rapidly relieved of some six guineas. Suspecting foul play he seized the dice, examined them, and found that they were loaded, being filled at one corner with lead.

Forthwith Hamilton presented to the Magistrates a petition

and complaint against his late playfellows, praying for a warrant to apprehend and incarcerate them until they should repeat (refund) the money of which they had robbed him, and pay a further sum in name of damages and expenses. Answers were lodged by the three respondents, who alleged that Hamilton had intruded himself upon their private game; that if anything were wrong with the dice they knew nothing about it, these being the property of, and supplied by, the house. Smith and Ainslie maintained that instead of winning, they had in fact lost; Brodie, that he had only won 7s. 6d. The petitioner himself, they averred, was a noted adept at gambling, and it was not very credible that he should have allowed himself to be imposed upon in the manner alleged. Irony is a great gift, and Mr. Hamilton possessed it in a marked degree, as witness these excerpts from his Replies to the respondents' Answers:—

> A wonderful story, indeed! Smith and Ainslie, two noted sharpers at the business, assert they were losers, and innocent Mr. Brodie avers he was only a gainer in this paltry trifle of 7s. 6d.; and yet the petitioner finds himself out of pocket near as many guineas as that gentleman says he received of shillings. Certain, however, it is that in their company, by undue means, he lost five guinea notes, two half-guineas in gold, and six shillings in silver, before he suspected the fraud.... Mr. Brodie knows nothing about, and is entirely ignorant of such devices, and always considered all dice to be alike....
>
> Miserable!—that the petitioner, a deemed sharper, should be taken in by a pigeon, to use the *lingua* of the Club. But so it has happened. Mr. Brodie knows nothing of such vile tricks—not he! He never made them his study—not he! Never was at either pains or expense to acquire them—not he, indeed! Mr. Brodie never haunted night-houses, where nothing but the blackest and vilest

arts were practiced to catch a pigeon; nor ever was accessory either by himself or others in his combination, to behold the poor young creature plucked alive, and not one feather left upon its wings—not he, indeed! He never was accessory to see or be concerned in fleecing the ignorant, the thoughtless, the young, and the unwary; nor ever made it his study, his anxious study, with unwearied concern, at midnight hours, to haunt rooms where he thought of meeting with the company from which there was a possibility of fetching from a scurvy sixpence to a hundred guineas—not he, indeed! He is unacquainted altogether with packing or shuffling a set of cards—he is indeed!

Mr. Brodie, in all his innocent amusements, never met with any person, who, after having been fleeced of money to the amount of a hundred pounds, and detected the vile and dishonest methods by which it had been abstracted from him, received as a return for his moral rectitude *a very handsome incision on the eye*—never he, indeed! He never was in such company, nor ever met with such accident—not he!

There is no record of the occasion on which the Deacon came by his retributive cut; but the resulting scar below his right eye is visible in his portraits by Kay, and is referred to as recent in the description of him issued by the authorities, aftermentioned. The petitioner at least, as the phrase goes, got some of his own back. All this, one would think, must have created a painful sensation among the Deacon's colleagues in the Town Council; but singularly enough nothing further is heard of the matter.

Brodie's next public appearance was in circumstances much more respectable, to wit, in the jury-box of the High Court of Justiciary, where five months later he was himself to stand at the bar. The case in which the Deacon was called upon to decide the issue of life or death was this: on 4th February 1788 an Excise officer and a soldier were tried for the murder of a ferryman at Dunoon. The ferryman had resisted the seizure of some illicit stills; the officer ordered the soldier to fire, and the man was killed. After hearing the evidence, the jury acquitted both prisoners. So the Deacon did his good deed for the day. One wonders whether it ever crossed his mind that his next view of that Court would be from the dock, with the same counsel for the Crown and the same Judges on the Bench—but with a very different conclusion.

## VII

The robbery of the Excise Office ought to have been Deacon Brodie's biggest job: the masterpiece that fittingly crowned his career, freed him from further association with his bad companions, and enabled him to retire from practice upon a comfortable competence. Long contemplated and carefully planned, it should, with any luck, have proved to such experienced hands an easy business. But, alas, it turned out instead a lamentable failure, involving everyone concerned in ruin and disgrace and costing its contriver his life.

As you go down the High Street, past the Nether Bow and the apocryphal manse of the Rev. John Knox—now with God or elsewhere furth of Scotland—you perceive on the south side of that thoroughfare a deep archway or *pend*, conducting to a spacious enclosure named Chessel's Court. A stately mansion faces you at the back of the court, fenced by ancient railings— the *palisadoes* of the trial. This, in old days, was the General Excise Office for Scotland, our Somerset House; the repository of the cash wrung from reluctant lieges throughout the land in name of His Majesty's revenue. Of course such moneys should have been lodged in bank, where they would have been secure from depredation; but in the simple practice of the time they were kept for a space in the office. The Deacon had often cast a covetous eye on this—as he deemed it—Robbers' Cave, to which he was minded to play Ali Baba. Over and above the rich harvest to be won, the opportunity to spoil the spoilers of their prey tickled his sense of humor. So after due consultation, as became the importance of the undertaking, the partners proceeded to business.

The Deacon had a relative who often came to town upon Excise matters, and with him Brodie took occasion to visit the office. Then, having noted the internal arrangements, he called one day with Smith on pretense of inquiring for his friend. While he held the cashier in conversation, Smith took an impression of the office key, which as usual hung behind the front door. Brodie made a drawing of the wards, and Smith filed therefrom a false key. Ainslie, being instructed to study the habits of the watchmen charged with the duty of warding the premises, reported that the office was left unguarded between 8 p.m., when it was closed for the day, and 10 p.m., when two watchmen alternately came on duty. The new key was tried; it readily opened the outer door, but the inner door of the cashier's room had a different lock. Mr. Brown was of opinion that this difficulty might best be overcome by direct violence; and on Friday, 28th February, we find him, accompanied by Ainslie and attended by Smith's black dog "Rodney," enjoying a country ramble at Duddingston Loch. Having suitably refreshed themselves in the village ale-house, they entered a field in which was a temporarily abandoned plough, from which they stole the coulter and two iron wedges. Returning by way of the King's Park, they concealed these souvenirs of their excursion among the rocks of Salisbury Crags. By Tuesday, 4th March, the company was ready to take the field, and Wednesday the 5th was to witness the carrying out of the great adventure. We learn from Mr. Smith what was the plan of campaign:—

> Ainslie was to keep on the outside of the office, hanging over the palisadoes in the entry with a whistle of ivory, which was purchased by Brodie the night before, with which, if the man belonging to the Excise Office came, he was to give one whistle, and if any serious alarm was perceived he was to give three whistles, and then make the best of his way to the Excise Gardens in the Canongate in order to assist the declarant [Smith], Brodie, and Brown to get out at the back window of the hall, it being determined in case of surprise to bolt the outer door on the inside and make the best of their way by the window.

Ainslie was armed only with a stick; Brodie had a brace of pistols, Smith a brace and a half, and Brown a brace. These arms were all loaded with ball, "as they were determined not to be taken, whatever the consequences." It was concerted by Brodie that in the event of interruption by any member of the office staff, they should secure him, "and personate smugglers who came in search of their property that had been seized"—a characteristic touch this—and he provided Smith with an old wig of his (the Deacon's) father for purposes of disguise. Brodie deposited with Smith sundry implements of his craft to be used in effecting the robbery, including a spur, which was to be left upon the scene of action, "to make it believed it had been done by some person on horseback." The coulter and wedges were retrieved by Brown and Ainslie from Salisbury Crags; and three crape masks were prepared for the use of the junior partners— the Deacon disdaining such disguise. The rendezvous was fixed for 7 p.m. at Smith's house in the Cowgate.

## VIII

At the appointed hour, in an upper chamber of Mr. Smith's modest dwelling, the three conspirators impatiently awaited the coming of their chief. Meanwhile they discussed a light supper of chicken and herrings, and drank success to the night's adventure in *black cork*, which Mr. Brown afterwards explained to mean Bell's beer—a popular local beverage. To them entered the Deacon, dressed in a light-colored greatcoat, a suit of black—instead of his ordinary "white" clothes—and wearing a cocked hat. Pistol in hand, he histrionically hailed his comrades with the famous Rogues' March from his beloved *Beggar's Opera*:—

> Let us take the Road.
> Hark! I hear the Sound of Coaches!
> The Hour of Attack approaches,
> To your Arms, brave Boys, and load.
>
> See the Ball I hold!
> Let the Chymists toil like Asses,
> Our Fire their Fire surpasses,
> And turns all our Lead to Gold.

Mr. Brown, like an Illustrious Personage on another occasion, was not amused. His was a mind severely practical; he had no use for play-acting and flash songs. Brodie was well-nigh an hour late and their business brooked no delay. The Deacon apologized; he had been giving a little dinner in his house in Brodie's Close; the last guest was but just departed, and he had only stayed to change his clothes. Now he was with them: heart and soul and dark-lantern. "Let us take the Road!" The order of their going was on this wise: Ainslie, carrying the coulter, went first to Chessel's Court, to hide behind the *palisadoes* and see that the coast was clear. He was followed by Smith with the false key; Brodie, armed, came next, and finally, with the requisite tools, Mr. Brown. Smith opened the outer door of the Excise Office, and Brown called for *Great Samuel*, as he playfully dubbed the coulter, which Ainslie handed to him through the railings. Brodie kept watch in the passage, while Smith and Brown dealt with the inner door, whose lock yielded to the persuasion of a pair of curling irons or "toupee tongs." The strong door of the cashier's room submitted to the forcible arguments of *Great Samuel*, and the contents thereof were at the robbers' mercy.

The night was one well suited to their purpose. It was appropriately dark; snow had fallen all day and it was freezing hard; a bitter wind kept most folks within doors. Out in the Canongate, the city lamps, few and far between, swung to and fro in the easterly blast, their tenuous gleam but making darkness visible. The court itself appears to have been unlighted. This, in his own words, is the sum of Mr. Ainslie's observations, as, grasping his ivory whistle, he shivered behind the *palisadoes*:—

> I took my station within the rail and leaned down, so that no person either going in or coming out could see me. Some short while after Brodie and Brown went into the office, a man came running down the close [entry from the street] and went in also. I gave no alarm, for before I had time to think what I should do, another man came immediately running out at the door and went up the court. In a very little afterwards, to my great surprise, a second man came out from the office. I got up and looked at him through the rails, and perceived that he was none of my three companions. I had not seen the other man who came out first so distinctly, owing to my lying down by the side of the parapet wall on which the

rail is placed, in order that I might not be observed. I was afraid that we were discovered; and as soon as the second man had gone up the close, I gave the alarm by three whistles as the agreed-on signal of retreat, and ran up the close myself.

What had happened was this: Mr. Bonar, Deputy-Solicitor of Excise, having left in his room certain papers which he required, went back to the office for them about half-past eight, thinking some of the clerks might still be there. As he hoped, he found the outer door on the latch, opened it, and entered the building. Here I have to make, vicariously, a humiliating and painful confession. No sooner did Mr. Bonar appear in the passage than the Deacon bounced out from behind the door. Now, surely, was the time to show his mettle, here at last was an opportunity to play the hero and emulate the great Macheath; never again would he have such a chance of rousing melodrama. He was armed; and if he were too humane to pistol the intruder, a shot fired in the air would be enough to scare him off the field. But instead of taking his cue, the Deacon brushed rapidly past the stranger, and in the terminology of his favorite sport, fled the pit, without regard for his confederates' safety! Mr. Bonar, deeming him to be someone connected with the office and being himself in haste, ran upstairs to his own room, got what he wanted, ran down again, and slamming the outer door behind him, hurried from the court. His entrance and exit account for the first and third of Ainslie's apparitions; Deacon Brodie, sad to say, was the second.

Meanwhile Messrs. Smith and Brown, those busy and burglarious bees, had been for half an hour feverishly ransacking the hive by the light of the Deacon's dark-lantern. Every press and lock-fast place likely to contain money was opened, some by violence and others with keys. All they could find were sixteen pounds odd in the cashier's desk with which, cursing their ill luck, they had to rest content. And the cream of the jest is this: in a secret drawer beneath that desk there lay, for the taking, a sum of *six hundred pounds sterling*! Mr. Smith afterwards stated:—

> That the declarant and Brown, when in the cashier's room, heard the outer door open, but trusting to Brodie's being at the door and staunch, they did not mind it; that the declarant and Brown, when coming out of the cashier's office, heard a person coming hastily down-stairs, which made them stop or they would have met him; that upon this the declarant said to Brown: "Here must be treachery; get out your pistols and cock them," which they did accordingly; that upon coming to the outer door they found it shut, they having seen the person that came downstairs smash the door after him when he went away.

Seeing no sign of their evasive companions, they followed his example.

## IX

With that touching faith in the virtue of an alibi so strongly held by old Mr. Weller, Deacon Brodie, having regained in safety his own house shortly before nine o'clock, changed into his usual dress, "of a marbled color and a round hat," and has-tened to the abode of his mistress, Jean Watt, where he spent the night. Libberton's Wynd was nearer Brodie's Close than Cant's Close, where Anne Grant lodged; wherefore, I suppose, Jean's hospitality was preferred. Perhaps, too, he deemed her a more pliant accomplice in the tampering with Time, which, like a later malefactor, he proposed to attempt. Next morning the Deacon called at Burnet's Close to confer with his partners as to the miscarriage of the night before. "He came in laughing," Ainslie reports, "and said that he had been with Smith, who had accused him of running away the previous evening." Brown and Ainslie expressed themselves strongly as of the same opinion; "but he said that he had stood true." After much mutual recrimination, it was agreed that they should meet next night at Smith's equitably to divide the spoil. So on Friday, 7th March, the members of the band met in the upper chamber in the Cowgate for the last time, each receiving four pounds odd as his share of the proceeds. Ainslie took the opportunity of pressing for payment of money which Brodie owed him, and the Deacon honorably discharged the debt. He, therefore, got less than nothing out of the great raid. Brown, so soon as he had received his dividend, went out like Judas, and with similar intent. Smith and Ainslie crossed the Bridge to the New Town, where they booked a seat for the following morning in the Newcastle stage, by which Mrs. Smith purposed to set forth to treat with Mr. Tasker of the Bird-in-Hand touching the goods stolen from Inglis & Horner's shop, consigned to him as before related. They paid for the ticket with a five-pound note of which we shall hear again.

The reader may remember that in connection with this earlier robbery there was offered a reward of £150 and a free pardon for discovery of the criminals, which had been daily advertised in the Edinburgh newspapers since 25th January. Of this handsome offer Mr. Brown now proposed to take advantage. Over his head still hung the sentence of transportation and it were well that he should come to terms with the authorities. He was also very sore about the Excise Office fiasco and the manner in which he considered the Deacon had let him down. So the crafty ruffian waited that same evening upon the Procurator-Fiscal, and made what he was pleased to call a clean breast of the whole business. It is remarkable that his confession contained no reference to Deacon Brodie, whose name he doubtless suppressed with a view to blackmailing that unfortunate gentleman so soon as Smith and Ainslie were got safely out of the way. The Fiscal welcomed the informer with open arms. That night he and his clerk, guided by Brown, went out to Salisbury Crags, where they took possession of the false keys used at the Excise Office, hidden there by Smith after the failure of the attempt.

Next day, Saturday, 8th March, events moved swiftly in the interests of justice. Smith, his wife, and their maidservant, together with Ainslie, were all apprehended and lodged in the Tolbooth, while Brown, accompanied by the Sheriff-Clerk, left for Chesterfield to recover the stolen goods from Mr. Tasker, who must have been unpleasantly surprised by their visit. The fact that they traveled by the very coach in which Mrs. Smith was to have performed the journey should have appealed to the Deacon's well-known sense of humor. But Mr. Brodie had other and more serious things to think about. That night all Edinburgh was humming with the great news; the robbers, who so long had terrified the town, were taken and thenceforth the citizens might sleep in peace. When these glad tidings reached the Deacon's ear, his first thought was at all costs to stop the prisoners' mouths as to his connection with the burglaries. So, having donned his finest raiment, he proceeded to the Tolbooth where, as a Town Councilor, he demanded to see the prisoners. Alas, the keeper respectfully refused; he had strict orders to admit no one. That night the Deacon, after reviewing the situation, decided to fly the country, an act as foolish and more fatal than his evacuation of the Excise Office. For Smith and Ainslie had been staunch. In their examinations before the Sheriff they had denied all knowledge of the robbery, so Mr. Brown remained uncorroborated; and the name of Deacon Brodie was mentioned by no one. But the wicked flee when no man pursueth; our hero disappeared from Edinburgh.

He stood not upon the order of his going, the manner whereof we shall learn later.

## X

Not until the prisoners in the Tolbooth heard that their chief had absconded did they follow the example of Mr. Brown in the matter of making a clean breast and disclose the whole depredations of the gang, giving the Deacon the full credit of his leadership. So on 12th March there was issued from the Sheriff-Clerk's office the following notice:—

TWO HUNDRED POUNDS OF REWARD.

WHEREAS WILLIAM BRODIE, a considerable House-Carpenter and Burgess of the City of Edinburgh, has been charged with being concerned in breaking into the General Excise Office for Scotland, and stealing from the Cashier's office there a sum of money—and as the said William Brodie has either made his escape from Edinburgh or is still concealed about that place—a REWARD OF ONE HUNDRED AND FIFTY POUNDS STERLING is hereby offered to any person who will produce him alive at the Sheriff-Clerk's Office, Edinburgh, or will secure him so as he may be brought there within three months from this date; and FIFTY POUNDS STERLING MORE, payable on his conviction by William Scott, procurator-fiscal for the shire of Edinburgh.

WILLIAM SCOTT.

DESCRIPTION.

WILLIAM BRODIE is about five feet four inches—is about forty-eight years of age, but looks rather younger than he is—broad at the shoulders and very small over the loins—has dark brown full eyes, with large black eye-brows—under the right eye there is the scar of a cut, which is still a little sore at the point of the eye next the nose, and a cast with his eye that gives him somewhat the look of a Jew—a sallow complexion—a particular motion with his mouth and lips when he speaks, which he does full and slow, his mouth being commonly open at the time and his tongue doubling up, as it were, shows itself towards the roof of his mouth—black hair, twisted, turned up, and tied behind, coming far down upon each cheek and the whiskers very sandy at the end; high topped in the front, and frizzed at the side—high smooth forehead—has a particular air in his walk, takes long steps, strikes the ground first with his heel, bending both feet inwards before he moves them again—usually wears a stick under hand, and moves in a proud, swaggering sort of style—his legs small above the ankle, large ankle bones and a large foot, high brawns, small at the knees, which bend when he walks as if through weakness— Was dressed in a black coat, vest, breeches, and stockings, a striped duffle great coat, and silver shoe buckles.

Surely never was issued a more minute description of a "wanted" man. The subject himself had opportunity to see it as he passed through London on his way to the Continent, and was by no means flattered. He attributed its painful precision to the malice of Mr. Brown. "I can see some strokes of his pencil in my portrait," he afterwards wrote. "May God forgive him for all his crimes and falsehoods!"

The task of tracing the fugitive devolved upon Mr. George Williamson, King's Messenger for Scotland. Edinburgh having been drawn blank, he first found the scent at Dunbar, whence he followed it to Newcastle and York, only to lose it in London. After eighteen days' fruitless search Mr. Williamson returned to Edinburgh, and had to acknowledge that Deacon Brodie had beaten him.

The hegira of the Deacon deserves a chapter to itself; but as I have elsewhere given a fully-documented account thereof, I shall confine myself here to a bare outline of his adventures. Reaching London on Wednesday, 12th March, he found refuge in the house of a lady, whom he describes as "an old female friend," where he abode in safety till Sunday, the 23rd. He twice met Mr. Williamson in the street, but eluded his notice, and saw with indignation in the reward bill what he calls his "picture," exhibited to public view. Through the good but grudging offices of his cousin, young Brodie of Milton, who was then in Edinburgh, he had been put in touch with Mr. William Walker, attorney in the Adelphi. The man of law arranged the details of his embarkation and furnished him with funds for the voyage. At that period and for long afterwards communication by sea between Edinburgh and London was carried on by small sailing vessels, known as Leith smacks. One such lay that Sunday at Blackwall, ready to set sail for Leith. Her only passengers were a Mid-Calder tobacconist and his wife named Geddes, who had been holiday-making in London and were now on their way home. At midnight the master, John Dent, who had spent the day ashore, came on board, accompanied by another passenger, "dressed in a blue greatcoat with a red collar, round wig, black vest, breeches, and boots. He was allotted a bed in the state-room near the fire, as he was sick." Next morning the *Endeavour* got under way, but she ran aground at Tilbury Point and did not clear the Thames for a fortnight! This did not trouble the tobacconist and his lady, who probably held a contract ticket, entitling them to meals for the duration of the voyage. Accompanied by their fellow-passenger, whose name they ascertained to be Mr. John Dixon, and attended by Captain Dent, they visited the neighboring villages and enjoyed their protracted holiday. When the *En-deavour* at length reached the open sea Mr. Dixon presented to the captain sealed orders from the owners, instructing him to sail for Flanders and land the bearer at Ostend. Owing to bad weather he failed to do so, and had to put into Flushing. On arriving at that port, "Mr. Dixon set off for Ostend in a skiff, which he hired for that purpose." Before he left the ship that gentleman, on saying good-bye to the Geddes couple—who seem to have borne him no grudge because of the uncon-scionable extension of their trip—entrusted to the tobacconist for delivery in Edinburgh three letters, respectively addressed to Mr. Michael Henderson, stabler in the Grassmarket, Mrs. Anne Grant, Cant's Close, and Mr. Matthew Sheriff, uphol-sterer in Edinburgh. Of all the writer's manifold indiscretions this "last fatal one" was for him the worst.

Mr. and Mrs. Geddes having completed at Flushing some private purchases of contraband articles, the *Endeavour* once more set sail and in due season arrived at the port of Leith, where the passengers with their foreign spoils were at last quit of her. As Mr. Geddes, anxious to make up for lost time, was reading the newspapers to see how things had gone at home while he had been abroad, his attention was arrested by the public advertisement relating to Deacon Brodie, printed above. There could be no possibility of mistake; Brown's portrait was only too good a likeness: Mr. John Dixon and William Brodie were the same person. Mr. Geddes's conscience was not un-duly tender, as witness his smuggling of lace, etc. He did not scruple to open the letters; what he read therein confirmed his suspicion, so he took them to the Sheriff and the fat was fairly in the fire. The information thus received was at once commu-nicated to the authorities in London; through the usual diplo-matic channels the Deacon was traced to Amsterdam, where, on his lodgings being searched, he was discovered hiding in a cupboard; he surrendered, and was imprisoned in the Stadthouse, to await the officers of the law from England. On 1st July Mr. Groves, Messenger-at-arms, left London to bring the captive back. After some delay due to difficulty in proving his identity, which the prisoner denied, he was extradited and was by Groves safely conveyed to London. At Bow Street, on 11th July, he admitted his identity and was committed to Bridewell, pending his removal to Edinburgh for trial. The two trunks, which constituted the fugitive's baggage, being opened, divers compromising papers were found; these were later produced in evidence against him. On the 17th the *Caledonian Mercury* informed its interested readers:—

> This morning early Mr. Brodie arrived from London. He was immediately carried to the house of Mr. Sheriff Cockburn, at the back of the Meadows or Hope Park, for examination. Mr. George Williamson, Messenger, and Mr. Groves, one of Sir Sampson Wright's clerks, accompanied Mr. Brodie in a post-chaise from Tothilfields Bridewell. He was this forenoon committed to the Tolbooth. They were only fifty-four hours on the road.

## XI

Meanwhile Smith and Ainslie were still languishing in the Tolbooth, wherein they had been confined since March. In May, however, they made a vigorous bid for freedom. Smith's cell was two stories beneath that of Ainslie. In the absence of his professional tools he contrived to convert "the iron handle of the jack or bucket of the necessary into a pick-lock, and one of the iron hoops round the bucket into a saw." With these imperfect instruments Smith managed to open two doors and join his companion; together they cut a hole in the ceiling of

Ainslie's cell, and were doing likewise by the prison roof, when unfortunately their operations dislodged some slates, which, falling upon the sentry below, apprised him that something was wrong. And so an attempt not unworthy of the great little Jack Sheppard himself was brought to nought. "In order to let themselves down from the top of the prison they had prepared 16 fathoms of rope, which they had artfully manufactured out of the sheets of their beds." This was a much better and brighter business than the Excise Office job and deserved success, but the luck of the firm had turned.

Their partner Mr. Brown, despite the favor which he had found with the authorities, was also provided with board and lodging in the Tolbooth, where he then underlay the charge of killing with a bottle one M'Arthur, an innkeeper of Halkerston's Wynd. But the consequences of this, and of other regrettable incidents in Mr. Brown's variegated past, were avoided by the granting to him on 28th July of His Majesty's most gracious pardon for these and all other offenses, to enable him to appear in pristine purity to bear witness against his late associates.

Deacon Brodie bore the rigors of his incarceration with cheerfulness and good humor. I have elsewhere printed a delightful letter which he wrote to one of his fellow-magistrates, complaining of the excessive growth of his nails, due to his being debarred the use of a knife, and asking the councilor to visit him thereanent. "You'll be sure to find me at home, and all hours are equally convenient." As apart from the evidence of Brown there was no direct proof of the charge, the Lord Advocate decided to accept Ainslie as King's evidence, and proceed only against Brodie and Smith. So on 11th August an indictment was duly served upon them, the trial to take place on the 27th. Smith proposed to plead Guilty, but was dissuaded from doing so by the advice of his law agent.

## XII

On Wednesday, 27th August 1788, at nine o'clock in the morning, this historic trial began. So great was the public interest in the proceedings that a detachment of the 7th Regiment of Foot from the Castle occupied the Parliament Close. The prisoners were "conveyed in chairs" from the Tolbooth to the Court, escorted by the City Guard. "Mr. Brodie was genteelly dressed in a new dark-blue coat, a fashionable fancy waistcoat, black satin breeches, and white silk stockings, a cocked hat, and had his hair fully dressed and powdered." His brave appearance was in marked contrast to that of his companion in misfortune, who was "but poorly clothed." On the Bench sat the Lord Justice-Clerk, the great Braxfield himself, with Lords Hailes, Eskgrove, Stonefield, and Swinton. The Lord Advocate, Ilay Campbell; the Solicitor-General, Robert Dundas; and two Advocates-Depute, appeared for the Crown. Brodie was defended by the Dean of Faculty, Henry Erskine; Alexander Wight; and Charles Hay, afterwards Lord Newton. John Clerk, afterwards Lord Eldin, and Robert Hamilton were counsel for Smith. Such a galaxy of legal luminaries is seldom met with in a single case. The indictment being read, both pannels (prisoners) pleaded Not Guilty; a jury, which included Creech, the publisher, and the respective founders of Fettes College and of Donaldson's Hospital, was empaneled, and the trial proceeded. As he gazed about the crowded Court the Deacon must surely have called to mind the song of his old hero, the Captain, upon a similar dread occasion:—

> The Charge is prepar'd; the Lawyers are met,
> The Judges all rang'd (a terrible Show!)
> I go, undismay'd.—For Death is a Debt,
> A Debt on Demand.—So take what I owe.

From the forensic point of view the star turn of the "show" was John Clerk. He had been called barely three years before, this was his first big case, and he distinguished himself by the fighting attitude which he adopted towards the Bench. Whether his client gained anything by the tactics he saw fit to employ is another matter. He objected to the production and founding upon of certain articles specified in the indictment; to the admission of Smith's wife as a witness; and, most vehemently, to the adducing of the evidence of Brown and Ainslie. The Justice-Clerk dealt roundly with him throughout, but the irrepressible young counsel, as we shall see, was no wise abashed by the judicial thunders.

The Procurator-Fiscal proved the prisoners' declarations. Mr. Longlands, a London solicitor, described the extradition proceedings of which the Deacon had been the subject. John Geddes and his wife gave an account of the vagrant voyage of the *Endeavour* and of their double-dealing with the Deacon's letters. Robert Smith, his foreman, told how Brodie gave him orders about his work before "going to the country." His master asked him "If there were any news about the people who had broke into the Excise?" He replied that George Smith was apprehended and that John Brown had been taken to England to recover Inglis & Horner's goods. "I added," says the witness, "that I hoped he, Mr. Brodie, had no concern in these depredations; but he returned no answer." Two clerks from the City Chamberlain's Office identified the letters produced as in the Deacon's handwriting, with which they were familiar. Mr. Dundas, "housekeeper of the Excise Office," the chief accountant, and the two official guardians of the premises, described the arrangements of the office and its condition after the robbery. They identified the coulter of the plough, the two iron wedges, and the spur, left behind them by the robbers. Mr. James Bonar told how, returning to the office on the night of the crime, he collided with the Deacon in the passage, and Janet Baxter, a servant in Chessel's

Court, said she had seen a suspicious person hiding behind the railings, to wit, Andrew Ainslie. The landlady at Duddingston identified Mr. Brown as one of two men who had a drink in her house on an afternoon of February, and James Kinnear, ploughman to Lord Abercorn, identified the coulter and wedges as those stolen from his plough on that occasion. He had noticed two men in the field that day; there was a black dog with them.[5]

Smith's servant said that her master entertained Ainslie and Brown to supper on 5th March, and described how, after they were joined by Brodie, they severally left the house that night. They all came back between ten and eleven o'clock; "Mr. Brodie had on at this time the whitish clothes he usually wore." She remarked to her mistress on the fact that earlier in the evening the Deacon should have worn "such a strange dress: his old black clothes." Mrs. Smith explained "that it was his frolick."[6] Mary Hubbart or Hubburt, spouse of George Smith, being called, John Clerk strongly objected to her evidence being admitted, and after long discussion the Court repelled the objection, holding that while she was incompetent as a witness for or against her husband, her testimony as regards the Deacon was good. But the defense had another and a stronger card to play; it was objected that the real name of the witness was Hibbutt, as proved by an extract from the parish register of her birth, and the witness was accordingly withdrawn. Two witnesses from Drysdale's Inn, "in the New Town," proved the purchase by Smith of a ticket in the mail-coach for his wife to

---

5. This was Smith's dog "Rodney," whose head is shown in Kay's drawing of the first meeting of Brodie and Smith. Kinnear, when confronted with Smith in the Sheriff-Clerk's office, failed to recognize him. The dog, pushing open the door, ran in and fawned on his master; whereupon Kinnear exclaimed: "There is the dog I saw in the field!"

6. It does not appear that the Deacon returned with them. The witness is confusing this with his visit on the following night.

Newcastle. He paid for it with the five-pound bank note produced. This note, as already mentioned, was part of the proceeds of the crime. Various officials from the Sheriff-Clerk's office proved the recovery, with the assistance of Brown and Smith, of the false keys and other implements used in the robbery. Search of the Deacon's house resulted in finding a dark "lanthorn" in the pen where he kept his game-cocks, and a brace of pistols hidden beneath the fire-place of a shed in his woodyard, together with several pick-locks. George Williamson, Messenger-at-arms, narrated his search for Brodie and, after that gentleman's capture, his bringing of the prisoner to Edinburgh.

Andrew Ainslie was next called. There must have been some good stuff in Andrew, for it appears from the debate as to his admissibility, that on his examination before the Sheriff he stoutly denied the Deacon's accession to the robbery, and that even when offered his own life if he would turn King's evidence against him. Not until the pardoned Mr. Brown was allowed to interview him in prison did Ainslie consent to implicate his old chief. The objection taken to him as an accomplice was repelled by the Court, the Justice-Clerk observing that "the allegeance [allegation] that the witness is a *socius criminis* implies that the pannel is guilty of the crime." So Ainslie was admitted, and told the story of the robbery as we have already heard it.

A stiffer fight was put up when the Lord Advocate called virtuous Mr. Brown. It was proved that he was in England a convicted felon, under sentence of transportation for life, and that he had been banished in Scotland as before mentioned; his evidence was accordingly objected to.

> The SOLICITOR-GENERAL.—My Lords, in answer to this objection, I here produce His Majesty's most gracious pardon in behalf of this witness, under the Great Seal of England, dated 28th July last, which by the law of England renders the witness habile and testable.

After long and vigorous debate the Court allowed the witness to be examined, reserving the credibility of his evidence to the jury. John Brown then told his tale, making everything as black as possible against the Deacon. A severe cross-examination by the Dean of Faculty and by John Clerk failed to make any impression on this treacherous scoundrel. On the conclusion of his evidence the following interesting passage occurred:—

> The LORD JUSTICE-CLERK.—John Brown, you appear to be a clever fellow, and I hope you will now abandon your dissipated courses, and betake yourself to some honest employment.
>
> WITNESS.—My Lord, be assured my future life shall make amends for my past conduct.

It is satisfactory to read in a contemporary note on an old account of the case: "He was afterwards hanged in England." There is no doubt it was he who hanged the Deacon.

This closed the parole or verbal proof; there remained the written evidence. This consisted of the several declarations of the pannels, and the letters and documents written by Brodie: those intercepted by the perfidious Geddes and others found in his trunks. Writing to his brother-in-law, Matthew Sheriff, from Flushing on 8th April, he tells him: "My stock is seven guineas. My wardrobe is all on my back, excepting two check shirts and two white ones, one of them an old rag I had from my cousin Milton, with an old hat (which I left behind); my coat, an old blue one, out at the arms and elbows, I also had from him, with an old striped waistcoat, and a pair of good boots. Perhaps my cousin judged right, that old things were best for my purpose." But he complains that his thrifty kinsman would not let him take his own best coat and greatcoat. "I could not extract a guinea from him, although he owes me £24 for three years past." And we can believe the writer when he adds: "Had Milton been in my place and me in his, my purse, my credit, and my wardrobe, my all, should have been at his disposal." He asks that his personal effects and an assortment of the tools of his trade—lawful, not nefarious—be forwarded to him in a chest to an address at New York, where he purposed to begin the world anew.

> What has been done or likely to be done with the two unfortunate men Smith and Ainslie, and the greater villain John Brown *alias* Humphry Moore? Was John Murray *alias* Jack Tasker brought from England? Whatever these men may say, I had no hand in any of their depredations *excepting the last*, which I shall ever repent, and the keeping of such company; although I doubt not but all will be laid to me. But let me drop this dreadful subject.

And in another letter he writes:—

> Pray write me what is become of Anne Grant and how is her children disposed of. Cecill is a sensible, clever girl, considering the little opportunity she has had of improving. My dear little Willie will be, if I can judge, a brave and hardy boy. Jean is her mother's picture, and too young to form any opinion of.
>
> What is to become of Jean Watt? She is a devil and a ———. I can form no opinion of Frank or his young brother; but pray write me how they are disposed of.

This gives us an interesting glimpse of the Deacon as a family man, but the reference to Jean Watt is rather ungrateful. There was also produced an Account or State of his Affairs, written by him aboard ship, showing a balance in his favor of £1840.

## XIII

For the defense, no evidence was adduced in behalf of Smith; and the "exculpatory proof" led for Brodie was designed to establish an alibi. The first witness was Matthew Sheriff, his brother-in-law, to whose admission it was objected that he was related to the pannel. The Court repelled the objection. Mr. Sheriff stated that he dined in company with the Deacon at his house in Brodie's Close at three o'clock on Wednesday, 5th March—the day of the robbery. He was with him continuously until the evening. At six o'clock they had tea, and witness left at a few minutes before eight. He went straight home to his own house in Bunker's Hill—now St. James's Square—which he reached a few minutes after eight. Cross-examined by the Lord Advocate, he was certain that Brodie never left the room while witness was there. He was dressed in lightish colored or gray clothes. Witness had a clock in his house and a watch in his pocket. He was positive as regards the time. Jean Watt stated that she was "well acquainted" with Mr. Brodie. On Wednesday, 5th March, he came to her house in Libberton's Wynd while the eight o'clock bell was ringing,[7] and remained with her until the following morning. Cross-examined, she remembered the date as being the last time Mr. Brodie slept at her house. Peggy Giles, her maidservant, corroborated. Cross-examined, she was sure it was the Tron Kirk bell she heard. Asked as to the situation of the Tron Kirk, witness said it stood in the Parliament Close—which was, topographically, absurd. Mrs. Wallace, who lived in the same wynd, stated that on the morning of Thursday, 6th March, she saw Mr. Brodie come down Mrs.

---

7. When auld Saunt Giles, at aught o'clock,
   Gars merchant lowns their chopies lock.

   —Robert Fergusson: *Caller Oysters*

Watt's stair at nine o'clock. She then had little Francis Brodie, his son, aged seven, by the hand; and as Mr. Brodie passed he put a halfpenny into the child's hand and clapped him on the head. The boy said his father had been in the house all night. Three other minor witnesses having been examined, the defense closed their case. It was then one o'clock on Thursday morning, and the prisoners had been standing—literally—at the bar since nine o'clock on that of Wednesday!

## XIV

As the addresses of counsel to the jury and the charge of the Lord Justice-Clerk are fully reported in my edition of the trial it is unnecessary to deal with them in detail. The Lord Advocate, having described the heinous nature of the crime and the position of Smith in relation thereto, observed:—

> The other prisoner, Mr. Brodie, is in a different situation. He is known to us all; educated as a gentleman; bred to a respectable business; and removed from suspicion, as well from his supposed circumstances as from the rank he held amongst his fellow-citizens. He was far above the reach of want and, consequently, of temptation; he had a lawful employment, which might have enabled him to hold his station in society with respectability and credit; he has been more than once officially at the head of his profession, and was a member of the City Council. If, therefore, he, too, be guilty, his situation, in place of alleviating his guilt, is a high aggravation of it. If he indeed prevailed upon himself to descend to the commission of the most detestable crimes, what excuse can be made for him? That he frequented bad company; that he had abandoned himself to gambling and every species

of dissipation; that he has by these means run himself into difficulties, is surely no apology.

His Lordship's speech was in the main a fair argument upon the evidence, but he pressed his case somewhat harder than is usual for a Scots prosecutor, the honorable tradition of the Crown being that of strict impartiality. His peroration was as follows:—

> Gentlemen, I shall only further add that if the prisoner William Brodie, a person who from the nature of his employment had frequent opportunities of being introduced into the houses of others, has been guilty of the crime laid to his charge and is allowed to escape punishment, the consequences to the inhabitants of this populous city may be of the most serious nature.

Here was an *argumentum ad hominem* indeed!

At two o'clock in the morning John Clerk rose to make his memorable address to the jury for George Smith.[8] It is recorded of him that before beginning his speech he drank a bottle of claret, then the recognized "refresher" of the Scots Bar. His client, he observed, was an Englishman; a stranger there, in great straits for his life. No one had a good word to say for him, though that great villain John Brown on leaving the box was highly complimented by his Lordship in the Chair. "Be short and concise, sir," growled Braxfield, "at this time of the morning." Presently Clerk fired his first shot: "I think a great deal of most improper evidence for the Crown has been received in this case." "That, sir," interrupted Braxfield, "is a most improper observation to address to the jury." And the other Judges chanted

---

8. Clerk's quaint peculiarities of character and appearance are admirably described and illustrated in *The Scottish Bar Fifty Years Ago*, by Robert Scott Moncrieff. Edinburgh: 1871.

in chorus: "A positive reflection on the Court"; "A flat accusation that we have admitted improper evidence"; "I never heard the like of this from a young counsel at the beginning of his career at this Bar." "With these admonitions, proceed, sir," said Braxfield grimly. Clerk did so, and developed a strong attack on "these twa corbies or infernal villains," Brown and Ainslie. Brown was a convicted felon in England and ought not to be received as a witness in any case within the British dominions.

> BRAXFIELD.—Mr. Clerk, please restrict your observations. The Court have admitted the witness.
>
> CLERK.—Yes, my Lord, I know that very well, but your Lordships should *not* have admitted him, and of that the jury will now judge.
>
> BRAXFIELD.—This is most indecent behavior. You cannot be allowed to speak to the admissibility; to the credibility you may.
>
> LORD STONEFIELD.—This young man is again attacking the Court.
>
> CLERK.—No, my Lords, I am not attacking the Court; I am attacking that villain of a witness, who I tell your Lordships is not worth his value in hemp.
>
> BRAXFIELD.—The Court, sir, have already decided that in law the objections to these witnesses should be repelled, and they were repelled accordingly; therefore you should have nothing more to say to us on that point.
>
> CLERK.—But, my Lords, the jury are to judge of the law as well as the facts.
>
> BRAXFIELD.—Sir, I tell you the jury have nothing to do with the law, but to take it *simpliciter* from me.
>
> CLERK.—That I deny.

"Consternation in Court!" But Clerk continued to maintain his point, until Braxfield told him he was talking nonsense.

"My Lord," retorted Clerk, "you had better not snub me in this way. I never mean to speak nonsense." Yet most assuredly he was then doing so. The next outbreak occurred with reference to Mr. Brown's pardon. "Gentlemen of the jury, I ask you on your oaths: Can His Majesty make a tainted scoundrel an honest man?"—a question which was greeted with loud applause in Court. The wrangle regarding the jury being the judges of the law as well as of the facts was then resumed.

> BRAXFIELD.—Beware of what you are about, sir.
> [Here Clerk sat down.]
> BRAXFIELD.—Are you done, sir, with your speech?
> CLERK.—No, my Lord, I am not.
> BRAXFIELD.—Then go on, sir, at your peril.
> LORD HAILES.—You had better go on, Mr. Clerk. Do go on.
> CLERK.—This has been too often repeated. I have met with no politeness from the Court. You have interrupted me, you have snubbed me rather too often, my Lord, in the line of my defense. I am positively resolved that I will proceed no further, unless I am allowed to speak in my own way.

Lord Braxfield then called upon the Dean of Faculty to commence his address for Brodie, which Henry Erskine respectfully declined to do. His Lordship was accordingly about to begin his charge to the jury, when Clerk sprang to his feet, and shaking his fist at the Bench, uttered this memorable defiance: "Hang my client if ye daur, my Lord, without hearing me in his defense!"

Only such as are acquainted with the grave dignity and decorum which mark the conduct of a trial in the High Court of Justiciary can conceive the terrific effect of this amazing outburst. The Bench was paralyzed, the Bar aghast; the jury trembled, the audience was dumbfoundered. The rich hues ebbed from the fiery faces of the City Guard warding the prisoners; yea, even from the purple visages of the very Macers. No man knew what was like to happen. Would the Court order Mr. Clerk into custody and threaten to strip the robe from his temerarious back? There was no precedent for a situation so appalling. Solemnly Lord Braxfield rose and with his brethren left the Bench, retiring to the robing room to hold a consultation. The Court-room hummed with agitated whispers. Presently my Lords returned; and Braxfield, instead of blasting the presumptuous junior with the fury of his wrath, merely requested him to continue his address. Plainly their Lordships saw that it would never do to have it go forth that the speech for the defense had been burked, but the pill must have been for Braxfield a bitter one to swallow. Thereafter Clerk was suffered to proceed in peace and finished without further interruption, for which, it must be admitted, he afforded ample opportunities. It is difficult to see nowadays how he expected his client to benefit by his pugnacity; but he was himself thoroughly proud of his performance, and was wont to declare that "having stuck up so well to Braxfield was the making of him at the Bar."

It was three o'clock in the morning when the Dean of Faculty rose to plead for Deacon Brodie's life. His speech— contemporaneously described as "a long and splendid oration" —made the best of a bad job; even the brilliant Harry Erskine could hardly make bricks out of the exiguous straws at his disposal. Finally, at half-past four o'clock the Lord Justice-Clerk had the last word. His charge, despite what had gone before, was an impartial review of the evidence, but it left the jury in no doubt as to his Lordship's own opinion as to the inference to be drawn regarding the prisoners' guilt. He is said never to have left the Bench, except for the Clerk interlude, since the beginning of the trial. At six o'clock in the morning the Court adjourned; the jury were inclosed till one o'clock that day, when they should deliver their verdict; and the pannels were taken back to the Tolbooth.

On Thursday, 28th August, the Court being met at the appointed hour, the jury announced their decision, which was unanimous. They found both prisoners Guilty of the crime charged against them. A last forlorn plea in arrest of judgment having been repelled, the Lord Justice-Clerk pronounced sentence of death, to be executed on 1st October, and the Court rose after a sitting of twenty-one continuous hours' duration! Smith's agent has recorded that his client was throughout much dejected. "Mr. Brodie, on the other hand, affected coolness and determination. When the sentence of death was pronounced, he put one hand in his breast and the other in his side, and looked full around him." It is said that he accused his companion of pusillanimity, and even kicked him as they were leaving the Court. The Deacon was disgusted at Smith's failure to play up to the occasion.

## XV

Of the last days of Deacon Brodie I have elsewhere given a full account. The prisoners were confined in the condemned cell of the Tolbooth, known as the Iron Room, which they occupied along with two other housebreakers then under sentence of death for robbing the Dundee Bank. Each was chained by one foot to an iron bar, called "the goad," which extended the whole length of the chamber, the several rings thereon allowing the captives to move about to the extent of their tether. "Brodie's chain is longer than the rest, as he can sit at a table and write by himself." Of this privilege the Deacon took advantage to approach divers great folk, begging their influence to get his sentence commuted to transportation. Henry Dundas (Lord Melville), the Duchess of Buccleuch, and his brother members of the Town Council were among the recipients of these petitions for a reprieve. But, alas, his prayers for mercy remained unanswered. While awaiting replies, he cut out on the dungeon floor the figure of a draught-board, upon which he was in use to play with the companions of his fate, or, in default of them, with his right hand against his left. A poor substitute, this, for the excitement of the old games at hazard. When the two Dundee burglars received a respite of six weeks, Smith remarked upon the shortness of the time. "George," cried the Deacon, passionately, "what would you and I not give for six weeks longer? Six weeks would be an age to us." But as a rule he was cheerful and apparently resigned, for he had good hopes of an unofficial scheme to effect a jail delivery in his favor. His friends were free to visit him, and a plan was concerted, whereby, with the assistance of a surgeon and certain mechanical devices after-mentioned, he might still contrive to "cheat the wuddy." The night before the execution he sang, as I have said, his last stave from *The Beggar's Opera*. He also made his will, a curious instance of posthumous humor, containing certain satirical bequests in favor of persons against whom he had conceived a grudge. On the morning of his death, in pursuance of the arrangement for his premature resurrection, Deacon Brodie wrote to his old chief the Provost, praying, as his last request, "that your Lordship will please give orders that my body be delivered to Mr. Alexr. Paterson, *and by no means to remain in jail*; that he and my friends may have it decently dressed and interred." The request was duly granted, but, as we shall find, the projected revival failed.

Of the many picturesque legends of old Edinburgh which, in defiance of truth, cling like ivy about her vanished past, one of the most persistent is that Deacon Brodie was the first to suffer upon the new drop which he himself designed. This myth, upon research, I found myself reluctantly compelled to disprove. He may have planned the "moveable platform for the execution of criminals," which the Town Council caused to be erected in 1786 at the west end of the Tolbooth; but it was certainly not of his construction, nor was he the first to benefit by its ingenuity. The place of execution was the roof of a low building which projected from the west gable of the prison— roughly where the Buccleuch statue now stands. A beam was drawn out from an aperture in the wall above the platform and from this depended the fatal rope.

Wednesday, 1st October 1788, was the day of Deacon Brodie's great adventure. He slept till eight o'clock, when he arose and, his chains being struck off, made a careful toilet. At one he ate his last dinner: a beef steak and divers glasses of port. "During this repast he made some ludicrous remarks to Smith," particulars of which have not come down to us. At two the guard formed up around the scaffold; the Magistrates in their robes of office and the attending clergy in their gowns and bands proceeded from the City Chambers and took their places beneath the platform. The immense crowd that filled the area of the Lawnmarket gazed breathlessly at the great door of the prison. Presently the prisoners appeared between their guards and marched to the scaffold, Deacon Brodie bowing courteously to the Magistrates and to the multitude. One of the former remarked that he was sorry to see him there. "What would you have?" replied the Deacon with a shrug; "It is *la fortune de la guerre.*" He wore a full suit of black, his hair dressed and powdered as for some gala function, and carried in his hand his cocked hat. Smith was grotesquely garbed in white linen, trimmed with black. The great bell of St. Giles' tolled solemnly at half-minute intervals.[9] The usual devotions over, Brodie clapped his companion upon the shoulder, saying: "Go up, George, you are first in hand"; whereupon Smith, whose demeanor is described as "highly penitential," slowly

9. But hark! I hear the Toll of the Bell.—*The Beggar's Opera*, Act III.

ascended the steps to the platform, followed by the Deacon, who mounted with briskness and agility. He examined with a professional eye the dreadful apparatus, and as the hangman was about to bind his arms, he asked that they be left free, which was done. He then deliberately untied his cravat, buttoned up his coat and waistcoat, and helped the hangman to adjust the noose. Turning to a friend who stood beside him, he bade him farewell and begged him to acquaint the world that he died like a man. Next, placing his left hand in his waistcoat—with him an habitual gesture—he drew the white cap over his head and dropped his handkerchief as the last signal.

Then a horrible thing happened. It appeared that the halter had been too much shortened and required readjustment. Brodie took off the white cap, came down from the platform to the scaffold, and talked to his friends while the necessary change was effected. He tolerantly remarked of the gibbet that "it was on a new construction, and wanted nothing but practice to make it complete." When all was ready he sprang up again to the platform, but the rope was still too short and he came down once more, showing, not unnaturally, "some little impatience," and observed that the hangman was but a bungling fellow, who ought to be punished for his incompetence—"but it did not much signify." A third attempt met with the proverbial success, and the double life of Deacon Brodie was ended.

■

Of the plans, various and futile, formed for the resuscitation of the Deacon there are two contemporary and competing versions. One is that the hangman was bribed to tamper with the rope, so as to give a short fall and avoid dislocation of the vertebræ of the neck. But by excess of caution that officer first made it too short and then too long. The body, when cut down, was placed in a cart and driven furiously round the back of the

Castle to the Deacon's woodyard at the foot of Brodie's Close, so that animation might be restored as in the historic case of "half-hangit Maggie Dickson," a lady whose departed spirit was recalled by similar Jehu methods. In his own workshop his veins were opened by a French surgeon, whose services had been retained to that end; but all the resources of science could not bring the Deacon back to life. According to another account, he had, before leaving his cell for the last time, been supplied with a small silver tube for insertion in his throat at the final ceremony in order to prevent suffocation, and wires were carried down both his sides from head to foot to counter-act the jerk of the fall. In spite of these precautions and of subsequent bleeding by a surgeon, his friends had reluctantly to admit that "Brodie was fairly gone." From all which it appears that an attempt of some sort was made to continue his interrupted career.

He was buried, it is said, in the north-east corner of the graveyard of St. Cuthbert's Chapel of Ease, now Buccleuch Parish Church; but so strong was the public interest in his fate that it was the common belief that he, who had broken into so many houses in his day, had successfully broken out of his long home. Folks said he had been seen and spoken with in Paris; and that on his grave being afterwards opened—when and in what circumstances we are not informed—"not a bone of him was to be found." The wish, we may take it, was father to the thought: the many admirers of Deacon Brodie would fain hope that their hero did, in the flesh, "win through" after all. Be the fact as it may, his fame is writ large in the romantic story of his native city, and is like to outlast the memory of many a more deserving indweller.

There was something lovable about the man. Save for his loss of nerve at the Excise Office he was a gallant fellow enough, gay, generous, and good-natured. Despite his forty-seven years he bore in his middle-aged bosom the light heart of a boy. A bad boy, I grant you, with an unquenchable love of mischief for mischief's sake and a fine contempt for the conventional virtues. Yet it is recorded of him that he was a devoted son and brother; a kind and affectionate parent to his irregular offspring. And he was hanged for stealing four pounds! Verily, he fell a victim to the ruthless ferocity of the penal code of his time. Nowadays a few weeks' imprisonment would have been the measure of his punishment. Or, peradventure, had the defense called some of our distinguished alienists, it would plainly have appeared that the unhappy Deacon suffered such "diminished responsibility" as freed him from the consequences of his misdeeds. So that although he was unsuitable for Borstal, a rest cure in a mental nursing-home might have met the case.

## THE WEST PORT MURDERS

*The friendless bodies of unburied men.*

—*The White Devil*, ACT V. SC. 4

HAUNTED EDINBURGH! YES; though shorn of her former dignity, bereft of her old-time charm; compassed about by bungalows, her stately mansions disembowelled to furnish flatlets for the New Poor; her venerable Castle converted into an illuminated advertisement; her ancient Palace lost amid competing picture palaces; the Royal Mile, desecrated and defaced, reverberant with the thunder of motor buses; Princes Street bedizened like unto Sauchiehall Street—still, despite these manifold and startling "improvements," a city of ghosts.

Queen of the ghosts by right royal is the fair phantom of Mary Stuart. I see her coming down the dark wynd through the February night beneath the flaming torches of the guard, on her way to the marriage masque at Holyrood; while up the neighboring close go my Lord Bothwell and his evil crew upon their bloody errand to Kirk o' Field. I behold her incredible off-spring, King James the Just, of pious memory, fleeing, breeches in hand, down the palace stairs in fear of a lesser, but to him more formidable Bothwell. Then in the great gallery, where the candles blaze and the bagpipes blare and all the beauty of Edinburgh bows in homage to her Prince, I too salute that gracious, gallant presence, holding his first and last Court in the deserted halls of his ancestors.

Next, those inferior and middle-class specters—for even in Ghostland there are social distinctions—whose shades I have elsewhere more or less successfully evoked, appear again. Down the West Bow the mob drags luckless Captain Porteous to his doom on the dyer's pole in the Grassmarket; the windows of Major Weir's house at the Bends are aglare with unearthly lights, the silence vibrant with the humming of his sister's ceaseless wheel. From out Tweeddale Court runs the unknown murderer as he pockets the bank notes, leaving poor Begbie, the bank porter, dead at the stairfoot, the knife yet sticking in his heart. Here Deacon Brodie hovers in the shadows of the High Street, with his dark-lantern and his false keys, about to pay a midnight call upon some unsuspecting friend. Little recks he of the near disaster of Chessel's Court, and the ensuing ceremony on the new drop of the platform in the Lawnmarket. In yonder bustling tavern the boy-poet Fergusson is reciting his latest poem, while the "couthie chiels," charmed by the magic of his verse, forget to drain their pint stoups. Across the Parliament Close near by, the burly figure of Lord Braxfield, wrapped in his old cloak, stumps sturdily home to his house in George Square. . . .

But I must no further indulge my fancy. There is grim business ahead; ghouls, rather than ghosts (howsoever profitable), are our grislier objective—those two nightmare shapes, the evil spirits of Burke and Hare, that haunt for all time the purlieus of the West Port.

I

Before me as I write lies an inch-square bit of brown leather—not, you would think, an inspiring subject for a tale. But perpend. This fragment of human skin, for such it is, has been since 1829 in the possession of three persons only: the original owner, my grandfather, and myself. Inconsiderable in size and unimpressive of aspect, it was nevertheless potent to influence the direction of my future studies. While yet a small boy, my grandfather would often show me by request this singular relic and I never wearied of hearing how he came by it. As a matter of history, its first proprietor, the late Mr. William Burke of Edinburgh, in the circumstances hereafter to be related, was publicly anatomized, his carcase thereafter flayed, his hide tanned, and his skeleton by order of Court preserved in the Anatomical Museum of Edinburgh University, where it remains as a memorial of his infamy even unto this day. Mr. Burke's integument being cut up into sortable parcels to suit buyers' tastes and exposed for sale by private bargain, my grandfather, who was then but a young man, invested in a modest shilling's worth. Wealthier purchasers bought larger lots—I have heard that the late Professor Chiene had a tobacco pouch made of this unique material. Personally, despite my predilection for crime, I prefer indiarubber. My grandfather kept his portion coffined in a wooden snuff-box; it was shrouded in a yellow scrap of paper, bearing in his autograph the contemporary inscription: "Piece of Skin tan'd from the Body of Burke the Murderer." (As I grew older I plumed myself on my superior orthography.) Thus in my blameless childhood did I first hear the horrid story of Burke and Hare.

The next thing I recall about my acquaintance with these monsters is the issue in parts, in the early eighties, of James Grant's admirable work, *Old and New Edinburgh*, and I still remember how eagerly I devoured the number relating to the

West Port murders. One sentence of that vivid account yet sticks in my memory, where dealing with the murderers' methods he writes: "More is not required—and all is still in that dark room *with the window looking out on the dead wall.*" In due course of nature I succeeded to my grandfather's snuff-box and its incongruous contents; and in the fullness of time it was my fortune to edit *Burke and Hare* in the series of Notable British Trials. Finally, in my friend Mr. James Bridie's most excellent play, *The Anatomist*, I have had the pleasure to see the protagonists of that old dreadful drama revived for my entertainment in their habit as they lived.

## II

In 1827 the official headquarters of anatomical instruction and research in Edinburgh were situate within the Old College on the South Bridge, under the direction of Professor Monro. But that authorized exponent of the mysteries did not have it all his own way. Six extra-mural rivals competed for the teaching of students of anatomy, and of these the ablest, the most popular with the students, and the most brilliant lecturer was the famous Dr. Robert Knox. The scale upon which this learned industry was then conducted in Edinburgh, the meager and wholly inadequate quantity of requisite raw material legitimately available, and the exuberant zeal of the young disciples in behalf of their respective masters, led to a lamentable state of affairs. In order to supply the constant and increasing demand for "subjects," there had grown up an ancillary branch of research, carried out behind the scenes by the professional riflers of graves, known by the expressive names of Body Snatchers or Resurrectionists. These subordinate ministers to the needs of science were by the nature of their calling persons of irregular and often drunken habits, as unreliable as they were greedy and unscrupulous; so it frequently happened that the students themselves had to do their own catering, lest the "table" of the "Chief" should lack its daily indispensable equipage. Many and gruesome are the tales told of their adventures, some not without a certain grisly humor; but one necessary result of such pursuits was a coarsening of the moral grain, an indifference to decent feelings, and a callous recklessness regarding human life which, as we shall see, was to bear fearful fruit. One might have thought that the manners of Dr. Knox's pupils would be ameliorated by the great gifts and prestige of their preceptor; as a matter of fact they were even more bold and aggressive than their fellows. For the Doctor treated his confrères with savage contempt and in his lectures ceased not to jeer at what he deemed their incompetence. Especially did he have his knife—and he was a ruthless operator—in his learned and orthodox colleague, Professor Monro. Wherefore was the jealousy of the several classes embittered and Dr. Knox's lads were at all costs prepared to maintain the supremacy of their master.

It chanced that on a certain dark November night of 1827 two shabby and disreputable-looking men were hanging about the quadrangle of the College, wherein were situated the anatomical rooms of Professor Monro. They accosted a student who was leaving the building, and asked him the way to the Professor's emporium. They had, it appeared, something to sell that might suit him. Now the student was one of Dr. Knox's pupils; guessing the nature of their wares and delighted to steal a march upon the University, he directed the inquirers to No. 10 Surgeons' Square, the opposition establishment. So the two men thanked him, crossed the road, and went down Infirmary Street to the old ill-famed square by the Cowgate. At No. 10 they were received by the three assistants on night duty, but being new to their trade they were rather bashful in coming to business. Finally it appeared that they were in lawful possession of a corpse, of which in the interests of science and for a suitable remuneration they were willing to dispose. Being told that Dr. Knox sometimes gave as much as £10 for such commodities, the neophytes in carrion registered surprise and pleasure. They hastened to deliver the goods, which, being approved by the Doctor himself, they parted with to him for £7, 10s.

Thus was constituted that terrible trinity whose names are indissolubly associated for all time in the annals of crime. The fate of the three assistants was happier: they were in after life to become those distinguished surgeons, Sir William Fergusson, Thomas Wharton Jones, and Alexander Miller, whose names are yet eminent in the temple of science. It is a strange world.

### III

The main entrance from the west to the ancient city of Edinburgh was by the West Port in the Grassmarket. The adjacent suburb was known as Portsburgh. The old gates in the city wall had long since vanished, and by the time of our tale the street of the West Port was become a drab thoroughfare of ugly tumbledown dwellings, abandoned to dinginess and decay, occupied by undesirable tenants of the lowest class. The fronts of the houses, as was common in old Edinburgh architecture, were broken at intervals by alleys—locally termed "closes"—leading to back tenements, yards, and waste land behind the street. Dismal and malodorous by day, they were at night both dark and dangerous, being "illuminated" by scanty oil lamps and unpatrolled by any regular police.

In one of the worst of these unattractive tunnels, Tanner's Close—so called from the tannery on the north to which it led—was a tramps' hostel, known as Log's Lodgings in memory of its late proprietor. His widow still carried on the business, with the assistance of an Irishman of singularly sinister aspect, named William Hare. The couple were not married, but the lady, from motives of delicacy, assumed the style and title of Mrs. Hare. The tariff of their hotel was reasonable: 3d. per night, with liberty to sleep three in a bed, of which there were available seven. It happened that prior to the demise of the late unlamented Log, Hare, being employed as a laborer on the construction of the Union Canal, made the acquaintance of a fellow-countryman similarly engaged, named William Burke. This gentleman also had for helpmate a putative widow, whose name was Helen Macdougal. The Hares and Burke were Irish Catholics; Macdougal, for what it was worth, was a Scots Presbyterian. When Mr. Burke and lady after various vicissitudes came to Edinburgh, it was natural that they should avail themselves of the privileges offered by Mr. Hare's hotel. Their characters were congenial, their tastes simple, their habits frugal. Potatoes, and whisky—which in those golden days cost little more than milk—formed the staple of their diet. In a small back room Burke practiced his art as a cobbler; Hare, ostensibly a hawker, kept his wife, if not his house, in order; Macdougal provided Mrs. Hare with what she had hitherto lacked—the company and support of a female friend.

Among the inmates of the lodging-house in Tanner's Close was an old army pensioner named Donald, who paid his board by means of a small pension. On 29th November 1827 this lodger, who had long been ailing, gave up his room for a more celestial abode. I hasten to add that his death was due to natural causes. Now it chanced that with the customary selfishness of invalids, the old man departed just before his quarter's pension was due. And he owed his benefactors £4! But Hare, much aggrieved by this sharp practice on the part of the deceased, determined to square the account by selling his body to "the Doctors," whose willingness to deal in such wares was a matter of common knowledge. He communicated his idea to Burke, who appreciating the humor and profit of the proposal, agreed to take a hand in the gruesome game; and so began the famous co-partnery whose firm-name was to echo for all time down the corridors of history. A pauper's funeral was arranged for, a shell procured; but before the coffin was "lifted" they unscrewed the lid, took out the corpse, and replaced it with a bag of bark, stolen from the neighboring tanyard. Thereafter, as we have seen, they made their market of the poor remains. Hare received his own with usury, Burke got his commission, and Dr. Knox his "subject." So the business was concluded to the satisfaction of all concerned.

When Burke and Hare delivered the body of the pensioner at Surgeons' Square they were told "*that they* (Dr. Knox's assistants) *would be glad to see them again when they had another to dispose of,*" an invitation which afforded the philosophic mind of Mr. Burke matter for reflection. The old pensioner, alive, was relatively worthless; dead, he was worth £7, 10s. Hitherto Burke and Hare had fought hard for halfpence; the hint from the young surgeons opened a rose-colored vista of easy money and light work. Nothing was needed but the stock in trade. Unfortunately, the guests frequenting the tramps' clearing-house in Tanner's Close were mostly birds of passage; it might be long ere another of these was timeously called to his account. Even in the abominable hygienic conditions there obtaining, the feeblest clung to life with regrettable obstinacy.

Pondering on this problem the partners had a brain-wave. Why await the tardy operation of Providence? Surely there were to be found in the purlieus of the city many homeless wanderers whom it were mere charity to relieve of the weary burden of existence, so as it could be done wisely and with safety. And presently the evil shadows of Burke and Hare flitted to and fro about the wynds and closes of the Old Town, seeking such waifs as were like to meet the requirements of the new firm. But either because of their inexperience or of the wariness of their vagrant prey, the first attempts to obtain material proved disappointing. Satan unaccountably failed to maintain his reputation.

## IV

After the customary Scots celebrations of the New Year were sufficiently recovered from, the firm of Burke and Hare, purveyors-extraordinary to Surgeons' Square, began business in earnest. During the nine months of their joint adventure they successfully carried through sixteen capital transactions. These at least were all that their native modesty would allow them to claim, but there is reason to believe they had other affairs to their credit. The firm kept no books, and those of Dr. Knox, which would have enabled us to check the sales, were not produced.

In the confusion caused by their bankruptcy and the legal proceedings following thereon, it is natural that the partners, who by then had no means of communicating with each other, should differ as to details and the precise sequence of events; but in the main they confirm one another in all essential particulars. The chief divergence relates to the first murder: Hare naming as the victim, Joseph the Miller, while Burke gives pride of place to the Old Woman from Gilmerton. There is extant an interesting letter of Sir Walter Scott to the publishers of the official report of the trial, in which, having ripely weighed the evidence, he ranks and prefers the Miller to the distinction. "It is not odd," writes Sir Walter, "that Burke, acted upon as he seems always to have been by ardent spirits, and involved in a constant succession of murther, should have misdated the two actions. On the whole Hare and he, making separate confessions, agree wonderfully." So, accepting Sir Walter's ruling, we begin with Joseph.

This man, a casual visitor to Hare's hotel, became ill of a fever, whereby his hosts feared that the house would get a bad name and the business be affected. To relieve the situation Burke held a pillow on the sick man's face, while Hare lay upon his body to keep down his arms and legs. The miller, who had been previously plied with whisky, made but small resistance; the partners "mentioned to Dr. Knox's young men that they had another subject"; a porter was sent to meet them that evening at the back of the Castle, to whom they delivered the goods in a chest; and they received from Dr. Knox £10 for their trouble. Another lodger, an English hawker "who used to sell spunks (matches) in Edinburgh," fell sick of the jaundice. Him they disposed of in similar fashion, sold his body to the same purchaser, and were paid a like reward. In these two instances, it will be noted, the deceased had really been ill, and the Doctor may conceivably have attributed death to natural causes. No such excuse is available in the fourteen further cases.

An indigent old woman named Abigail Simpson lived precariously at the village of Gilmerton, whence it was her weekly custom to walk into town to uplift the pension charitably allowed her: eighteenpence and a can of "kitchen fee," *i.e.* edible odds and ends. Returning from her errand one February afternoon in 1828 she was accosted by Hare, who invited her to rest and refreshment in Tanner's Close. When the whisky gave out, Mrs. Hare bought the guest's can of scraps for 1s. 6d., to be expended on an additional supply of liquor. The old woman waxed merry in her cups; she boasted much of a fair daughter, whom Hare jocosely offered to marry, "and get all the money amongst them." Overcome by the unwonted hospitality, old Abigail presently became unconscious and was put to bed. How she was permitted to live through the night is astonishing; her hosts must themselves have been too drunk for action. Next morning she was persuaded to take a parting glass—or glasses; and when suitably bemused, Hare held her mouth and nose, Burke lay across her body, "and she never stirred." The ritual of the porter and the tea-chest duly observed, the corpse was carried to the classroom. "Dr. Knox came in when they were there. The body was cold and stiff. *Dr. Knox approved of its being so fresh, but did not ask any questions.*" He paid them £10 for it. The two next transactions dealt with a couple of stray women, who severally spending a night at Hare's hotel, were no more seen save by Dr. Knox and his disciples. They fetched £10 apiece.

Now that the partners were in receipt of a regular income their respective shares fell to be apportioned. Of the £10 commonly received from their surgical customer, Hare appropriated £5 to his own use; Burke had to rest content with £4, as he had to pay Mrs. Hare £1 a head, being a sort of pole tax exacted by that lady as proprietrix of the shambles. The marked improvement which had taken place in the financial circumstances of the joint household did not escape the notice of their neighbors. The mean little house at the foot of the close was become a place of riot and revelry; feasting and fighting were the order of the day and night, and the perpetual gurgling of a flow of whisky was heard in the land. This merriment and joy they gave out to be the fruits of a substantial legacy; but public opinion, doubtless influenced by the recurrent passage of the tea-chest, held that Burke and Hare's fortune had been found by them buried in the earth—that they were in fact Resurrectionists, a recognized and lucrative, though hardly respectable calling. But as the Hares kept open house and Burke was always willing to stand his hand, the dwellers in Portsburgh were prepared to wink at such irregular means of livelihood, and for the time, in the picturesque phrase of Mrs. Nickleby's admirer, "all was gas and gaiters."

## V

Wednesday, 9th April 1828, is one of the three leading dates in the case, for upon that day was committed the murder of Mary Paterson, a deed which struck not only the popular imagination, but a new note in the hideous symphony of these crimes. Heretofore Burke and Hare had preyed upon broken folk, frail, aged, and obscure, whose disappearance from the stream of life left no ripple on the surface. But emboldened by success and assured of the countenance of their patrons, they were now to fly at bigger game.

For the profession of Mary Paterson the Elizabethans had a short title, no longer, my dictionary warns me, in decent use. I shall therefore veil it classically as that of an hetaira. A beautiful girl of eighteen, famed for the perfection of her form, well-educated, amiable, and intelligent, her manifold charms had proved her undoing, and by this time she was squandering them on the streets of Edinburgh. Her parents were dead, relations she had none, and her only friends were casual males and girls as unfortunate as herself. Among the former, as we shall find, was one of Dr. Knox's assistants, in after years a baronet and Surgeon to Queen Victoria (who would have been vastly shocked by the association); of the latter, the most intimate was one of her own age, Janet Brown, with whom she shared a room in Leith Street.

On the evening of 8th April these two girls, being apprehended in the exercise of their calling, were lodged for the night in the Canongate watch-house. At 6 a.m. next day they were discharged and they immediately sought comfort in a neighboring public-house, kept by a man named Swanston, where they ordered a gill of whisky. Another early customer, a stranger to them, was taking his "morning"—rum and bitters—at the bar. The damsels found favor in his sight; he introduced himself to them by means of further drinks offered and accepted. The affable unknown then invited them to breakfast at his lodgings. Mary, ever rash and reckless, was nothing loath; Janet, more cautious, demurred. The stranger said he had a pension, "and could keep her handsomely." So in the end both girls agreed to go with him.

Burke—for the astute reader will have penetrated my little mystery—had a brother, Constantine, holding humble office as a city scavenger, and living with his wife and family in Gibb's Close, Canongate. Thither did Burke escort the two young ladies, having presented each of them with a bottle of whisky in token of his regard. On arrival at the house they found the inmates still abed. Burke, in his assumed role of lodger, damned their indolence and bade his "landlady" rise and prepare the morning meal, which she did; and presently the guests sat down to a good and plentiful Scots breakfast: tea, bread, eggs, and Finnan haddocks. Thereafter Constantine went off to his manurial duties, Mrs. Constantine busied herself with household matters, and Burke and his visitors turned their attention to the whisky. Soon Mary, a victim to undue hospitality, slept in her chair; Janet, either because she drank less or had the stronger head, was comparatively sober. Perceiving this, her host prescribed a breath of fresh air, which was obtained in an adjacent tavern and washed down with porter. Doubtless his medical experience suggested the exhibition of mixed drinks as tending to promote repose. Returning from this excursion they found Mary still sound asleep in her chair, and were proceeding to deal with the residue of the whisky, when suddenly the curtains of the bed were flung asunder and from out of it leapt the formidable figure of Burke's domestic partner, Helen Macdougal. She had chanced to pay a morning call on her illegitimate sister-in-law, and learning what was afoot, concealed herself as above for the confusion of her faithless lord. Mrs. Constantine, whispering to Janet that this was the gentleman's wife, left the house to fetch Hare as peacemaker. Meanwhile the virago fell upon the girl, charging her with attempted seduction of her "husband." Poor Janet apologized; she knew not that her entertainer was a married man. Finally, to pacify his outraged mistress, Burke reluctantly let the girl go, which, little dreaming how much she owed to Macdougal's jealousy, Janet, somewhat sobered by fright, confusedly did.

She sought counsel of one Mrs. Lawrie, who lived at hand and with whom she had formerly lodged. This lady, hearkening to her tale, became suspicious of the purity of Mr. Burke's intentions; so she at once sent Janet back, supported by her own servant, to bring Mary Paterson away. When, having been absent some twenty minutes, Janet with her escort returned to the house, she found there only Macdougal and the two Hares: Mary had vanished. They explained that she was out with Burke but would soon be back and invited her to stay. The servant was dismissed, and Janet, furnished with the inevitable dram, sat down to await the coming of her friend, whose dead and still warm body lay covered with a sheet in the bed behind her chair! Hare in the absence of his partner (who had gone to Surgeons' Square to give the usual intimation and invitation) acted as host, and already looked on Janet as stock worth £10. But Mrs. Lawrie, her suspicions confirmed, sent her maid back to the rescue, and Hare had the mortification of seeing this valuable asset withdrawn from the firm's custody and control.

The next we see of Mary Paterson—you note that I have discreetly refrained from drawing back the bed-curtains—is upon the table in Dr. Knox's dissecting-room, four hours after her death, where she has just been delivered by Messrs. Burke and Hare in the accustomed tea-chest. "She had twopence-halfpenny, which she held in her hand," Burke tells us; and they had some trouble with small boys in the High Street, who pursued him and the porter, crying: "They are carrying a corpse!" but they reached Surgeons' Square in safety. Dr. Knox is charmed with the beauty and freshness of the goods; but Mr. Fergusson, his assistant, despite his experience of such affairs, receives a shock: *he knew the girl, and named her.* He asked Burke where they had got the body. The merchants explained that they had bought it "from an old woman at the back of the Canongate," which in the circumstances was accepted as sufficient. Burke begged leave to cut off, as his perquisite, the girl's magnificent hair, "and one of the students gave him a pair of scissors for that purpose." They then departed, leaving Dr. Knox to expatiate to his admiring class upon the manifold merits of the "subject." So proud was the Doctor of the symmetry of the body, that he caused an artist to make a drawing of it (reproduced in my former account of the case), and kept the corpse undissected in spirits for three months, seemingly from sentimental motives. Even so strong a man as Dr. Knox had his little weaknesses.

Meanwhile Janet Brown, equally lucky and loyal, ceased not to make inquiry for her missing friend. The Constantine Burkes said she had gone to Glasgow with a packman; but as no word came from her and her poor belongings still lay in the lodgings, Janet could make nothing of it. So often as she met Constantine upon his municipal labors she would ask whether there was no word yet of Mary? "How the hell can I tell about you sort of folk?" retorted the virtuous scavenger. "You are here to-day and away to-morrow." Such was Mary Paterson's epitaph.

## VI

Two more murders committed that spring may be mentioned briefly. They are commonplace compared with the slayings of Mary Paterson, of Daft Jamie, and of Mrs. Docherty—the three outstanding peaks in this monstrous range of crime. One was an old cinder-wife—"Burke thinks her name was Effie"—who used to sell him for his cobbling such scraps of leather as she unearthed when "raking the backets"; the other a drunk woman whom, being haled to the lock-up, Burke prevailed upon the watchman to commit to his more tender care, saying, with truth, that he would "see her home." In each instance the firm's profits were increased by £10.

One day in June Burke met in the High Street a sturdy old Irishwoman, holding by the hand a little boy, her grandchild, who was dumb. She had tramped from Glasgow in hope to find certain friends in Edinburgh. By a fortunate chance Burke knew their address and offered to take her to them; but first, as a countrywoman of his, she must go home with him and drink his health. At Tanner's Close she was ushered into the fatal guest chamber, "that dark room with the window looking out on the dead wall"; Mr. Hare dropped in for a friendly glass, and the door was shut. Meanwhile the dumb boy remained in the kitchen with the two she-wolves. He became frightened and restless at the continued absence of his "granny," and the gang consulted as to what should be done with him. It was at first proposed that, being incapable of speech, he should be "wandered" in the streets at night; but this would provoke inquiry, so it was decided that he must follow his grandmother. While Hare went out to fetch some receptacle of greater capacity than the tea-chest, which was inadequate to the double freight, Burke, in the back room where the dead woman lay, took the boy on his knee and, in his own expression, "broke his back." Of all the damnable deeds whereby his conscience was branded this is the only one that troubled it: he was haunted o' nights by the piteous look in the dumb boy's eyes. Hare having procured an empty herring barrel, the bodies were crammed into it, and the horse and cart which he kept for his pretended trade of a hawker were requisitioned to convey the cargo to Surgeons' Square. But the horse was on its last legs; halfway along the Cowgate it collapsed, and despite the blows and curses of its humane proprietor it could go no farther. A crowd began to gather, so, damning the expense, they hired a passing porter with a "hurley," to which the barrel was safely transferred. £16 was paid for the contents, the students complaining of the tightness with which the goods were packed. The horse, a less marketable commodity, was sold to a knacker. "He [the unhappy quadruped] had two large holes in his shoulders stuffed with cotton, and covered over with a piece of another horse's skin to prevent them being discovered," says Burke; the price received for *him* was negligible and is not recorded.

That month Burke, feeling the need of a holiday—it is satisfactory to know that he slept very badly and had horrible dreams—accompanied Helen Macdougal on a visit to her late husband's relatives in Falkirk. Before they set out, Mrs. Hare took Burke aside and suggested that Macdougal, whom as a Scotswoman she distrusted, should be by him converted into merchandise for behoof of the firm, he to write to Hare that she had died and been buried in the country! Burke resenting this proposition as in bad taste, a coolness was in consequence engendered. Matters became still more strained by his ascertaining, on their return to town, that Hare had been doing a bit of business on his own account. Hare indignantly denied the fact, but inquiry at Surgeons' Square proved that he had sold a woman's body for £8 and appropriated the price. A violent quarrel ensued; unable to forgive this breach of faith, Burke removed himself and Macdougal from the Hare *ménage*, and took a room in the house of a cousin, John Broggan, in the basement of a tenement a few doors east of Tanner's Close. But personal ill-feeling had to yield to the exigencies of business; funds were low, and the partners, pocketing their respective grievances, agreed, though still living apart, to resume practice.

The reunion was precipitated, surprisingly enough, by the delicacy of Burke's feelings. A young girl named Ann

Macdougal came from Falkirk on a return visit to her kins-woman; he regarded her favorably as a suitable "subject," but told Hare that being a relative, "*he did not like to begin first on her.*" So the initial steps were taken by that expert, Burke, despite his scrupulosity, assisting at the finish. The country cousin was, in due season, sent to end her visit with Dr. Knox, who paid £10 for her. Mr. Broggan, commenting on the abrupt departure of the visitor, was given £3 to stifle his curiosity.

The next item in the frightful catalogue was an old char-woman named Mrs. Hostler, who, having been employed to clean up the house, was slain by Burke and Hare during the celebrations incident to the happy confinement of Mrs. Broggan. "She had ninepence-halfpenny in her hand," Burke observes, "which they could scarcely get out of it after she was dead, so firmly was it grasped." The body, concealed in the coal-cellar till the merry-making was over, was only valued by Dr. Knox at £8.

A familiar but unreverend figure in the back streets of the city was old Mary Haldane, a retired harlot, who was solacing her remaining years with gin. She had a daughter, Peggy, re-grettably following in her mother's footsteps. One day Burke saw Mary standing at a close-mouth in the Grassmarket in the condition described as sober, and sorry for it. Sympathizing with her state he invited her to refresh herself at his expense, and she willingly accompanied him to Tanner's Close. There she was royally entreated by the women, and being overcome by the extent of their libations, was permitted to sleep awhile in Hare's stable. The sleep became eternal, and she was shortly on her way to Surgeons' Square. "She had but one tooth in her mouth, and that a very large one in front," Burke records of this aged Rahab. As we have seen, he was curious in such minutiæ.

Peggy Haldane became alarmed at her mother's continued absence. Hearing that the old woman had been seen to enter

Hare's hotel, she sought that sinister hostelry in quest of her. She was received by the ladies of the house, who denied that Mary had ever darkened their door, and after some general observations upon the undesirability of disreputable persons entering respectable establishments, they proceeded to cast highly offensive aspersions in particular upon the walk and conversation of mother and daughter. Peggy gave as good—or rather, bad—as she got; the war of words was at its height, when the door of the back room opened and Hare, with a significant glance at the viragoes, mildly asked what was amiss. Peggy, invited within to state her case, was assured that her aged relative had gone to Mid-Calder; Burke appeared opportunely with the indispensable dram. That afternoon poor Peggy joined what remained of her mother in Dr. Knox's rooms, and her introducers got £8 for her.

## VII

The murder of Daft Jamie in October 1828, one of the worst and most audacious of the series, shows that Burke and Hare were become so daring by reason of their repeated successes, that they believed they could do what they pleased without fear of detection.

James Wilson, a "natural" of eighteen, was intellectually a Peter Pan. But though in mind he remained a child, physically he was a fully-developed man, big and strong for his age, active, and incapable of fatigue. He had, however, a marked malformation of the feet, of which we shall hear again. Following upon the discovery of his untimely death an interesting account of his life was published, with many quaint and curious anecdotes of his eccentricities on which I here lack space to enter, though elsewhere I have done justice to his engaging personality. He was one of Old Edinburgh's many "characters," and indeed the most harmless and amusing of them all; and his face and figure were as familiar to the citizens as was the Mercat (Market) Cross. Vitiously to intromit with such a one proves that the murderers had surely incurred the curse of the gods. And yet, amazingly, by favor of Dr. Knox they got away with it! Though Jamie had a mother and sister in the town, he did not live under their roof, preferring to rely on the chance hospitality which all who knew him seem willingly to have afforded. This was the "kenspeckle" and popular being whom Burke and Hare had the effrontery to choose from the inhabitants of Auld Reekie as a suitable "subject" for the exercise of their art.

Mrs. Hare, having one day enticed Jamie upon some pretext to visit the house in Tanner's Close and left him there in conversation with her lord, set forth in search of Burke, with whom returning, she thereafter locked the door on the outside and pushing the key beneath it, discreetly departed. Macdougal was absent. Jamie, though he "liked fine a dram," was in capricious mood; despite the pressing of his hosts he would drink but one glass of whisky. He was induced, however, to take a rest on the pallet in the little back room, and presently in his childish fashion fell asleep. Hare lay down beside him to watch the case, Burke "sitting at the foreside of the bed." In their diverse accounts of the atrocious scene that followed so soon as they perceived Jamie's slumber to be sufficiently sound for their purpose, each ruffian sought to assign to the other the leading role in what they found to be an unpopular tragedy. It is plain that poor Jamie, endowed with the strength of insanity, put up a desperate resistance to his destroyers, and had he fought for life against a single adversary, would surely have come off victorious. But the combined attack of his base assailants proved too much for his pluck and prowess, and after a fierce and prolonged struggle they effected their hellish aim. Even these devils were moved to admiration: Hare says Jamie

"fought like a hero"; Burke describes his courage as "terrible."
After stripping the body, Hare took the brass snuff-box and
Burke the accompanying spoon, Daft Jamie's sole and greatly
prized possessions. The clothes Burke presented to his small
nephews in Gibb's Close, and the remains were disposed of to
Dr. Knox at the usual rate of exchange.

Now although I do not wish to anticipate what will have to
be said regarding the responsibility of that distinguished
anatomist in the premises, while the facts are yet fresh in the
reader's mind I would point out: (1) that the deadly struggle as
described by both the murderers must inevitably have left
*some* traces upon the victim's body; (2) that so soon as it was
unpacked from the tea-chest it was at once recognized as that
of Daft Jamie by the janitor of the rooms, and by several of the
students then present; *"but Dr. Knox persisted all along that it
was not Jamie"* until the hue and cry arose, when, contrary to
the regular rotation of "subjects," he ordered its immediate
dissection; and (3) that Mr. Fergusson, the senior assistant,
forthwith possessed himself of the feet, which owing to their
notorious malformation—for Jamie went always bare-footed—
would have furnished indisputable and ready proof of identity,
while another assistant made away with the head, as equally
susceptible of recognition. Thus, had the attention of the authorities been directed to Surgeons' Square, they could have
found no clue to the mystery of Daft Jamie's disappearance.

Vainly did the mother and sister perambulate the city
ways, seeking some tidings of the missing lad; none knew or
had seen anything of him, and they ceased not from their
search until the sudden rending of the veil which for nine
months had hidden the horror of the West Port murders revealed in the clear light of justice their hideous features and
unparalleled extent.

## VIII

The Portsburgh murder factory had met with such favor in scientific quarters that the time was now deemed ripe for extending and consolidating its operations. It was definitely arranged that the managing partners should receive a fixed sum for all such "subjects" as they were able to supply: £10 in winter and £8 in summer. Further, a third partner—popularly believed to be David Paterson, Dr. Knox's janitor—was to be assumed, with whom Burke was to proceed to Ireland, with a view to increasing the firm's output by opening up a fresh market, or in the words of that expert: "to try the same there, and to forward them to Hare, and he was to give them to Dr. Knox." But before this promising project could be put into execution, another execution had put its promoter permanently out of business, and he was himself converted into a "subject" for the benefit of that science to which he had offered so many vicarious sacrifices. The irony of the situation should have appealed to his native sense of humor.

In perpetrating what proved to be their last murder, Burke and Hare reverted to their earlier methods. It was for them quite a humdrum affair after the sensational and foolhardy slayings of Mary Paterson and Daft Jamie: only a little old beggar woman, frail and friendless, a stranger within the city gates: one, in their view, too inconsiderable for anybody to bother about. Yet the business, trifling as it seemed to them, was in fact the last straw. On Friday, 31st October 1828, this humble instrument of Providence entered Rymer's spirit shop, at the head of Tanner's Close, begging for alms. At the counter Mr. Burke chanced to be taking his morning dram. Perceiving by her speech that she was Irish, he haled her as a countrywoman; and learning that her name was Docherty—which he alleged to be also that of his mother—he claimed her for a kinswoman. Invited to make his home her own during her sojourn in Edinburgh, the little old woman joyfully accepted and was cordially received there by the genial and kind-hearted Macdougal. Burke then went out to inform Hare "he had got a 'shot' in the house for the Doctor," and to bespeak his cooperation in the requisite arrangements.

It was Hallowe'en; and to that time-honored festival, as holden in the Burke home, the Hares had been invited. His partner, he judged, would have no objection to combine business with pleasure. The accommodation of the house was limited: a single room, 16 feet 2 inches by 7 feet 5 inches; and its resources were already overtaxed by the presence of an ex-soldier named Gray, who with his wife and child were there for a week as paying guests. It was accordingly agreed and provided that they, the Grays, should for that night remove to the Hare hostelry. (The firm desired to keep in touch with them; they might be useful in the way of business later.) So in that small and bloody chamber was spent a jovial evening. There was abundance of whisky, Burke was in excellent voice, delighting his guests with the songs of their native land, and as the spirits—animal and alcoholic—rose amain, the parties began to dance. Sounds of mirth and revelry echoed through the basement flat; to these succeeded the noise of brawling and fighting, too common to attract attention or to cause interference. Then about midnight was heard a cry of "Murder!" and a violent beating from within upon Burke's door. A neighbor went out to look for a policeman, but failing to find one, returned to bed.

Next morning, when the Grays came back, the little old woman was gone. They asked what had become of her, and Macdougal replied that being "ow'r friendly" with Burke, she had kicked her out of the house. After breakfast Mrs. Gray, in pursuance of her unladylike habit, lit her morning pipe. At the foot of the connubial couch was a heap of straw, on which the lodgers slept. Approaching this to look for her child's stockings, she was sharply rebuked by Macdougal, who bade her "keep out of there." Burke, too, expressed much annoyance at her harmless action, alleging his fear of fire. This unusual inhibition aroused Mrs. Gray's curiosity, which, woman-like, she determined at the first opportunity to satisfy. Not until the late afternoon was she able to do so. Burke went out for more liquor, Macdougal was reposing on the bed, and beside it sat a young lad named Broggan, the landlord's son, whom Burke, before he left, ordered not to stir from the chair until his return. But when Macdougal arose and went forth, Broggan rashly forsook his post, and the couple were at last alone. They went instantly to the forbidden corner, and lifting the straw, uncovered the dead and naked body of the little old woman. Horrified, they hastily caught up their small belongings and hurried from the house. Macdougal, returning, met them in the passage. They told her what they had seen. The terrified hag fell on her knees, imploring them not to "inform"; she offered present money, and swore it would be "worth £10 a week to them" if only they kept silent. But the Grays were proof against temptation; they left the house and communicated with the police. The upright conduct of Gray, a penniless and homeless man, to whose integrity alone the unmasking of the murder gang was due, met with most inadequate reward. A subscription opened in his behalf produced under £10. The public was less lavish of its money than Macdougal.

When the police reached the house at 8 p.m. they found the birds of prey about to fly their foul nest. Asked as to the present whereabouts of the little woman, Burke stated that she had gone away at 7 *a.m.* and that Mr. Hare had witnessed her departure; Macdougal, separately interrogated, said the woman had left at 7 *p.m.* In view of these conflicting statements, and of the fact that there was seen upon the straw a quantity of fresh blood, the pair were apprehended. Early next morning the police paid their long overdue visit to Dr. Knox's rooms.

The janitor produced a tea-chest, delivered the evening before in the ordinary course of business. On being opened it was found to contain a dead body, identified at once by the Grays, and later by others, as that of the little old woman. Their next call was upon Mr. and Mrs. Hare, whom they surprised in bed and took into custody. When confronted with the corpse of their victim the prisoners one and all swore that they had never seen the woman before, alive or dead. A post-mortem examination of the remains proved inconclusive. It was made by Mr. Black, the police surgeon, and by the eminent Dr. (afterwards Sir Robert) Christison, Professor of Medical Jurisprudence in Edinburgh University. No indications of death from natural disease were found, and certain superficial injuries were plainly due to the forcing of the body into the tea-chest. The appearances were *consistent* with death by suffocation, but of that there was no positive *proof*. Repeatedly examined, the four prisoners continued to deny all accession to the murder.

What, in these aggravating circumstances, was the Crown to do? Nothing was as yet definitely known regarding the commission of the other crimes, but there was a feeling that the accused could if they chose throw a light upon the many mysterious disappearances which, during the last nine months, had caused so much uneasiness in official quarters. The Lord Advocate, Sir William Rae, came regretfully to the conclusion that there was no sufficient proof either of the murder or of the actual perpetrator; he therefore, with extreme reluctance, decided to take one or other of the accused as witness against the rest, rather than that the whole four miscreants should escape. The desirability of getting information, otherwise unobtainable, as to the suspected further crimes was an additional factor in his Lordship's decision. Burke was believed rightly or wrongly to be the ringleader, so he was not approached. Macdougal refused to turn King's evidence; but Hare gladly, nay enthusiastically, accepted the part. As he could not bear witness against his spouse, her testimony had also to be accepted. The pair proved only too ready to tell their horrible tale; but as the witnesses of truth, they showed a regrettable eagerness to shift as much of the responsibility as they could on to the shoulders of their former partner. Still, without the information—howsoever affected by the modesty with which they sought to minimize their own share in the transactions— that they were willing to furnish, the Crown would have known nothing of the fate of Mary Paterson and of Daft Jamie.

After considering upon which items of the ghastly catalogue Burke and Macdougal should be tried, the Lord Advocate decided to charge them with three: the murders of Mary Paterson, of James Wilson, and of "Madgy or Margery or Mary M'Gonigal or Duffie or Campbell or Docherty," under which imposing style and title the reader will hardly recognize the little old woman. In her case, at least, his Lordship was in a position to produce a tangible *corpus delicti*.


IX


The trial—which was to rank as Scotland's most famous criminal cause—began on Christmas Eve. As I have elsewhere furnished a verbatim report of the case I shall do no more here than mention such facts as are needful to continue the narrative.

"It may surprise the young barristers of to-day," writes Lord Kingsburgh in his strangely deficient volume of reminiscences, "to know that the Law Room, which they now frequent for study, was the Second Division Court Room, to which the bow-window at the corner was added later, and that in that confined space the celebrated trial of Burke and Mrs. Macdougal took place, the Judges stimulating their jaded nerves by drinking coffee on the Bench during an adjournment in the middle of the night. This I learned from an eyewitness." The Senators who suffered this painful experience were the Lord Justice-Clerk (Boyle), Lords Pitmilly, Meadowbank, and Mackenzie. The Lord Advocate and three Advocates-Depute conducted the prosecution. Though it was a "Poor" case, *i.e.* one in which there were no fees, hence commonly conducted by an inexperienced junior, the sporting instincts of the Scots Bar supplied the pannels (prisoners) with the services of some of its most distinguished members. Burke was defended by the Dean of Faculty (Moncreiff), Patrick Robertson, Duncan M'Neill, and David Milne; Macdougal, by Henry Cockburn, Mark Napier, Hugh Bruce, and George Patton. Of these, some rose to highest judicial office as Lord President, Lord Justice-Clerk, and Lords of Session; others achieved literary fame.

The indictment being read, counsel for the defense objected to the accumulation of charges, and after long debate the Court held that the three must be tried separately, allowing the Lord Advocate to choose whichever he liked to take first. His Lordship decided to begin with the last charge: the murder of Mrs. Docherty; and to that the proof was accordingly restricted. The effect of this course was in many ways lamentable; but the most unfortunate result was this: of all the sixteen murders, *the only "subject" which had not been seen and personally examined by Dr. Knox was the one selected.* Had either of the two other charges been taken, the Doctor and his assistants must have been called as witnesses in order to prove the death, and would themselves have become "subjects" for cross-examination. But as a conviction was obtained on the third charge, the others were not gone into at all. This state of matters was very strongly resented by the public and by the Press, and we shall presently see the attempts that were made to remedy it.

Certain of the neighbors having deponed to seeing the old woman in Burke's house on Hallowe'en, David Paterson, Dr.

Knox's janitor, stated that Burke called at his house, No. 26 West Port, at midnight that day. Witness accompanied him by request to his abode, where he found Macdougal and the Hares. Burke pointed to the straw, saying "he had procured something for the Doctor." Witness did not offer to inspect it, but told him to communicate with Dr. Knox direct. Next morning Burke and Hare had a meeting with the Doctor in his rooms; he then instructed witness to receive any package brought by them. At 7 p.m. Burke and Hare returned with a porter and a tea-chest, which, it being Saturday night, was deposited unopened in the Doctor's cellar by Mr. Jones, the assistant on duty. Thereafter Jones and witness walked out to Dr. Knox's house at Newington to report—Burke, Hare, and the two women following. The Doctor gave witness £5 for the men, the balance to be paid on Monday, when the condition of the goods had been ascertained. Witness then described the coming of the police to the dissecting-rooms next morning (Sunday), and the opening of the chest in their presence. Cross-examined, he admitted he knew Burke and Hare. They acted "conjunctly," and Dr. Knox had often dealt with them before for dead *unburied* bodies. All the parties were the worse of drink when he called at Burke's house that night.

The Grays told their tale; and the porter said that, being employed by Burke "to carry something," he helped to pack the body into the chest. "A good deal of pressure was required for putting the lid on."

When the Lord Advocate called his next witness there was "sensation in Court" indeed. Hare entered the box with a grin and gave his evidence with unblushing effrontery. At the Hallowe'en party Burke and he quarreled and fought. The old woman was frightened and twice ran out of the house, calling "Murder!" Each time she did so, Macdougal fetched her back. She stumbled over a stool and was too drunk to rise. Burke fell upon her and held her down until she ceased to breathe.

During the murder, witness sat in a chair the whole time, looking on. Henry Cockburn rose to cross-examine. His first question was: "Have you been connected in supplying the doctors with subjects on other occasions?" The Lord Advocate promptly objected; the question was allowed, but the witness was told he was not bound to answer so as to incriminate himself. Hare then replied in the negative, but admitted that he "saw them doing it." Cockburn next successively asked: How often? Was this the first murder he had been concerned in? Was a murder committed in his house in October? (Daft Jamie). Witness, duly warned as before, declined to answer. Mrs. Hare corroborated. So soon as Burke attacked the old woman, she and Macdougal withdrew into the passage. On their return to the room, fifteen minutes later, they saw nothing of the guest. "I had a supposition that she had been murdered," said the witness, coolly; "I have seen such tricks before." Asked why she did not seek assistance from the neighbors, she tartly replied: "The thing had happened two or three times before, and it was not likely I should tell a thing to affect my husband." This truculent and forbidding hag held the while in her maternal grasp a wretched infant, then in the throes of whooping-cough, which, as Cockburn afterwards reminded the jury, "seemed at every attack to fire her with intenser anger and impatience, till at last the infant was plainly used merely as an instrument for delaying or evading whatever question it was inconvenient for her to answer."

The medical evidence came practically to this: in chief, that death was probably due to suffocation by violence; in cross, that the appearances were merely suspicious.

To the long and elaborate addresses of counsel and the able charge of the presiding Judge I cannot here do justice; the reader may study them at length in my report of the trial. The Dean of Faculty, for Burke, began his speech at three o'clock in the morning, the proceedings having already lasted seventeen hours! Cockburn started at five, and spoke for an hour in behalf of Macdougal. The Justice-Clerk's charge, the weight of which was heavily against both pannels, occupied over two hours. At half-past eight, on the morning of Christmas Day, the jury retired to consult, and in fifty minutes returned to Court with their verdict: Burke, Guilty; Macdougal, Not Proven. Turning to his companion in the dock, Burke remarked: "Nellie, you are out of the scrape." The Justice-Clerk, in pronouncing sentence of death, said his only doubt was whether Burke's body should not be hung in chains, but he directed that it be publicly dissected and anatomized. His Lordship further expressed the hope that his skeleton would be preserved as a memorial of his atrocious crimes. All which, as we know, was well and truly done. The Court then rose, having sat continuously for four-and-twenty hours.

## X

The universal joy on the conviction of Burke, tempered by grief for the acquittal of Macdougal, was well-nigh discounted by the disappointment, wrath, and indignation felt at the escape of Hare. The non-appearance in the witness-box of Dr. Knox himself and his three assistants was very bitterly resented. "Vengeance on Hare!" cried the people; "Where are the doctors?" These sentiments were vehemently reechoed by the Press; never, as far as I know, has so fierce a newspaper campaign been fought over any murder trial.

Meanwhile Macdougal, having been set at liberty, with unbelievable boldness or stupidity went back to her home in Portsburgh. The rumor of her return quickly spread, a huge crowd besieged the house, and but for the intervention of a strong force of police she would infallibly have been torn in pieces. Secured for a time in jail, she subsequently effected her escape unnoticed, and so passes out of the story. Mrs. Hare, after undergoing similar exciting experiences at the hands of the enraged populace, contrived to reach Greenock whole. Sailing from that seaport for her native country, she vanishes from our view. The disposal of Hare furnished the authorities with a more difficult problem. To let him loose meant, in the then state of public feeling, certain death, so he was kept in the Calton Jail until my Lord Advocate could make up his mind what to do with him.

On 3rd January 1829 Burke, in the condemned cell, made what is known as his "official" confession; on the 21st he confided to an enterprising journalist a further and much fuller statement, called the "*Courant*" confession, from the title of the journal in which, after the author's death, the manuscript was published.

At eight o'clock in the morning of the 29th, at the head of Libberton's Wynd—the site of the gallows is still marked by two reversed sets in the paving of the High Street, at the northwest corner of the County Buildings—in presence of a vast crowd, estimated at 25,000 and said to be the largest that had ever assembled in the streets of Edinburgh, William Burke, the murderer, was sent to his account. The rascal multitude had waited patiently all night, in pouring rain, so as to be in good time for the performance; the élite of Edinburgh society (including, as I have elsewhere shown, Sir Walter Scott) viewed the entertainment in relative comfort from the windows of the towering tenements overlooking the scaffold.

The measure of Burke's punishment was felt to be peculiarly appropriate: like his victims, he met his death by stifling; like theirs, his remains formed a "subject" for scientific research. On the following day his body was delivered to Professor Monro, who in terms of the sentence dissected it in public. The show started with a private view, admission to which was by ticket, a privilege highly resented by the students. The precincts of the Old College were beset by indignant undergraduates, determined to get into the classroom; there was a riot in the quadrangle; finally the authorities gave way, and they were allowed in by batches of fifty. Next day the public were admitted, and from 10 a.m. till dark a continuous stream of sightseers enjoyed the edifying spectacle, the total attendance numbering 30,000. "Who is he," asks Sir Walter in his *Journal*, "that says we are not ill to please in our objects of curiosity?" Thereafter, as I have told, Burke was flayed, his skin tanned, his body salted and, with exquisite propriety, packed into a barrel for purposes of future lectures, and ultimately his articulated bones were set up to grace the University museum. Never was murderer more comprehensively disposed of; never was justice more amply satisfied; never was "subject" more effectually "burked."

## XI

There remained the burning question: What was to be done with Hare? To Press and public the answer seemed simple: he had been examined in Court as a witness in one charge only; he must now be brought to trial on the two other charges, regarding which he had given no evidence. But the Lord Advocate, after long and careful consideration of the whole matter, felt bound to dissent from the popular judgment. In view of the immunity given to Hare by his authority, his Lordship was of opinion that he was legally barred from prosecuting the informer further.

When all hope of forcing the Crown to take action had to be abandoned, a movement was made to institute against Hare a private prosecution for the murder of Daft Jamie, generally regarded as the most flagrant of the crimes, at the instance of his mother and sister. The necessary funds being readily raised, a law agent was instructed and Francis Jeffrey retained as counsel. On 16th January a petition was presented to the Sheriff by the private prosecutors, Mrs. and Miss Wilson, praying that Hare, who was still in custody, be examined upon the charge, and a precognition of other witnesses taken. Hare countered by a petition applying to be released and to have the proposed precognition stopped. The case was argued before the Sheriff, Duncan M'Neil appearing for Hare, when his Lordship decided in favor of the Wilsons; but in view of the novelty of the point, allowed Hare to apply to the High Court of Justiciary. This was accordingly done by Bill of Advocation, Suspension, and Liberation. The Court ordered intimation of the Bill to be made to the Crown; and the Lord Advocate in his answers thereto explained that the assurance given to Hare was unqualified, and was meant to be understood as excluding the possibility of future trial or punishment for any of the crimes concerned. At the hearing before the High Court, the case was debated at great length and with equal forensic learning and ingenuity. On 2nd February it was advised: the Lords, by a majority of four to two, held that Hare could not be prosecuted for the murder of Daft Jamie, ordered him to be set at liberty, and quashed the proceedings taken against him by the Wilsons.

Any criminal prosecution being now out of the question, a final attempt was made to punish Hare by means of a civil action by the Wilsons, claiming an assythment (damages) of £500 for the murder of their relative. They alleged that Hare was *in meditatione fugæ* (about to flee the country), and prayed for his commitment until he should find caution (security) for his appearance to defend the action. Upon this point Hare was examined, and refusing to answer any questions either as to the murder or his own prospective arrangements, was committed to prison until he found caution as required. It being obvious that he could never do so, let alone pay the assythment were it found due, the warrant was withdrawn, and on 5th February Hare was finally let loose. The proposed action can hardly have been serious; probably it was meant merely to give him as much annoyance and to keep him in jail as long as possible.

On his release Hare was conveyed in a hackney coach to Newington, where, without pausing to pay his respects to Dr. Knox, he joined, in disguise, the southward mail. At the first stage the passengers alighted at the inn for supper. Among them, by a strange chance, was the junior counsel for the Wilsons, who disclosed to his fellow-travelers the identity of their companion. So, when the mail-coach reached Dumfries, the news was soon all over the town, and presently the King's Arms, in which Hare had sought sanctuary, was beset by an angry crowd, impolitely shouting in concert the alliterative slogan: " 'Burke' the ———!" While, in order to distract the attention of the mob, a chaise was ostentatiously brought round to the front door, Hare was smuggled out of the house by a back window and safely lodged in prison. This maneuver being detected, the mob next attacked the jail, the riot continuing throughout the night; but eventually, by persuasion of the batons of a hundred special constables, the crowd was dispersed. Very early next morning, escorted by a sheriff-officer and a guard of militiamen, the odious visitor was conveyed out of the town. By daybreak he was beyond the Border, and nothing further of his adventures is recorded.

There is a tradition that, having been identified by some fellow-workmen as the West Port murderer and consequently cast into a lime pit, whereby he lost his sight, Hare survived for many years as a blind beggar in the streets of London; and naughty children were admonished by nurses that unless they were "good," they would be delivered into the hands of that fearsome miscreant.

## XII

There are three incidents connected with the dreadful drama which, though in themselves inconsiderable, seem to me significant and typical as regards the psychology of the principal performers. When Hare, being in the prison yard, was informed of the result of the trial, he capered about in fiendish glee at having himself escaped justice at the cost of his accomplice's life. The malevolence and hideous levity of the wretch shocked even the hardened warders. When he sands of time were for him well-nigh sunk, Burke, who since his condemnation had shown no emotion whatever, was seen to be sensibly perturbed. His ghostly counselor, believing his conscience to be at length awakened, hopefully asked what was worrying him. "I think," said Burke musingly, "I am entitled, and ought to get that five pounds from Dr. Knox which is still unpaid on the body of the woman Docherty." "Why," exclaimed the other, "Dr. Knox lost by the transaction, as the body was taken from him!" "That was not my business," sharply retorted the penitent. "I delivered the subject, and he ought to have kept it." He explained that he needed the money for a new coat, as he wished on his last public appearance "to be respectable"! The blend of callous selfishness and conceit is noteworthy. When Dr. Knox first met his students after the Christmas recess and the revelations of the trial, he announced to his class in his introductory lecture, with reference to the widespread censure of his conduct in relation to the crimes: "I will do just as I have done heretofore." The intellectual arrogance of the man, his colossal egoism, and imperviousness to adverse criticism are all summed up in that amazing pronouncement. Thus will it be seen that the three protagonists had something in common over and above the similarity of their taste in "subjects."

## XIII

Seldom is the life of a great and good man written with such gusto and devotion as is the biography of Dr. Knox by his admirer and former student, Dr. Lonsdale. Dr. Knox had but one eye, and never saw more with it than suited his convenience; Dr. Lonsdale, equipped with the usual number, fails totally to see either spot or blemish in the fair character of his hero. Yet none of us is perfect, and the partiality of the author for his "subject" has blinded him, as we shall find, to sundry wrinkles in the Doctor's moral make-up. At the time of the trial, when the fierce light of publicity was turned upon his professional pursuits, the domestic atmosphere of Dr. Knox remained obscure. The day's work done, he shut the door of his house at No. 4 Newington Place, and Edinburgh knew nothing of him until he appeared next morning in Surgeons' Square, brilliant, flamboyant, and pre-eminent in his art as usual. Of social relations he neither had nor desired to have any; he was secretly married "to a person of inferior rank"—perhaps a euphemism for his cook—by whom he had a small family; his private life was a thing apart and looked upon askance by the respectable. His sinister countenance and repulsive manner, his loud attire, his cynical and caustic speech, his avowed scorn of creeds and churches, were little likely to commend him to the self-righteous and conventional inhabitants of the strait-laced city of Edinburgh. Even among his medical confrères he had no friends; for it was his amiable custom on every possible occasion to hold them up to ridicule and contempt, and such references in his lectures as have been preserved to Professor Monro, Liston, and other rival teachers of anatomy, are so virulent as almost to baffle belief.

On the credit side is the unquestioned fact that he was the idol of his classes; his disciples swore by him, and for them, as his biographer justly claims, Knox was *primus et incompara-*

*bilis.* And they stuck at nothing to enhance the fame of their preceptor. "He lived to lecture," says Dr. Lonsdale; his class numbered over 500 students; he had to deliver his lectures thrice a day, and he spared neither time nor money (some have added, conscience) in the endeavor to maintain his pre-eminence as a demonstrator. Dr. Lonsdale states that in one session alone he spent above £700 on "subjects," and boasts that "No. 10 Surgeons' Square had a supply which no other establishment possessed." A Notice of Course of Lectures for that fatal winter session of 1828–9 (a copy of which I have reproduced elsewhere) contains the suggestive intimation: "Arrangements have been made to secure as usual an ample supply of Anatomical Subjects." All this told heavily against the Doctor when the crash came and one source of his supply was "demonstrated" to a horrified world.

Robert Knox was born at Edinburgh in 1791. His father was a mathematical master at George Heriot's, his mother was a German. To maternal heredity has been ascribed certain of his less lovable traits. Educated at the High School, he left it in 1800 as Dux and Gold Medalist, and joining the medical classes of Edinburgh University, devoted himself specially to the study of anatomy. But he deserted the orthodox professor for Dr. John Barclay, the brilliant extra-mural lecturer, whose best pupil he soon became. Graduating in 1814, he began his life-long contributions to medical journals; in 1815 was attached to the military hospital in Brussels and attended the wounded from Waterloo; and in 1817 sailed for South Africa, as surgeon of the 72nd Highlanders. His sporting record while at the Cape is remarkable, rivaling in thrills the surprising adventures of a later medical traveler, Dr. Pritchard. One hopes, however, that they are more authentic. On his return to England, having left the army, he spent the years 1821–2 studying anatomy in the medical schools of the Continent; and 1823 saw him settled in Edinburgh, his whole time being given to dissection. In the following year he formed a Museum of Comparative Anatomy in Surgeons' Hall, and was appointed its Conservator. In 1825 he joined as colleague and successor his old chief, Dr. Barclay, and began the first course of his famous lectures in the winter session of 1825–6. Such in briefest outline is the distinguished career which, whether from lack of judgment or by willful fault, was so wantonly wasted and destroyed.

Let us glance for a moment at the sort of criticism which Dr. Knox ignored and affected to despise. The *Caledonian Mercury*, Edinburgh's leading "organ," likened his relations with Burke and Hare to those of Macbeth with the murderers of Banquo, and the other local newspapers were equally plainspoken and defamatory. Professor Wilson, "Christopher North," wrote thus of him in *Blackwood's*: "He is ordered to open his mouth and speak, or be for ever dumb. Sixteen uninterred bodies—for the present I sink the word murdered—have been purchased within nine months by him and his, from the two brutal wretches who lived by that trade. Let him prove to the conviction of all reasonable men that it was impossible he could suspect any evil; that the practice of selling the dead was so general as to be almost universal among the poor of this city; and that he knew it to be so; and then we shall send his vindication abroad on all the winds of heaven." Yet Dr. Knox continued, in the modern phrase, to carry on as if nothing out of the way had happened, and beyond the declaration in his opening lecture already mentioned, took not the least notice of the grave accusations thus made publicly against him.

The people of Edinburgh, who could not give literary vent to their feelings—for the following popular quatrain can hardly be described as literature:—

> Up the close and doun the stair,
> But and ben wi' Burke and Hare.

Burke's the butcher, Hare's the thief,
Knox the boy that buys the beef—

also manifested their appreciation of his position in more practical form. On the night of 12th February a great crowd gathered upon the Calton Hill, where a life-size figure of the Doctor, garbed in raiment of the well-known gaudy hues and bearing on its back a label: "Knox, the associate of the infamous Hare," was the object of the meeting. Thence it was carried in procession to Newington, and having been solemnly hanged upon a tree in the front garden of No. 4 Newington Place, the residence of the original, was thereafter consumed by fire. The windows of the house were smashed with stones, and it was long before the police, who got access by the back, succeeded in driving off the assailants. Meanwhile the Doctor, who had donned his old military cloak and armed himself with a brace of pistols, a sword, and a Highland dirk, was with difficulty restrained from sallying forth to give battle in defense of his principles and property; but persuaded at length of the futility of engaging single-handed so fierce a mob, he consented to retire from the field by the back door, and for a space left the city.

The same night an attack upon his dissecting-rooms in Surgeons' Square was repulsed with loss, certain of the rioters being taken and subsequently fined for breach of the peace. Even Portobello, that blameless bathing-place, under suspicion of harboring the obnoxious surgeon, was moved to take action, and he was once again hanged and burnt in effigy at the head of Tower Street, on the site of the old-time gibbet. When things were quieter, Dr. Knox returned to town and resumed his lectures. But it was necessary for him to be attended by a bodyguard of students, lest the common folk, notoriously intolerant of scientists, should give forcible expression to their views.

Something had to be done about it; for the credit of the city and the University, things could not remain as they were; accordingly it was announced that a committee of gentlemen had undertaken the rather invidious task of inquiring into Dr. Knox's relations with the Wolves of whom, in popular belief, he was the shepherd. "The rank, station, and character of these individuals [the gentlemen, not the Wolves]," observed the *Scotsman*, "assure us that they will act with the strictest impartiality." Doubtless they did so; yet the form and manner of their proceedings left much to be desired. The members were nominated by the Doctor himself; the investigation was conducted in private; neither the names of such witnesses as were examined nor the nature of their evidence was disclosed; and the chairman, the Most Noble the Marquess of Queensberry, resigned before the hearing, which occupied six weeks, was completed, no reason being given for his withdrawal. When the report was ready it was communicated to the Press by its originator, who, in sending it for publication, broke for the first time his long silence. He stated that he had taken opinion of counsel regarding the calumnies of which he had been the object; that the Dean of Faculty had advised him "there was no want of actionable matter"—an opinion in which, if I may say so, I respectfully concur; but he refrained from seeking legal redress, because the disclosure in Court of dissecting-room methods might "shock the public and be hurtful to science"! Of the much more important matter, his personal dealings with Burke and Hare, Dr. Knox makes no mention.

The committee's report satisfied nobody except its begetter. While admitting, as they were bound to do, that the circumstances in which the subjects were furnished by the murderers "appear calculated to excite suspicion," they "found no evidence of their actually having excited it in the mind of Dr. Knox or of any other of the individuals who saw the bodies." Still, they thought the Doctor had acted throughout "in a very incautious manner," and regarded as "unfortunate" his orders to his assistants to make no inquiries, as likely "to diminish or divert the supply of subjects." They regretted that the practice of his rooms was such as "unintentionally" to facilitate the disposal of the victims of the murders. The point was afterwards very fairly put by Sir Robert Christison, who as Dr. Christison was the leading medical expert at the trial: "Knox, a man of undoubted talent but notoriously deficient in principle and in heart, was exactly the person to blind himself against suspicion and fall into blameable carelessness." None is so blind as he who will not see. Let us leave it at that.

His students, of course, were overjoyed at the "acquittal" of their idol and his vindication from the blasphemies of the profane. They presented him with a golden cup in commemoration of his triumph. In accepting this tribute, the Doctor said he did so as evidence of how all reasonable men regarded "the absurd imputations against me by which the public has been industriously misled." In certain colored caricatures of the day the cup is represented as filled with an ominous fluid —not wine.

Paterson, the janitor, also at this time bulked largely in the public eye, by reason of a pamphlet which he published on the late "horrid transactions," entitled: *Letter to the Lord Advocate, disclosing the Accomplices, Secrets, and other Facts relative to the late Murders . . .* By the Echo of Surgeons' Square (Edinburgh: 1829). He had in his degree participated in the popular opprobrium attaching to his principal, and maintained that he had been made "the scapegoat for a personage in higher life." But his contention, as elaborated in a series of letters to the Press, is not convincing. Paterson had the effrontery to suggest to Sir Walter Scott that they might collaborate in a book about Burke and Hare! which caused the Author of *Waverley*, not without warrant, to damn his impudence.

The subsequent history of Dr. Knox makes but sorry

reading, and I do not propose to dwell on it. His once crowded classes gradually dwindled; "the tide was on the ebb," Dr. Lonsdale sadly records, "and the growing animosity of his contemporaries rendered the ebb more and more apparent." In 1837 he applied for the Chair of Pathology, vacant by the resignation of Dr. John Thomson, whom, having held other professional preferment, Dr. Knox in his pleasant way called "the old chair-maker." He was not appointed; and in a later application for the Chair of Physiology he was also unsuccessful. In 1839 he gave up his old rooms in Surgeons' Square to become a lecturer on anatomy in the Argyle Square Medical School—a marked declension. His next move was to Glasgow, where he tried to establish himself again as a teacher; but the enrolments for his class were so few that he returned the fees. In London, his final resort, he was for a time, according to his biographer, in general practice at Hackney; and "one of his last occupations," Sir Robert Christison tells us, "was that of lecturer, demonstrator, or showman, to a traveling party of Ojibbeway Indians." He died on 20th December 1862 at the age of 71, and was buried at Working. Recalling their relative positions, his fate was as terrible as that of Hare and less merciful than Burke's.

■

Even the dark cloud that so long lowered over Edinburgh had its silver lining. In 1832 the passing of the Anatomy Act, due to the revelation of the West Port atrocities, abolished forever those secret sources of supply which brought about the downfall of the brilliant but unconscionable scientist. And should anyone have found interest in this plain composition and desire a more colored treatment of the theme, I counsel him to read that grim fantasia by Robert Louis Stevenson, *The Body Snatcher*, wherein he shall breathe the very atmosphere of those fearful times. Or if he would see Burke and Hare, Mary Paterson and the Janitor, above all, Dr. Knox himself, in actual flesh and blood, let him take occasion to witness a performance of Mr. Bridie's "lamentable comedy," *The Anatomist*.

# TO MEET MISS MADELEINE SMITH

*Where there's a beautiful woman in the dock, it makes a Criminal Court trial so much more amusing!*

—AUGUSTUS MUIR: *The Bronze Door*

THEY SAY THAT even of a good thing you can have too much. But I doubt it. True, such good things as sun-bathing, beer, and tobacco may be intemperately pursued to the detriment of their devotees; yet, to my mind, one cannot have too much of a good murder.

For example, my friend and criminous colleague, Mr. Edmund Pearson—I wonder, by the way, what has happened to the intervening "Lester" of his earlier title-pages?—told in his first and most excellent book in this vein, *Studies in Murder*, the attaching tale of the incomparable Lizzie Borden, a New England maiden, charged, in the nineties, with the unfilial massacre of her parents by means of an ax, and surprisingly acquitted by a sympathetic jury of her fellow-countrymen.

And in later works Mr. Pearson has returned to the "charge," and given us further aspects of his favorite heroine's personality and unique achievement, manifestly to his own delight and to the equal joy of such readers as share his admiration for the gentle Lizzie.

So that although the story of Madeleine Hamilton Smith has often been, with more or less competence, set forth—the latest and best account being that by Miss Tennyson Jesse, in her admirable introduction to the Madeleine volume of the Notable British Trials series—and the name of that engaging fair one is become, for such as savor legal mysteries, familiar in our mouths as household words, I venture to think the subject not yet exhausted, and that in fact we can never have enough of her and of the Mystery of Blythswood Square.

Any time I chance to be in Glasgow with an hour or so to spare—which, in view of the grievously inadequate miscalled "connections" afforded by the railway companies to Clyde-bound travelers from the east coast, often happens—I make my way to that respectable and dignified enclosure, and pausing at the second basement-window in the by-street, round the corner of the Square, ponder awhile upon what the iron stanchions could tell me an they would. For this very window once gave light to the chaste mysteries of Miss Madeleine's bedroom, and the space between the sill and the pavement, below the level of the street, was used by the lovers as their letter-box. And it was through these rusty bars that the white hand of Madeleine was wont to proffer for the refreshment of her unpleasant wooer those midnight cups of cocoa or chocolate, of whose baneful effects he complained to his complaisant confidante, Miss Perry.

It is hard to account for the spell which even unto this day Madeleine Smith unquestionably casts upon her votaries. Hers was an unlovely nature: false, self-centerd, wholly regardless of the rights and feelings of others, so far as these conflicted with her own desires; and her treatment of her blameless suitor, Mr. Minnoch, was flagrantly perfidious. Miss Tennyson Jesse, to whose recondite knowledge of the mysteries of her sex I respectfully take off my hat, has sought to excuse these shortcomings on the ground of the sex-suppressions by which Victorian virgins were cabined and confined. But it humbly appears to me that Madeleine was essentially, in the phrase of Andrew Lang, "other than a good one"; and that even in the wider freedom offered by this golden age of lipstick, cocktails, and night clubs, she would infallibly have gone wrong.

Professor Saintsbury, in his graceful preface to *Pride and Prejudice*, has wisely observed: "What is the good of seeking for the reason of charm? it is there." And he instances, from the novels of the last hundred years, five young ladies with whom it might be a pleasure to fall in love. "Their names are, in chronological order, Elizabeth Bennet, Diana Vernon, Argemone Lavington, Beatrix Esmond, and Barbara Grant. I should have been most in love with Beatrix and Argemone; I should, I think, for mere companionship, have preferred Diana and Barbara. But to live with and to marry, I do not know that any one of the four can come into competition with Elizabeth." For the benefit of would-be admirers lacking his encyclopaedic acquaintance with our fiction, I may mention that the shyest of these maids is to be found concealed in the *Yeast* of Charles Kingsley.

In like manner I too have, in my own line of reading, my darker favorites, who, following the Professor's order, I name our Madeleine (1857), Jessie M'Lachlan (1862), Florence Bravo (1876), Adelaide Bartlett (1886), and Mrs. Maybrick (1889). Of three of the five I have elsewhere treated at large; Miss Smith and Mrs. Maybrick are for me—figuratively speaking—virgin. Despite the superior social standing, the richer hues and higher romantic value of Madeleine, I give my vote, as a "case," for Jessie, whose attractions, though physically inferior to those of her more brilliant rival, are morally of much greater appeal. And yet Madeleine has many "points" to which the humbler genius of Jessie can make no claim. Her amazing correspondence —to Victorian ears so outrageously outspoken; her equally astounding courage, coolness, and seeming unconcern in a situation fraught with such danger and disgrace; and more notable than all in one of her age and sex, her complete lack of sensibility, her callosity of heart, in face of the ruin and devastation which she had wrought upon her hapless kinsfolk.

Apart from personal and professional feeling, I am moved to return to this old tale by the circumstance that I have before me a report of the case, which a former owner has "embellished" by the insertion of divers cuttings from the contemporary Press, relating to the nine-days' wonder of the trial. These are of value as giving us some notion of how the affair was regarded at the time. Although I have been living with Madeleine—I hasten to add, merely in a literary sense— for many years, they are to me instructive "news"; so I have thought it worthwhile to give some excerpts from them for the benefit of readers like-minded with myself. They do not solve the mystery, but they lighten a little our darkness as to the reactions of her fellow-citizens to the startling features of her case.

While I have neither wish nor intention to journey over again the traveled road of the evidence, it occurs to me as possible—having regard to the precedent of a learned Judge's historic question to counsel: "Who is Connie Gilchrist?"— that some readers of this inconsiderable essay, whether by ill-luck, inadvertence, defective education, or other cause to the present writer unknown, may never even have heard of Madeleine Smith! Such ignorance is to be deplored, and so far as may be in the space at my disposal, remedied. I shall, therefore, furnish first an outline of the general question at issue, which will enable these benighted persons to appreciate the situation. Those acquainted with the facts and circumstances of the case need not read it, but it may prove of service to such as know not Madeleine.

## I

The daughter of an architect of position in Glasgow, Madeleine Smith at nineteen was a dashing damsel, accomplished and attractive, an ornament of middle-class society in that city. Her charms caught the roving eye of a young Frenchman, Pierre Emile L'Angelier, clerk in a commercial house, and he contrived through a common friend an introduction to her in the street. This ill-omened meeting occurred in 1855. Socially, of course, L'Angelier was impossible; but he was a good-looking little "bounder," and the girl fell in love with him. They corresponded constantly, with that amazing mid-Victorian voluminosity which, happily, is a lost art, and met as often as circumstances permitted. No one in Madeleine's set knew of their intimacy; but a romantic spinster friend of L'Angelier, Miss Perry, acted as go-between, and one of the Smiths' maids connived at their clandestine meetings.

In the spring of 1856 the flirtation developed into an intrigue, the changed relations of the lovers being reflected in the tropical and abandoned tone of the fair correspondent. They addressed one another as "husband" and "wife," and there can be little doubt that in the belief of L'Angelier, as well as by the law of Scotland, they actually were married. An elopement was anticipated, but the gallant's official salary amounted only to ten shillings a week and the young lady was quite dependent on her parents, so the prospect was none of the brightest. In November 1856 the Smiths occupied a main-door corner house, No. 7 Blythswood Square. The stanchioned windows of Madeleine's bedroom in the basement, as I have said, opened directly upon, and were partly below the level of the pavement of the side street; it was the lovers' custom to converse at these, the sunk part formed a convenient receptacle for their respective letters, and when the coast was clear she could take him into the house.

In the flat above lived a gentleman named William Minnoch, who began to pay his charming neighbor marked attentions. Whether or not the copiousness of her draughts of passion had induced satiety, Madeleine was quick to realize that her position as the wife of a prosperous Glasgow merchant would be very different from her future with the little French clerk, so she gave her responsible suitor every encouragement. On 28th January 1857, with the approbation of her parents, she accepted his hand. Meantime her correspondence with L'Angelier was maintained at the accustomed temperature, till, early in February, she made an effort to break the "engagement," and demanded the return of her letters.

Rumors of Mr. Minnoch's attentions had reached L'Angelier; he suspected what was afoot, taxed her with perfidy, and refused to give up the letters to anyone but her father. The mere suggestion drove Madeleine well-nigh crazy. The letters were indeed such as no parent ever read and few daughters could have written. She poured forth frantic appeals for mercy and solemnly denied that she had broken faith; she besought him to come to her and she would explain everything. L'Angelier stood firm. He has been called blackguard and blackmailer; as I read the facts, it was neither revenge nor money that he wanted, but his wife. "I will never give them [her letters] up," he told his friend Kennedy; "she shall never marry another man so long as I live," adding with prophetic significance: "Tom, she'll be the death of me!"

A reconciliation was effected on 12th February, the correspondence was resumed on the old footing, and L'Angelier became again "her love, her pet, her sweet Emile." He told Miss

Perry he was to see Madeleine on the 19th. That night he left his lodgings, taking the pass-key as he intended to be late; next morning his landlady found him writing in agony on his bedroom floor, with all the painful symptoms of irritant poisoning. Whether the lovers had met or not is disputed, but in his diary, production of which at the trial was disallowed, L'Angelier wrote: "Thurs. 19. Saw Mimi a few moments—was very ill during the night." He recovered, but was never afterwards the same man.

At 4 a.m. on Monday 23rd, L'Angelier rang for his landlady, who found him suffering from another similar attack. The diary records: "Sun. 22. Saw Mimi in drawing-room—Promised me French Bible—Taken very ill." This meeting is otherwise established under Madeleine's own hand: "You did look bad on Sunday night and Monday morning. I think you get sick with walking home so late and the long want of food, so the next time we meet I shall make you eat a loaf of bread before you go out." L'Angelier said to Miss Perry: "I can't think why I was so unwell after getting coffee and chocolate from her [Madeleine]," referring, according to that lady, to *two* separate occasions. "If she were to poison me I would forgive her." He also told his friend Towers that he thought he had been poisoned *twice*, after taking coffee and cocoa.

Now, prior to the first illness, Madeleine had made an abortive attempt to procure prussic acid—"for her hands"— but no arsenic could then be traced to her possession. The day before the second attack, however, she bought from Murdoch, a druggist, *one ounce of arsenic*, "to send to the gardener at the country house"—Mr. Smith's summer villa, Rowaleyn, near Row, on the Gareloch.

On 5th March, L'Angelier, whose jealousy was reawakened, wrote insisting on knowing the truth about Mr. Minnoch. That day Madeleine purchased from Currie, another druggist, *a second ounce of arsenic*—"to kill rats in Blythswood Square";

and on the 6th she went with her family for ten days to Bridge of Allan. Mr. Minnoch was of the party, and the wedding was fixed for June.

L'Angelier, on sick leave, had gone to Edinburgh, impatiently awaiting Madeleine's return, when everything was to be explained. On the 19th he followed her to Bridge of Allan; but Madeleine had come back on the 17th, and next day she obtained from Currie *a third ounce of arsenic*—"the first was so effectual."

On the evening of Sunday 22nd, L'Angelier returned to his lodgings: a letter forwarded to him from Glasgow had brought him home in hot haste. He looked well and happy, and after a hasty meal hurried away, saying he might be out late. At 2:30 a.m. his landlady, aroused by the violent pealing of the doorbell, found him doubled up with agony upon the threshold. He was put to bed and she sent for a doctor, who formed a hopeful prognosis. "I am far worse than the doctor thinks," cried the patient. He said nothing as to the cause of his sudden seizure, but asked to see Miss Perry. When that lady arrived upon the scene L'Angelier's lips were sealed forever. In his vest pocket was found the last letter of a remarkable series:—

> Why my beloved did you not come to me. Oh beloved are you ill. Come to me sweet one. I waited and waited for you but you came not. I shall wait again to-morrow night same hour and arrangement. Do come sweet love my own dear love of a sweetheart. Come beloved and clasp me to your heart. Come and we shall be happy. A kiss fond love. Adieu with tender embraces ever believe me to be your own ever dear fond MIMI.

The postmark was Glasgow, 21st March. A facsimile will be found in Miss Tennyson Jesse's edition of the trial.

L'Angelier's half of the fatal correspondence was discovered; Madeleine fled to Row, and was brought back by her fiancé; an examination of the body pointed to poison, and she was apprehended. In her declaration she said that she had not seen L'Angelier for three weeks; the appointment was for Saturday, 21st March; he came neither that night nor the next; her purpose in making it was to tell him of her engagement to Mr. Minnoch! As to the arsenic, she used it all as a cosmetic, on the advice of a school-friend. She admitted giving cocoa to L'Angelier once, at her window.

Of the nine-days' wonder of her trial at Edinburgh in July I have small space left to speak. No less than 88 grains of arsenic were found in the body, and the defense made much of the fact that this was the greatest quantity hitherto detected, arguing that so large a dose indicated suicide rather than murder. The unsoundness of this contention is proved by two subsequent English cases,[1] where 150 and 154 grains respectively were recovered. As regards the two first charges—of administration—the Crown was handicapped by the exclusion of L'Angelier's diary; and in the murder charge, by inability to prove the actual meeting of the parties on the Sunday night. There was proof that L'Angelier had talked once or twice in a vaporing way of suicide, but none that he ever had arsenic in his possession. The prisoner's account of her object in acquiring arsenic was contradicted by her old school-fellow, and the fact that what she obtained was, in terms of the Statute,[2] mixed with soot and indigo, rendered it strangely uninviting for toilet purposes. On the other hand, the Crown doctors noticed no coloring matter in the body, but to this point their attention was not then directed. On the question

---

1. *R.* v. *Dodds*, 1860, and *R.* v. *Hewitt*, 1863.

2. 14 Vict. c. 13, s. 3.

of motive, it was maintained that the accused had nothing to gain by L'Angelier's death if her letters remained in his possession. These, however, having neither address nor any signature except "Mimi," afforded little clue to the writer's identity. But surely it was his *silence* that was for her the supreme object, and how could that be ensured save by his death?

Lord Advocate Moncreiff's masterly address, strong, restrained, convincing, was then, as now, unduly eclipsed by the brilliant, emotional speech of John Inglis for the defense, held to be the finest ever delivered in a Scots court. The one appealed to the head, the other to the heart; each pledged his personal belief in the righteousness of his cause. Lord Justice-Clerk Hope's charge favored an acquittal; the jury found the pannel Not Guilty of the first charge; the two others, Not Proven. In the popular verdict: "If she did not poison him, she ought to have done it," I am unable to concur.

The amazing self-command with which the prisoner faced her ordeal, no less than her youth and beauty, inspired the pens of contemporary scribes. During the trial she received many proposals, lay and clerical. Her fiancé was not an offerer....

II

Such is the abridgment of the case which I wrote for a chapter on Scottish poisonings in *Glengarry's Way*, a collection of essays first published in 1922. I make no apology for reprinting it here, because I am rather proud of it, as presenting in minimum compass the essential facts. The book was dedicated to my friend Mr. Hugh Walpole, who, in acknowledging the copy I sent him, thus referred to my inadequate treatment of Miss Smith:—

PENDRAGYN, CURY,
S. CORNWALL, JUNE 1, '22.

My dear Roughead,

I've just finished *Glengarry*, and I do congratulate you. I only wish it had been three times as long. I don't know what to pick out when it is all so good. But I think the "Locusta" chapter is perhaps the best, a really wonderful summary that must have been the Devil itself to do. When I had finished it I swore I'd never eat porridge in Scotland again—a decision good for my figure, if I could only hold to it.

Any mention of my little pet and favorite Madeleine Smith always thrills me to the bone; but do you give her letters quite sufficient literary credit? They seem very fine compositions to me, and I would have been almost in L'Angelier's place might I have received them. And is it true that there is someone alive in Edinburgh today who saw the poor young man on the fateful night leaving Madeleine's window? . . .

Thanking you once more for your splendid book and the honor you did me in connecting my name with it,

Yours very sincerely,
Hugh Walpole.

I admit that I did not do justice to the pen-flowers of Madeleine's indefatigable culture, but to have done so was, in the circumstances, impossible: they would require a volume to themselves. The rumor that L'Angelier was seen at her window that Sunday night was current at the time and has persisted even unto this day. I have often heard it asserted, but have never been able to verify the fact.

Madeleine's letters are painful reading, as well materially as

139

morally. She wrote the large, angular hand—I believe it was termed Italian—then affected by well-bred young ladies. Six to eight pages was her average allowance, half of which, in the damnable fashion of the day, she "crossed," with the result that her MS. presents at first sight the appearance of a Chinese puzzle. And when we reflect that the unfortunate L'Angelier received, and presumably perused, no less than 198 of these cryptographic missives—I had almost written "missiles"— which an expert at the trial stated were so difficult to decipher that he had to use a magnifying lens, the theory of suicide suggested by the defense seems, after all, less untenable than it otherwise appeared.

To show the versatility of Madeleine as a correspondent and the remarkable range of her epistolary gift, here is a letter written by her to her husband-elect, on parting from him at Bridge of Allan, *but five days before she wrote to her lover the impassioned appeal above quoted*. The contrast in style is not less striking than instructive. Posted at Stirling on 16th March, it is addressed to "William Minnoch, Esq., 124 St. Vincent Street, Glasgow," and runs as follows:—

My dearest William,

It is but fair, after your kindness to me, that I should write you a note. The day I part from friends I always feel sad. But to part from one I love, as I do you, makes me feel truly sad and dull. My only consolation is that we meet soon. Tomorrow we shall be home. I do wish you were here today. We might take a long walk. Our walk to Dumblane [*sic*] I shall ever remember with pleasure. That walk fixed a day on which we are to begin a new life—a life which I hope may be of happiness and long duration to both of us. My aim through life shall be to please you and study you. Dear William, I must conclude, as Mama is ready to go to Stirling. I do not go with the same pleasure as I did the last time. I hope you got to Town safe, and found your sisters well. Accept my warmest kindest love and ever believe me to be

Yours with affcn.,
Madeleine.
MONDAY,
PROSPECT VILLA.

When "dearest William" read the letters she had written to his rival, as disclosed at the trial, he must have had his doubts concerning the mutual happiness promised by his fiancée, had their marriage gone through as arranged. As it was, he behaved with conspicuous loyalty; when the blow fell and she fled in panic to Row, he followed her at once, found her on board the Helensburgh boat at the Broomielaw, brought her back to her parents' house, and gallantly stood by her until the revelations of the trial. These, however, proved too much even for his generosity. In the last of her letters which we have, that written to the Edinburgh prison matron four days after her release—I shall later have occasion to quote it in full—, she thus refers to the man who, despite the unspeakable wrong she had done him, treated her to the end like a gentleman: "My *friend* I know nothing of. I have not seen him. I hear he has been ill, which I don't much care [*sic*]."

The only complete verbatim text of the famous letters in book form is to be found in the appendix to Miss Tennyson Jesse's definitive edition of the trial. Madeleine had destroyed her share of the correspondence, and of L'Angelier's letters we have only a few, of which he kept copies. But the cunning little cad carefully preserved every line she ever wrote to him. The full text thus for the first time made generally available—there is an American unexpurgated edition, issued in 1857 and much sought after by the curious—furnishes less lurid reading than the judicial fulminations would lead one to expect. Naïvely outspoken in matters sexual, while they may be termed indelicate, to class them as pornographic is absurd. The fault lies in their unconventional frankness; and the mid-Victorians deemed it unseemly to call a spade a spade. "Candor such as this," justly remarks Miss Tennyson Jesse, "was felt to be perfectly shocking from a young woman, and to do the spirit of the time justice it would probably have been felt to be just as shocking had the parties been married. Love-making was a mysterious arrangement on the part of Providence, which was necessary to gentlemen and which a good wife accepted as her bounden duty. It was not a pagan festival such as Madeleine found it."

If Madeleine's phraseology was upon occasion ungenteel, the sentiments expressed by her lover, so far as we are permitted to know them, were perfectly correct—indeed, surprisingly so in one of his age and race. For example, the so-called seduction took place in the garden at Rowaleyn one June night in 1856. After his departure, Madeleine, in a long letter to him dated, amazingly, "*Wednesday morning*, 5 *o'c*," refers to the episode with engaging *épanchement*: "Tell me, pet, were you angry at me for letting you do what you did—was it very bad of me? We should, I suppose, have waited till we were married. I shall always remember last night...." To which L'Angelier, also at great length, very properly replied: "I was not angry at you allowing me, Mimi, but I am sad it happened. *You had no resolution*. We should indeed have waited till we were married, Mimi. It was very bad indeed. I shall look with regret on that night." The reproaching of Mimi for her moral weakness is a charmingly characteristic touch.

Although the Lord Justice-Clerk's strictures on the tone of the letters was as severe as the most acidulous virgin could desire, in charging the jury his Lordship dealt with the very formidable case for the Crown in a manner that, despite the dictum of a certain doctor of laws at Padua, somewhat strained the quality of mercy. But his Lordship was apt to be lenient, as witness another *cause célèbre* on which he presided: the trial of Dr. Smith of St. Fergus in 1854, for the murder by shooting of a young farmer friend, whose life he had insured and by whose death he stood to profit to the tune of £2000. Yet, notwithstanding most damning evidence against him, the Judge practically directed the jury to acquit him of the charge, which, to the extent of Not Proven, they obediently did. There is an irreverent tradition that the Justice-Clerk, besides being an able lawyer, was a good judge of feminine charms, and that Madeleine, being possessed of a neat foot and an undeniable ankle, was advised not to conceal those assets from the purview of the Bench, a display facilitated by the crinoline of the day. But no such tactics were available to the physician of St. Fergus.

Gratitude, as appears, was not one of Madeleine's strong points; she described the Lord Justice-Clerk, to whose charge she was so largely indebted, as "a tedious old man." As showing the incredible coolness exhibited by her during the trial, where everyone else concerned was in a state of intense feverish excitement, it is recorded that on the conclusion of the Lord Advocate's deadly address for the Crown she was asked what she thought of it. "When I have heard the Dean of Faculty I will tell you," she placidly replied; "I never like to give an opinion till I have heard both sides of the question!"

### III

There can, I think, be little doubt that the withholding by a majority of the Court—2 to 1—of L'Angelier's diary from the knowledge of the jury was the determinant factor in the case. Had they been allowed to see, under the dead man's own hand, the recorded fact of his meetings with Madeleine on the nights immediately preceding his two first seizures, it would probably have turned the scale against her. The last entry in the diary is of Saturday, 14th March; it was on the night of Sunday the 22nd that the Crown alleged he got from her his third and fatal dose. Morally, we can be fairly certain they did meet that night. He had come hot-foot from Bridge of Allan on her urgent invitation, he left his lodgings for that express purpose, he was seen in the near vicinity of her house; but, legally, there was no proof of their meeting. In like manner, on the occasion of the two first attacks, it was not proved that they had met. There the diary supplies the missing links.

It is idle to suggest that L'Angelier fabricated these entries with a view to inculpate Madeleine, for, as Miss Tennyson Jesse has acutely pointed out, he had only to breathe to his landlady during his last illness a suspicion that it was due to the attentions of his "intended," and the game was up. But he spoke no word as to the cause of his condition. Then, as regards the suicide theory, whoever heard of anyone taking three separate doses—on 19th and 22nd February and on 22nd March —as a means of self-destruction, of so agonizing a poison as arsenic? And his last words: "If I could only get a little sleep I think I should be well," are scantly indicative of a wish to take his own life.

Too little attention has been paid to Madeleine's other medicinal shopping: her attempt to procure, on an unspecified day in the second week of February, "a small phial of prussic acid," coinciding as it does with L'Angelier's first threats of exposure, and curiously anticipating the similar failure of Miss Lizzie Borden to obtain the same death-dealing substance, whereby she was driven to adopt the more crude expedient of an ax. "She said she wanted it for her hands," says Madeleine's boy-messenger. In her declaration she does not state, as she did of the arsenic, that its use as a cosmetic was recommended to her by a school-friend; the matter is not mentioned. Yet the applicability of prussic acid to toilet purposes is so novel and startling as surely to call for some explanation. Madeleine's notions of beauty-treatment were, to say the least, peculiar.

It is sad to think that we possess no picture of those marvelous and compelling charms which she thus sought superfluously to enhance. The woodcut portraits published in the illustrated papers at the time of the trial are singularly unattractive, depicting a horse-faced female of repellent aspect. But from the correspondence it would seem that she was actually photographed, although unfortunately no copy of the result is known to exist. Writing to L'Angelier in November 1856 she says: "Emile, I know you won't look on my likeness with pleasure—it is so cross—but, love, when it was done I had been in the horrid man's place from 12 o'c., and I had it closed at 4 o'c. [sic]. I had had no food from the night before and I was very furious." So protracted a time-exposure on an empty stomach must have been a trying ordeal. The form of photography then in use was the daguerreotype, which was taken on glass. Most of us possess grim and ghostly presentments of our forebears, surrounded by gilt tin frames, commonly preserved in little velvet-lined leather cases. That Madeleine's was of this sort appears from her next letter, sending the portrait to her lover: "I have put up this likeness in an old book, so that it may not be felt to be glass." And in later letters she writes: "I hope ere long you will have the original, which I know you will like better than a glass likeness"; "Tell me what Mary [Perry] says of my likeness. It is horrid ugly." Finally, in February 1857, when she made her first attempt to break the bonds wherein she was entangled, she wrote to him: "I shall feel obliged by your bring me [sic] my letters and likeness on Thursday eveng. at 7. Be at the area gate, and C. H. [the maid, Christina Harrison, who was privy to the intrigue] will take the parcel from you." But *this* appointment, at any rate, L'Angelier failed to keep, and the "likeness or portrait" was found in his repositories by the police on 31st March, and is included in the Crown list of productions (exhibits). What became of it afterwards I cannot tell. Probably the family applied for it and got it back.

My regret for the lack of a "likeness" was shared by Henry James, who, surprisingly in one of his delicate and fastidious taste, was fond of a good murder. I once presented him with a copy of the official report of the trial by Forbes Irvine (Edinburgh: 1857). In accepting my gift he made most interesting reference to the case, and his characteristic comments will be welcome to Madeleine's admirers. Here is his letter:—

> 21 CARLYLE MANSIONS,
> CHEYNE WALK, S.W.
> JUNE 16TH, 1914.

My dear Roughead,

Your offering is a precious thing and I am touched by it, but I am also alarmed for the effect on your fortunes, your future, and those (and that) who (and which) may, as it were, depend on you, of these gorgeous generosities of munificence. The admirable Report is, as I conceive, a high rarity and treasure, and I feel as if in accepting it I were snatching the bread perhaps from the lips of unknown generations. Well, I gratefully bow my head, but only on condition that it shall revert, the important object and alienated heirloom, to the estate of my benefactor on my demise.

A strange and fortunate thing has happened—your packet and letter found me this a.m. in the grip of an attack of gout (the 1st for 3 or 4 years, and apparently not destined to be very bad, with an admirable remedy that I possess at once resorted to). So I have been reclining at peace for most of the day with my foot up and my eyes attached to the prodigious Madeleine. I have read your volume straight through, with the extremity of interest and wonder. It represents indeed the *type* perfect case, with nothing to be taken from it or added, and with the beauty that she precisely didn't squalidly suffer, but lived on to admire with the rest of us, for so many years, the rare work of art with which she had been the means of enriching humanity.

With what complacency must she not have regarded it, through the long backward vista, during the time (now 20 years ago) when I used to hear of her as, married and considered, after a long period in Australia, the near neighbor, in Onslow Gardens, of my old friends the Lyon Playfairs. They didn't know or see her (beyond the fact of her being there), but they tantalized me, because if it made me feel very, very old it now piles Ossa upon Pelion for me that I remember perfectly her trial during its actuality, and how it used to come to us every day in *The Times*, at Boulogne, where I was then with my parents, and how they followed and discussed it in suspense and how I can still see the queer look of the "not proven," seen for the 1st time, on the printed page of the newspaper. I stand again with it, on the summer afternoon—a boy of 14—in the open window over the Rue Neuve Chaussée where I read it. Only I didn't know then of its—the case's—perfect beauty and distinction, as you say.

A singularly fine thing *is* this report indeed—and very magnificent the defense. She was truly a portentous young person, with the *conditions* of the whole thing throwing it into such extraordinary relief, and yet I wonder all the same at the verdict in the face of the so vividly attested, and so fully and so horribly, sufferings of her victim. It's astonishing that the evidence of what he went through that last night didn't do for her. And what a pity she was almost of the pre-photographic age—I would give so much for a veracious portrait of her *then* face.

To all of which absolutely inevitable acknowledgment you are not to *dream*, please, of responding by a single word. I shall take, I foresee, the liveliest interest in the literary forger-man. How can we be sufficiently thankful for these charming breaks in the sinister perspective? I rest my telescope on your shoulder and am

> Yours all gratefully,
> Henry James.

The "forger-man," by the way, was that skillful penman known as "Antique Smith," of whose nefarious career I was then preparing an account[3]; but Henry James found him rather colorless, after his brilliant namesake—and no wonder.

Another literary friend of mine supplied a further reminiscence of Madeleine. Andrew Lang told me how he was at school with her brother, and that one day he and some of the other boys saw on a newspaper bill the striking announcement: "Arrest of Young Glasgow Girl for Murder." Whereupon, turning to his companions, Lang jokingly remarked: "That'll be Jim Smith's sister," which proved to be the truth!

Once upon a time I thought I had secured the prize. A middle-aged young lady of my acquaintance advised me that her venerable mamma was possessed of a water-color drawing of Madeleine Smith, executed from the life and given to her by the artist. She set no value on such things, and would doubtless let me have it for the asking. An appointment was made; I

3. First published in the *Juridical Review*; later reprinted in *The Riddle of the Ruthvens*, 1919 (new edition, revised, 1936).

waited upon the lucky dowager, a frosty-faced and crusted person with a mischievous eye, and preferred my request. She replied that I would have been welcome to the sketch, had she not unfortunately, when clearing out some "rubbish"—save the mark!—committed it to the flames. When I was sufficiently recovered I took my leave, expressing my fears for the future welfare of one capable of committing such a crime, and withdrew, followed by the unhallowed chuckles of that malevolent old woman.

From another survivor of that dim epoch, who as a girl had seen Madeleine in the flesh at "parties" in Glasgow, I learned that she was ever the belle of the ball, extremely handsome, dark and dashing, alluring to the male; but in style and manner what the language of the day termed "bold." Which was just as well, looking to all she was later called upon to outface.

### IV

I have been a long time in reaching the Press-cuttings that I promised. The earliest is from the *Glasgow Herald* of 3rd April 1857. It is headed: "Painful Event—Charge of Poisoning," and is the first blast of the trumpet against the fair fame of Madeleine Smith. "For the last few days the recital of an event of the most painful character has been passing from mouth to mouth, and has become the subject of almost universal excitement and inquiry. So long as the matter was confined to rumor and surmise we did not consider that we were called on to make any public allusion to it; but now that a young lady has been committed to prison on a most serious charge, and the names of the respective parties are in the mouths of everyone, any further delicacy in the way of withholding allusion to the case is impossible. At the same time we fervently trust that the cloud which at present obscures a most respectable and estimable

household may be speedily and most effectually removed."
The article proceeds to give a long and well-informed narrative
of the facts, so far as then ascertained, and concludes: "Though
she should be found pure and guiltless, as we trust may be
the case, the family will have suffered deeply by having had
one of their household even suspected of a crime so odious. We
may add that Miss Smith, who, we understand, was judicially
examined at great length before the Sheriff on Tuesday last,
has comported herself throughout with perfect calmness." The
*Glasgow Mail* also reports: "The utmost coolness is stated to
have been manifested by the prisoner ever since she was placed
in custody."

We learn from *The Times* that "The prisoner is granddaugh-
ter of the late Mr. David Hamilton, the celebrated architect of
Glasgow Exchange and Hamilton Palace"; and I have somewhere read, although I cannot recall the reference, that she was
akin to the ducal house of Hamilton.

"All sorts of rumors are afloat," says the *Morning Advertiser*, "bearing on the character of Miss Smith and the young
Frenchman L'Angelier, whom she is accused of having poisoned. It is, of course, out of the question to place any reliance
upon these stories, but it is said that the evidence at the trial
will be of a very startling nature—so much so indeed that it
may be deemed advisable to conduct the case with closed
doors." An unnamed correspondent, who had talked with Miss
Smith on the day of L'Angelier's death, informed the journal
"that the young lady was then as gay and fascinating as he had
ever seen her."

"The trial is now fixed for the 30th of the present month
[June]," says the *Mail*. "It may be premature and unfair to pre-
judge the case, but we cannot help remarking that we can see
nothing for it but that the jury must bring in a verdict of 'Not
Proven.' No one can prove that Miss Smith administered the
poison; there is an hour at least unaccounted for between

L'Angelier's leaving her and reaching his lodgings; circumstantial evidence, too frequently faithless, is all that the prosecution can be based upon." It is interesting to note that the writer admits, *pace* the Dean of Faculty, the meeting of the lovers on the fatal night. He goes on to outline the cosmetical defense; suggests that L'Angelier, on his way home, may have fallen in with somebody "who treated him with infinitely less kindness that his *inamorato* [sic]"; and concludes with the statement that the majority of Miss Smith's fellow-citizens believe her to be entirely innocent. And a word of warning is uttered for the Judge and jury: to remember "the maxim of our immortal dramatist," touching the quality of mercy. As we have seen, the Lord Justice-Clerk seems to have taken the editorial hint!

After the trial, a public subscription was got up for L'Angelier's mother in Jersey, of whom he was said to have been the sole support, and the *Herald* published an open letter from her, invoking the blessing of the Almighty on the generous contributors. The amount raised was £89, 9s. 3d. It is stated by the *Sentinel* "that a few of the leading citizens of Glasgow subscribed largely for the defense of Miss Smith. We understand that a sum of not less than £5000 was raised for this purpose." Thus substantially did the Glasgow public back their opinion.

The *Courier* states that, after her discharge from the bar, she left Edinburgh, unobserved, by train for Glasgow. "Miss Smith, on getting out at Stepps Station, near Glasgow, immediately drove to Rowaleyn House, where she arrived a little after ten o'clock. We regret to learn that Mrs. Smith (the mother) is in a very critical condition, and is rapidly sinking under the calamity which has been brought upon the family by the unfortunate daughter."

Only the pen of a Dostoevsky could describe the harrowing scene of the unrepentant Magdalen's—I beg pardon, Madeleine's—return to the family bosom. It was in truth a tragic homecoming. She had cast down the Great Goddess Respectability, that idol of the Victorian home; she had blasphemed her worship and defiled her altars. We, with our looser bonds and less exalted standards, can hardly realize the devastating outcome of her sacrilege. But though the pen of the great Russian master of pain and sorrow is not available, we are fortunate to possess a first-hand account from that of the heroine herself. Four days after her release she wrote to the matron of Edinburgh prison a letter, which, as Miss Tennyson Jesse has justly observed, is "far more profoundly shocking than any of her violent epistles to L'Angelier":—

Dear Miss Aitken,

You shall be glad to hear that I am well—in fact I am quite well, and my spirits not in the least down. I left Edinburgh and went to Slateford, and got home to Rowaleyn during the night. But, alas, I found Mama in a bad state of health. But I trust in a short time all will be well with her. The others are all well.

The feeling in the west is not so good towards me as you kind Edinburgh people showed me. I rather think it shall be necessary for me to leave Scotland for a few months, but Mama is so unwell we do not like to fix anything at present.

If ever you see Mr. C. Combe [the Foreman of the jury] tell him that the "pannel" was not at all pleased with the verdict. I was delighted with the loud cheer the Court gave. I did not feel in the least put about when the jury were out considering whether they should send me home or keep me. I think I must have had several hundred letters, all from gentlemen, some offering me consolation, and some their hearths and homes. My *friend* I know nothing of. I have not seen him. I hear he has been ill, which I don't much care [sic].

I hope you will give me a note. Thank Miss Bell and Agnes in my name for all their kindness and attention to me. I should like you to send me my Bible and watch to 124 St. Vincent Street, Glasgow, to J. Smith.

The country is looking lovely. As soon as I know my arrangements I shall let you know where I am to be sent to. With kind love to yourself and Mr. Smith, ever believe me,

> Yours sincerely,
> Madeleine Smith.
> MONDAY, 13TH JULY.
> ROWALEYN,
> GARELOCH.

To comment upon this unconscionable missive were to paint the lily. A facsimile of it may be seen in Mr. Duncan Smith's edition of the trial.

But even more repellent is her letter to the prison chaplain, first published from the original MS. as communicated to the *Scotsman* on 15th June 1933:—

Dear Mr. Rose,

After the kind interest you showed me, I think it is but fair I should let you know of my safe arrival at home. I am very well, and my spirits are good. I found Mama far, far from well, but I trust she will soon be convalescent.

The feeling here is, I rather fear, strong against me, so I rather think I shall have to leave Scotland for a few weeks, but the poor state of Mama's health renders it impossible for me to make any arrangements at present.

I was not at all pleased with the "verdict," but I was charmed with the loud cheer the Court gave me. I got out of Edinburgh in the most private manner possible. I trust that painful, unhappy affair may tend to do us all great good—I see a different feeling pervades our family circle already. I am so glad that they all view it as an affliction sent from God for past errors and crimes, and if this be the means of drawing a family to the feet of Christ, I shall not grumble at the pain that sad event has cost me.

I may live to hear the family exclaim that it was the most blessed day of their life—the day I was cast into prison. God grant it may be so. I shall ever remember your kindness to me.

Receive my deepest, warmest, and heartfelt thanks, and with kind regards, believe me,

Yours sincerely,
Madeleine Smith.
JULY 15TH '57
ROWALEYN,
GARELOCH.

Again, comment is needless: the letter speaks for itself. But one would like to have known the nature of those "past errors and crimes," committed by *other* members of the family, that so merited Divine punishment.

V

Resuming our newspaper researches, we find the reporter of the *Daily Express* giving a minute, but by no means flattering, portrait of the fair prisoner at the bar. Under the heading:

"Personal Appearance of Madeleine Smith," he thus antici-
pates the methods of his modern journalistic successors: "The
figure in the dock is small in stature, slight, and finely-formed,
with the elasticity of youth and healthful upbringing. It is attired in a manner which shows how the most refined elegance
may be united with the quietness of a Quakeress. Madeleine
Smith, it is plain to every eye, is an artist in matters of dress. . . .
But with her dress and figure admiration ends. Her countenance is striking, but not pleasant. A projecting brow, a long
prominent nose, and a receding chin, impart to her sharp features a hawk-like aspect; and if her eye is large and lustrous, no
spring of sensibility gleams from beneath those long, drooping
lashes. . . . The brow is narrow and low; but the head, swathed
in a profusion of dark brown tresses, swells upwards in the region in which phrenologists place the bump of firmness, and
broadens behind to an extent that corresponds exactly with the
mental weakness and moral depravity developed in her love
epistles." But here, I think, our reporter is wise after the event;
and how he was able to define her "bumps" beneath the
"small, straw bonnet, trimmed with white ribbon, of the fashionable shape," does not appear. "Her mouth," he continues,
"is significantly large, the upper lip projecting far over the one
beneath, which, when she is moved, droops away from its
companion, and has a tendency to reveal the rising tide of
emotion, so that more than once she has been seen to catch
her lips tightly between thumb and forefinger, to hide the feeling that she did not wish to show. Her head embodies, more
than we have ever seen before, the union of intellectual weakness with strong propensities and unbounded firmness." Our
reporter is better at description than deduction, for the charge
of "intellectual weakness" is grotesquely unfounded: Madeleine had the brains of a man, and a clever one at that. "Her
eye, which fears to meet no other, and which is always the
last to be withdrawn, is one which compels us to believe

the statement she made in prison—that she never shed a tear."
If this forbidding portrait be indeed a true "likeness," we can
but exclaim with Dr. Faustus of immortal Helen—

> Was this the face that launched a thousand ships
> And burnt the topless towers of Ilium?

The reporter's unfavorable account, however, is confirmed
by that of a brother scribe, who, under the style and title of
"An Eye-Witness," furnishes his impressions of the trial.
"Apart from the unhappy associations then, now, and there is
too much reason to fear, alas! for ever likely to be inseparably
connected with her appearance anywhere, the pannel was a decidedly handsome, lady-like figure, of fully average height and
development for a female, with a very graceful carriage. Most
erroneously, in some sketches, she has been called a 'little,
slim girl.' Her countenance has been termed 'pretty' and 'beautiful,' and designated by other hackneyed phrases, but was not
according to our taste in female beauty. From the brow to the
chin, a very long face, very small features, nose prominent, but
unclassable among any of the three chief varieties of that organic protuberance; splendidly rich, dark gray eye—physically
considered—of pure and sparkling lustre, but to a degree un-
pleasing, nay forbidding in its expression; bad lips, mouth, and
chin. We thought it fox-like, unattractive, cunning, deceitful,
and altogether unprepossessing."

The truth is that none of us would show to advantage in the
dock. It is a trying situation in which nobody looks their best. I
have often noted how quite faceable, ordinary folk, viewed
in that dread environment, take on a sinister aspect at once.
Had a Cleopatra or a Mary Stuart sat within that narrow,
railed-in pen, there would not have been lacking those who
perceived flaws even in their loveliness. And, curiously, the
accepted portraits of the Scottish Queen exhibit the same

long face, prominent "organic protuberance"—I thank thee, "Eye-Witness," for teaching me that word—and oblique eyes, which seem to have been leading features of our Madeleine. Doubtless the charm of each resided in the play of their expression: a subtile smile, a swift-flashing glance, the rich tones of a fine contralto voice—such may have been the secret of their allure. But it is idle to speculate; I had better get on with my cuttings.

The *locus classicus* regarding the accused's demeanor during the trial is the oft-quoted description in the *Ayrshire Express*, which I have italicized: "In the midst of all this excitement, passing through the eager crowd from and to prison, seated at the bar with hundreds of eyes fixed steadily upon her, Madeleine Smith is the only unmoved, cool personage to be seen. From the first moment to the last she has preserved that undaunted, defiant attitude of perfect repose which has struck every spectator with astonishment. She passes from the cab to the Court-room-or rather, to the cell beneath the dock—*with the air of a belle entering a ballroom*. She ascends the narrow staircase leading into the dock with a jaunty air, an unveiled countenance"—(why, by the way, do reporters never say, "face"? Is there anything indecent in the word?)—"the same perpetual smile—or smirk, rather, for it lacks all the elements of a genuine smile; the same healthy glow of color, and the same confident ease. . . ."

It is also recorded of her that day by day, when the Court rose for the luncheon interval, the prisoner refused either to leave the dock for the temporary privacy afforded by the cells below, or to take anything either to eat or drink, declining even a proffered packet of sandwiches. Inmmediately on the retiral of their Lordships, the official silence was broken and the tongues of the spectators were loosed. From the packed seats arose a continuous hum of many voices, discussing the evidence and commenting on such incidents as caught the popular fancy. Less abstemious than the accused, the eager crowd, with appetites whetted by excitement, munched steadily from paper bags or lunch cases, and athirst in the July heat of the stuffy Court-room, refreshed themselves, according to their degree, from surreptitious bottles or flasks. And amid this restless babel sits Madeleine Smith unmoved, calm and composed as if alone in her Mamma's quiet drawing-room in Blythswood Square! Verily, whatever else we may think of her, we must applaud her prodigious pluck.

From a lively article, headed "Notes on the Trial," I take the reporter's thumb-nail sketches of one or two of the principal figures. "Of all the witnesses, 'dear' Mary Perry seemed the most general favorite, her indiscreet patronage of the young lovers notwithstanding. No one, when they saw her, could believe the stories of her that had come from Glasgow. Folks expected a dashing young creature, a second string to the bow of the facile L'Angelier. Fancy the surprise when a little old maid, in quiet black bonnet and brown dress, with an intellectual cast of countenance, and a pair of spectacles imparting quaintness to her face, entered the witness-box! For the young Jersey man she had evidently at first entertained an affection more than Platonic. Her case was probably one of those in which we so frequently find old-maid friendship crossing the borderland of mere friendship, and shading insensibly away into the region of something warmer and more endearing.

"Mr. William Minnoch was the witness whose appearance created most interest in anticipation. He is a man of apparently thirty-five years, though a fair complexion makes him look younger. He is short and slim, perhaps one of the best-dressed men on 'Change in Glasgow and with a keen-cut and more lady-like face than that of the woman to whom he was betrothed. His coolness in the witness-box was remarkable; all the symptoms of agitation which he displayed were an occasional cough, evidently to clear his throat when his voice was becoming husky, and a somewhat frequent appeal to a glass of water, which lay conveniently at hand, when his lips were becoming dry. But his coolness could not help but inspire the spectator with the notion that had he and Miss Madeleine Smith been married, they might have taken up house at the North Pole without much inconvenience to either." (It is elsewhere recorded that never once did he allow his eyes to light upon the figure in the dock, although she stared fixedly at him while he gave his evidence.)

"The youthful sister of the accused could not have been recognized as a relative from any family resemblance; her features were less prominent, and displayed much less force of character.

"Mr. Robert Baird, the young gentleman who introduced L'Angelier to Miss Smith, and was thus the most important actor in the first act of the tragedy, seemed to be about twenty years of age, and looked an ordinary enough specimen of young Glasgow—the best man in the world to cut a figure in Buchanan Street, or in any other fashionable promenade of the west country 'swells'; the last to shine in the most tragic Scottish tale of the nineteenth century."

## VI

Of the acting of the leading lady in the dramatic scene, the same writer gives us some enlightening glimpses, particularly as regards her reactions to the Lord Advocate's address. At first she leant forward on her elbow, the more favorably to mark his words and to watch the impression made by them upon the jury. But her interest soon relaxed, and while his Lordship was dealing with "the horrible and disgusting details which had been placed before them," she was gazing intently at a face that had attracted her attention in one of the galleries, and seemed not to hear the biting words in which her moral failings were described. "It was when the word *arsenic* occurred in the speech that she was most attentive. In whatever direction she might be looking, however intently she might be studying the motions of someone, the bare utterance of that word seemed to have a magic influence over her, and she at once turned round to the speaker from whose lips the sibilant came. But no sooner had the word passed out of use, than the smallest matter apart from the speech sufficed to secure her attention. . . . The first allusion to her letters made her eye dilate to its fullest extent, and so it remained through all the extracts from, and comments upon her extraordinary literary productions; and this dilation of the eye, which many remarked, although it increased the striking appearance of her countenance, did not by any means give it a more prepossessing effect."

The reporter gives a graphic sketch of the final scene, after the jury had retired to consider their verdict. "Every spectator has risen from his seat in the feverish expectancy of the moment. The Court is like a beehive with the buzz and hum of voices. Amidst all this, the prisoner sits calm and quiet, only at intervals you may note her lips tightly compressed. Her color neither comes nor goes. . . ." A short half-hour passes, yet it seems an age; then the jingle of the jury-bell is heard: it sounds like the Last Trump. Solemnly the fifteen messengers of destiny file into the box; one is seen to smile, so the omens are propitious—though perhaps it is only due to nervousness. Then, in the breathless silence, the voice of the Chancellor [Foreman] announces an acquittal. So soon as the last "Not Proven" has issued from his lips, the decorum of the Court is shattered. "Loud cheers and huzzas and hand-clappings and ruffing rend the rafters, drowning the cries of purple-faced officers of court and deafening the angry Judges, who strive in vain to still the tumult." Friends gather round her to congratulate her on her escape; her law agent grasps one hand, the female warder the other. She smiles once—"a strange, sad, unlovely smile." But the great Dean of Faculty, to whose efforts she owes her freedom, remains seated at the table in the well of the Court, his head sunk in his hands. He neither looks at her nor smiles. The gate of the dock is thrown open, the trapdoor is lifted, and for the last time Madeleine Smith, with her wonted elegant composure, slowly descends the stair, followed to the end by the eager gaze of the multitude, and so passes from the ken of her contemporaries.

Well do I recall being present at the finish of another famous trial thirty-six years later, namely, that of A. J. Monson, charged with the murder of Cecil Hambrough at Ardlamont. Splendidly defended by that admirable advocate, John Comrie Thomson, the accused, was acquitted in like manner to Madeleine, though the verdict was received with less enthusiasm. In beginning his address to the jury, Comrie Thomson made telling reference to the fact that, as a young counsel, he had listened in the same Court-room to the historic speech of John Inglis in behalf of Madeleine Smith, and quoted with much effectiveness the masterly opening words of that celebrated appeal: "Gentlemen, the charge against the prisoner is murder, and the punishment of murder is death; and that simple statement is sufficient to suggest to you the awful nature of the occasion which brings you and me face to face."

I was struck by a further coincidence. When, upon the pronouncement of the verdict, Not Proven, the prisoner stood up, smiling, in the dock, his two junior counsel went forward to the rail and shook hands with him. Comrie Thomson left the Court without so much as a glance at his late client. The parallel is instructive.

## VII

In their joy at the triumph of innocence, and with intent further to whitewash the besmirched fame of the popular heroine, certain newspapers of the baser sort made a cruel and unwarrantable attack upon the behavior of Mr. William Minnoch. That gentleman had, one would think, suffered sufficiently by reason of his connection with the case and might have been allowed to quit the stage without a hostile demonstration. But I am glad to see that one voice at least was raised in his defense. This well-founded protest was made by a correspondent of the *Northern Whig*, who addressed that journal as follows: "An article appeared in your columns of the 11th instant, censuring, in very strong terms, the conduct of Mr. Minnoch during the late trial at Edinburgh. I, therefore, take the liberty of writing to set you right on one or two points—or rather to lay before you facts that will induce you to alter your opinion of that gentleman. In the first place, you condemn him for consenting to appear as a witness at the trial. Upon Miss Smith's being arrested, so firmly was he convinced of her innocence that he declared his intention of marrying her as soon as she was acquitted. In the meantime he left Glasgow, giving up his business for a month, in order to avoid the chance of being subpoenaed [cited] as a witness; but it was represented to him that it would go against Miss Smith if he refused to give evidence. And, besides this, I think that you will allow that the situation in which he was placed—that of an accepted lover giving evidence against his affianced bride—was a most painful one, and not one that any man would willingly have courted.

"After he had given his evidence, he did not return home, as might have been expected, but remained at Edinburgh, and there awaited the issue of the trial; and as soon as Miss Smith was released he escorted her, not only back to Glasgow, but the whole way down to her father's country house, Rowaleyn.

"The next thing we hear of him is, that he has put down his name for £500 to a subscription which was got up for the purpose of defraying the expenses of the trial—a delicate way of testifying to poor Mr. Smith his esteem for him, and his sympathy with him during his affliction. What his private conviction with regard to Miss Smith's innocence may have been I am at a loss to say; but this is a point on which Mr. Minnoch has a right, and ought to judge. If he thought her guilty, it only renders his conduct all the more meritorious. The whole affair is involved in the deepest mystery, and forms a problem for moralists to speculate upon—a problem which will, perhaps, not be solved until the day when all things shall be made known."

The reader will remember that in her letter to the prison matron Madeleine says she has not seen her "friend" since her return; but she is by no means a reliable witness, and having taken her safely home, he may then have left her for good and all. Or it may be that the writer, though he seems to be otherwise well-informed, has confused this journey with the earlier one, when she fled to Rowaleyn and Mr. Minnoch brought her back. At any rate it would doubtless occur to him, as a man of affairs, that if his betrothed could do what she was alleged to have done to one whom she had so passionately loved, what might she not do in the end to one whom she had never loved and was marrying for his money?

## VIII

From the many notices of this extraordinary case published in newspapers and journals after the trial, I must content myself with quoting one or two extracts from a leading article in the *Saturday Review*, which seems to me the best of the lot: "The verdict in Madeleine Smith's trial is 'Not Proven.' It declares nothing. The case, then, as they say in Germany, shifts from the actual to the ideal. The guilt or innocence of the accused will henceforth be like Queen Mary's guilt or innocence—it will be a moot point for moralists. If we seem to assume the alternative of guilt, Madeleine Smith is to us only *nominis umbra*. She is an historical and debatable character, and an inquiry into her criminality becomes a question of purely moral and psychological interest. . . ."

Upon this assumption, the writer finds that in the matter of motive the chief interest of the case resides. "Yet it is not," he remarks, "any one single and simple passion—revenge, or lust or avarice—which can end in such a catastrophe as this. It is in the mixture of motives, the complexity of passions, the conflict of sins—the seven devils wrestling with each other as well as with the victim—that the unearthly grandeur as well as horror of the deed with which she was charged consists. Passion leads many a man to murder his mistress; jealousy leads many a woman to murder her lover, even in the very frenzy of affection; cold-blooded ambition and interest prompt to murder, in order to get rid of an inconvenient obstacle to respectability and a fair standing with the world. But on the hypothesis of Madeleine Smith's guilt, we have each and all, and yet none of them, as adequate motives. The problem to solve—and it is inscrutable, because, as far as we know, absolutely without example—is the coexistence of that burning intensity of mere sexual passion which indisputably led Madeleine Smith to discard every restraint, even of common decency, that frailty so generally throws over the acts of sin, with a cool, settled malignity of self-possession, a deliberate hypocrisy in counterfeiting rapturous affection, which, for the credit of human nature, is unparalleled. And yet this must have been so, if she be guilty. The counsel for the defense never accounted for the fact—an indisputable one—that the letters to Minnoch and the last letters to her seducer (if that is to be the word), with all the old passion at least pretended, were of the same date. Whether Madeleine Smith poisoned L'Angelier or not, her parallel correspondence with him and with Minnoch in March is established; and this is the moral anomaly in presence of which the fact of murder is a mere sequence.... Madeleine Smith was not convicted because it was not proved that she and L'Angelier met on the night before his death. This single circumstance compelled the verdict."

Commenting on the Dean of Faculty's telling point as to the improbability of this burning, passionate girl being suddenly transformed into a cold, deliberate murderess,[4] the writer observes that the miracle might well have been worked by L'Angelier's character: "His was just the sort of mind to work this horrible change in Madeleine Smith. A meaner and more contemptible scoundrel it would be difficult to conceive; and probably his low, selfish character prompted that sort of unhappy popular sympathy with Madeleine Smith which seems to prevail, at any rate in Edinburgh. A profligate, vain adventurer, boasting of his *bonnes fortunes*, and trafficking with this *liaison*, as perhaps with others, as a means of advancement—this is what L'Angelier was.... We believe that as a further knowledge of his miserable character broke upon Madeleine Smith, the insight into the man who could hold this girl's shame over her, and who could resist the terrific pathos of her shuddering, shivering appeals for mercy—appeals

---

4. "Gentlemen, I will not say that such a thing is absolutely impossible; but I shall venture to say it is well-nigh incredible. He will be a bold man who will seek to set limits to the depths of human depravity; but this at least all past experience teaches us: that perfection, even in depravity, is not rapidly attained, and that it is not by such short and easy stages as the prosecutor has been able to trace in the career of Madeleine Smith, that a gentle, loving girl passes at once into the savage grandeur of a Medea, or the appalling wickedness of a Borgia. No, gentlemen, such a thing is not possible."—Speech for the Defense.

unequaled in the whole range of tragic vehemence—may account for this moral change. The deep fountains of her passion were, on discovering her paramour's character, frozen up. She found that she had ventured everything upon an unworthy object; and the very depth of her love was changed, on the complete and perfect sense of utter loss, into the corresponding depth of hatred."

And the writer proceeds to argue, with skill and cogency, that such satisfied hate, such vengeance fulfilled, would explain the strange indifference of the prisoner, which so baffled all beholders—

> The deed is done,
> And what may follow now regards not me.

## IX

Every now and then, from that day to this, the fate of Madeleine Smith has furnished a paragraph for an all-wise and sleepless Press. She emigrated to America, Australia, and New Zealand; she lived her life in London, she settled in Staffordshire; she contracted divers marriages, with issue and without; she never married at all. *Enfin*, she frequently died and was as often resurrected. Amid such contradictory pronouncements it was difficult to discern the truth.

The earliest authentic account of her subsequent adventures appears to be that communicated by Mr. A. L. Humphreys to *Notes and Queries* (II S. IV. Oct. 14, 1911). It begins, however, with the customary false report of her death, this time at Melbourne in 1893, on the authority of an obituary notice in the *St. James's Gazette* of 20th November. According to Mr. Humphreys, she married in the year of the trial a surgeon, named Tudor Hora, whom she accompanied to Melbourne.

Four years later, the marriage having been dissolved—whether by natural or legal process is not stated—she returned to the old country, and in 1861 made a fresh matrimonial venture. Her second husband was Mr. George Wardle, an artist, then living at 5 Bloomfield Terrace, Pimlico, the bride's address being given as 72 Sloane Street, Chelsea. The wedding was celebrated at St. Paul's, Knightsbridge, on 4th July 1861; the officiating clergyman was the Rev. Robert Liddell; the witnesses were H. Hoverlock and James Smith, her brother. Of the truth of these facts there is, in the familiar words of Don Alhambra del Bolero, "no probable, possible shadow of doubt" —I have seen an extract of the marriage certificate. Mr. Wardle, I understand, was associated later with William Morris and William de Morgan in their artistic pursuits.

It appears, from an article in the *Scotsman* of 4th January 1926, that Madeleine was then alive, at the age of 90, in the United States of America. Her husband, Mr. Wardle, was a man of much distinction, who was not only highly talented, but possessed of a good social position and considerable wealth. "She very soon made for herself a position in the literary and Socialist circles of London in those days, being well known to some still alive, whose reputation is world-wide, and who knew and guarded the tragic secret of her life."

The last word is with *The Times* of 18th April 1928. Madeleine is there stated, on good authority, to have died in America in the preceding week at the ripe age of 92. "Her husband, Mr. Wardle, was one of the first members of the Social Democratic Club in London, and her identity was known to most of the members. When well on in years she went to America, and it was only last year that her identity leaked out. Some cinema promoters suggested the exploiting of the story of the crime by the production of a film drama, in which Madeleine Smith would take the leading rôle; but she refused. Pressure was brought to bear on her, and a threat made that if she declined to fall in with the suggestion, steps would be taken to have her sent back to Britain as an undesirable alien. As a result of the publicity that ensued, however, more humane counsels prevailed, and Madeleine was permitted to remain. Her death took place last week."

So the long tragedy ended in a farce, and Madeleine, despite her venerable age, was not immune from the ruthless realism of Hollywood. It is pathetic to think of that ancient woman—she was born in 1836, the year before Queen Victoria's accession—coerced into playing again the part of the wondrous girl who had thrilled the susceptibilities of three bygone generations. Surely, those responsible for this grotesque outrage lacked equally a sense of decency and of humor. But the spirit of the age knows neither.

X

In addition to figuring so largely in the law reports, Madeleine Smith has her niche in polite letters. Miss Emma Robinson, the gifted but neglected author of *Whitefriars* and other historical fictions, told the old tale in novel form: *Madeleine Graham* (London: John Maxwell and Company, 1864). Though marked, or marred, by the flamboyant style then in vogue, the three volumes, charming in format, afford an enthralling study of the facts; the characters of the heroine, of Camille Le Tellier (L'Angelier), and of George Behring-bright (Mr. Minnoch), are drawn with much insight and skill—Madeleine herself being uncannily lifelike.

And in our own time a sister-writer, Miss Winifred Duke, has made of the story a grim little play: *Madeleine Smith: A Tragi-Comedy* (Edinburgh: William Hodge and Company, 1928). It is in two acts; the first shows Madeleine at a dinner-party on the day of L'Angelier's death, when the ghost of the miserable

Frenchman troubles, like that of Banquo, the peace of the board; the second, the Smiths' drawing-room at Rowaleyn, on the night of the prodigal daughter's return. Here again, her character is drawn with subtlety and effect.

And so we take leave of Madeleine Smith, as she sits alone beside the dying fire—the family having "retired" to rest, after delivering their several opinions on her impropriety; and letting the dead past bury its dead, surveys, rather wearily, the gray vista of the years to come. Had she been able to trace in the embers the tedious course of her pilgrimage, even that indomitable spirit might well have faltered.

# CONSTANCE KENT'S CONSCIENCE

## I
## THE PROBLEM

*When murderers shut deeds close, this curse does seal 'em:*
*If none disclose 'em, they themselves reveal 'em!*
*This murder might have slept in tongueless brass*
*But for ourselves, and the world died an ass.*

—Cyril Tourneur: *The Revenger's Tragedy*

IN THE PALMY days of the sixties, the memory of which is preserved for us in the evergreen pages of *Punch;* when skirts were wide, minds were narrow, and whiskers did prodigiously abound; when ladies veiled their graces in chignons and crinolines, and gentlemen, inexpressibly peg-topped, fortified their manly bosoms with barricades of beard; when the cultured delighted in wooden woodcuts of gilt-edged table books, and the vulgar worshipped albums of painfully realistic family photographs; when the outside of cup and platter received much attention, and due regard was had to the whitening of sepulchres, and whatever was "respectable" was right; *enfin*, about that sincere and engaging period, there resided—to employ the appropriate contemporary term—at Road Hill House, near Trowbridge, in Wiltshire, one Mr. Samuel Saville Kent, gentleman.

Mr. Kent had been twice married. His first wife was a Miss Maryanne Windus, whom he wedded in January 1829. He was then in business in London, and lived near Finsbury Square. There were born to him three children: Thomas, Maryanne, and Elizabeth; only the girls grew up, the boy dying of convulsions. In 1833 Mr. Kent received a Government appointment as sub-inspector under the Factory Act, and the family removed to Sidmouth. In 1835 Mrs. Kent gave birth to her fourth child, a son named Edward Windus, who survived to enter the mercantile marine, and died of a fever abroad in 1858. Shortly after the birth of this boy Mrs. Kent developed symptoms of insanity. She became subject to delusions; wandered aimlessly out of doors with the children, and lost her way near her own house; further (*horresco referens!*), she would tear out and destroy plates from books in her husband's library —a form of criminal lunacy, I regret to find, in some quarters condoned under the style of Grangerizing. Her mental malady growing in gravity—a knife was found concealed beneath her bed—the family doctor suggested that an alienist be called in; and as the result of their consultation Mr. Kent was advised to place his wife under restraint. To this course, however, that gentleman would by no means consent, being averse from incurring the stigma of madness in his family. If private persons would, in such circumstances, realize their public duty to safeguard their afflicted relatives, much misery and crime might be avoided, as we learn in many similar cases, from that of

Major Sir Archibald Gordon Kinloch in 1795, down to that of Ronald True in 1922.

It is a singular instance of Victorian "respectability" that this unfortunate lady was during the next five years (1837–42) encouraged to produce four more children, all of whom died within a year of their birth; and that in each of the years 1844 and 1845 she was again a mother. These, the last of her children, Constance Emilie and William Saville, survived. It had been better, for one of them at least, that they had never been born.

Mrs. Kent died in 1852, a victim of madness and maternity. As for twenty years before her death she had been wholly incapable of performing the duties of a mother—other than the mere mechanical one indicated above—Mr. Kent had engaged a Miss Mary Pratt, of Tiverton, to discharge those functions and to manage his household. In 1853 this lady was promoted to be the second Mrs. Kent. In the following year, as the result of an accident, she was prematurely delivered of a still-born child. But Mr. Kent, confident in his role of Dostoevsky's hero, "The Eternal Husband," was nowise discouraged by these several calamities. In 1855 Mrs. Kent gave birth to a daughter, Mary Amelia Saville, in 1856 to a son, Francis Saville, and in 1858 there was another little girl, while in 1860 the mother was expecting the arrival of yet a further addition to her well-stocked nursery! Verily, like Mrs. Morland in *Northanger Abbey*, Mr. Kent's helpmates were "much occupied in lying-in."

When Edward, the eldest son of the first marriage, returned from sea to find the governess installed in his dead mother's room, he expressed strong resentment, quarreled with his father, and left home for good.

In 1855 the family removed from Baynton House, Wilts, where they had been living for the last three years, to Road Hill House in the same shire. In July of the following year, Constance, being then thirteen, and William, aged eleven, fled from their father's house. They were home for the holidays, Mr. Kent was absent on business, and the day before his return the children disappeared. Much alarm was caused and fruitless search made, but next morning it was learned that the fugitives were in safe-custody at Bath, and a manservant was sent to bring them back. What had happened was this: after lunch, on the day of the adventure, Constance went to a disused closet in the shrubbery, where she had already secreted certain old clothes of her brother's; into these she changed, and cut off her hair,[1] which, together with her discarded dress, she thrust into the vault of the closet, whence they were afterwards recovered. Taking the little boy by the hand, she then set off to walk to Bath, ten miles distant, where the pair that evening presented themselves at the Greyhound Hotel and asked for beds. It reminds one of Dickens's small couple in "The Holly Tree Inn." The unusual appearance of the travelers aroused the landlady's suspicions; but she could get nothing out of Constance, whose manner is described as self-possessed and insolent. William, by reason of his tenderer years and less Spartan qualities, proved more amenable to cross-examination: he broke down, wept, confessed, and was comfortably put to bed. As his sister continued recalcitrant, she was handed over to the authorities and spent the night in the police-station. Even in the dread shadow of the law, so terrifying to the childish mind, Constance maintained a dogged silence; neither kindness nor scolding made any impression upon her hard composure. Nor, on regaining the paternal roof, could she be brought to admit the least regret for her behavior. The only light she would vouchsafe regarding her escapade was, that "she wished to be independent" and

---

1. I do not remember to have seen the point noted, but I think there is little doubt that Dickens had this incident in mind when describing in *Edwin Drood* the similar action of Helena Landless. Wilkie Collins, as we shall find, used some later features of the case for *The Moonstone*.

meant to make for Bristol, with a view to leaving England. The force of character and fixity of purpose thus exhibited by a child so young are truly remarkable, and of these traits, as we shall see, she was afterwards to furnish further and more startling proof.

Beyond the advent of the customary little stranger, nothing noteworthy occurred for the next few years in Mr. Kent's family. On the night of Friday, 29th June 1860, the household consisted of the following persons: Mr. Kent and his wife, the three surviving daughters and one son of his first marriage, the three children of his second, and three female servants: nurse, housemaid, and cook. These all slept in the house. Three male servants: coachman, gardener, and pantry-boy: presumably for fair propriety's sake, were lodged in the outbuildings. The house, a handsome and commodious mansion of three stories, stood in its own grounds, at a genteel remove from the public road. On the left of the entrance hall was the library, with behind it the drawing-room; on the right the dining-room, which formed a wing by itself, having no building above. Beyond the hall were the domestic offices. On the first floor, above the library, was the connubial chamber of Mr. and Mrs. Kent, with a dressing-room communicating. Their eldest child lay in her parents' room. In the nursery, over the hall, slept the nurse, Elizabeth Gough, with the younger girl in a crib beside her bed, and the little boy, four-year-old Francis Saville, in a cot on the other side of the room. On the second floor, three rooms to the front were respectively assigned to the two eldest girls, to Constance, and to the cook and housemaid. The boy, William, slept in a room to the back. Thus the first family were relegated to the second floor, while the second occupied the first.

One by one the several members of the household, in the language of the day, retired to rest. The master was always the last to go to bed; it was his habit to perambulate the premises with a dark-lantern to see that the doors and windows were properly secured. After performing his customary round and finding that all was well, Mr. Kent joined his spouse above-stairs, and silence fell upon the sleeping circle.

At five o'clock next morning, Saturday, 30th June, the nurse, Elizabeth Gough, awoke. The sun was shining into the room, and she could see the little girl beside her, still sound asleep. Raising herself in bed, she looked across the room at the boy's cot: it was empty. The child had been given medicine the night before; she assumed that he had been restless and that his mother had taken him into her own room. Elizabeth herself was very tired; she had had a hard day's house-cleaning on the Friday—the establishment was obviously under-staffed, and there was constant trouble with servants—so she lay down again and fell asleep forthwith. On waking the second time, at half-past six, she rose and went over to the cot. The bedclothes were neatly folded back; nothing else was displaced or dis-arranged. She went at once across the landing and knocked twice at her mistress's door, but getting no response returned to the nursery. She then dressed herself and the little girl, said her prayers, read a chapter in her Bible, and went again to call Mrs. Kent. This time she was bidden to come in. "Please, ma'am," said she, "have you got Master Saville? He is not in his cot." "No; we have not got him," cried the mother; "where is he?" Where, indeed! Gough ran upstairs to ask the two eld-est girls whether they knew, and Constance, nearly dressed, opened her door to see what was the matter. It now appeared that the housemaid, Sarah Cox, who the night before had locked the door and fastened the windows and shutters of the drawing-room as usual, had that morning found the door ajar, the shutters open, and the window slightly raised. Surely someone must have thus entered the house and carried off the child, doubtless for purposes of ransom. Mr. Kent ordered his carriage and drove to Trowbridge to inform the police.

Meanwhile the news that the little boy was missing spread to the village, and many of the neighbors volunteered to assist in the search. Among them one Benger, with a man named Nutt, beating the grounds, came to the disused closet in the shrubbery, once, as we have seen, the base of Constance Kent's early operations. Looking in, he noticed a pool of blood upon the floor; and lifting the lid, saw wrapped in a blanket the dead child, his head practically severed from his body. They carried him into the house, and the news was broken to the bereaved mother. Mr. Peacock, the rector of the parish, then set out for Trowbridge to tell the father what had happened; he met him on his way back and gave him the dread intelligence. Soon afterwards Superintendent Foley, of the Trowbridge division, accompanied by several officers, arrived on the scene, and the house was taken possession of by the police.

On Monday, 2nd July, the inquest was opened before Mr. Coroner Sylvester in the Red Lion Inn at Road. Mr. Rodway, solicitor, Trowbridge, watched the proceedings on behalf of Mr. Kent. The body having been viewed, divers witnesses were examined. Sarah Cox, the housemaid, told how she fastened the drawing-room window on the Friday night and found it open next morning. There were no marks of blood or footprints in the room, and the furniture was undisturbed. Mr. Kent was the last to go to bed that night; it was his habit so to sit up. Elizabeth Gough spoke to putting the child to bed and waking to find him gone. She thought that Mrs. Kent, hearing him cry, had taken him. She was a very heavy sleeper and had been up the whole day. Thomas Benger, farmer, said that, learning that the boy was missing, he and Nutt searched the grounds and found the body in the closet.

> The child was lying on the splashboard. It had only its little nightdress on and a flannel waistcoat. Its throat was cut, but it looked pleasant and its eyes were shut.

He carried it into the kitchen, and then the family came to look at it. If it had not been for the splashboard, the body would have fallen down into the vault.[2]

William Nutt, shoemaker, corroborated. Stephen Millet, butcher, produced a piece of *The Times* newspaper, stained with blood, which he had found outside the closet. The quantity of blood in the closet amounted to about three half-pints. He then gave his professional opinion as to the manner of the slaying. Superintendent Foley produced a piece of flannel, found by him in the closet. No blood-stains had been discovered in any other part of the house or grounds. Joshua Parsons, surgeon, Beckington, who had examined the body, deposed as follows:—

Deceased had two small cuts on his left hand, from which no blood had flowed; the throat was cut to the bone by some sharp instrument—a single clean cut, without being jagged; it severed the skin, all the blood-vessels, and the nerves. He afterwards found a stab, evidently made with a sharp, long, strong instrument, which cut through the flannel shirt, entered the body below the pericardium, and extended three-quarters of the width of the chest. It was in his judgment inflicted by a pointed instrument: *it could not have been done by a razor*. The internal parts were healthy; the child had evidently not been drugged. He believed the child had been dead at least five hours. His opinion was, that so large a quantity of blood was not accounted for as was likely to be produced by cutting the throat of a child so large and well developed as the deceased.[3]

---

2. *The Great Crime of 1860*, by J. W. Stapleton, surgeon, Trowbridge, p. 122. London: 1861.

3. Ibid., p. 123.

Here the Coroner proposed to close the evidence, but the jury said they wished to have the two younger children of the first marriage examined. The Coroner thought that to do so would inflict unnecessary pain on the family, but yielded the point, provided that, to spare the feelings of those concerned, the examination should take place at their own home. An adjournment was accordingly made to Road Hill House, where the two children were severally examined.

*Constance Emilie Kent*, sworn, said: I am sixteen years of age, and am sister to the deceased. I knew nothing whatever of his death until he was found. I retired to bed about half-past 10 o'clock on Friday night last. I did not hear anything during the night. I slept soundly. It was between 8 and 9 o'clock on Saturday morning when I first heard anything about the occurrence. I arose about half-past 6 in the morning. I did not leave my bed or hear any noise or anything unusual until then. I know nothing whatever of the murder. I know of no particular disagreement in the house between the members of the family. I found the nursemaid generally quiet and attentive, and perform her duties in every respect as could be wished.

*William Saville Kent*, sworn, said: I am fourteen years of age, and brother to deceased. I retired to bed on Friday night at half-past 10 o'clock. I slept all night soundly and got up at 7 o'clock the following morning. I did not hear of this circumstance till I was coming out of my room. I did not get out of my bed at all during the night of Friday. I did not sleep on the same floor as the deceased, but on the floor above. I knew nothing nor heard anything of this circumstance till the morning—I wish I had. The deceased was a great favorite with all. I have always found the nursemaid very kind and attentive. I know nothing whatever of the murder. I do not sleep with my bedroom door locked: but I did lock it last night from fear.[4]

On the resumption of the sitting the Coroner summed up the evidence, remarking that it was the most mysterious and atrocious crime of which he had ever heard. The cause of death was apparent, but the mystery lay in the motive that could have induced the perpetrator of the deed to murder this young child. He suggested that some person or persons, having malicious feelings towards some of the family, might have secreted themselves in the house for the purpose of wreaking their vengeance. It would have been a satisfaction to have traced this crime to the perpetrator; but as they could not do that, they would return as their verdict that the murder was willfully committed by some person or persons unknown.

A JURYMAN.—There is a strong suspicion on my mind, for it is clear no one could have got into the house from the outside.

THE CORONER.—Whatever suspicion you may have in your mind must not influence you in giving your verdict. You must remember that suspicion is not proof. We have no direct evidence before us whatever.[5]

The jury then returned an open verdict, and were thereupon discharged.

---

4. *The Road Murder: a Complete Report and Analysis*, by a Barrister-at-Law, p. 7. London: 1860.

5. Ibid., p. 8.

## II

### GUESSWORK

*"The fact is, we have all been a good deal puzzled because the affair is so simple, and yet baffles us altogether."*

*"Perhaps it is the very simplicity of the thing which put you at fault," said my friend.*

—EDGAR ALLAN POE: *The Purloined Letter*

The suspicions of the jury that the murderer was to be sought for within the four walls of Road Hill House were shared by the police and by the public, though naturally not by the family, who from the first stoutly maintained that a strange hand had done the deed.

> The medical man, who had been examined and who had resumed his seat [writes Mr. Stapleton in his account of the inquest], afterwards made a voluntary statement, attested by no valid reason and unsupported by any sufficient explanation, that from certain appearances which he had observed (but which he had not even mentioned at the post-mortem examination) it struck him that the child might have been partially suffocated.

This theory was later disproved: the discoloration of the mouth being due to post-mortem hypostasis; but the pathological spark was sufficient to kindle into a blaze the heap of doubts and difficulties accumulating about the case. Well-nigh every inmate of the house that night was at one time or another the object of popular denunciation, and the Press, instead of guiding or restraining the flood of wild surmises and extravagant suggestions, did all in its power to promote the deluge by which the hapless family was finally overwhelmed.

Elizabeth Gough, the nurse, was the first victim. She was a good-looking girl of three-and-twenty, who had been ten months in Mr. Kent's employment. Her parentage was respectable, and she enjoyed a perfectly blameless record. But there were in her statement certain points of singularity on which the public attention was not slow to fasten. How came it that a stranger could enter and leave her room in the night, open and close the creaking door, and remove the child in its blanket, all without disturbing her repose? Why, when she wakened at 5 a.m. and missed the child, did she not instantly raise an alarm, instead of going to sleep again? Why, when re-awakening at 6:30, did she not then rouse the house, instead of giving an inaudible tap on her mistress's door and spending another hour in her physical and spiritual ablutions? This skepticism, in the light of the medical hint, assumed a darker hue. The girl, plainly, had a lover, who visited her on the fatal night; the little boy was wakened and had seen those things which he ought not to have seen; he was old enough to tell tales and must at all costs be silenced; so he was promptly smothered and taken to the closet, where the wounds were inflicted in order to conceal the true cause of death. Who, then, was this sanguinary Romeo? Horrible to relate, it was broadly whispered that the child's own father was the culprit. One would have thought that his affections were shown to be otherwise sufficiently and legitimately engaged; but it speaks volumes for middle-class mid-Victorian morals that this view was at once accepted as affording a natural explanation of the tragedy. The more charitable considered that Mr. Kent, having discovered that he was not the father of the child, had sought to wash out in blood the stain upon his honor. But these were the minority: "the paramour-surprised" theory held the field.

The authorities in London were by no means satisfied with the handling of the case by the local police, and on 14th July Inspector Whicher, of Scotland Yard, descended from the Metropolitan machine to take charge of the inquiry. On the 16th he privately informed the magistrates that he suspected the crime to have been the act of Constance Kent. By the 20th he had so far strengthened his case against her as to apply for a warrant for her arrest, which was granted, and Constance was committed to Devizes jail. On the 27th she was brought before the Road magistrates, charged with the murder of her brother.

> When this young lady entered the room she hastened to meet her father, and affectionately kissed him. She wore deep mourning, and appeared to be much afflicted, but perfectly quiet and composed.[6]

Another contemporary reporter notes:—

> She looks to be about eighteen years of age, though it is said she is only sixteen. She is rather tall and stout, with a full face, which was much flushed, and a dimpled forehead, apparently somewhat contracted. Her eye is peculiar, being very small and deep set in her head, which perhaps leaves rather an unfavorable opinion on the mind. In other respects there is nothing unprepossessing in her appearance. The young lady wore a black silk dress and mantle, trimmed with crape, and kept her veil down throughout the proceedings.[7]

The prosecution was represented by Captain Meredith, chief constable of the county, Inspector Whicher, and Super-intendent Foley; Mr. (afterwards Sir Peter) Edlin appeared for the prisoner. The first witness was Elizabeth Gough, who repeated the

6. *The Great Crime of 1860*, p. 125.

7. *The Road Murder*, p. 8.

evidence given by her at the inquest. Cross-examined by Mr. Edlin, she never heard the prisoner say anything unkind about the little boy or behave otherwise than kindly to him. She saw her playing with him the day before the murder. She did not miss the blanket from the cot until it was brought in with the dead body. William Nutt described in greater detail the finding of the body in the closet. In cross-examination, he said that he had "predicted" they would find a dead child, though they were only told to look for a stolen one. Emma Moody said she was a schoolmate of the accused at Beckington, about a mile from Road. Had heard her say she disliked the child and pinched it; she said she liked to tease the younger children. Witness understood she was jealous of them, because the parents showed great partiality. "Won't it be nice to go home for the holidays so soon?" witness had asked her; she replied, "It may be, to *your* home; but mine's different," adding that the second family were much better treated than the first. "Mamma will not let me have anything I like; if I said I should like a brown dress, she would let me have a black: just for contrary." Cross-examined, the prisoner had been a boarder for the last half-year. She took the second class prize for good conduct. Inspector Whicher had called upon witness regarding the case; she was very surprised to see him. Mr. Parsons, Beckington, gave further particulars of the postmortem examination. The throat was cut from ear to ear, dividing it all down to the spine. There was a stab on the left side, cutting through the cartilage of two ribs. The mouth had a blackened appearance and the tongue protruded between the teeth: "I think this was produced by forcible pressure during life." There were two slight incisions on the right[8] hand, which appeared to have been made after death. When he saw the body at 8:30 a.m. rigidity was complete; he judged it had been dead at least five hours. The

---

8. At the inquest he said the left.

injuries were inflicted with a long, pointed knife. In presence of Superintendent Foley he had examined the linen in the accused's bedroom. The nightcap and nightgown on the bed were free from blood-stains. The nightdress was very clean; he could not say how long it had been worn. Cross-examined, it might have been worn for a week. The deceased was an exceptionally heavy child for his age. It would require great force to inflict the stab through his clothing. He saw a clean nightdress in the prisoner's drawer. Louisa Hatherall said she was at school with the accused, who had spoken of the partiality shown by her parents for the younger children. William was made to wheel their perambulator, which he disliked doing. The father used to say how much finer a boy his youngest son, Saville, was than William.

All this was but a weak groundwork on which to base so terrible an accusation, but Inspector Whicher held a stronger card. Sarah Cox, the housemaid, said that she collected the soiled linen from the bedrooms on Monday mornings. Miss Constance threw her nightgown out on the landing as usual on Monday, 2nd July, and witness took it to the lumber-room on the same floor, along with the other dirty linen. She then called the eldest Miss Kent to enter the weekly washing in the laundry book, in which that nightgown duly figured. She perfectly remembered putting it in the laundry basket.

> Miss Constance came to the door of the lumber-room after the things were in the basket, but I had not quite finished packing them. She asked me if I would look in her slip pocket and see if she had left her purse there. I looked in the basket and told her it was not there. She then asked me to go down and get her a glass of water. I did so, and she followed me to the top of the back stairs, as I went out of the room. I found her there when I returned with the water, and I think I was not gone a

minute. She drank the water and went up the back stairs to her own room.[9]

The cross-examination of this witness occupies two closely-printed pages of the report, which shows how much weight Mr. Edlin attached to her statement. But Sarah was not to be shaken. She said that Miss Constance's nightdresses were easily distinguishable from those of the other ladies, as hers had plain frills and theirs lacework. Miss Constance had three, including the one put into the basket. That week three nightdresses were entered in the laundry book, of which hers was one. On the Tuesday the laundress sent a message to say that there was one nightdress short; witness said that must be a mistake, for she herself had put in three. There was nothing unusual in Miss Constance's manner on the discovery of the murder. Witness had never seen her unkind or unsisterly to her little brother. Esther Holly said that she was in the habit of washing for the family. On the Monday after the murder she got the clothes as usual in a basket. When she got home and compared them with the list, she found there was a nightdress missing. On her reporting the fact, Mr. Kent said he would take out a search-warrant if the nightdress was not returned within forty-eight hours. It had never been found, and her connection with the family had ceased. In cross-examination, she said the only two articles that had ever been lost at the wash before were a ragged duster and an old towel. "Mrs. Kent forgave me the towel." Inspector Jonathan Whicher said he had been engaged in investigating the case.

From information received,[10] I sent for Constance Kent on Monday last to her bedroom, having just examined

---

9. *The Great Crime of 1860*, p. 132.

10. It is probable that Whicher obtained his first clue from the previous association of Constance with the closet.

her drawers and found a list of her linen, which I produce, in which were enumerated three nightdresses, belonging to her. I said, "Is this a list of your linen?" She replied, "Yes." I said, "In whose writing is it?" She said, "It is my own writing." I said, "Here are three nightdresses: where are they?" She said, "I have two; the other was lost in the wash the week after the murder." She then brought me the two which I produce. I also saw a nightdress and a nightcap on her bed. I said, "Whose is this?" She said, "That is my sister's." The two she had before brought me were soiled: I mean they had been worn.[11]

When arrested on the charge of murder she wept and repeatedly said, "I am innocent."

Whicher's theory as to the nightdresses was this: Constance had done the deed in the nightdress—let us call it A—which she was wearing on Friday, the night of the crime; it was bloodstained, and on regaining her room she burnt or otherwise destroyed it; she then took from her drawer a clean nightdress, B, in which she slept during the nights of Saturday and Sunday, and put it out for the wash on Monday morning, in order that it might be entered in the laundry book as A. By sending the maid for the water, she contrived to recover B from the basket and took it up to her bedroom, thus avoiding the necessity for using her third and only remaining nightdress, which might have attracted notice and inquiry.

Mr. Edlin then addressed the Bench. He demanded the instant liberation of his client, against whom no title of evidence had been adduced. This young lady had been the subject of a judicial murder not less atrocious than that with which she was charged. She had been dragged to jail like a common felon, on the mere suspicion of a police inspector, actuated

---

11. *The Road Murder*, p. 9.

by hope of earning the offered reward. The matter of the missing nightgown—the little peg upon which alone this fearful charge depended—had been disposed of to the satisfaction of everyone. The meanness of hunting up the girl's schoolfellows reflected ineffable disgrace upon the person responsible. The Bench would fail in their duty if they did not at once restore this injured young lady to her home and friends. "The learned gentleman resumed his seat amidst the loud applause of the audience"—a curious example of the psychology of crowds: these same people had but lately been clamoring for her blood. The magistrates, after a brief consultation, announced that the prisoner would be discharged, on her father entering into recognizances of £200 for her appearance if called upon.

So Constance was free once more to "listen to the merry village chime." She returned in triumph to the family bosom, and *The Times* shed tears of printers' ink over the touching scene of her reunion with her parents. No one, however, had a good word to say for poor Whicher. His fate affords a palmary example of the unhappiness of the policeman's lot, as described by a popular playwright. He had to pay the penalty of those whose genius is in advance of their time; his brilliant bit of inductive work was upon all hands held up to ridicule, and he himself retired from the case, buried beneath a weight of obloquy and contempt. The *Annual Register* pontifically pronounced his epitaph:—

> The grounds on which this accusation was made were so frivolous, and the evidence by which it was attempted to be supported so childish, that the proceeding can only be described as absurd and cruel. . . . The other evidence to support the charge was singularly empty and vexatious. . . . By this indiscretion, the exertions of the detectives, so far from having tended to the discovery

of the criminals, had rather diminished the chance of success.[12]

Public opinion, thus satisfied of the innocence of Miss Constance, was now in full cry after her father and the nurse. A memorial was presented to the Home Secretary, praying for the appointment of a special commission to investigate the circumstances of the crime, but this application was refused. On 3rd September Sir George Lewis intimated that he would not be justified in advising Her Majesty to create an exceptional and extraordinary tribunal for the purpose of interrogating persons suspected of the murder. The inaction of the Home Office was strongly condemned by the Press, with the characteristic British result that the Government unofficially authorized a private inquiry to be conducted by one Mr. Slack, a solicitor of Bath, at the instance of the Wiltshire magistrates. There is no pleasing some people. The *Spectator* remarked: "Sir George Lewis gets rid of the difficulty by a side wind, for it appears now that although he refuses to initiate any proceedings, he yet sanctions another course, taken by the local magistrates, utterly subversive of every principle of justice." On 26th September Mr. Slack, having concluded his inquiry, the result of which was never published and which seems to have consisted in the re-examination of the whole household, reported the proceedings to the magistrates, and applied for a warrant for the arrest of Elizabeth Gough. This step was taken after consultation with the Attorney-General, Sir Richard Bethell, who was of opinion that there was sufficient evidence to justify the charge. Superintendent Foley—again in command, *vice* Whicher, dismissed with ignominy—must have been gratified to have his opinion thus backed by so competent an authority.

---

12. *Annual Register*, June 1860, p. 101.

On 1st October the prisoner was brought before the magistrates at Trowbridge; Mr. T. W. Saunders, of the Western Circuit, appeared for the prosecution, Mr. Ribton represented the accused, and Mr. Edlin watched the case on behalf of Mr. Kent. In opening the case, Mr. Saunders gave an account of the former investigations, and referred to the fact that "another party was apprehended at the instance of a detective from London—a young lady, a member of the family in which this murder was committed. He was happy to have an opportunity of saying that from first to last there was not the slightest ground for entertaining suspicion against her, and he believed that young lady went forth to the world as clear of suspicion as any gentleman he had the honor of addressing." This would be pleasant hearing for Miss Constance, then present in Court. After reviewing the circumstances of the crime, with which the reader is already familiar, he said that they could fix the time of the murder at about one o'clock in the morning of Saturday, 30th June. With regard to the nature of the injuries inflicted, "the conclusion he had arrived at was that the child's throat was cut to mislead, and for the purpose of diverting suspicion and inquiry from the proper quarter." It was clear that no one broke into the house; it was highly improbable that anyone was secreted there.

> The probabilities were that whoever committed the murder, and took the child out and deposited it where it was found, got out through the back door, was let out by a person in the house, and afterwards returned. It may be suggested that it was done by one person only. Whether it was done by one or more, it was clear almost to demonstration that the prisoner must have been concerned.[13]

---

13. *Bristol Daily Post*, 2nd October 1860.

But one person could not have taken the child from the cot, lifted the blanket from between the sheet and counterpane, and carried both off, leaving the bedclothes smoothly rearranged. There must have been a second person there. Was it likely that two strangers went into that room to do it? Were they not forced to the conclusion that if there were two persons, one at least must have been the nurse? Counsel then considered most unfavorably her behavior when she found the child gone, and commented on her unexplained failure to give the alarm. Before the discovery of the body, she had told Mrs. Kent that the blanket was missing; but afterwards, perceiving the danger of that admission, she declared that she did not know it until the body was brought in. Beneath the body in the closet was discovered "a triangular piece of chest flannel, worn by females"; it was found to fit exactly the prisoner's chest. It had been proved by actual experiment that from her bed, as she described, she could not have seen whether or not the boy was in his cot. The case was fraught with such grave suspicion that justice demanded the prisoner should be sent for trial.

Mr. Samuel Saville Kent was then called and examined by Mr. Saunders. He described the extent of his family and the accommodation of his house. He slept soundly on the fatal night and did not wake till a quarter past seven. He set off for Trowbridge so soon as he heard the child was missing. The house could not have been entered from without except by violence, of which there was no trace. He knew before he left for Trowbridge that the blanket was missing, and told the turnpike-keeper at Southwick so. On the Saturday after the murder it was arranged that two policemen should pass the night in the house. He admitted them at 11 p.m., after the household had gone to bed; put them in the kitchen, well provided with refreshments; *and locked them in without their knowledge.* These vigilant officers were presumably so occupied in refreshing themselves that they were unaware of their predicament till 2 a.m., when they made such a noise at the door that Mr. Kent came down and unlocked it. Pressed for an explanation of this strange proceeding, he now explained: "I bolted the door that the house might appear as usual, and that no one might know there were policemen in the house." He kept a large Newfoundland dog for protection of the premises and let it loose at night. He did so at 10 p.m. on the Friday. He was often awakened by its barking, but that night he heard no bark. The dog did not bark at the inmates. Cross-examined by Mr. Ribton, he might have expressed to the police the opinion that no one could have got into the house from the outside. He made no search himself before going to Trowbridge. He had refused to allow a plan of the premises to be taken. He did not interrogate the nurse on the morning of the murder, nor did he enter the nursery on that occasion. The only reason he had for supposing, before he searched the premises, that the child was stolen, was that he was told it was missing.

Mrs. Kent described how she gave her boy a pill at eight o'clock on the Friday night and saw him put to bed. When she went to bed herself at eleven she shut the nursery door. It creaked, unless shut carefully. Owing to her condition, she was very restless and awoke frequently during the night. She heard no sound from the nursery. Mr. Kent did not leave his bed till 7:30 next morning. Early in the morning she heard the drawing-room shutters opened, but did not call her husband's attention to that as he was asleep. She was not alarmed; she thought it was done by the servants. She did not hear the dog bark during the night. Witness then stated how the prisoner informed her of the child's disappearance.

> I asked her why she had not told me sooner: she said she did not come, as she thought I had heard him cry and had fetched him. I replied, "How dare you say so? You know

I could not carry him." ... I had never gone and taken the child from the room when the nurse was asleep.

After discovery of the murder, when accused was brushing her mistress's hair, she exclaimed, "Oh, ma'am, it's revenge!" Cross-examined, Mrs. Kent said that the nurse was particularly kind to the child, who was very fond of her. After his death she often spoke of him with sorrow and affection. In re-examination, witness said that the boy was a general favorite; she knew of no one who had any vengeful feeling against him or the family. On concluding her evidence witness asked leave to make a voluntary statement, which was refused. One wonders what she wanted to say.

Sarah Cox, the housemaid, was then called and examined, but contributed nothing to our knowledge of the facts. At the conclusion of her testimony the Court rose. The solid body of spectators, who had waited outside all day, "hooted and hissed every carriage that left, believing it to contain the Kent family."

Next morning the examination of witnesses was resumed. The cook, the gardener, and the two eldest Miss Kents succeeded each other in the box without adding anything material to the issue. Then Miss Constance Emilie Kent was called.

On Friday the 29th of June I was at home. I had been at home about a fortnight. I had been previously at school, as a boarder, at Beckington. The little boy who was murdered was at home also. I last saw him in the evening, when he went to bed. He was a merry, good-tempered lad, fond of romping. I was accustomed to play with him often. I had played with him that day. He appeared to be fond of me, and I was fond of him.

On the Saturday night she slept in the same nightdress she had worn all that week. She put on a clean one on the Sunday or Monday night. Her third nightdress was missing; she did not know what had become of it. Cross-examined, she heard from the nurse that the child's blanket was missing, but whether before or after the discovery of the body she could not remember. Morgan and Urch, two local constables, spoke to visiting the nursery on the Saturday morning. Prisoner showed them the child's cot, with the bedclothes folded back and the impression of his head on the pillow. She stated that the blanket had been removed. Urch said that, along with another officer, he was told by Mr. Kent to remain in the kitchen all night. They afterwards discovered that they were locked in, and "made noise enough to wake the house" until he released them. Benger and Nutt described the finding of the body, and were needlessly badgered in "cross" as to their "prediction." Superintendent Foley told how he had put two officers at Mr. Kent's disposal. "They were, I understood, to have the whole range of the house, but they only had the kitchen range." "A laugh" is the recorded tribute to the superintendent's pleasantry.

> I never received any information from the prisoner that was of any service. She said she was sure it was not Miss Constance, and I said, "Was it you?" She said, "No." I said it must have been somebody in the house: "Was it Mr. Kent?" She said it must have been some person concealed in the house. I said, "That story won't do."

Superintendent Wolfe, of Devizes, had interviewed the prisoner on Monday, 2nd July. She said, "The first time I missed the blanket was after the child was found; I went and looked at the crib when I went to do Mrs. Kent's hair." She had frequently repeated that statement. He had tried the experiment of kneeling on the nurse's bed and looking towards the cot; it was impossible from that position to see whether the child was in it or not. In reply to his question, prisoner told him, "Mr. Kent has never alluded to the matter [of the murder] to me since it occurred, from first to last. The young ladies have, and so has Miss Constance, and Master William has often cried over it."

The third day's hearing began with the evidence of Master William, who had nothing to tell, and of other witnesses, who were in the same situation. Then Mr. Parsons, the surgeon, gave an elaborate account of the post-mortem, at which it now appeared that Mr. Stapleton, the historian of the case, assisted. He was more positive about the appearance of the mouth: "It had been pressed for a considerable time—say, from five to ten minutes, and by a soft substance."[14] His final opinion was that the child died from suffocation, and that the several injuries were inflicted *after* death. The remainder of the sitting was occupied by witnesses of no importance. Mrs. Dallimore, wife of a Trowbridge constable, who seems to have been placed by Foley as a spy upon the nurse, gave an account of divers conversations had with her, as well before as after her apprehension. Gough, however, while maintaining her own innocence, had steadily refused to inculpate anyone else, to the manifest annoyance of the policewoman.[15] This expert alleged that the "chest flannel" found in the closet fitted Gough alone of all the female inmates, but denied that it fitted herself equally well. She was much discredited in cross-examination.

The fourth and last day of the proceedings was devoted to Mr. Ribton's long and eloquent address for the defense, into which I have no space to enter. He contended that the evidence showed

14. Mr. Stapleton was of opinion that the wound in the throat amounted, physiologically, to decapitation. It would at once abolish all feeling and preclude all resistance. "One murderous cut had drained the large vessels in a few short seconds of their blood"; but that from the smaller vessels, filtering downwards, produced the distention and suffusion of the face, erroneously regarded as evidence of suffocation.—*The Great Crime of 1860*, p. 62.

15. She did, indeed, express the opinion that the crime was due to "jealousy," and she may well have had her own reasons for saying so.

the murder to have been committed by a stranger secreted in the house,[16] and that the sole point made against his client—her varying statements as to when she missed the blanket—was accounted for by her natural confusion in so shocking a situation. He concluded with a strong appeal for her immediate discharge. The magistrates, after half an hour's deliberation, discharged the prisoner, upon recognizances of £100.

As, according to the stage tradition of the day, melodrama and pantomime were commonly conjoined in the same playbill, it was fitting that the tragedy of which these abortive investigations were the theater should be followed by a farce. On Saturday, 3rd November, Mr. Saunders, a Wiltshire magistrate—not the barrister of that name whom we have already met—began a season at the Temperance Hall, Road, with an entirely new and original comedy, of which he was at once the author, producer, and first comedian. The proceedings, in that they were without lawful authority instituted by himself, were private, but in another sense public; for he welcomed to the witness-stand any busybody who cared to come. The village idiot—locally, as appears, a noun of multitude or signifying many—responded with gusto to the invitation; and all who had a grudge against the Kent family, a relish of gossip and scandal, or an itch for self-advertisement, trooped joyously to the Temperance Hall. There they found Mr. Saunders, in all the majesty of self-appointed office, presiding at a table covered with documents. Anticipating but cold comfort from the dry character of the Court-house, the president produced from his pocket a bottle, containing what looked very like brandy—"it might have been cough mixture," is the charitable comment of the *Daily Post* reporter—poured an adequate dose thereof into a tumbler, slightly tempered the same with water, and dur-

---

16. About the only thing the evidence *did* establish was that the deed was done by an inmate, familiar with the premises.

ing the progress of the sederunt, had frequent recourse to this specific. He then "opened" in an address teeming with such ludicrous irrelevancies and idiotic observations as these:—

> If I mistake anything, it is unwittingly, and let me, for God's sake, be corrected by somebody and interrupted. If I am correct in my impression—and I am happy to say, from the investigation I took, I have most of the facts at my fingers' ends—I think there was a person who volunteered evidence that Mr. Kent—evidence, I mustn't say—made a statement that Mr. Kent was at church on the previous Sunday, Midsummer Day, with the little boy who was unfortunately found afterwards in the receptacle. That person, I now think, was Mrs. Webley: is she here? Is she near at hand? If anybody goes for her, let them call on Silcox, who lives near the lane that leads up to the pound, with my personal respects.[17]

The dame, with much difficulty and waste of time, being produced and testifying to Mr. Kent's Sunday observance—though to what purpose, Heaven and Mr. Saunders only knew—the learned gentleman remarked:—

> I am much obliged to you. Is there anyone here can give me any account of Mr. Samuel Saville Kent's proceedings on the Monday after Midsummer Day? Is there anybody in this room who saw Mr. Kent on the 25th of June? Let him speak out, without fear, favor, or affection, and be kind enough to make that inquiry among his friends. Is there anyone here that knows anything of his proceedings on the Tuesday? Let him make a like inquiry among his friends. Is there anyone here who said

---

17. *Bristol Daily Post*, 6th November 1860.

anything about Kent's proceedings on the 27th June? Is there anybody—is there anybody—do they know anybody? My memory fails me.

As it is possible that the reader's patience is in similar case, we shall leave Mr. Saunders to conduct, or rather misconduct, his extrajudicial inquiry, ungraced by our presence. But, by a strange chance, from the heaps of chaff thus winnowed by this egregious husbandman, a new and startling grain of evidence *did* emerge. It appeared that one of the police, who searched the house on the morning after the murder, found in the boiler-furnace of the scullery a woman's blood-stained shift. He showed it to Foley, who said "he shuddered to think the man that found it was so foolish as to expose it." So it was put back again, and the superintendent's sensibilities were doubtless appeased by its disappearance, for it vanished and was no more seen. This explains why Foley that night placed two men in the kitchen: it was to watch whether anyone attempted to recover the garment. He had carried his delicacy so far as to make no mention of the matter to Inspector Whicher, who, when the fact came out, wrote on 27th November to the Trowbridge magistrates, indignantly complaining how he had been kept in the dark by his colleague.[18] The magistrates held an investigation into the affair of the suppressed chemise, as the result of which, while Foley's conduct in the business was declared "regrettable," the fineness of his feelings was commended. This ensanguined *trouvaille*, by the way, though less welcome than the flowers of spring, resembled them, as afterwards appeared, in having "nothing to do with the case."

The last official attempt to discover the secret of Road Hill

---

18. It is clear that the relations of Foley and Whicher suggested to Wilkie Collins those of Superintendent Seegrave and Sergeant Cuff, in connection with the mystery of *The Moonstone*.

House, made on 24th November by Her Majesty's Attorney-General, in the Court of Queen's Bench, Westminster, was no more successful than its forerunners. This was an application for a writ *ad melius inquirendum* touching the death of Francis Saville Kent—in other words, for a rule to quash the Coroner's inquisition and to grant a new inquiry before special commissioners—the grounds being misdirection of the jury and the exclusion of evidence. The offending functionary was represented by Sir Fitzroy Kelly, and the matter was debated at vast length.[19] The real question was, whether the Coroner had been guilty of judicial misconduct in failing to examine Mr. Kent. Finally, on 30th January 1860, the Court found that he had not, and Lord Chief-Justice Cockburn discharged the rule. Thus the final effort to reopen the inquiry failed, and the arraignment of the Road murderer was remitted to the knowledge of the Great Assize.

# III
## THE SOLUTION

*Still with unhurrying chase,*
*And unperturbèd pace,*
*Deliberate speed, majestic instancy,*
*Came on the following Feet,*
*And a Voice above their beat—*
*"Naught shelters thee, who wilt not shelter Me."*

—FRANCIS THOMPSON: *The Hound of Heaven*

It is among the lamentable consequences of great crimes that the just and the unjust are alike involved in one common ruin;

---

19. A verbatim report of the discussion is given in *The Great Crime of 1860*, Appendix v. p. 329.

that the innocent kinsfolk of the criminal must pay a portion of the price. Road Hill House had to be abandoned by the unfortunate family, who vainly sought in Wales a refuge from the scandal and disgrace which was to follow them through life. The outbreak of the American Civil War in the ensuing year provided the newspapers with ample copy, and the familiar headline "The Road Murder" no longer figured as a daily item in their columns.

Constance Kent had ceased to be a member of the home circle. Her early desire for independence met with qualified fulfillment: she went into retreat in a French convent, where she remained for the next three years. The reason for this singular relaxation of the bonds of mid-Victorian domesticity may be inferred from the following paragraph:—

> It is not generally known that nearly a year afterwards [1861], in consequence of an alleged confession of the crime by Miss Kent to one of her relatives, another attempt to investigate the matter was made by the detective officers, who had incurred the censure of a large proportion of the Press and the public for their proceedings in the case. They found it unadvisable, however, to act upon the fresh information which had reached them: and it subsequently transpired that Miss Kent had been sent to a convent in France.[20]

So the wicked Whicher had not yet ceased from troubling; but the object of his malevolent persecution was now beyond his reach. In August 1863 Constance Kent returned to England, and was admitted an inmate of St. Mary's Home, Brighton, an

---

20. *Annual Register*, April 1865.

Anglo-Catholic hostel for devout women, under the ghostly
ward of the Rev. Arthur Wagner, perpetual curate of St. Paul's
Church there. In April 1865, while being prepared for Confirmation, Constance confessed to Mr. Wagner, as her spiritual
director, that she was in truth the murderess of her brother.
Shortly thereafter she avowed her intention to make public
confession of her guilt; and on 25th April, accompanied by the
clergyman and by the Lady Superior of the institution, Constance came to London and gave herself up to the authorities.
The same day she was brought before Sir Thomas Henry at
Bow Street, when, the charge having been taken,

> Sir Thomas, addressing the prisoner, said,—Am I to
> understand, Miss Kent, that you have given yourself up
> of your own free act and will on this charge?
>
> MISS KENT.—Yes, sir.
>
> SIR THOMAS.—Anything you may say here will be
> written down, and may be used against you. Do you
> quite understand that?
>
> MISS KENT.—Yes, sir.
>
> SIR THOMAS.—Is this paper, now produced before
> me, in your own handwriting and written of your own
> free will?
>
> MISS KENT.—It is, sir.
>
> SIR THOMAS.—Then let the charge be entered in her
> own words.

The confession was accordingly read as follows:—

> I, Constance Emilie Kent, alone and unaided, on the night
> of the 29th of June 1860, murdered at Road Hill House,
> Wiltshire, one Francis Saville Kent. Before the deed was
> done no one knew of my intention, nor afterwards of

my guilt. No one assisted me in the crime, nor in the evasion of discovery.[21]

The Rev. Arthur Wagner, sworn, deposed that the confession was entirely voluntary; he had not in any way induced her to make it. He had neither persuaded her to confess nor dissuaded her from doing so. It was her own free act. Constance was then remitted in custody to the Wiltshire magistrates for examination. Next day she was brought before the local Bench at Trowbridge, and after some formal evidence was committed for trial at the ensuing assizes.

At Salisbury, on 20th July 1865, in a thronged Court and amid intense popular excitement, Constance Kent made her last appearance in public. The great John Duke Coleridge, afterwards Lord Chief-Justice of England, had been retained for the defense by Mr. Rodway, the Kent family solicitor. "Before taking the very unusual course of acquiescing in a plea of Guilty to a capital charge," says Mr. Atlay in his admirable article on the Road Mystery, "Mr. Coleridge desired to have his instructions direct from his client; and, in accordance with his wish, he received the following letter, written in a firm, precise, feminine hand:—

Sir,—I announced my determination yesterday to Mr. Rodway to plead guilty, and then if the judge should consider that a trial would conduce to clear those who are unjustly suspected, I would consent and leave the case in the hands of my counsel for that purpose. If the case is not gone into, it will not be believed that my confession is a true one, and I am persuaded that nothing

---

21. *Annual Register*, April 1865.

will tend to clear the innocent so completely as my conviction.—Yours truly,

Constance Kent."[22]

Coleridge, in a letter to which the above is a reply, had advised his client, *if she was really determined to plead guilty*, not to allow any other plea to be recorded. "If you plead Not Guilty, then whatever I can do shall be done for your acquittal. If you plead Guilty, anything I can say to set others right shall be said. But I advise you against any intermediate course."[23] The prisoner decided to be ruled by counsel's advice, but Coleridge must prepare for either event. His diary contains the following entries regarding the case:—

> July 20.—Saw Miss Kent, the sister, and William Kent, and then sat up till near three, getting up my speech which, after all, I shall not deliver.
>
> July 21.—Poor Constance Kent pleaded guilty. I said a few words and *there* an end. It was very solemn.[24]

Mr. Justice Willes presided; Mr. Karslake, Q. C., appeared for the Crown, Mr. Coleridge, Q. C., for the defense. The prisoner, being required to plead, replied in a low voice, "Guilty." Twice did the Judge repeat the question; twice did she return the same answer. So the plea was duly recorded. Then, amid the tense silence of the crowded Court-room, "silver-tongued" Coleridge rose to address the Judge:—

---

22. *Famous Trials of the Century*, by J. B. Atlay, p. 131. London: 1899.

23. *Life and Correspondence of John Duke, Lord Coleridge*, ii. 412. London: 1904.

24. Ibid., ii. 39.

My Lord, as counsel for the defense, acting on the prisoner's behalf, before your lordship passes sentence, I desire to say two things—first, solemnly in the presence of Almighty God, as a person who values her own soul, she wishes me to say that the guilt is hers alone, and that her father and others who have so long suffered most unjust and cruel suspicion are wholly and absolutely innocent: and secondly, she was not driven to this act, as has been asserted, by unkind treatment at home, as she met with nothing there but tender and forbearing love: and I hope I may add, my lord, not improperly, that it gives me a melancholy pleasure to be the organ of these statements for her, because on my honor I believe them to be true.[25]

Mr. Justice Willes, who was deeply affected, pronounced the inevitable sentence.[26] "The prisoner at the bar, who up to this time had maintained the greatest composure, burst into a passion of tears, which was audible in every part of the Court and produced a profound impression upon all who witnessed the scene." She was thereupon removed, and the brief proceedings were over.

Had the case occurred in later and more enlightened times, Constance Kent, availing herself of the Prisoners' Evidence Act, could have told in the witness-box her own story and would have been cross-examined upon it, thus probably preventing the fulfillment of her prophecy that her confession would not otherwise be believed—a prediction which, as we shall see, has been verified. There is an interesting letter, written in 1890, by Lord Coleridge to Mr. Gladstone, with refer-

---

25. *Annual Register*, 1865, p. 228; *Life and Correspondence*, ii. 411.

26. The capital penalty was afterwards commuted for that of penal servitude for life.

ence to the present case, regarding the law applicable to the sanctity of confession to a clergyman. The Rev. Mr. Wagner, had the trial gone on, was to have been a witness; and if Karslake put the question to him and Coleridge objected, the Judge was prepared to uphold the objection. "He said he had satisfied himself that there was a *legal* privilege in a priest to withhold what passed in confession. . . . Whether the English Judges would have upheld Willes's law I own I doubt."[27]

Miss Tennyson Jesse, in her brilliant study of the case, has noted it "as an example of the gulf that divides present-day thought from that of 1860":—

> None of the problems of adolescence, with which a modern counsel for the defense would have made such powerful play, were invoked by Constance Kent's advocate. It is quite certain that the doctrines of Freud and his followers could not have been left out of a similar trial taking place nowadays, but in Constance Kent's day it was considered that justice had been sufficiently tempered with mercy when the woman of twenty-one was sentenced to penal servitude for life for the crime committed when an ill-balanced girl of sixteen.[28]

But the authorities were not wholly heartless. By instruction of the Home Office, Dr. Bucknill of Rugby[29] examined the

---

27. *Life and Correspondence,* ii. 365.

28. Murder and Motives, by F. Tennyson Jesse, p. 75. London: 1924.

29. Dr. (afterwards Sir John Charles) Bucknill was one of a well-known Rugby family. His grandfather, Samuel Bucknill, surgeon there, was, curiously enough, also concerned for the prosecution in another local *cause célèbre*: that of Captain John Donellan, convicted at Warwick Assizes in 1781 of the murder of his young brother-in-law, Sir Theodosius Edward Allesley Boughton of Lawford Hall.—See *The Fatal Countess and Other Studies,* p. 103. Edinbugh: 1924.

prisoner before the trial as to her mental condition, with a view to a possible plea of insanity, but he was unable to advise that she was not fit to plead. After commutation of the sentence, Dr. Bucknill, by request of the convict and her family, published in *The Times* the following letter, giving a detailed account of the manner of the murder, as communicated to him on that occasion by Constance Kent herself:—

Sir,—I am requested by Miss Constance Kent to communicate to you the following details of her crime, which she has confessed to Mr. Rodway, her solicitor, and to myself, and which she now desires to be made public.

Constance Kent first gave an account of the circumstances of her crime to Mr. Rodway, and she afterwards acknowledged to me the correctness of that account when I recapitulated it to her. The explanation of her motive she gave to me when, with the permission of the Lord Chancellor, I examined her for the purpose of ascertaining whether there were any grounds for supposing that she was laboring under mental disease. Both Mr. Rodway and I are convinced of the truthfulness and good faith of what she said to us.

Constance Kent says that the manner in which she committed her crime was as follows: A few days before the murder she obtained possession of a razor from a green case in her father's wardrobe and secreted it. This was the sole instrument which she used. She also secreted a candle with matches, by placing them in the corner of the closet in the garden, where the murder was committed. On the night of the murder she undressed herself and went to bed, because she expected that her sisters would visit her room. She lay awake watching until she thought that the household were all asleep, and soon after midnight she left her bedroom and went downstairs and opened the drawing-room door and window shutters. She then went up into the nursery, withdrew the blanket from between the sheet and the counter-pane, and placed it on the side of the cot. She then took the child from his bed and carried him downstairs through the drawing-room. She had on her nightdress, and in the drawing-room she put on her goloshes. Having the child in one arm, she raised the drawing-room window with the other hand, went round the house and into the closet, lighted the candle and placed it on the seat of the closet, the child being wrapped in the blanket and still sleeping, and while the child was in this position she inflicted the wound in the throat. She says that she thought the blood would never come, and that the child was not killed, so she thrust the razor into its left side, and put the body with the blanket round it into the vault. The light burned out. The piece of flannel which she had with her was torn from an old flannel garment placed in the waste bag, and which she had taken some time before and sewn it to use in washing herself. She went back into her bedroom, examined her dress, and found only two spots of blood on it. These she washed out in the basin, and threw the water, which was but little discolored, into the foot-pan in which she had washed her feet overnight. She took another of her nightdresses and got into bed. In the morning her nightdress had become dry where it had been washed. She folded it up and put it into the drawer. Her three nightdresses were examined by Mr. Foley, and she believes also by Mr. Parsons, the medical attendant of the family. She thought the blood-stains had been effectually washed out, but on holding the dress up to the light a day or two afterwards, she found the stains were still visible. She secreted the dress, moving it from place to place, and she eventually burnt it in her own bedroom, and put the ashes or tinder into the kitchen grate. It was about five or six days after the child's death that she burnt the nightdress. On the Saturday morning, having cleaned the razor, she took an opportunity of replacing it unobserved in the case in the wardrobe. She abstracted her nightdress from the clothes basket when the housemaid went to fetch a glass of water. The stained garment found in the boiler-hole had no connexion whatever with the deed. As regards the motive of her crime, it seems that, although she entertained at one time a great regard for the present Mrs. Kent, yet if any remark was at any time made which in her opinion was disparaging to any member of the first family, she treasured it up, and determined to revenge it. She had no ill-will against the little boy, except as one of the children of her stepmother. She declared that both her father and her stepmother had always been kind to her personally, and the following is the copy of a letter which she addressed to Mr. Rodway on this point while in prison before her trial.

DEVIZES, MAY 15.

Sir,—It has been stated that my feelings of revenge were excited in consequence of cruel treatment. This is entirely false. I have received the greatest kindness from both the persons accused of subjecting me to it. I have never had any ill-will towards either of them on account of their behavior to me, which has been very kind.

I shall feel obliged if you will make use of this statement in order that the public may be undeceived on this point.—I remain, sir, yours truly,

Constance E. Kent.

To Mr. R. Rodway.

She told me that when the nursemaid was accused she had fully made up her mind to confess if the nurse had been convicted; and that she had also made up her mind to commit suicide if she was herself convicted. She said that she felt herself under the influence of the devil before she committed the murder, but that she did not believe, and had not believed, that the devil had more to do with her crime than he had with any other wicked action. She had not said her prayers for a year before the murder, and not afterwards, until she came to reside at Brighton. She said that the circumstances which revived religious feelings in her mind was thinking about receiving the Sacrament when confirmed.

An opinion has been expressed that the peculiarities evinced by Constance Kent between the ages of twelve and seventeen may be attributed to the then transition period of her life. Moreover, the fact of her cutting off her hair, dressing herself in her brother's clothes, and leaving her home with the intention of going abroad, which occurred when she was only thirteen years of age, indicated a peculiarity of disposition and great determination of character, which foreboded that, for good or evil, her future life would be remarkable.

This peculiar disposition which led to such singular and violent resolves of action, seemed also to color and intensify her thoughts and feelings, and magnify into wrongs that were to be revenged any little family incidents or occurrences which provoked her displeasure.

Although it became my duty to advise her counsel that she evinced no symptoms of insanity at the time of my examination, and that, so far as it was possible to ascertain the state of her mind at so remote a period, there was no evidence of it at the time of the murder, I am yet of opinion that, owing to the peculiarities of her constitution, it is probable that under prolonged solitary confinement she would become insane.

The validity of this opinion is of importance now that the sentence of death has been commuted to penal servitude for life, for no one could desire that the punishment of the criminal should be so carried out as to cause danger of a further and greater punishment, not contemplated by the law.

> I have the honor to remain your
> very obedient servant,
> John Charles Bucknill, M.D.
> HILLMORTON HALL, NEAR RUGBY,
> AUG. 24.[30]

This statement, which was "broadcasted" by the British Press, can have had few more interested readers than Inspector Whicher, who in 1863 had retired from the force—"presumably to grow roses," as Mr. Atlay pleasantly remarks in allusion to the hobby of Sergeant Cuff.[31] We all like to be proved right; and thus to be justified in the event must have given the intelligent officer legitimate joy.

Thirteen years later Dr. Bucknill, in a lecture on insanity delivered by him at the Royal College of Physicians in April 1878, made the following further revelations:—

The most remarkable case in which I have been concerned was the case of Constance Kent, who murdered

---

30. *The Times*, 28th August 1865.

31. During the great Tichborne case, Whicher came out of his retirement to assist the family, and it was he who discovered the claimant's famous visit to Wapping on Christmas Day 1866, which led to the identification of that personage with Arthur Orton.

her young brother and escaped detection. After an interval of several years, a truly conscientious motive led her to confess, and the most painful and interesting duty fell to my lot of examining her for the purpose of ascertaining whether it would be right to enter the plea of "Not guilty on the ground of insanity." I was compelled to advise against it, and her counsel, Mr. (now Lord) Coleridge, on reading the notes of my examination, admitted that I could not do otherwise. By her own wish, and that of her relatives, I published a letter in *The Times* describing the material facts of the crime; but, to save the feelings of those who were alive at the time, I did not make known the motive, and on this account it has been that the strange portent has remained in the history of our social life that a young girl, not insane, should have been capable of murdering her beautiful boy brother in cold blood and without motive. I think the right time and opportunity has come for me to explain away this apparent monstrosity of conduct. A real and dreadful motive did exist. The girl's own mother, having become partially demented, was left by her husband to live in the seclusion of her own room, while the management of the household was taken over the heads of the grown-up daughters by a high-spirited governess, who, after the decease of the first Mrs. Kent, and a decent interval, became Constance Kent's stepmother. In this position she was unwise enough to make disparaging remarks about her predecessor, little dreaming, poor lady, of the fund of rage and revengeful feeling she was stirring up in the heart of her young stepdaughter. To escape from her hated presence, Constance once ran away from home, but was brought back; and after this she only thought of the most efficient manner of wreaking her vengeance. She thought of poisoning her stepmother, but that, on reflection, she felt would be no real punishment, and then it was that she determined to murder the poor lady's boy. A dreadful story this; but who can fail to pity the depths of household misery which it denotes? At her arraignment, Constance Kent persisted in pleading "Guilty." Had the plea been "Not Guilty," it would, I suppose, have been my most painful duty to have told the Court the tragic history which I now tell to you, in the belief that it can give no pain to those concerned in it, and that it is mischievous that so great and notorious a crime should remain unexplained.[32]

Even allowing that Constance Kent was, according to the dimmer scientific lights of her day, technically sane, yet to the lay reader it would seem that the monstrous character of the crime, the pitiful inadequacy of the alleged motive, and the hideous heritage of the mad mother, jointly and severally predicate a mind diseased. There can be, of course, no adequate motive for murder, but there may be at least one humanly comprehensible; and that a normal young lady could, by the gibes of an ill-mannered and partial stepmother, be moved to cut off her baby half-brother's head, is a proposition which I confess I have some difficulty in accepting.

Confinement had not the baneful effect on the convict's mental health which Dr. Bucknill anticipated. During the period of her detention at Portland, she executed some of the mosaics which enrich St. Peter's Church. She survived, without apparent damage, a twenty-years' residence there and in that particular penitentiary of which, in *The Princess Casamassima*, Henry James has given us so grim a picture. Brief glimpses of her prison life are afforded by Major Arthur Griffiths, under

---

32. *Celebrated Crimes and Criminals*, by W. M. [Sir Willoughby Maycock, C.M.G.]. p. 154. London: 1890.

whose guardianship at Millbank Constance served a measure of her time. She was at first employed in the laundry and later as a nurse in the infirmary.

> A small, mouse-like little creature, with much of the promptitude of the mouse or lizard surprised, in disappearing when alarmed. The approach of any strange or unknown face, whom she feared might come to spy her out and stare, constituted a real alarm for Constance Kent. When anyone went the length of asking, "Which is Constance?" she had already concealed herself somewhere with wonderful rapidity and cleverness. She was a mystery in every way. . . . No doubt there were features in her face which the criminal anthropologist would have seized as suggestive of instinctive criminality—high cheek-bones, a lowering overhanging brow, and deep-set small eyes; but yet her manner was prepossessing and her intelligence was of a high order, while nothing could exceed the devoted attention she gave the sick under her charge as nurse.[33]

Elsewhere he records:—

> Constance Kent was like a ghost in Millbank; flitting noiselessly about, mostly invisible, but certainly so when any strange visitor appeared and she scented the smallest danger of being made a show. She spoke to no one, no one addressed her, the desire to efface herself was always respected, and her name was never mentioned.[34]

---

33. *Secrets of the Prison-House*, by Arthur Griffiths, ii. 10. London: 1894.

34. *Fifty Years of Public Service*, by Arthur Griffiths, p. 219. London: [n.d.].

Major Griffiths' testimony confirms the view expressed on other grounds by Miss Tennyson Jesse: that Constance "was not —as the congenital female criminal invariably is—a poseuse. She did not commit the crime for the sake of notoriety."[35]

Constance Kent was released on license in 1885. She is believed to have gone abroad, and history knows nothing further of her fate. Of the many legends begotten by the case the most intriguing is that Constance was a niece of Queen Victoria, her father having been an illegitimate son of His Royal Highness the late Duke of Kent, whose acquaintance it was the boast of Major Bagstock to enjoy. The physical resemblance between Constance and her august kinswoman is alleged to have been striking, but I have not been able to verify the relationship.

A word in closing as to the fidelity of her confession. As there will always be a certain type of mind which refuses to accept plain facts, preferring to the simple truth some subtle supposition, so in this case there have been divers skeptics who held that Constance deliberately damned herself, here and hereafter, to screen her guilty parent. "A certain barrister," says Mr. Ellis, "expressed his conviction of Constance Kent's entire innocence, maintaining that she made a bogus confession in order to divert suspicion from her father, who was regarded with mistrust by his neighbors."[36] There can be no question that the local feeling against Mr. Kent was intensely bitter and persistent. There must surely have been something in the personality of that respectable inspector of factories which aroused popular prejudice. But an exhaustive examination of the facts has satisfied me that he was a much-wronged man. I find no proof whatever of his alleged intrigue with the nurse, upon which is based the superstructure of suspicion.

---

35. *Murder and its Motives*, p. 97.

36. *A Mid-Victorian Pepys*, by S. M. Ellis, p. 24. London: 1923. An eminent criminological authority known to me also holds this view.

Had such a liaison existed, there must have been among the mass of testimony collected some trace of familiarities, of which there is none. Again, it is said that the drawing-room window required two people to open it; if that were so, it is remarkable that counsel at the nurse's trial did not avail himself of a fact so easily established and of such importance to his case: that two persons were concerned in the crime. And why should Constance postpone for five years the filial duty to vindicate her father's ruined reputation? Had she made her vicarious sacrifice at the time, it might have proved acceptable; as it is, I see no purpose to be served by so belated an oblation. There is nothing against Mr. Kent except the virulent and vindictive gossip of the village in which, for his sins, his lot was cast, and the misguided ingenuity of subsequent investigators.

In dealing with this dramatic and most sensational case I have eschewed, as will be seen, any attempt at pyrotechnics, whether psychological or literary, being content merely to collect and present such particulars as might enable each reader to form his own judgment upon the facts, so far as these are known to us. Of the verdict of the majority I am not in doubt.

# THE SANDYFORD MYSTERY

*"Alas! I had na the wyte [blame] of it."*

—LAST WORDS OF THE MASTER OF GOWRIE

I AM DOUBLY in debt to Mrs. Jessie M'Lachlan. She provided me with a case of high interest and importance; one which affords an instance unique in our juridical annals, namely, that of a person charged with murder, whose defense is that the crime was committed by the chief witness for the Crown! This surely is a situation sufficiently startling and dramatic to outgo even the most bold of fictionmongers. Then, my report of the trial being duly completed—not, as Mr. Sapsea remarked of his famous Epitaph, without some little fever of the brow, for in fact it was a tough job—and the volume having taken its place in the series to which it belongs, it chanced to meet the eye of that fine connoisseur in matters criminal, the late H. B. Irving. He fell in love at first sight with my Jessie, and for her sake sought an introduction to her biographer, which effected, led to a friendship greatly prized by me and subsisting until his untimely death. My account of the case became for him a bedside book—his nerves were in such circumstances of the strongest; and he told me that it was the best murder he had ever read. This, from one of his wide acquaintance with the literature of the subject, was praise indeed and made me very proud. That was over twenty years ago, and in re-telling to-day the old story for a new audience I am heartened by the remembrance of his approval.

In the Glasgow of the early sixties the Sandyford Mystery (with a capital M) was the topic not only of the hour, but of the year. The Second City, in mid-Victorian times, was singularly rich in wrongdoers of the most attaching type. There was the wonderful Miss Madeleine Smith in 1857, there was the poisonous Dr. Pritchard in 1865; and between these twain, in 1862, a first-class case, bristling with sensation and strange surprises; possessing everything requisite to a great criminal drama and constituting, in my submission, an ideal murder. For to do one's self the deed of which by means of your evidence another is convicted, is a veritable triumph of naughtiness only to be compassed by a past-master of the art of homicide. Little wonder, then, that such of the public as credited James Fleming, that curious old gentleman, with having achieved this feat at the expense of his former maidservant, Jessie M'Lachlan, were lost in admiration of the veteran's prowess. But there was an opposing faction that held old Fleming to be the blameless victim of a wicked woman, seeking to cast upon his venerable shoulders the weight of her own blood-guiltiness. So the interest of the case resides in this conundrum: Which of these solutions is the right one?

# I

Sandyford Place is a respectable street in the West End of Glasgow, and in the summer of 1862 there lived at No. 17 a suitably respectable accountant named John Fleming, together with his respectable son young John, who occupied a stool in the paternal office. Mr. Fleming was a widower; his house was presided over by his sister, and he had two young daughters. These ladies were also highly respectable. But there was in the background another member of the family whose respectability was not on a par with that of the rest. This was Mr. Fleming's aged parent, James Fleming, who had been a hand-loom weaver in Cumbernauld and claimed to be eighty-seven, though it was afterwards averred that he was in fact but seventy-eight. The point is of importance in connection with his alleged activities. Now old Fleming, as he was familiarly known throughout the subsequent proceedings of which he may or may not have been the occasion, had failed to attain the high standard of respectability of which his descendants were in their own persons so justly conscious. Despite their rise in the social scale, the grandfather remained a man of the working class. He spoke broad Scots, his habits were homely, his manners rude and unpolished, and he was difficult to fit into the genteel middle-class circle of which the Fleming family was an ornament. His ways were not their ways; he took his meals in the kitchen, lived largely below-stairs, and consorted chiefly with the maidservants. Now it was not mere snobbery that caused the refined Flemings thus to relegate to the basement their unattractive progenitor: the old man's character exhibited certain traits abhorrent to his self-respecting issue. If drink were available he got drunk, and in his cups he was apt to be amorous after a fashion painful to his relations and most unseemly in one of his advanced years. Nay more, in 1852 he had a child by a domestic servant, and in respect of this patriarchal lapse was rebuked by the Kirk Session of Anderson United Presbyterian Church, of which he was the oldest member, for "the sin of fornication with Janet Dunsmore." But having showed becoming contrition, he was restored to the full fellowship of the Church. This regrettable incident occurred ten years before the date of our story.

Mr. John Fleming, like most prosperous Glasgow folk, had a country house on the Clyde, whither in the summer months the establishment removed, one servant being left in town to look after the house and attend to the grandfather, as also to the father and grandson during the week, the two Johns going down to Dunoon from Saturday to Monday. Thus at the weekends the sole occupants of the house in Sandyford Place were old Fleming and the maid in charge. At the time in question this was a young woman named Jess M'Pherson, who had been for some years in Mr. Fleming's service with complete satisfaction to her employer.

Friday, 4th July 1862, is the leading date in the case. That morning after breakfast Mr. Fleming and his son left for the office in St. Vincent Street as usual and went down to Dunoon by the afternoon steamer. They returned to town by "the first boat" on Monday the 7th, going straight to the office in pursuance of their regular custom. At half-past four o'clock young John went home. The door was opened to him by his grandfather. This was quite unusual, and the lad exclaimed: "Where is Jessie?" to which the old gentleman rejoined: "She's away; she's cut. I haven't seen her since Friday, and her door's locked." "Why didn't you have it opened?" naturally asked young John, to which the patriarch replied that "he thought she was away seeing her friends and would be back again." Mr. Fleming, arriving at the moment, was told by his son of the situation. "She may be lying dead in her room," said the lad, "for anything he [the old man] knows." So the three generations descended to the basement, the grandfather making no further comment. The maid's door was locked and the key missing. Mr. Fleming tried that of the pantry adjoining; it opened the bedroom door and they all entered the room. It was in partial darkness; the blinds were down and the shutters half-shut. On the floor beside the bed lay the dead body of the unhappy maid, practically naked, with a piece of carpet covering the head. There was much blood about the room. With singular acumen the old gentleman touched at once the very kernel of the case: "*She's been lying there all this time,*" he exclaimed, holding up his aged hands, "*and me in the house!*" They then went upstairs, and Mr. Fleming ran for the doctor, Dr. Watson, who lived hard by in Newton Terrace. Dr. Watson at once accompanied him back to Sandyford Place. Having looked at the body, he remarked, with respect to the injuries which he saw: "This is evidently not a suicide; you had better call in the police," which was done; and Dr. Joseph Fleming, surgeon of police, was promptly on the scene of the tragedy, arriving there before five o'clock.

The two doctors examined the body and then turned their attention to the condition of the basement flat. In the kitchen, which immediately adjoined the bedroom, a good fire was burning. Obvious blood-stains were seen upon the "jaw-box" (sink); upon the inside of the door; and on the door-post, four or five feet above the floor. The door-mat was soaked in blood and sticking to the threshold. Along the lobby, from the kitchen to the bedroom, was a trail of blood, suggesting that the body had been dragged from the one apartment to the other. There were many other blood-stains about the flat, notably in the bedroom, of which we shall hear again. But the strangest discovery made by the doctors was this: the floors of the kitchen and bedroom, respectively of stone and wood, and the flags of the lobby, as also the face, neck, and chest of the dead woman, *had all been washed*. "The lobby was perfectly moist," said Dr. Fleming at the trial; "it was very damp, as if it had been recently washed. The kitchen floor was drier, *but still there was a damp appearance.* They had the appearance of not having been done on the same day." When that night at ten o'clock the superintendent of police and two detective officers made a thorough examination of the premises they found that the kitchen floor, though appearing to have been lately washed, *was then dry.*

Next day, 8th July, Dr. Joseph Fleming and Dr. (afterwards Professor) G. H. B. Macleod, by instructions of the Sheriff, conducted a post-mortem examination of the body, the results of which were embodied in a joint report. The doctors, *inter alia*, stated:—

> The body was lying on its back on the floor, close to and in front of the bed, the clothes of which were heaped together and in many places deeply stained with blood. The lower limbs of the deceased lay fully exposed, and a piece of carpet was thrown carelessly over the head and trunk. On removing the carpet the body was seen to be dressed in a chemise and a knitted worsted jacket. *These clothes were all quite damp,* and much stained with blood. *The neck and chest appeared to have been partially washed.* The furniture of the room was in confusion. Large drops of blood were seen on the floor, and that even at a distance of 6 feet from the body. On further examination it became apparent that the body had been dragged from the kitchen (where evidence of a severe conflict was obtained) along the lobby to the apartment in which it was found, and also that imperfect attempts had been made to obliterate the traces of this removal.

The head was horribly mangled. There were three deep *transverse* wounds upon the face: one across the forehead and two across the bridge of the nose. On the right side of the head and neck were eleven distinct incised wounds. The right ear was destroyed and the right-half of the lower jaw broken into fragments. All these wounds, in distinction to the transverse wounds on the face, *sloped from above downwards and from behind forwards*. Both the hands and wrists were mutilated, there being nine distinct wounds on each. The body was otherwise healthy and free from disease or injury. From these appearances the reporters drew the following conclusions:—

1. That this woman was murdered, and that with extreme ferocity.
2. That her death had taken place within three days.
3. That a severe struggle had taken place before death.
4. That such an instrument as a cleaver or a similar weapon was the most likely to have caused the fatal injuries found.
5. That the injuries had been inflicted before or immediately after death.
6. That all the wounds on the neck and head, with the exception of those on the nose and forehead, had apparently been inflicted by a person standing over the deceased as she lay on her face on the ground.
7. That the comparatively slight degree of strength shown in the blows would *point to a female or a weak man* as having inflicted them; and

Lastly, that the body had been drawn by the head with the face downwards along the lobby from the kitchen to the front room.

As regards the lobby, there were spots of blood on the lower steps of the stair leading to the floor above, and on the *front* of the steps marks which seemed to have been made by blood-stained skirts. There were finger-prints on the corner of the wall; a blood-smear on the inside at the top of the press door beside the kitchen; and blood behind the back door to the yard. In a room used by the patriarch as a dressing-room—he slept in the flat above—there was upon the floor a mark of blood, and some of his clean shirts in a chest of drawers were spotted with blood. In the dead woman's bedroom there was blood on the basin-stand and blood-stained water in the basin; the servant's box lay open and rifled, "as if some bloody hand had been working amongst the contents." Strangest of all, on the bare floor, beyond the margin of the washed area, were plainly to be seen three several bloody imprints of a naked foot. Finally, in a drawer of the kitchen dresser was found a butcher's cleaver, eminently adapted to produce the injuries; clean, but as afterwards appeared, bearing traces of blood.

## II

There were missing from the servant's box two silk dresses, one black and one brown, a silk "polka" or jacket, and other garments. There were also missing from the dining-room side-board sundry silver and plated spoons, etc., which the maid had out for daily use. A valuable silver tea-service was left there untouched. The cruet bottles were upon the sideboard, but the cruet-stand was found near the body in the servant's room. Particulars of the missing articles were published in all the Glasgow newspapers and issued in official handbills.

Despite the *prima facie* appearance of burglary presented by these facts, old Fleming, as the last person to see the dead woman alive and having spent three days in this bloodstained house without raising any alarm, was very properly in-terrogated by the police; and so unsatisfactory did his account of his behavior seem to the official mind, that on 9th July he was apprehended on a warrant from the Sheriff on the charge of being concerned in the crime. The Sheriff of Lanarkshire, before whom he was brought for examination, was Sir Archibald Alison, the distinguished historian, who justly observes of old Fleming's conduct after the murder that it was "extremely suspicious." His examination lasted for four hours and on its conclusion he was committed to prison. That is all we are permitted to know about the matter, though in view of later developments it were vital to have heard the old man's original version. In England he would, of course, have been a witness at the inquest and his evidence fully reported; in Scotland, however, the preliminary investigation into a criminal case is conducted in private by the Procurator-Fiscal, as Crown prosecutor, and the result is kept secret from the vulgar. While I consider that as a general rule our system is the better one, like all rules it is subject to exception, a fact of which the Sandyford case forms undoubtedly a flagrant instance. Superintendent M'Call, who apprehended Fleming, stated in cross-examination at the trial: "He made a statement to me. He said he had been wakened by screams, *which he attributed to loose characters at the back of the house*; that he looked at his watch and saw that the time was 4 a.m." Lord Deas stopped at this point the line of cross-examination, which he thought "might lead to the contradiction of what had been said out of the box"!

The obvious difficulties of the patriarch's position were these: Having heard such screams in the night and finding the maid missing in the morning, with her bedroom door locked, he did nothing whatever about it, raised no alarm, made no inquiries, and carried on as if everything were all right. Yet he admitted noticing that morning the spots of blood on his shirts. In these circumstances he lived alone in the house for three days without saying a word about the matter to the several persons with whom he had occasion to talk, particularly an admirer of the maid, who called twice to see her! Finally, the noticeable blood-stains in and about the kitchen where he passed his time; and the *recent* washing of the kitchen floor and of the lobby.

Meanwhile the boards of the bedroom floor containing the bloody footprints were removed for skilled examination. Dr. Macleod found that the impressions were totally different from the feet both of old Fleming and of the deceased. In his judgment they were those of a female.

The advertisements speedily bore fruit. On the 9th the police learned from a pawnbroker in East Clyde Street that the missing plate had been pledged for £6. 15s. at midday on Saturday, the 5th, by a woman who gave a false name and address. On the 13th the police, acting upon information received —plainly from the patriarch—went to a house in the Broomielaw and took into custody a sailor named James M'Lachlan and his wife, Jessie M'Intosh or M'Lachlan, as being concerned in the crime. The apprehension of the mariner was merely a device of the authorities to get him to testify against his wife, seeing they were then aware that he had been in Ireland with his ship at the time of the murder. Mrs. M'Lachlan, being judicially examined, denied that she had been at Sandyford Place on the night of 4th–5th July. She said that the plate in question had been given to her by old Fleming the day before, with instructions to pawn it as he was short of money. After she had done so, he called again, gave her £4 for her trouble in the matter, and received from her the balance. He warned her to tell no one of this curious transaction. She was examined at vast length on this and two subsequent occasions as to her own dresses and those of the deceased, and the tactics of the Fiscal were successful in involving her in a mass of falsehoods and contradictions. Strong objection was at the trial taken by the defense as to the manner in which these "voluntary" declarations were extorted from the accused. Its gross unfairness is manifest from the shabby trick played upon her at her third examination. The Fiscal, having found the box in which she had sought to conceal the missing clothes, questioned her in detail as to Jess M'Pherson's wardrobe. She denied that she had lately seen any of the items referred to; whereupon the Fiscal confronted her with the recovered garments, which she then said had been given to her by the deceased to be altered and dyed. This official trap-laying would have seemed to Mr. Sapsea "un-English," and is certainly foreign to Scots practice. We shall hear the true history of the dresses later.

It was further ascertained by elaborate tests that hers was the foot which had undoubtedly left the bloody imprints in the dead girl's room, a fact held conclusively to prove that Mrs. M'Lachlan had a hand—or rather a foot—in the affair. Now while her concern in the matter was obvious, this in nowise affected the "extremely suspicious" behavior of old Fleming, and in the circumstances both prisoners ought to have been indicted for the murder and jointly have been tried therefor. But the authorities took a different view—it was said at the time that the Fiscal was an intimate friend of the Flemings—so the old man was set at liberty to bear witness, whether true or false, against his fellow-prisoner. As was well observed by the *Spectator* in an admirable article on the case:—

> Strange to say, the Glasgow authorities seem to have adopted at once, and with an almost personal bias, the latter, and to our minds we will not say the least probable, but the more improbable of these two hypotheses. The fact of Mr. Fleming's innocence was assumed as an axiom, and the object of the prosecution appeared to be not so much to prove that Jessie M'Lachlan was guilty of the murder as that Mr. Fleming had no concern with it whatever.

The Press on the whole, with the exception of the *Glasgow Herald*, which held from the first a brief for "the old innocent," was of the same opinion.

### III

The case was set down for trial at the Glasgow Autumn Circuit. This course was highly prejudicial to the accused. The crime had aroused unprecedented excitement in Glasgow, and to meet the popular demand the local newspapers of the day anticipated the most unscrupulous methods of modern journalism. Detectives were dogged by reporters and the results of their discoveries regularly published; witnesses examined by the Fiscal were waylaid and their proposed evidence printed in full, with editorial comments; correspondents were encouraged to air the most fantastic theories as to how the accused committed the murder, to suggest all sorts of motives, and to asperse with irresponsible spitefulness her character and previous conduct. So profitable proved this scandalous campaign, that since the publication of the precognitions [witnesses' statements] began, the circulation of certain of the daily papers rose from 10,000 to 50,000! In these disgraceful circumstances it was manifestly impossible that the accused could have a fair trial in Glasgow. Six years earlier fortunate Miss Smith, and three years later pious Dr. Pritchard, though their alleged crimes were committed in Glasgow, were each tried at Edinburgh. And *they* were both popular prisoners, courteously treated by the local Press. *A fortiori* Mrs. M'Lachlan should certainly have been tried before the same Court, where, by the then existing practice, her case would have been presided over by the Lord Justice-Clerk and two Lords of Justiciary. As it was, it was dealt with by a hostile jury and a single Judge.

Unfortunately for his judicial reputation, it fell to the lot of

Lord Deas to try the Sandyford murder case. His Lordship was a senator of strong character, high integrity, and great experience; powerful in personality, masterful in mind, learned in the law; but so far from being of counsel with Portia in the article of mercy as to be termed by the profane a "Hanging Judge." The prosecution was conducted by an Advocate-Depute —the chief law officers of the Crown do not attend the Circuit Courts—Adam Gifford (afterwards himself a Judge), assisted by a junior. Andrew Rutherfurd-Clark (later a well-known Senator of the College of Justice), with two juniors, appeared for the defense. The trial took place in the Old Court in Jail Square, and the proceedings lasted from 17th to 20th September 1862. As I have elsewhere devoted to these an entire volume,[1] in which the evidence and speeches are printed at length, together with the additional evidence taken at a subsequent inquiry, and other documents relative to this most amazing case, all that I need do here is to give the reader a brief narration of what happened at and after the trial.

The Court-house was besieged, and those concerned in the case had literally to fight their way into Court. The prisoner, who was quietly dressed and perfectly composed, was placed at the Bar. She pleaded Not Guilty to the charge, and her counsel lodged a special defense: "that the murder alleged in the indictment was committed by James Fleming." John Fleming and his son having given their account of the discovery of the crime, James Fleming entered the witness-box. Nothing could have been more respectable than the appearance presented by "the old gentleman," as Lord Deas termed him. Of grave demeanor, attired in his best Sunday blacks, bald, aquiline, silver-whiskered, he looked a typical Free Kirk elder of the old school. He was wearing spectacles, but let out that they

---

1 *Trial of Jessie M'Lachlan.* Notable British Trials series, 1911; second edition, 1925.

had only been given to him that very morning, and admitted that he could see "gey weel" without them! So they may be regarded as part of his excellent make-up. The only infirmity of age to which he pleaded guilty was being "a little dull o' hearing."

The patriarch gave his evidence in broad Scots and his testimony is reported in the vernacular, tempered slightly by the shorthand writer for behoof of the Sassenach reader—the only instance of the kind known to me. He told the following tale. He was employed by his son to look after certain house property in the Briggate. He knew the deceased. On Friday, 4th July, he was alone with her in the house. He went to bed at half-past nine; the girl was still busy with her work in the kitchen: it was washing-day. At four o'clock next morning he was awakened by three loud "squeals," which suggested to his mind that the maid had a sister spending the night with her! He slept again till six, from which hour he lay waiting for the servant to bring him his porridge according to her daily custom. She did not do so, and at nine he arose and dressed. On research, he found her bedroom door locked and "gied three chaps" (knocks) which met with no response. The pantry window, giving upon the area, was open and he closed it. He made up the kitchen fire. His first caller was a maid from next door, who requested "the len' [loan] o' a spade," with which he was unable to oblige her. This was at eleven, and he then noticed that the front door, though closed—"just snecked, ye ken"—was unlocked. The next person to call was the baker, from whom he accepted a half-quarter loaf. At twelve he repaired to the office, did some business in the Briggate, and so home by bus at two o'clock. He made himself a "bit dinner." At seven came a third ring at the bell. This was the maid's young man, who had arranged with her to call and was disappointed to learn from the patriarch that she "wasna in." Leaving his name he went his way. The old man then put away his clean

shirts, which, since the maid had washed them, had been drying on a "screen" before the kitchen fire. He noticed "there was two marked with blood on them." He supped at eight and retired at nine. "On Sabbath morning the bell was rung by the milkman, *but I did not answer.*" After breakfast—tea and a boiled herring—he went to church as usual, speaking to a neighbor by the way. Fortified by a dinner of bread and cheese, he attended divine service in the afternoon. That evening the maid's young man repeated his call and was surprised to hear that she was out again. At half-past nine the patriarch sought his couch. Monday was a busy day, for then the tenants paid their weekly rents. The old man was up and doing by eight o'clock, went off to the office for his books, thence to the Briggate "to lift what he could," returning to the office in the afternoon to lodge with the cashier the proceeds of his industry, and going home at two o'clock. It should be noted that to none of the several persons with whom he spoke on the Saturday, Sunday, and Monday did he say one word as to the mysterious disappearance of the servant. Having described the finding of the body and identified the pawned plate, which he denied giving to the accused, he said that he knew her when in his son's service three years before and had visited her once at her own house since. With that single exception he had never seen her after she left until confronted with her on his examination before the Sheriff—when, as was stated in the Press at the time, he denied that he ever knew her!

"Was your watch right that Saturday morning?" was Mr. Rutherfurd-Clark's first question on rising to cross-examine the venerable witness, for this matter of *time* was to be the touchstone of the truth or falseness of his story. He stuck to it that he did not rise till nine and that the first person he spoke to was the girl for the spade, who called at eleven. The front door was not on the chain when he opened it to her. Then Mr. Clark put his crucial question, which in the sequel was to

become historic: *"Did the milk come that Saturday morning?"*
Surely an easy enough question for one of the witness's remarkable power of memory, though strange to say he found
the greatest difficulty in replying to it. But Mr. Clark would
have an answer. Seven separate times the witness swore that
the milkboy did *not* call that morning. Finally, he was brought
to admit that the boy *did* call—"betwixt eight and nine," that
he opened the front door "on the chain" and said he did
not need any milk, and that he was then dressed. Being reminded that he had sworn he did not rise till nine, the patriarch paused for a space and slowly replied: "Whether I
was dressed or not I cannot charge my memory." To the next
question: "Why did you not let Jessie open the door as usual
when the milkboy rang?" the old man returned the startling
answer: "ON SATURDAY MORNING, YE KEN, JESSIE WAS
DEID; SHE COULDNA OPEN THE DOOR WHEN SHE WAS
DEID!" Asked whether he then knew that she was dead? he
replied, sharply and with emphasis, that he did not. In further cross-examination, being reminded of the cries of distress
heard by him in the night, the servant missing, her door
locked, and the blood upon his shirts, did he not suspect some
evil had befallen her? he said he "never thocht onything was
wrang"—which, as we shall presently see, implies a lack of
interest strangely at variance with his proved character. None
of the significant appearances in the kitchen and lobby attracted his attention during that weekend; neither did it occur
to him to inform the police or have the maid's door opened;
not to tell the milkboy, the baker, the servant from next door,
Jessie's young man, his friends at church, or the people at the
office that the maid had vanished. He never thought that she
had run away; yet his first mention of her to anybody was:
"She's away, she's cut!" Old Fleming was the only witness
in the case to whom the Judge put no questions; but his Lordship made many observations very helpful in relieving him

from the undue pressure and inconsiderate persistence of Mr. Rutherfurd-Clark.

Before leaving this branch of the case it may be convenient for the reader to know how far the evidence of the old gentleman was supported by the sworn testimony of other witnesses. I have summarized the proven facts as follows:—

1. That old Fleming was notoriously of an abnormally suspicious and inquisitive disposition; that nothing could take place in the house without arousing his curiosity; that the door-bell could not be rung without his knowing the cause, and that he would even rise from his bed to look out of the window on such occasions; that if a servant left the house upon an errand he must know where she had been and what she did; that he devoted much attention to acquiring a full knowledge of such visitors as came to see the servants, and if possible personally interviewed them; that he extended the sphere of his observations to the servants next door, so far as he had opportunity of spying upon their movements; and that in everything relating to the deceased girl, who enjoyed a special share of his attentions, he was known to be peculiarly interested.

2. That the milk was usually delivered at the house not later than twenty minutes to eight in the morning; that prior to the Saturday in question he had never answered the door to the milkman; that at 7:40 a.m. on that day the milkboy rang the bell once as usual; that there was no delay in answering his ring; that the boy heard the chain being taken off the door; that old Fleming, dressed in black clothes, himself opened the door, and said "he was for nae milk"; and that never before that morning had milk been refused at that house.

233

It will thus be seen that not only was the patriarch uncor-roborated, but that his evidence was in all vital points flatly contradicted.

The movements of the accused on that eventful night were proved by certain friends and neighbors. She made no secret of her intention to visit Jess M'Pherson that evening, and arranged with a woman to look after her young child during her tem-porary absence. Another woman, who chanced to call as she was dressing to go out, accompanied her part of the way to Sandyford Place. She left her own house at ten o'clock, remark-ing that she always went late so as to let old Fleming be in bed. She returned at nine o'clock next morning, carrying a large bundle, and was admitted by the neighbor who was attending to her child. She was then wearing a brown dress different from that in which she had gone out. That day she paid her ar-rears of rent: £4, and pawned the plate for £6. 15s. The clothes of the deceased she packed in a box and dispatched by rail, ad-dressed: "Mrs. Darnley, Ayr." The clothes she herself had worn that night she sent off in a trunk, addressed: "Mrs. Bain, Hamilton." Both were labeled: "To lie till called for." It need hardly be added that these apocryphal consignees had no exis-tence. They were the creatures of Mrs. M'Lachlan's imagina-tion, as was the immortal Mrs. Harris of Mrs. Gamp's. The accused went later personally to Hamilton, uplifted the trunk, which she left at a saddler's to be repaired, and walked out into the country, carrying a bundle. Near where she was seen to go there were afterwards found in a hedge certain torn pieces of clothing, blood-stained, which were identified as the skirt and petticoat worn by her on the night of the murder. Finally, she had burnt her crinoline in the fire and given the wires thereof to a lady friend; these also, despite the cleansing process, re-tained traces of blood. So in addition to the footprints, there was clear evidence of the prisoner's presence in the house at the time of the crime.

Among other witnesses called for the Crown was the servant from next door, who had proposed to borrow a spade from old Fleming. She stated that she did so on the Saturday afternoon *between two and three o'clock*. The door was opened by the patriarch, whom she accompanied downstairs to the back door. He went out to the washing-house, and returning said that it was locked. She suggested searching the kitchen for the key, but he said he had looked there already, so she was not admitted to the kitchen. The deceased's young man stated that he called for her twice: on the nights of Saturday and Sunday. On the first occasion old Fleming, in reply to his questions, admitted that "Jessie had been out a good while"; on the second, when witness said she was surely very often out, he made no reply. A fellow church member stated that he had a conversation with old Fleming on the Sunday, and the cashier at the office described his interviews with him on the Saturday and Monday. To neither of these witnesses did the patriarch make mention of the maid's disappearance. Mr. Clark asked the elder if he were aware that the venerable adherent had been up before the Kirk Session, but Lord Deas, very jealous for the old gentleman's repute, disallowed the question. Of the medical evidence given by Drs. Watson, Fleming, and Macleod we have heard the general purport. They spoke to the remarkable character of the wounds: the three *transverse* cuts across the face, the multiple injuries to the back of the head and neck, and the incisions upon the hands and wrists: all which could have been inflicted with the cleaver produced. They also described the extraordinary appearance of the body: the underclothing quite damp, the face, neck, and chest washed with water; and the partial washing as well of the bedroom and kitchen floors as of the lobby between them. The only expert from whom we have not yet heard was Professor Penny of the Andersonian University, who examined the remains of the accused's apparel, recovered from Hamilton as already mentioned; the crinoline wires; and the cleaver, upon each and all of which he found stains and clots of blood.

To the admission of the prisoner's declarations, which it was then proposed to read, Mr. Clark strenuously objected as having been extorted from the accused by questions; in respect of the inordinate length of her examinations; and on account of the traps laid for her by the Fiscal as before narrated. Lord Deas repelled the objections, holding that there was no ground in law for refusing to admit these declarations. They were read to the jury accordingly; but in the legal journals of the day the soundness of his Lordship's ruling was questioned. Here endeth the case for the Crown.

IV

The evidence of the witnesses for the defense, though brief, was cogent. George Paton, milkman, who had been long in use to supply the Flemings' daily wants, stated that on Tuesday, the 8th, he heard of the servant's death. On the previous Saturday he stopped his cart as usual at No. 17 Sandyford Place between half-past seven and twenty minutes to eight in the morning. His boy Donald went up to the door and rang the bell. It was immediately answered, witness could not see by whom, as the door was only opened "a small bit." No milk was taken in. The same thing happened on the Sunday and Monday mornings. These were the only occasions when milk had not been taken in at that door.

Donald M'Quarrie, the milkboy, stated that he went his rounds with his master's cart on the Saturday in question, reaching No. 17 at the accustomed hour: about twenty minutes to eight.

I went up and rang the bell. Old Mr. Fleming answered it. I did not ring more than once. I had not to wait any time before it was answered. The first thing I heard after ringing the bell was the chain coming off the door.

Are you quite sure of that?—Yes. After the chain came off, the door was opened by old Mr. Fleming. I saw him. He was dressed. He had on black clothes. He said "he was for nae milk." Witness never knew of old Fleming answering the door before.

Mrs. Mary Fulton or Smith stated that she had known the deceased intimately for some six years. She also knew the accused as a friend of the dead girl, who always spoke of her in most affectionate terms. She last saw Jess M'Pherson alive on 28th June, when walking in Sauchiehall Street with her husband, and noticed that she seemed unwell. "I do not feel very happy or comfortable with old Mr. Fleming," Jess told her, "for he is actually an old wretch and an old devil." This she said very seriously. Witness remarked that she was looking ill and asked what was wrong with her. "I cannot tell you what the cause is," she replied, "because Sandy is with you"; but she promised to come to tea next Sunday, the 6th, her day out. "And then," said Jess, "there is something I would like to tell you." The secret was plainly of a nature so delicate that it could not be communicated in the hearing even of a married man. What it was Mrs. Smith never learned, for on her next Sunday out poor Jess was indeed gone out—forever.

Mrs. M'Kinnon, a sister of the deceased, stated that Jess and the accused were affectionate friends. A month before the murder witness called on her sister and asked why she never came to see her. She said she had too much to do, adding "that her heart was broken by the old man, who was so inquisitive that the door-bell never rang but he must see who it was and know all about them." Martha M'Intyre, another servant of

Mr. Fleming's stated that the old man was most curious as to the maids' doings—particularly so in all that related to the deceased. Witness had known him get out of his bed to see who had rung the door-bell. Ann M'Intosh, sister of the accused, stated that James M'Lachlan, her husband, earned 30s. a week, which he invariably gave to his wife. (He must have been an ideal husband.) The accused's brother also contributed to her needs; he gave her money after every voyage and had given her 25 sovereigns last November. (He must have been a model brother.)

Robert Jeffrey, criminal officer, who conducted a search of the premises after the murder, stated that he found in old Fleming's bedroom a canvas bag, having on one side of it a bloody mark. He also found under a chair a strip of cotton, spotted with blood. On Mr. Rutherfurd-Clark asking what had become of these significant finds, of which the defense now heard for the first time, witness said they were handed by him to the Procurator-Fiscal, who gave him a receipt therefor. It seems that subsequently they disappeared from the case, presumably as not forming links in the chain wherewith the Crown sought to bind the prisoner to the crime. Lord Deas suggested that the marks might have been other than bloodstains, but witness declined to accept his Lordship's hint. Superintendent M'Call, who saw and examined the stains, corroborated.

The last witness examined was a police constable, who alleged that between 8:30 and 9 p.m. on Saturday, 5th July, he saw two women come out of the front door of 17 Sandyford Place. They stood talking together for five minutes; then one went away and the other re-entered the house. (He seems to have mistaken the night.) Here endeth the case for the defense.

## V

Before we glance at the addresses of the learned counsel and the charge of the presiding Judge, it were well to remind the reader of certain proven facts whereof the case for the prosecution, as presented, offered no explanation. Such were the washing of the body, the dampness of the clothes, and of the lobby and the kitchen floor, the three footprints—on which alone the Crown could prove the presence of the prisoner in the house —so considerately left intact by the criminal when washing the rest of the bedroom floor, the trifling value of the articles abstracted, and finally the inexplicable lingering of the accused on the scene of her alleged crime: the murder being committed, according to old Fleming, at "exactly four o'clock—a bonny, clear morning," and Mrs. M'Lachlan not going home with her bundle till nine. Should it be said that she did so in order to remove from the vigilant and then unspectacled eye of old Fleming the damning traces of the deed, it may be answered that while this might be so as regards the kitchen and the lobby, it is inapplicable to the cleaning up in the bedroom, the door of which was locked and the key missing. If that kitchen floor were washed by the accused before nine o'clock on the Saturday morning, how came it to be still moist at five o'clock on the Monday afternoon, though dry by ten that night? It was a stone floor and, we are told, would dry rapidly, there being a good fire. But for none of these anomalies could the prosecution satisfactorily account.

The Advocate-Depute handled his case delicately. In view of the obvious stumbling-blocks in the prosecutor's path caused by the peculiarities of his chief witness, it behoved him to emulate King Agag. He relied for a conviction mainly upon the footprints of the accused, her all-night absence from her home, her pawning of the plate, her dealing with the deceased's garments, and her disposal of her own blood-stained raiment. Mr. Gifford's white-washing of old Fleming, essential to a verdict adverse to the accused upon the charges as libeled, was surprisingly half-hearted and inadequate. The old gentleman, said he, had been aroused at 4 a.m. by cries of distress, had lain awake from 6 to 8, and risen at 9—although it was clearly proved that he was up and dressed before 7:40! (As the accused did not leave the scene till 8:30, it would never have done for the patriarch to admit an earlier rising.) With reference to these facts, and to what Mr. Gifford termed "the extraordinary circumstances of this case, which distinguish it from all others": the presence of old Fleming in the house at the time of the murder and his behavior during the ensuing three days: he justly observed that "*the gravest possible suspicion attached to such a person so acting,*" and the jury could not wonder that he was apprehended and charged with being concerned in the crime.

> But the guilt of James Fleming is not the subject of inquiry at all. It is possible, in crimes of this kind, that more than one person is connected with it. If guilt be brought home to one, it will not be enough to say: "Somebody else had a share in it." If there were more murderers than one, and if the prisoner was one of them, you must find a verdict against her. For the question is, and it is the only question: Is the prisoner guilty or is she not guilty?—not had she confederates, not was she alone?

Even the prosecutor could not put it higher than that. He spoke for over two hours; and at 7:30 p.m. on the third day of the trial, Mr. Rutherfurd-Clark rose to address the jury. As a defending counsel in criminal causes, like his gifted successors, the late Lord Aitchison and Mr. Macgregor Mitchell, he had no equal at the Scots Bar, and the fine fight which three years later he was to put up for wicked Dr. Pritchard is still recalled with admiration. But in the M'Lachlan case, as we shall soon see, he was hopelessly handicapped by the tactics which the accused's advisers, in their mistaken attempt to do the best for their client, had seen fit to adopt; and his argument, though brilliant and resourceful, was vitiated by his knowledge of its essential hollowness. On the conclusion of his address, which occupied an hour and a half, the Court rose.

The fourth day of the trial, Saturday, 20th September, began with the Judge's charge to the jury. His Lordship's handling of the case was not the least of the remarkable features by which it is distinguished. The charge had a bad Press. "The conduct of Lord Deas," observed the *Law Magazine and Review*, "has been almost universally censured. . . . Instead of maintaining a proper judicial equilibrium, and holding the balance of justice even, he put his foot fiercely into one scale and kicked at the other. We shrink from the unpleasant task of analyzing his charge. . . . It lasted four hours, and from beginning to end of it there is not one observation favorable to the prisoner; not one fair consideration of a doubt in her favor; not one suggestion that any fact renders her guilt a matter of the least doubt. On the contrary, facts that in our humble opinion tell strongly in her favor are either quietly ignored or disposed of by reckless assertion of the most transparent sophistry. . . ." The grave censure thus expressed by this responsible legal journal is mild in comparison with the torrent of adverse criticism poured forth by the popular Press, always excepting the *Glasgow Herald,* which rejoiced at the judicial vindication of "the old innocent." His Lordship's treatment of the evidence incompatible with the innocence of Fleming was a conspicuous element of this singular charge: the patriarch was too stupid to notice the condition of the basement flat or to make any inquiries; the milkboy had mistaken the time; what the deceased meant by calling him an "old devil" was that he might "look a little sharply" after the maids, and so on, and so forth. But the masterpiece of this judicial gloss upon the proven facts was his Lordship's explanation of the secret which the dead girl could not tell her friend Mrs. Smith in the presence of that lady's husband: *"What she might have to say was that she was going to emigrate"*! The fact that when Lord Deas took his seat that morning he carried in his hand and laid down upon the Bench before him the Black Cap, the symbol of the prisoner's doom, showed plainly that he was prepared for the worst; and the jury, following his Lordship's lead, and having presumably weighed the three-days' evidence with that scrupulous care and caution requisite to a matter of life or death, *after an absence of fifteen minutes* returned to Court with a unanimous verdict of Guilty.

## VI

And now I am free to disclose an astonishing incident with which I have been longing to confound the reader, a surprise so unlooked for and dramatic as would make the fortune of any writer of fiction—although I do not expect that it will make mine. The Advocate-Depute moved for sentence; and while the verdict was being recorded and the Court hummed with suppressed excitement, the prisoner summoned her counsel and earnestly spoke with him for a space. Whereupon Mr. Clark announced that his client wished to make a statement, either by her own or by his lips, and Lord Deas said she could do so. Then for the first time the voice of Jessie M'Lachlan was heard in that chamber. Throwing back her veil and standing up in the dock she said loudly and distinctly: "I desire to have it read, my Lord. I am as innocent as my child, who is only three years of age at this date."

Amid a thrilling silence Mr. Rutherfurd-Clark rose to read

one of the most remarkable documents ever read in a court of justice. I shall have much to say about it later; meantime the reader should note that it, the statement, was made by her to her law agents on 13th August, so soon as she learned that old Fleming had been set at liberty, and was by them taken down to her dictation and signed by her. She told how on that fatal night she set forth to visit her friend. Contrary to his custom and to her expectation, she found old Fleming still up and sitting with Jess in the kitchen. The patriarch hospitably produced a bottle and they had each a dram. Reference was made to Mr. John Fleming having commented on the undue consumption of his whisky, which the patriarch had accounted for by saying it had been used by young John. "However," said he to Jess, "if ye'll haud your ill tongue, I'll gi'e ye half a mutchkin, if ye'll sen' for't." To which overture the girl replied: "Aye, I've a tongue that would frighten somebody if it were breaking loose on them"—a dark saying. The bottle giving out, Fleming asked the visitor to have it replenished and handed her 1s. 2d. for that purpose. He let her out at the back door into the lane. It was then hard upon eleven o'clock, and when she reached the public house in North Street, she found it closed. Returning empty-handed to the house, she saw in Elderslie Street one Mrs. Walker, whom she knew by sight, talking to a friend. She found the back door shut; none answered her knock, and she looked in at the kitchen window; the gas was lighted but she saw nobody. The more important passages of the statement must be given in her own words.

> I rapped at the door with the lane door key, and after a little old Mr. Fleming opened the door. He told me he had shut the door on "them brutes o' cats." I went into the kitchen, and put the money and bottle on the table. The old man locked the door and came in after me. I told

him the place was shut and I could get nothing. I then said: "Where's Jessie? It's time I was going home." He went out of the kitchen, I supposed to look for her, and I went out with him. When in the passage, near the laundry [bedroom] door I heard her moaning in the laundry [bedroom] and turned and went past the old man, who seemed at first inclined to stop me. I found Jessie lying on the floor, with her elbow below her and her head down. The old man came in close after me. I went forward, saying: "God bless us, what is the matter?" She was stupid or insensible. *She had a large wound across her brow and her nose was cut*, and she was bleeding a great deal. There was a large quantity of blood on the floor. She was lying between her chest and the fire-place. I threw off my bonnet and cloak, and stooped down to raise her head, and asked the old man what he had done this to the girl for? He said he had not intended to hurt her—it was an accident. I saw her hair all down, and she had nothing on but a polka and her shift. I took hold of her and supported her head and shoulder, and bade him fetch me some lukewarm water. He went into the kitchen. I spoke to her and said: "Jessie, Jessie, how did this happen?" and she said something I could not make out. *I thought he had been attempting something wrong with her*, and that she had been cut by falling. He did not appear to be in a passion and I was not afraid of him. He came in again, bringing lukewarm water in a corner dish. I asked him for a handkerchief and some cold water, as the other was too hot. He brought them in from the kitchen, and I put back her hair and bathed away the blood from her face and saw she was sore cut. I said to the old man: "However did he do such a thing to the girl?" and he said he did not know, and seemed to be vexed and put about by what had happened. I asked him to go for a doctor, but he said she would be better soon, and he would go after we had got her sorted. The old man then went ben the house again, and I supported her, kneeling on one knee beside her. In a little she began to open her eyes and come to herself, but she was confused. She understood when I spoke to her, and gave me a word of answer now and then, but I could get no explanation from her, so I just continued bathing her head. I bathed it for a long time, until she got out of that dazed state and could understand better. I asked her whether I would not go for a doctor, and she said: "No, stay here beside me." I said I would. While I was sorting at her head, the old man came into the room with a large tin basin and soap and water in it, and commenced washing up where the blood was all round about us, drying it with a cloth and wringing it into the basin. I had raised Jessie up and was sitting on the floor beside her. As he was near us, he went down on his elbow and spilt the basin with a splash. *He spilled the water al' over my feet and the lower part of my dress, and my boots were wet through.*

Jess asked to be put into her bed, and as Mrs. M'Lachlan was unable alone to lift her—she was a big, heavy woman—old Fleming lent a hand. As she seemed to be getting weaker Mrs. M'Lachlan again begged him to let her fetch a doctor. He looked at the patient, and said: "There was no fears; he would go for the doctor himself in the morning." She lay with her eyes shut till the day was beginning to break—about three o'clock. The old man was in and out of the kitchen making up the fire and preparing tea. Mrs. M'Lachlan took off her wet boots and stockings, and carried them "ben" to the kitchen to dry. During old Fleming's absence Jess regained consciousness. She told her friend that some weeks before the old man had been out on the spree with a brewer of his acquaintance and came home at 11 p.m. "gey tipsy." During the night he entered her room and bed, and attempted to take advantage of her. Upon her "outcry" he desisted, and withdrew to his legitimate couch. Next morning she threatened to tell his son, her master, of the outrage, but he begged her not to do so, attributing his lapse to drink taken, and promising not so to offend further. There had been "words" between them about it ever since; old Fleming continuing in terror lest his backsliding should be revealed. That night, so soon as Mrs. M'Lachlan had left for the half-mutchkin, there arose between them an angry scene, the patriarch construing her reference to her tongue breaking loose as a threat to disclose to her friend his naughtiness.

> She had given him some words in the kitchen, and he was flying and using bold language to her in the lobby after she was in the room, and she was giving it him back while loosening her stays; when he was there and going to take them off she went and shut the door to in his face, and *he came back immediately after, and struck her in the face with something and felled her....* She also asked me if she was badly cut, and I said she was, and she said when the doctor came in the morning she would need to tell some story or other how she got it.

Without telling old Fleming that she now knew the truth, Mrs. M'Lachlan again asked him why he had struck the girl? He said he was sorry and would make it up to Jess, and that if she, Mrs. M'Lachlan, would never mention what she had seen, he "would not forget it to her," whereupon she justly observed that it was a great pity she had anything to do with it. Jess said she must tell what had happened to the doctor or to Mr. John

Fleming. "No, no, Jess," said the patriarch; "ye'll no' need to do that," adding that if they held their tongues he would "put everything to rights."

> He would not rest content till I would swear it, and he went upstairs and brought down the big Bible with a black cover on it, and he made me swear on the Bible by Almighty God that I would never tell to man, woman, or child anything I had seen or heard between him and Jess that night. He said that he would make her comfortable all her life. After this he sat at the bedside.

Jess having occasion to rise, the old gentleman was requested to leave the room. She was very stiff and weak, and complained of being cold; so Mrs. M'Lachlan put a blanket round her, recalled the patriarch, and between them they got her into the kitchen and laid her on an improvised couch before the fire. Between four and five she grew rapidly worse and asked her friend to go for a doctor. The old man was then upstairs. Mrs. M'Lachlan put on her boots and Jess's French merino dress over her own, which was "all wet and draggled," and went up to the front door, but found it locked and the key removed. She asked old Fleming to let her out as the girl was dying. He refused. She then went into the back parlor and threw up the window to see if she could see anyone whose aid she could invoke, but saw no one.

> I was leaving the parlor to go into the dining-room to look out in front when I heard a noise in the kitchen. I turned downstairs as fast as I could, and as I came in sight of the kitchen door *I saw the old man striking her with something which I saw afterwards was the meat chopper. She was lying on the floor with her head off the pillow, and he was striking her on the side of the head.*

> When I saw him I skirled [shrieked] out and ran forward
> to the door, crying to him; and then I got afraid when he
> looked up, and I went back up part of the stair, where I
> could go no further, as I got very ill with fright and palpi-
> tation of the heart, to which I am subject.

Holding to the wall, without power of motion, she stood
crying: "Help! help!" The old man came to the stair foot and
looked up at her. "Oh, let me away, let me go," she cried; "for
the love of God, let me go away!" He came up and took her by
the cloak, and said: "I kent frae the first she couldna live," and
that if any doctor should come he would have to answer for
her death, as she would have "told." "Don't be feart," he continued; "only, if you tell you know about her death you will
be taken in for it as well as me. Come down, and it can never
be found out." She was terrified, alone in the house with the
murderer and his dead victim, and knew not what to do. "My
life's in your power," said the tempter, "and yours is in mine";
if both would keep the secret, both were safe. But if she informed on him, he would deny the deed and charge her with
the crime. He asked her to help him to wash up the blood upon
the kitchen floor, but she was incapable of action.

> He took the body by the oxters [arm-pits] and dragged it
> ben into the laundry [bedroom], and took the sheet and
> wiped up the blood with it off the floor. When he took
> up the sheet I saw the chopper, all covered with blood,
> lying beneath it. I beseeched and begged of him to let me
> go away and I would swear never to reveal what I had
> seen, in case of being taken up for it myself as well as
> him. *He said that the best way would be for him to say
> that he found the house robbed in the morning, and to
> leave the larder window open.*

The old man then gave her certain of the dead girl's gowns, instructing her to send them by rail to some out of the way place to lie till called for. Afterwards he brought down the plated spoons, etc., and directed her to pawn them in a false name—all this to simulate a burglary.

He got some water at the sink in a tin basin and washed himself. He had taken off his coat and was in his shirt sleeves since after the time he killed the girl. His shirt was all blood when he took it off to wash himself, so he put it in the fire. He put on a clean one off the screen, and went ben to his own [dressing] room and changed his trousers and vest. He went down to the cellar for coals, brought them up, and put them on the fire. *The bell rang. He bade me open, but I said: "No, I'll not go to the door; go you."* IT WAS THE MILKBOY. *The old man took up no jug with him. He was in his shirt sleeves when he went up, but in a coat when he came down again. He brought no milk with him.*

He presented her with £1. 7s., which she agreed to accept, together with the other articles, promising never to breathe a syllable of what had passed. He said he would never see her want and would set her up in a shop. About 8:30 he let her out at the back door into the lane, and she made her way home in safety. She declared that she never had any quarrel with Jess; they were always most affectionate and friendly.

The reading of this document, which occupied forty minutes, was listened to by the crowded audience with breathless and intense excitement. No one knew what would happen in a situation at once so surprising and unprecedented. But Lord Deas was equal to the occasion. Having narrated at length the manner in which he conceived she had done what he termed "her bloody work" and barbarously butchered her bosom friend, his Lordship expressed his entire concurrence in the verdict. "There is not upon my mind a shadow of suspicion that the old gentleman had anything whatever to do with the murder." As counsel and Judge he had never known statements made by prisoners after conviction to be other than false. A person who had committed a crime such as that of which the prisoner had been convicted was capable of saying anything. "Your statement," said his Lordship in conclusion, "conveys to my mind a tissue of as wicked falsehoods as any to which I have ever listened; and in place of tending to rest any suspicion against the man whom you wished to implicate, I think *if anything were awanting to satisfy the public mind of that man's innocence, it would be the most incredible statement which you have now made.*" Lord Deas then assumed the Black Cap and passed sentence of death, ending with the formal commendation of the prisoner's soul to the mercy of the Almighty. "Mercy!" exclaimed the doomed woman in the dock, "aye, He'll hae mercy, for I'm innocent!"

## VII

Lord Deas's dictum as to the effect of the Statement upon the public mind proved unsound. The Press, not only of Glasgow, but of London and the provinces, was loud in denunciation of the conduct of the trial, the verdict, and the attitude which the Judge had seen fit to adopt throughout, especially with reference to the prisoner's Statement. Only the *Glasgow Herald* rejoiced at the complete vindication of "the old innocent." Sir Archibald Alison, who as Sheriff of Lanarkshire had conducted the preliminary inquiries, has well observed: "She had not a fair trial; the minds of the jury were made up before they entered the box." And he comments on the indecency of a verdict returned in fifteen minutes after a judicial charge lasting four hours. In his judgment there was a miscarriage of justice. "The Statement," he points out, "bore the mark of truth, coincided in a remarkable way with the evidence, and explained much in the case which was otherwise inexplicable."

Immediately upon her conviction Mrs. M'Lachlan's law agents, a reputable firm of Glasgow writers, addressed to the Press a letter describing the circumstances in which their client had made to them her Statement. From the time of her arrest she insisted "that Mr. Fleming would surely [certainly] clear her." When she learned from them of the old man's release, she was so greatly astonished that she would not believe it, until she sent for her husband to confirm the fact. She then informed her agents that she had a communication to make to them, and on 13th August the famous Statement was made. *The indictment was not served till the 30th*. On the 13th, therefore, they knew not what evidence would be brought against her, nor had they seen any of the witnesses for the prosecution. They had nothing to go on but the newspaper reports, for Mrs. M'Lachlan would give them no information whatever. The Statement was most anxiously considered by her counsel and agents; the former were of opinion that as the Crown might fail to prove her presence in the house that night, her admission to the contrary must at all costs be suppressed. But it was decided to lodge a special defense that old Fleming committed the crime. Before the Court met on the last morning of the trial Mrs. M'Lachlan sent for her counsel and agents, and insisted that her Statement should be read aloud in open Court. Mr. Rutherfurd-Clark's decision to suppress it was much blamed at the time, and as things turned out this was certainly a grave error in tactics; but it is easy to be wise after the event. The fact, however, greatly hampered him both in his cross-examination of old Fleming and in his address to the jury.

Now that the cat was out of the bag, public opinion ran

strongly in favor of the condemned woman's story; and the demand was urgent that its truth or falsity must be determined before she was sent to her death. Memorials were addressed to the Home Secretary both by her counsel and agents and by the general public. Committees were formed, meetings were held, even sermons were preached, for the purpose of securing a reprieve. Deputations waited upon the Lord Advocate and the Home Secretary. Never in any trial before or since was there such an ebullition of public feeling. Sheriff Alison and the Lord Provost of Glasgow lent the weight of their authority to a petition for further inquiry; and the eminent Professor (later Lord) Lister wrote to the editor of the *Herald*—who must have been much annoyed—expressing his opinion "that the medical features of the tragedy are in remarkable accordance with the prisoner's statement." On 3rd October a respite was granted from Whitehall to allow of time for some further investigation; but it was intimated that if such failed to confirm the truth of the prisoner's Statement, "*no hope can be held out to her of commutation of the capital sentence.*"

Meanwhile the venerable cause of all this fuss was confined to the house by reason of the popular resentment. On leaving the Court he had been assailed by groans, hoots, and hisses from an angry crowd, and hardly escaped undamaged from their hands. He fled to the villa at Dunoon, where the *Herald* described him as reading with much interest the printed comments upon the trial; but other papers proclaimed him the object of hostile demonstrations, and on occasion, like an early martyr, he was even stoned. So late as November he was reported to be mobbed at Greenock. What Lord Deas thought about this treatment of his protégé is not recorded.

Mr. George Young, who had been Solicitor-General the year before, and afterwards became a distinguished Judge, was appointed Crown Commissioner to conduct the investigation, which opened on 17th October. The proceedings, invidiously known as "The Secret Inquiry," were held in private; the Crown being represented by the Procurator-Fiscal and the prisoner by one of her agents, Mr. Dixon. The Commissioner had no power to compel the attendance of witnesses nor to administer the oath to such as were called before him; and the order of their coming was arranged by the Procurator-Fiscal, who, as the official instigator of the recent prosecution, seems hardly the ideal person to inquire into his own conduct.[2] The investigation was concluded on the 20th and the result communicated to the Home Secretary. On the 28th the convict was respited "until further significance of Her Majesty's pleasure." On 6th November the death sentence was commuted to penal servitude for life.

This illogical and anomalous conclusion pleased nobody. Had the case occurred to-day and been reviewed by the Court of Criminal Appeal, Mrs. M'Lachlan could have been allowed to give evidence in her own behalf and been cross-examined as to its veracity; old Fleming, too, could in the witness-box have been treated with a freer hand than Mr. Clark was able to use at the trial. But the patriarch remained in seclusion at Dunoon, and the Fiscal refrained from intruding upon his retirement. His law agents, however, were very indignant at the Secretary's decision, which they held—and justly—"led to the inference that, in his judgment, Mr. Fleming was other than innocent of the murder." The Secretary intimated that he "must decline to express any opinion on that point," and the matter came to nothing. But when we remember that the first respite was granted on the express stipulation that unless the truth of her story were established the woman must be hanged, the commutation had indeed in his agents' words, "brought suspicion

---

2. These Gilbertian conditions curiously anticipated those under which a similar Official Inquiry was, subsequent to the trial, held in the case of Oscar Slater by the Sheriff of Lanarkshire at Glasgow in 1914.

on the hitherto unblemished character of Mr. Fleming"! But I think that in the circumstances "the old gentleman" did not do so badly after all. Whatever happened, having been accepted as a witness for the prosecution, he could never be arraigned at mortal bar. How it might fare with him at that of a Higher Tribunal does not concern us.

## VIII

The Sandyford Mystery was the subject of two long debates in the House of Commons, in the course of which the Home Secretary defended the action of the Crown. The Statement, he said, was corroborated in many respects by the subsequent inquiry; admittedly Mrs. M'Lachlan was an accessory after the fact, and as such had now received suitable punishment. The Lord Advocate (Moncreiff) explained for the benefit of his English critics the reason why, according to Scots law, old Fleming could not be put on trial for the crime.

Subsequently the papers called for in the debate and ordered to be printed were laid before the House, and formed the subject of further discussion, not only in Parliament but in the Press. Seventy-six witnesses had been examined at the trial; sixty-nine were called at the inquiry. Most of these had testified before, but some were new. The prisoner's law agents told how she made her famous Statement. They knew nothing of the milk episode until she mentioned it, and only then got into touch with the milkboy and his master. The Flemings, father and son, had nothing material to say; but they admitted that there were openly in the house two silver tea-services, which were untouched, and that the whisky had a habit of disappearing. Old Fleming's hour of rising was nine. The deceased never had anyone staying the night with her. Mr. Stewart, their next-door neighbor, said that on the night of the murder he went to sleep at eleven and was awakened two hours later by a scream from the Flemings' house. Mrs. Walker and friend said they saw the accused in a gray cloak go into the lane at a quarter past eleven. Another woman corroborated these twain, and further stated that on passing No. 17 thereafter, she heard a wailing cry, as of someone in great distress, and saw that the windows in the area—those of the servant's bedroom—were lighted. Three sisters, going home from a dance, saw the dining-room gas alight at four o'clock in the morning. The milkboy and the milkman repeated their former evidence. The man had looked at his watch while the boy was at the door: it was exactly twenty minutes to eight. They called as usual on the following Sunday and Monday mornings. On each occasion old Fleming answered the bell and refused to take delivery of the milk.

One of the most interesting of the new witnesses was Miss Mary Brown, aged sixteen years. She said the deceased used to employ her to wash the steps and go errands. She called by her appointment at nine o'clock on the Saturday morning. Old Fleming opened the door upon the chain, let her in, and put up the chain again. He was dressed in black and had on a "Sunday" coat. He asked her to wash the upper hall near the head of the stair, and gave her a cloth and a pail of water for that purpose. The floor was dirty, "as if trampled on by persons having *soot* on their feet." She smelt soot at the time. She saw no marks of blood, but one mark of a naked foot. The old man stood beside her all the time, and when her job was done and she was going downstairs to empty the pail, he bade her leave it where it was. "He spoke only once, when I was going away. *He catched a grip of me by the hand and put his hand on my waist, and said I was a nice girl.*" He then gave her sixpence for her trouble and dismissed her. She told her mother, who said she must hold her tongue "for fear she might get into some hobble about it." Mrs. Jane Pollock or Brown corroborated her daughter's evidence. Now if, as the *Herald* averred, little Mary were telling lies, she was surely an artist in fiction: the passage which I have italicized, if invented, is a masterstroke.

The three Crown experts were re-examined with reference to the medical features of the Statement. These were entirely consistent with all the appearances observed by them. The wounds on the face might have been received while the deceased was standing; they would fell and stun her. The other injuries were inflicted while she lay on the floor. Dr. Macleod still stuck to the evidence of a struggle, which he said he observed in the kitchen: there was nothing else he saw contradictory of the Statement. Certain of the Briggate tenants, from whom on the Monday old Fleming had collected rent, stated that he then wore his best black clothes, not those he wore "for ordinary," that his manner was "raised like," and they thought something had happened to agitate him. Daniel Paton, clothes dealer, denied the fact, sworn to by Fleming at the trial, that he had sold to him an old brown coat. Much evidence was given by the friends and neighbors of the prisoner to the effect that she was of a very mild, gentle, and kindly disposition, neither thriftless, extravagant, nor prone to drink; and that she was a woman who, in the quaint Scots phrase, "enjoyed" but poor health.

Mrs. Mary Smith, re-examined, said that the prisoner and the deceased were almost like sisters. Jess often told her how she was tormented by old Fleming and could not get quit of him. She frequently said he wanted to marry her; she seemed disgusted by his attentions. On the last occasion of their meeting, a fortnight before her death, witness said: "She was looking very ill; I never saw her looking so melancholy . . . She said: 'I'm no' weel. You don't know how I am situated; I live a miserable life. He [James Fleming] is just an old wretch and an old devil.' I said: 'Tell me the right way of the story; what has he done to you?' She said: 'I have something to tell you, but I cannot tell you just now before your husband.' She made the remark that she was well enough when the family was at home, and that *her misery began when she was alone with him.*" Witness was positive there was something gravely wrong from the serious tone in which Jess spoke. It is reassuring, however, to know from Lord Deas that it only denoted a purpose of emigration.

Mrs. M'Kinnon, sister of the deceased, said that a month before her death Jess told her that her heart was broken by old Fleming, whom she described as "an auld deevil," adding that she intended to give up her place at the end of the six months. Witness never spent the night with her sister, and old Fleming had no reason to suppose so. A fellow-servant of the deceased stated that Jess spoke of the old man as *"a nasty, dirty body"*; witness understood he had behaved indecently to her. The gardener at Dunoon stated that Jess told him old Fleming was very anxious to marry her, "and would give her all he had if she would do it." The brewer friend, with whom the patriarch had a day out as already mentioned, denied that old Fleming went home tipsy: "he was hearty and in good spirits." But the cabman who drove him home said he was so drunk he had to be helped up the steps. The ministers and elders of that Presbyterian temple in which old Fleming was as a polished corner, deponed reluctantly to the patriarchal lapse before referred to. A sheriff-officer, who had sifted the ashes of the kitchen fire, stated that he found therein a shirt button. Many other witnesses were examined, but these are those who contribute chiefly to our knowledge of the facts.

The outcome of the inquiry was this: on each and every point in which Mrs. M'Lachlan's statement was capable of confirmation, its truth was clearly established; in no single instance was it in any respect contradicted. It fitted the proven facts so perfectly as to render its fabrication incredible. If it were false, then in Mrs. M'Lachlan we have lost a fictionist more marvelous than Defoe; one so adroit as to foresee and account for facts and circumstances which it is humanly impossible she could have known she would be called upon to meet. And this masterpiece of mendacity, this feat of fraudulence, this dexterity in deceit was achieved by the illiterate authoress of those clumsy and idiotic declarations, concocted in her early efforts to escape from the meshes of the net wherein she had been so cunningly entangled—which, as Euclid would say, is absurd. On literary grounds alone, apart from all question of corroboration, the statement, in my judgment and *pace* Lord Deas, warrants belief. Only a supreme artist could have supplied the numberless minute touches, the telling strokes, which produce the lifelike effect of the figured scene. If these be lies, then indeed, as an humble tiller of the field of letters, I admire Mrs. M'Lachlan's genius as greatly as I do that of her so gifted sisters, Miss Austen and Miss Ferrier.

## IX

For fifteen years Jessie M'Lachlan "dreed her weird" within the gloomy precincts of H. M. General Prison of Perth. She was a model convict. Years afterwards the chaplain told me her conduct was exemplary, and that throughout the long term of her punishment she ceased not to proclaim her innocence of the deed for which she had been condemned. On 5th October 1877 the gates of her prison-house were opened and she was released on ticket-of-leave. For the leading of a new life she was provided with a sum of £30, the wages due to her in respect of her penitentiary labors. She was in her four-and-fortieth year. After the trial her husband had emigrated with her child, now a lad of eighteen, and was living in the United States.

At first she sought refuge with a cousin in Greenock, where

she hoped gradually to recover the sense of a living world. Looking backward across the gulf that separated her from the dreadful past, it must have seemed to her impossible that those old dim happenings should be still remembered. So much was changed, so many things had since befallen, that none could yet bear in mind the memory of her tragedy. But she knew not the inexhaustible persistence of a public-spirited and resourceful Press! Word of her release "transpired"; speedily she was pursued, run to earth, and taken captive by enterprising journalists in quest of copy. She was paragraphed and interviewed, and only escaped the camera's fire because it had not yet occurred to our reporters to shoot their prey. The victim of newspaper enthusiasm found life a burden to her; so, seeing that in Scotland there was no rest for even the relatively wicked, she fled her native country and rejoined her husband in America. How she fared in the Land of Freedom is not recorded. She died at Port Huron, Michigan, on New Year's Day 1899, as her son intimated to the Greenock cousin, in the sixty-sixth year of her pilgrimage. Her death was due to an old affection of the heart, from which in her Glasgow days she had been wont to suffer. Whether or not in another and a better world she met once more her ancient enemy, who had long preceded her beyond the veil, is a matter of conjecture.

Should this partial and imperfect outline of her most attaching case arouse in some sympathetic bosom any interest, I would counsel the owner thereof to read the verbatim report of the trial. No mere abridgment can do justice to its manifold attractions. Indeed, as regards the Statement, none can possibly appreciate its merits who has not studied it *in extenso*. To compare her story of the crime with the facts established at the trial and the inquiry, will furnish an intellectual pastime more entertaining and worthier the effort than the solving of many cross-word puzzles. But in an age of short-cuts and substitutes, when the part is esteemed greater than the whole, I have small hope that anybody will take my advice. If not, why then so much the worse for us both: the loss is his, and mine— or rather, my publishers'.

■

Twice have I had occasion to call at Sandyford Place and, like the heroic milkboy, to ring the bell of No. 17. The first time was while collecting my material; the second, to introduce Mr. Irving, who, having read my book, desired to view the *locus* of a crime which peculiarly appealed to him. He was bred to the Bar, and in such cases had the advantage of the popular crimi- nologist: he was an expert in his subject. We were courteously received by a genial physician, for thirty years the tenant of the house, which despite its grisly history he deemed a most desir- able abode. Although the surroundings were different the house itself was unaltered; just the same as when gazed at long ago by morbid-minded crowds, a twelve-months' wonder to the curious. The grim little kitchen, the narrow lobby, the ill- lit bedroom within the shadow of the area—all were un- changed since that fatal Friday night on which was staged by its three protagonists the dreadful drama of the murder. We were cautioned not to discuss the case before the maids when we explored the basement flat, as they were happily ignorant of its darker associations. Probably they took us for sanitary inspectors, which indeed, in a sociological sense, we were.

"H. B." conceived the notion of having a play written upon the tragedy; but alas, it never came to birth. He himself was keen to impersonate the patriarch, in whom he perceived a character study after his own heart. Doubtless he could have done so to the life, as far as acting and make-up were con- cerned. But I am afraid that old Fleming's broad Scots would have proved too strong for him in the end. Someone has since made a fiction out of the old facts, transferring the scene and the actors to England, and raising the social status of the parties to a degree that would have been most gratifying to the Flemings. But I doubt whether Jessie gains anything from her enhanced gentility, while I am sure that "the old gentleman" loses much by dressing for dinner.

## THE BALHAM MYSTERY

*I know your mind, and here I have it for you.*
*Put but a dram of this into his drink,*
*Or any kind of broth that he shall eat,*
*And he shall die within an hour after.*

— ARDEN OF FEVERSHAM

THERE IS NOT much mystery about Balham nowadays—
unless it be why anyone should wish either to go or stay there;
but in the summer of 1876 it was a name to conjure with, a
word of sinister significance and power, compelling for many
months the attention of the English-speaking race. The Bedford Hotel, strange stage of this strange drama, was occupied,
in other than the common sense, by votaries of the Bar; its
precincts were invested by an army of Pressmen, its doors be-
leaguered by the clamorous lieges; and the presiding Coroner,
like an apostolic Christian, was compassed about by so great a
cloud of witnesses that he knew not which way to turn. The

case, which conferred upon an uninteresting suburb a temporary distinction, still keeps its proud position as the prize puzzle of British criminal jurisprudence; and this despite the fact that while murder was indisputably done, no trial followed, neither was any person charged with the crime, though the guilty party was certainly a member of the dead man's household, and testified in the flesh at the inquest! In our leading Scots poisoning case, of which the heroine was the matchless Madeleine Smith, the chief mystery for me has ever resided in the amazing fact of her acquittal; which likewise is my sole perplexity regarding that of her English rival, Adelaide Bartlett. More doubt attaches to the conviction of Mrs. Maybrick, whom I am disposed to deem the victim of a miscarriage of justice. But the Balham Mystery continues an unsolved riddle, a problem presented by Providence to the ingenuity of the posterities. Of course, the law officers of the Crown, and those charged with the duty of conducting the investigation, had no doubt at all where the guilt really lay; but the circumstances were such as to afford immunity to the murderer, and the sword of Justice remained undrawn.

In every poisoning case with which I am acquainted it was the possession or acquisition of the means of death that brought home the crime to the criminal; here, however, there is not the slightest evidence of either. A large dose of antimony—*pace* Dr. Pritchard, an unusual and unlikely poison for the purpose—had been introduced into the body of the murdered man; but where and when that antimony was obtained, by whom it was procured, and how administered, were points upon which there was no clear light. The one solid fact to which a study of the evidence inevitably leads is, that Charles Bravo did not commit suicide, and that death by misadventure is out of the question. He was willfully slain by someone within his gates, by someone whose enmity he had no reason to fear and in whom he had perfect confidence, by someone who, favored by a unique combination of chances, as well as by great coolness and cunning, contrived, in the Scots vernacular euphemism, to "cheat the wuddy" after all.

The case has been in our day admirably dealt with by an eminent hand[1]; but having become possessed of a verbatim contemporary report of the whole affair, illustrated by most intriguing woodcuts,[2] I am tempted to re-tell the story after my own fashion. That story I venture to think one of the strangest chapters in the history of crime, and as such it can hardly be told too often, so that it be told well. I shall do my best; should it fail of interest, be mine the blame.

I

On 7th December 1875, at All Souls, Knightsbridge, Charles Delaunay Turner Bravo, barrister-at-law, was married to Mrs. Florence Campbell or Ricardo, widow. Both were on the sunny side of thirty, handsome, healthy, born of rich city folk; Fortune, in the fullest sense, seemed to smile upon their union. The bridegroom, who to his own name of Turner had added that of his wealthy stepfather, lived with his people at No. 2 Palace Green, Kensington. After a creditable school and college career, he had been called to the Bar, where he was diligently building up a practice, occupying chambers in Essex Court, Temple. The bride was the daughter of Mr. Robert Campbell, of Buscot Park, Berks, and No. 37 Lowndes Square. She had married in 1864, at the age of nineteen, a young officer of the Guards, named Ricardo, but the venture turned out badly.

1. *The Bravo Mystery and Other Cases*, by Sir John Hall, Bart., pp. 1–104. London: 1923.

2. *The Balham Mystery: a Complete Record of the Bravo Poisoning Case*. In seven parts with eighty engravings. London, No. 39 Bedford Street, Strand: n.d. [1876].

There were faults on both sides. The Captain proved more attentive to his bottle than to his bride; the lady consulted her elderly physician, and availed herself of his pharmacy to an undue extent. Divorce was spoken of; but in the end the parties agreed to a voluntary separation, the wife receiving an annual allowance of £1200. In 1871, when the warrior finally laid down his arms, it was found that he had omitted to revoke the will made in his wife's favor on their marriage, so his widow was consoled by an income of between £3000 and £4000 a year. Mrs. Ricardo then lived at Streatham Hill; and in 1874 she removed to a larger house, The Priory, Bedford Hill Road, Balham. Included in the new establishment was a lady friend, also widowed, named Mrs. Jane Cannon Cox, who had been for some years her paid companion. This lady, who hailed from Jamaica, where her husband had died, leaving her with little money and a small family, received assistance and advice from Mr. Joseph Bravo, the well-to-do stepfather of the barrister, who himself had large interests in the island. At his suggestion she invested her inconsiderable means in renting a house in Lancaster Road, Notting Hill, with a view to letting it furnished; he also placed her three boys in St. Anne's Asylum School at Streatham. Thus, by the benevolent aid of Mr. Bravo senior, Mrs. Cox's burden was substantially lightened, and she added to her resources by going out as a daily governess. Among the pupils privileged to enjoy her educational career were the children of Mrs. Ricardo's solicitor, Mr. Brooks, at whose house the ladies met and liked one another; and their intimacy increasing, Mrs. Ricardo offered Mrs. Cox the position of companion, with a salary of £100 a year. That the middle-aged, unprepossessing, indigent gentlewoman should be attracted to the rich and beautiful young widow is not surprising; what Florence Ricardo saw desirable in the West Indian relict is another story. Be the facts as it may, it was, for her, a fatal hour when she first set eyes upon the uninviting countenance of

Jane Cannon Cox. That lady had indeed, as the phrase is, fallen on her feet. She passed at once from toil and penury to a luxurious and easy life. The housekeeping at The Priory was on a lavish scale: men and maidservants in plenty, horses and carriages enow; all the amenities of a wealthy middle-class Victorian home: verily, the ex-governess had secured what is vulgarly termed a soft job, one which she was little likely voluntarily to relinquish. And she was not treated as a dependent; her footing was that of a dear and valued friend (plus the salary); the ladies called each other by their Christian names.

Now it came to pass that one day Jane was moved to pay a visit of gratitude to Mr. Joseph Bravo, her benefactor; and Florence drove her up to town, arranging to call for her later. When the carriage returned to Palace Green, Mrs. Bravo invited Mrs. Ricardo to come in; she did so, and was by Mrs. Cox introduced to the family, including the son of the house, who happened (for his sins) to be present. Soon afterwards, when the ladies went to Brighton for a change, whom should they meet in the King's Road but young Charles Bravo, who had followed them from town. So rapidly did the acquaintance ripen that when in the autumn the Brighton episode terminated, Charles and Florence had become engaged. The path of true love presenting none of the customary obstacles—the widow was handsomely dowered, and Mr. Joseph Bravo settled on his stepson £20,000, payable on the death of the last surviving parent—there was nothing to delay their happiness, so the couple were married in a month. The sole discordant note was struck by Mrs. Bravo senior, who disliked her daughter-in-law from the first, and declined to attend the wedding. But the beautiful bride did not trouble her head about the old lady's maternal jealousy. The honeymoon was spent at Brighton, and after a duty visit to their respective people, the happy pair took up house at The Priory in the beginning of January 1876. They were welcomed home by the faithful Mrs. Cox, for Florence had stipulated, and Charles with a lover's complaisance had agreed, that the indispensable dame should continue to afford them the comfort of her company on the old terms.

In the opinion of friends and acquaintances, as well as in the judgment of the Vehmgericht of the servants' hall—that grim tribunal that sits upon us all impartially—the marriage was a success. The young couple were obviously, in the language of the day, attached; they "wrote home" enthusiastically of their mutual happiness and affection; the omens seemed wholly propitious. Mr. Bravo was inclined to be "close," and looked somewhat too narrowly at both sides of a penny; but with their ample means this idiosyncrasy was negligible. He went up to town every day, to attend the Courts or to visit his chambers, returning at eventide to dinner; his wife, whose domestic duties devolved upon her capable companion-housekeeper, drove her smart pony phaeton and pair, of which she was extremely proud, and employed the aimless leisure of a lady of that genteel period in unnecessary shopping and the paying of perfunctory calls. But even into the most placid stream it is the practice of Fate to cast an occasional stone: Mrs. Bravo had a miscarriage in January, and again on 6th April her hope of becoming a mother received a second check. She suffered severely and made a slow recovery; it was proposed that when she was convalescent she should be taken for a change to Worthing.

Let us pause for a moment to consider the kind of house in which Charles Bravo had thus so comfortably hung up his hat. Situated at the end of Bedford Hill Road and abutting on Tooting Bec Common, The Priory is described in the contemporary account as "a stuccoed structure of that bastard style of Gothic architecture which Horace Walpole may be said to have inaugurated by the erection of Strawberry Hill." The grounds, which covered some ten acres, were well arranged and kept; there were pineries, vineries, and melon pits; and a five-acre paddock for the saddle and carriage horses, of which husband and wife were equally fond, though Charles was but an indifferent horseman. Two entrance lodges respectively accommodated coachman and gardener. The house was of three stories, but we are here concerned only with the ground and first floors. The former contained, on the one side, the drawing-room and the dining-room; on the other, the morning-room and the library. Above the dining-room was the chamber of the married pair, next to which, over the drawing-room, was the bedroom whither, pending his wife's recovery from her indisposition, the husband had been relegated. Across the landing were two dressing-rooms, appropriated to the wedded couple. Mrs. Cox commonly slept upon the third floor, but since her friend's temporary divorce she had shared with her the conjugal couch. It should be borne in mind that the doors of Mrs. Bravo's bedroom and of that occupied by Mr. Bravo immediately adjoined, and that both faced the head of the main staircase from the hall.

## II

Tuesday, 18th April 1876, is the crucial date in the case. At nine o'clock that morning the indefatigable Mrs. Cox might have been observed (by a reader of Mr. G. P. R. James) setting forth, fortified with a flask of sherry, upon her way to Worthing, to look for a furnished house. An hour or so later Mr. and Mrs. Bravo, attended by coachman and footman, drove in the landau to town. She dropped him at the Turkish Baths in Jermyn Street, and then went on to the Stores, where she bought "some very choice tobacco" for her lord, of whose customary brand she disapproved, returning to The Priory at two o'clock to "partake," in the language of the time, of a champagne luncheon. Meanwhile Mr. Bravo, after a more modest repast, which he described as "a jolly lunch," consumed with an uncle of his wife at St. James's Restaurant, walked to Victoria accompanied by a barrister friend, whom he invited home to dinner. Most unfortunately, this friend was engaged, but he promised to go down to The Priory next day to try the new tennis court. Mr. Bravo got home at four o'clock; cheerfully and affectionately kissed his wife, who was resting on a sofa in the morning-room; changed, and then went for an hour's ride on the Common. He was, as I have said, a bad rider; his horse bolted with him, and he came back so shaken and stiff that his wife prescribed a warm bath before dinner—quite an adventure, as appears, in mid-Victorian days.[3]

The dinner hour was half-past seven; Mrs. Cox had not then returned; but after they had waited for her a few minutes, she arrived, and having no time to dress, immediately joined her hosts at table. The meal consisted of whiting, lamb, poached eggs on toast, and a bloater-paste savory, of all which, excepting the fish, Mr. Bravo "partook." The wine decanted for the occasion by the butler comprised one bottle each of Burgundy and Marsala, and two bottles of sherry—surely a generous provision for three persons. Bravo alone drank Burgundy, of which he had three glasses; the two ladies, between them, disposed of the sherry—a bottle apiece![4] After a brief adjournment to the morning-room, the ladies, at a quarter to nine, retired to rest. Mrs. Bravo was still, officially, an invalid; Mrs. Cox had had a tiring day; and this "intolerable deal of sack" may well have

---

3. As an instance both of Mr. Bravo's thrift and of his intention to survive, he told the housemaid to leave the water in the bath, "as it would do for him in the morning."—*The Balham Mystery*, p. 51.

4. The butler afterwards deposed that between 11th March and 18th April the average fortnightly consumption of wine amounted to over thirty-three bottles; one hundred and thirty-four bottles for the eight weeks! Even the genteel Victorians could "do it" when they liked.

induced a desire for repose. The servants were then at supper, and Mrs. Bravo asked her friend to fetch her another drink, which that obliging dame did, in a tumbler, from the dining-room. Next, Mary Ann Keeber, the housemaid, came up to the dressing-room with a can of hot water; and her mistress, who was now undressed, bade her bring "a little Marsala." As the girl left the dining-room with the tumbler of wine, Mr. Bravo came out of the morning-room, looked at her without speaking, and went up to his wife's room. There, addressing her in French, presumably because of the maid, he said, "You have sent downstairs for more wine: you have drunk nearly a bottle to-day"; a just observe, to which Mrs. Bravo made no response. He then went into his own bedroom and shut the door. There-after, for some fifteen minutes, Mary Ann was busy putting away her mistress's clothes in the dressing-room, after which she went into the bedroom to ask whether anything further was required, and was told by Mrs. Cox, who was still up and fully dressed, to take away the pet dogs for the night. Mrs. Bravo was in bed, apparently asleep. As the maid stood on the staircase calling the dogs, her master's bedroom door sud-denly opened and he appeared on the landing in his nightshirt, shouting loudly: "Florence! Florence! hot water! hot water!" Realizing that something serious had happened, Mary Ann rushed into the ladies' room, announcing to Mrs. Cox—who, curiously, had heard nothing of these cries for help uttered within a few feet of her—that Mr. Bravo was taken ill; and fol-lowed by the maid, that lady came out to see what was amiss. Mr. Bravo had gone back to his room and was vomiting vio-lently out of the window. Capable Mrs. Cox at once sent Mary Ann for hot water and mustard; when the girl returned her master had collapsed on the floor, and Mrs. Cox was rubbing his chest. What passed between that ministering angel and the sufferer, during the maid's brief absence and before he lost consciousness, will be discussed later. Mrs. Cox then went downstairs herself, and ordered the butler to send the coach-man for Dr. Harrison of Streatham Hill—instead, as one should have expected from one of her capacity, for the nearest doctor.

Meanwhile Mary Ann had wakened Mrs. Bravo, and told her that Mr. Bravo was very ill. Twice crying, "What is the matter?" the wife threw on her dressing-gown and hastened to her husband's assistance. She was horrified to find him lying insensible on the floor by the window: "he was looking like death." The moment she heard that Dr. Harrison had been summoned from Streatham, she said to Mrs. Cox, "Why didn't you send for Dr. Moore?" who lived hard by. Running down-stairs, she met the butler as he returned from his message to the lodge. She was crying, he says, and seemed sincerely anx-ious. She bade him fetch Dr. Moore forthwith, which he did. When Dr. Moore came shortly after ten he found the two ladies with the patient, who had been lifted into a chair; he was totally unconscious, the pulse barely perceptible. "He looked like a person who was under the influence of poison," but what poison, the doctor failed to ascertain. He was put to bed, and Mrs. Bravo asked whether his condition was danger-ous; being told to expect the worst, she burst into tears, her grief appearing to Dr. Moore to be perfectly genuine. Some half-hour later Dr. Harrison arrived. He was met at the door by Mrs. Cox, who was more communicative to him than to his confrère; she informed him of the vomiting at the window and of the administration of the mustard emetic, adding: "*I am sure he has taken chloroform.*" After consulting with Dr. Moore, Dr. Harrison saw the patient, who was in a state of collapse and quite insensible; he was given an injection of brandy. In consequence of Mrs. Cox's statement the doctors searched the room; they found three bottles: one of chloroform, another of laudanum, and a third of camphor liniment: these were the only visible drugs.

The physicians were nonplussed; they suggested getting another opinion, to which Mrs. Bravo at once agreed, sending her carriage to bring from Harley Street Mr. Royes Bell, surgeon, a cousin of her husband and his intimate friend. At 2:30 a.m. (Wednesday, 19th April) that gentleman, together with his colleague Dr. (afterwards Sir George) Johnson, Senior Physician of King's College Hospital, reached The Priory; they consulted with the other two doctors and saw the patient, who at 3 a.m. recovered consciousness. They were satisfied that he was dying of a powerful irritant poison. Dr. Johnson asked him what he had taken; he said he had rubbed his gums with laudanum for neuralgia, and might have swallowed some. Dr. Johnson said, "Laudanum won't explain your symptoms"; to which the patient replied, "I have taken nothing else; if it was not laudanum, I don't know what it was." Mr. Bell was then called out of the room by Mrs. Cox, who said she had a communication to make to Dr. Johnson. To him she stated that when she first entered Mr. Bravo's room he said to her. *"I've taken some of that poison, but don't tell Florence."*[5] Dr. Johnson naturally replied, "Did you not ask him what he had taken, when he had taken it, and why he had done so?" She said, "No; he told me nothing more than that."[6] Dr. Johnson then returned to the bedside. "Mrs. Cox tells us you have spoken to her of taking poison," said he; "what's the meaning of that?" "I don't remember having spoken of taking poison," said Bravo. "Have you taken poison?" asked the doctor; the patient repeated his former statement as to the laudanum. Asked whether there were any poisons about the house, he said, "Yes; chloroform, laudanum, and rat poison in the stable." He was perfectly

---

5. It was, presumably, to keep the matter secret from his wife that a few seconds earlier he had shouted on the landing, "Florence! Florence!"

6. This statement, Dr. Johnson learned later from Drs. Harrison and Moore, had been withheld from them during their four hours' anxious attendance upon a dying man.

conscious, and the doctor was satisfied that he understood every word that was said to him.

Meantime the symptoms—abdominal pain, vomiting, and purging—continued their distressing course.[7] At 5:30 a.m. Dr. Johnson left, taking with him certain ejected matters, which he tested for *arsenic* with negative results. Mr. Bell remained in charge of the case. Between 11 and 12 on the Wednesday forenoon the dying man, being somewhat easier, asked his wife, Mrs. Cox, and the doctor to pray with him; he said the Lord's Prayer, in which they all joined. He then dictated to Mr. Bell his will, leaving his whole property to his wife and appointing her his sole executrix. Seeing him still restless, Mr. Bell asked whether he had anything on his mind, to which he answered, "No"; adding, "I have not led a religious life." Rowe, the butler, who was devoted to his master and did all he could in the sickroom, gives us the following graphic glimpse of the situation: "Every now and then they [the doctors] asked him what else he had taken, saying that laudanum would not account for his symptoms; but every time, he said he had only taken laudanum. He was asked so often that he seemed to get angry at last, and then he said, 'If I knew what I was suffering from, why the devil should I send for you?' "—which, to me, has about it the ring of truth.[8]

That morning Mrs. Bravo had telegraphed to her father and mother-in-law, who were at St. Leonards, and they arrived in the afternoon, bringing with them Mr. Royes Bell's sister, and old Mrs. Bravo's maid, Amelia Bushell, who had known Charles half his life. They took charge of the sickroom, Florence making no objection; she was, Bushell tells us, pale and weak, and quite unequal to the nursing. Till then she had been constantly

---

7. Strangely enough, cramp, a usual feature of antimonial poisoning, was not present.

8. *The Balham Mystery*, p. 14.

in the room, her husband often asking her to kiss him and calling her by a pet name. "What a bother I am to you all, Florrie," said he in the intervals of his pain; and he begged her to "bury him without fuss." "What have you taken, Charlie, to make you so ill?" she asked; but such was his anguish that he could only call upon his Savior for mercy.

Next day, Thursday, 20th April, the doctors informed the family that the case was hopeless and they could do no more. Mrs. Bravo then said, "You have had your way, you have given him up; now I must have my way as his wife," and she told them she had been advised—by whom, will presently appear—to try a mustard poultice, and small doses of *arsenicum*—a homeopathic drug. Dr. Johnson objected to the poultice on the ground that the patient was already sufficiently tormented, but permitted the *arsenicum*, which, Mrs. Bravo claimed, relieved the sickness. It was obtained from Mrs. Cox's medicine chest. Dr. Johnson next brought down Mr. Henry Smith, surgeon, of King's College Hospital, whose wife was a sister of Mrs. Joseph Bravo and who had known Charles from a boy. He asked the patient no questions and had nothing to suggest as to treatment.

Meanwhile Mrs. Bravo, having lost faith in the five medical experts, regardless of professional etiquette had sent Mrs. Cox to London with a note to the great Sir William Gull—who, with the unqualified assistance of Providence, had five years before saved the life of the Prince of Wales—to come and see if he could help her husband. Mrs. Cox, curiously, told him nothing as to the nature of the illness. Sir William, in the circumstances—he knew Mrs. Bravo's people—was willing to waive ceremony, and accompanied Dr. Johnson to The Priory. They differ, as we shall find, in their accounts of what occurred. "This is not disease," said Sir William, after examining the patient; "you are poisoned; pray tell me how you came by it?" He said he took it himself: laudanum. "You have taken much more than that," said Sir William; and then solemnly adjured

him to tell what it was, as it might help them to find an anti-
dote. "Before God," said the dying man, "I took only laudanum."
"If you die without telling us," Dr. Johnson warned him, "someone may be suspected of having poisoned you." "I know that,"
was the reply, "but I can tell you nothing more." Sir William,
having heard of the vomiting from the window, looked out,
and saw lying on the leads a portion of the ejected matter
—there had been heavy rain overnight, and much of it was
washed away. What remained was collected with a spoon and
placed in a sealed jar for subsequent analysis. That none of the
other doctors had thought of doing this is surprising. After the
great physician had left the room the patient insisted on his
being recalled. What followed is described by Miss Bell: "The
deceased moved himself in the bed and said, 'Sir William, I
wish to tell you now that I have told you the truth, and nothing but the whole truth.' Sir William said, 'You must consider
the gravity of your situation, and of all that you say and do.'
Deceased said, 'I know that; I know I am going to appear before
my Maker. I have told them all so [i.e. that he had taken nothing but laudanum], and they will not believe me.'. . . Deceased
asked them if they could not give him something to relieve his
pain, and was there really no hope? Sir William said, 'There is
very little life left in you—in fact, you are half-dead now.' "[9]
Thereafter the patient gradually sank and died at 5:20 a.m. on
Friday, 21st April, some fifty-six hours from the onset of the

---

9. *The Balham Mystery*, p. 18. Sir William, who represented Mrs. Bravo's family
and the suicide interest, was very intolerant of cross-examination: he thought Mr.
Lewis's questions "unbecoming." He maintained that he expected to see a case of
disease and that *he* diagnosed poison; Dr. Johnson said he fully explained the matter on the drive down. Sir William also alleged that he was recalled to the sickroom merely to be asked by the patient if he were dying; Dr. Johnson and other
witnesses agree with the version given by Miss Bell. One of Sir William's reasons
for assuming suicide was the patient's failure to express surprise on being informed by him that he was poisoned; but as Mr. Bravo had been told so by the

symptoms. His last words were: "Be kind to my darling wife, Mother; she's been the best of wives to me." The old lady's guarded reply was, "I am never unkind to anyone."

As none of the six medical men concerned saw his way to grant a death certificate, an inquest was inevitable, and the Coroner's officer received in the handwriting of Mrs. Cox the following hospitable invitation:—

THE PRIORY, BALHAM, APRIL 23. [1876].

Mrs. Charles Bravo writes to say that she wishes the inquest to be held at The Priory, where she will have refreshments prepared for the jury.[10]

The inquest, held on 25th April in the dead man's dining-room, had quite the air of a family party. The Coroner was an old friend, and it seems to have been understood that Mr. Bravo's regrettable suicide, so painful to the survivors, should be disposed of with the minimum of scandal. The proceedings were private and no reporters were present. Mr. Joseph Bravo having given formal evidence of the death, Mrs. Cox described the onset of the illness. She had told Dr. Harrison when he came what the deceased said to her about having taken poison. Mr. Bravo did not explain why he took the poison. He was on affectionate terms with his wife and had no reason for committing suicide. She could give no opinion as to why he should do so. Amelia Bushell and Mary Ann Keeber described the

---

other doctors the day before, we need be no more surprised than he. That the great man was not infallible is shown by the fact of his stating that he had no previous knowledge of Mrs. Bravo; whereas (I am advised by Sir John Hall) it appears from other evidence that that lady, during her first coverture, was under Sir William's professional care in 1869.

10. *The Balham Mystery*, p. 38.

course of the illness so far as they knew it; Dr. Harrison and Mr. Bell recounted the symptoms, which were those of an acrid poison, and told how the deceased, though repeatedly questioned, denied having taken anything but laudanum. Dr. Payne, who conducted the post-mortem, said he saw no sign of natural disease to account for death. He removed certain organs for further examination. Professor Redwood stated that he had analyzed the several matters submitted to him and found antimony in the vomited matter, in the excreta, and in the intestines. It had been taken in the form of tartar emetic, which was readily soluble in water and practically tasteless. Mr. M'Calmont, the barrister friend whom the deceased on the day of his seizure had invited to dinner, said that Mr. Bravo was then in the best of health and spirits, and was in his judgment a most unlikely man to commit suicide. Here the Coroner closed the inquiry. He refused to hear Drs. Moore and Johnson, who were present and wished to testify, and he declined to call Mrs. Bravo. He summed up, on the evidence of Mrs. Cox, for *felo de se*; but the jury returned as their verdict "that the deceased died from the effects of poison—antimony—but we have not sufficient evidence under what circumstances it came into his body." So Charles Bravo was laid to rest in Norwood Cemetery; and his widow, with her devoted confidante, retired to Brighton for a season. Their *villégiature* was to suffer a rude interruption.

### III

When the facts of the case became public property there was deep and widespread dissatisfaction with the result of the inquest, and an agitation for a fresh inquiry began in the Press. The *Lancet* published a medical history of the case by Dr. Johnson, together with Dr. Payne's report of the post-mortem and Professor Redwood's of the analysis. On 16th May Mrs.

Bravo, through her solicitor, offered a reward of £500 to anyone who should prove the purchase of the antimony that killed her husband. On the 17th the Coroner's jury met to consider the situation. Certain singular features in the evidence of Mrs. Cox were commented upon, as also was the inadequacy of the information laid before them. "A jury less determined to do their duty," said the Foreman, who presided, "might have been induced to return a verdict of suicide or of death by misadventure." To the ladies at Brighton the news, from the peculiarity of their position, was disappointing. Mrs. Bravo wrote to her father-in-law that a letter she had received from Mr. Royes Bell "fully confirms my suspicions as to poor Charlie's committing suicide. . . . We have Sir William Gull's evidence, and I shall not allow the living to be under any imputation such as is cast upon them by such a wicked verdict." But the matter was to be taken out of her hands.

On 18th May the question was raised by Serjeant (afterwards Sir John) Simon in the House of Commons, and the Home Secretary (Mr., later Lord, Cross) replied that he was ready to do all in his power to elucidate the mystery of Mr. Bravo's death. Mr. Stevenson, Solicitor to the Treasury, thereupon held a private inquiry at which some thirty witnesses were examined, but neither Mrs. Bravo nor Mrs. Cox was invited to attend. The significance of this omission was not lost upon the legal advisers of those ladies, who, after consultation with their respective solicitors, tendered their evidence to the Treasury. This was permitted, on the understanding that their statements were entirely voluntary and that they would not be questioned thereon. What these statements were we shall hear when we come to the evidence; meanwhile it is sufficient to note that a new and startling element was imported into the case by Mrs. Cox. That lady now averred that when examined at the first inquest, from a mistaken idea of shielding Mrs. Bravo's reputation, she did not tell "the full particulars,"

279

which she was anxious to do. What Mr. Bravo had really said to her on the fatal night was this: *"Mrs. Cox, I have taken poison for Gully. Don't tell Florence."* Who "Gully" was, and what cause Charles Bravo had for jealousy of him as alleged by both ladies, we shall see in the sequel.

On 19th June the Attorney-General (Sir John Holker) made application to the Court of Queen's Bench for a rule to quash the Coroner's inquisition and to grant a fresh inquiry—the grounds being the exclusion of Dr. Johnson's evidence (whose affidavit was read to the Court, in which he expressed his "decided belief" that Mr. Bravo did not knowingly take poison), and the new matter introduced by Mrs. Cox in her statement to the Treasury:—

> THE LORD CHIEF JUSTICE [Cockburn].—There is no use in shutting our eyes to the fact that in your view it is not a case of suicide.
>
> THE ATTORNEY-GENERAL.—If it turned out to be a murder, as I suspect it was, I hope we should be able to elicit facts which would justify a charge against someone.[11]

The Court quashed the inquisition and ordered the Coroner to hold a new inquiry.

We may take advantage of this interval between the acts to identify the skeleton thus evoked by Mrs. Cox from the cupboard of her friend and benefactress. Dr. James Manby Gully, who graduated at Edinburgh in 1829, and so may have attended Dr. Knox's lectures and witnessed the execution of the murderer Burke, was sixty-eight years of age when Mr. Bravo died, having been born in 1808 in Jamaica.[12] After successfully

---

11. *The Balham Mystery*, p. 6.

12. It is a curious coincidence that Jamaica was the theater of the elder Mr. Bravo's fortune, of Mrs. Cox's matrimonial adventures, and of Dr. Gully's birth.

practicing hydropathy at Malvern for thirty summers, he retired in 1872. Some two years previously he had professionally attended Captain Ricardo's young wife, whom he had known since she was twelve, and an "attachment" was then formed between the elderly physician and his fair patient which was to prove equally fatal to both, and of which there will be more to say. "The aged if vigorous medico," as he was picturesquely termed in the Press, had throughout his career exercised upon the opposite sex a powerful attraction. Even Mrs. Cox, that demure matron, confessed to finding him "a fascinating man, one who would be likely to interest women very much"; and Mrs. Bravo frankly said of him, "No one could grow tired of his society, he is so intellectual." This fine spirit, housed in a short stout tabernacle of flesh, triumphed over its unromantic casing to the beguilement of its female worshipers: the doctor, a fat little man with a charming manner, had a way with the women.

The second inquest, which opened on 11th July in the Bedford Hotel, hard by Balham Station, was a much more formidable affair than the homely inquiry at The Priory. The Coroner sat with a legal assessor; the Treasury was represented by Her Majesty's Attorney-General, with Mr. (later Sir John) Gorst, and Mr. (later Sir Harry) Poland; Mrs. Bravo, by Sir Henry James (afterwards Lord James of Hereford) and Mr. Biron; Mrs. Cox, by Mr. Murphy; and the Bravo family, by Mr. (later Sir George) Lewis, of the famous firm in Ely Place. At a subsequent stage Mr. Serjeant Parry and Mr. (afterwards Justice) A. L. Smith appeared for Dr. Gully. So strong was the public interest in the proceedings that these were reported with a fullness, and attended by an audience, much greater than usual in such inquiries, while the presence of the chief law officer of the Crown, a bevy of Queen's Counsel, and London's smartest solicitor was, in the circumstances, unique. The business was to occupy twenty-three working days and was to cost the parties fifteen thousand pounds; what it cost the community, goodness (and the Treasury) only knows. Yet for all this expenditure of time and money no one benefited excepting the purveyors and consumers of scandalous revelations, against which doubtsome profit must be set the abasement of Mrs. Bravo, the disgrace of Dr. Gully, the involuntary exile of Mrs. Cox to Jamaica, and the demonstrated insolubility of the Balham Mystery.

Now, by reason of the conflicting interests involved, the noble army of lawyers engaged, the introduction of so many side issues, and the admission of so much irrelevant matter, due to the extrajudicial character of the inquiry, a consideration of the evidence is beset with difficulties unknown to the student of regular criminal trials. The witnesses, put up apparently at random, had to sustain as best they might the cross-fire of half a dozen counsel, as greatly to their own confusion as to that of the result. We lack, moreover, the aid of addresses to the jury, presenting and commenting on the nature and value of the evidence from the standpoint of the respective parties; while the Coroner's summing up, in view of the extent and complexity of the proof, forms but an indifferent substitute for the expert charge of a trained Judge. Hence the reader of the evidence as reported, groping his way through a jungle of facts and circumstances more or less relevant to the issue, instead of pursuing the beaten track of ordered judicial procedure, may well exclaim with Webster's immortal Duchess:—

> Wish me good speed,
> For I am going into a wildernesse
> Where I shall find nor path nor friendly clewe
> To be my guide.

Such a monitor, so far as my ability and space permit, it has been my humble purpose to supply. If, courteously, you have followed me so far, you will know the salient features of the case, so that it only remains for me to deal with such points as seem to throw light upon the radical question: How came Charles Bravo to swallow the poison by which his death was caused? This, the sole object of the investigation, was largely lost sight of in exhaustive attempts to find in the three persons suspected—Mrs. Bravo, Mrs. Cox, and Dr. Gully—some *motive* for perpetrating the crime. The matter imported into the case by Mrs. Cox in her memorable disclosure to the Treasury was, in a sense very different from her intention, generally accepted as furnishing the key to the mystery, and popular opinion at the time succinctly expressed itself in the following parody of certain familiar lines:—

> When lovely woman stoops to folly
> And finds her husband in the way,
> What charm can soothe her melancholy,
> What art can turn him into clay?
>
> The only means her aims to cover
> And save herself from prison locks,
> And repossess her ancient lover,
> Are Burgundy and Mrs. Cox.[13]

---

13. For this gem I am indebted to the research of Sir John Hall (*op.cit.*, p. 87). Other bloody versicles known to me include the tribute to the Gill's Hill crime of 1823, which so intrigued Sir Walter Scott:—

> They cut his throat from ear to ear,
> His brains they battered in;
> His name was Mr. William Weare,
> He dwelt in Lyon's Inn.

The West Port murders of 1828 are thus poetically enshrined:—

> Up the close and doun the stair,
> But and ben wi' Burke and Hare.

Whether or not this view of the case is warranted by the facts it is now our business to consider.

## I V

Mrs. Cox, in her statement to the Treasury of 2nd June, said that when she received Mr. Bravo's confession of suicide "for Gully" she remarked, "How could you do such a thing?" but he only screamed for hot water. Before that came, he was sick out of the window. She then smelt chloroform and rushed to the bottle, which she found nearly empty.[14] She did not tell Dr. Moore, as it would have caused "such a scandal," though she did tell Dr. Harrison: if Mr. Bravo had recovered he would have been "so angry" at her telling.[15] Mrs. Bravo had had no communication with Dr. Gully since her marriage. She (Cox) "conscientiously believed" their friendship, though very imprudent, to be entirely innocent. On Good Friday (14th April) Mrs. Bravo came downstairs for the first time since her illness. Mr. Bravo

---

> Burke's the butcher, Hare's the thief,
> Knox the boy that buys the beef.

Finally, the case of Miss Lizzie Borden in 1893, America's super-murder trial, is embalmed in a quatrain which was a favorite of President Roosevelt:—

> Lizzie Borden took an ax
> And gave her Mother forty whacks;
> When she saw what she had done,
> She gave her Father forty-one!

The admirable brevity of the bard is beyond praise; volumes might have contained less matter. Would that he had my present job—or I, his gift!

14. Both Dr. Moore and Dr. Harrison state that there was no smell of chloroform.

15. Dr. Harrison states that on his first examination of the patient he told Mrs. Cox that he (Bravo) "would not live for an hour"; and further, that she never mentioned poison to him.

objected to her lying on the sofa to rest, saying she was a self-ish pig; he further said that he would no longer live with her, was going away, and wished she were dead. He often said he hated Gully and wished *he* were dead. "Let her go back to Gully!" said he, when Mrs. Cox expostulated with him on his unreason. On another occasion he rushed out of the house and was with difficulty persuaded by her to return. She always made peace between husband and wife. Before his death he asked her, "Why did you tell them? Does Florence know I have poisoned myself? Don't tell her." He was jealous of Gully, "though he knew everything before marriage."[16]

Mrs. Bravo, in her statement of the same date—they were plainly acting in concert—corroborated Mrs. Cox as to Mr. Bravo's retrospective jealousy of Dr. Gully. Another cause of dissension was that before their marriage he (Bravo) had kept a woman at Maidenhead, to whom he still paid money and for whom he had borrowed £500. He was very passionate, and once actually struck her (his wife). His meanness was such that he required her to put down her own maid, and wished her to give up the cobs and *to turn away Mrs. Cox*, whereby he anticipated a saving of £400 a year. During one of their quarrels he jumped out of bed and threatened to cut his throat. Her "attachment" to Dr. Gully began at Malvern in 1870. When she went to Streatham he took a house opposite hers, and on her removal to Balham he came to live within five minutes' walk of The Priory. She informed Mr. Bravo before marriage of her intimacy with the doctor. This "attachment" was quite innocent, and nothing improper had ever passed between them. It was agreed that the matter should never be mentioned; yet after the marriage, though she had neither seen nor heard from Dr. Gully since, Mr. Bravo spoke of him "morning, noon, and night," abusing him and calling him "that wretch."

16. *The Balham Mystery*, p. 6.

They quarreled about him on the drive to town on the morning of the seizure, and Mr. Bravo said, "You will see what I will do when I get home!" Nothing was said to her about poison till Sir William Gull came. Mr. Bravo did not tell her that he had taken poison; he made no inquiry as to the cause of his illness.[17]

To the picture here painted of the dead man's inveterate, if groundless, jealousy of his wife's former friend, designed by the ladies to supply a motive for his taking his own life, there was a reverse side which they had overlooked. A husband so base as thus to abuse his wife, and so mean as to compass the casting out of her faithful companion, might be deemed to have invited reprisals. Both ladies had, since the first inquest, received anonymous letters, denouncing them as jointly and severally responsible for his taking off, and good Mrs. Cox was even by one optimistic correspondent presented with a portrait of herself suspended from a gibbet! It was, therefore, essential to their convenience and safety that they should suggest some other explanation of the tragedy. Let us see what support is afforded to their story by the evidence of impartial witnesses.

It appears from the unanimous testimony of relatives, friends, and servants that Charles Bravo was a strong, active fellow, in perfect health, of a lively and cheerful disposition, famed for his high spirits, and full of fun: the last man, as all agree, to commit the cowardly crime of suicide. Similarly, his relations with his wife seemed happy and affectionate: no one (except Mrs. Cox) ever saw the slightest cloud between them, none of the servants ever heard him mention Dr. Gully's name. In particular, coachman and groom heard nothing of the alleged quarrel in the open carriage on the last drive to town. Further, Bravo's demeanor to his wife during the long-drawn agony of the death chamber—when all vain pretenses must

---

17. *The Balham Mystery*, p. 44.

be laid aside—was that of a loving, considerate, and confiding spouse. Of course, many an imperfectly matched pair may present to the world an harmonious front; yet I defy a couple, living on the footing here described of violent opposition and mutual distrust, not to afford their intimates an involuntary glimpse of the cat in the marital bag, nor wholly to stifle the cries of that indignant captive. But to the Gully-Ricardo motif I shall in due course revert.

With reference to the suicide theory, Mr. Bravo senior explained that the Maidenhead incident was amicably closed, that the deceased had £1100 at his credit, "and had only to ask for more." His barrister friends proved him to have had some knowledge of medicine and to be well read in medical jurisprudence; one, Mr. Atkinson, deposed: "He was a very clearheaded man, with a great deal of common sense and very little sentiment, and no feeling for any woman would make him take a painful and uncertain poison, with the effect of which he was thoroughly acquainted"—"a dreadful death," as one of the doctors described it. And indeed if Charles Bravo did take antimony with suicidal intent, it is admitted that he established a record which no one has ever attempted to break.

As to the vehicle of the poison, the same gentleman, from his intimate association with the deceased, supplied a valuable clue. He and Bravo had shared rooms together at Oxford in 1866–68, and also chambers in the Temple for three years. It was Bravo's invariable custom to take before going to bed a deep draught of cold water from the bedroom water-bottle, without using a tumbler. He had noticed the same habit later, when staying with Mr. Bravo's people, and also on a recent visit to Paris in his company.[18] Keeping an eye on the water-bottle, we find that it was filled nightly by the housemaid (Keeber), and

---

18. *The Balham Mystery*, p. 30. This "inveterate habit" would, of course, be known to his wife, who may have mentioned it to her companion.

was always used; particularly that she filled it on the night in question, after dinner. The doctors saw in the bedroom no vessel from which poison had apparently been taken. In view of the amount absorbed—thirty or forty grains, according to Professor Redwood's estimate—the bottle must have contained at least ninety grains. The popular attribution of the poison to the Burgundy at dinner is for two reasons improbable: the wine would have become turbid, and the butler says that his master was something of a connoisseur, with a critical palate: the experts state that the poison would act in fifteen minutes, in which case Mr. Bravo would have been sick at table.[19] Forty grains of tartarized antimony in four ounces of water were exhibited by the Professor to the jury: the mixture could be held in the mouth without taste or feeling. Thus the probabilities all point to the water-bottle as the medium. But Dr. Harrison remembered that at midnight on the Tuesday he drank in the bedroom nearly a tumblerful from a water-bottle, *which was three parts full*; and Dr. Moore recalled that he had used some earlier to cool the hot brandy-and-water injection. Neither could identify the bottle produced, which was of a common type, nor say that the butler did not bring up fresh cold water with the tray.[20]

To the general accord as to Mr. Bravo's previous good health there is one noteworthy exception. A month before his death, as the butler puts it—early in March, according to his stepfather—Mr. Bravo was sick after breakfast and asked the butler

---

19. As to what became of the residue of this Burgundy there is no evidence.

20. Why the butler (Rowe) was not recalled to speak to this does not appear. If there were but one bottle, and if Mr. Bravo had taken his usual "deep draught" and Dr. Moore had used some, how came it to be *three-quarters full* when Dr. Harrison assuaged his thirst? Nay, more; Mrs. Cox, before they came, took half a tumblerful for camphor drops for the sufferer! Either there were *two* bottles, or, more probably, the bottle was emptied and refilled—by whom can only be conjectured—*before the arrival of the doctors*.

for brandy. Between nine and ten o'clock he called at Palace Green, and there complained of being sick. He told his stepfather that on coming up the lane from his house to Balham Station he had vomited so much that he was afraid people would think he had been drunk the night before. He looked very ill, was given some curaçao, and, feeling better, went his way to Westminster. It is a remarkable coincidence—though it may be no more—that at this very time the vexed question of Mrs. Cox's departure became acute. To herself, to his wife, to his mother-in-law, and to divers friends Mr. Bravo had announced his intention to dispense with her further services. Her salary, traveling expenses, dress, and board cost him, he considered, £300 or £400 a year: "he might keep another pair of horses for that." Mr. Bravo was a self-willed man, one who would carry out his purpose despite all opposition, *unless he were rendered incapable of action.* On 11th April a letter came from Mrs. Cox's aunt in Jamaica, who had opportunely taken ill, begging her niece to come out to her forthwith. This seemed to solve the difficulty; but that lady said it would be "inconvenient" for her to go; and although Mr. Joseph Bravo expressed a strong opinion that she should at once do so, and "urged in every way the propriety of her going," she steadfastly refused to vacate her post.

The only proof of the presence of antimony on the premises rests upon the evidence of George Griffith and his wife. This man had been eight years with Dr. Gully as coachman, and from May 1875 to January 1876 was in service with Mrs. Ricardo, being dismissed before her second marriage for careless driving. His wife had been her own maid, and they occupied one of the lodges at The Priory. He stated that he was in the habit of using for his horses a lotion of antimony which he made up himself, as prescribed in *The Pocket Farrier*; that he kept it in a pint bottle, labeled "Poison," in an open cupboard in the stables; that he poured out what remained of it when he left; and that he had bought the antimony at Robertson's and Smith's, respectively chemists at Streatham and Balham. He produced his expense book, showing two entries in July and August 1875, of 1s. 6d. and 3d. for "horse medicine," which he said referred to those purchases. Mr. Robertson deposed that he found no such entries in his poison register, but admitted that certain leaves were missing and that there was an anonymous entry of two drachms of tartar emetic, sold "to be administered to horses." Mr. Smith and his assistant denied ever selling to Griffith any tartar emetic. Mrs. Griffith deposed that her husband had an ounce of antimony in a box in a drawer, which she put in the fire as she wanted the box. She remembered him saying later that he was "going to fetch some poison" from Smith's, to make a lotion for his horses. It appears that Griffith resented his dismissal, and remarked of his mistress's new husband: "Poor fellow, I wouldn't like to be in his shoes; he won't live four months!"—a strange prediction.[21] My own idea is that the fatal dose—so "greatly diluted"—came from this lotion in the bottle in the stable cupboard, from which, before it was emptied by Griffith, some politic person, attracted by the label, had taken a sample as a provision against contingencies. One never knows when one may find a use for a thing.

V

The two ladies and the doctor divided between them the honors of the inquiry. Mrs. Cox, moral considerations apart, was a

---

21. It was proved that in July 1869 Griffith bought two ounces of tartar emetic from a Malvern chemist, whose books described the purchase as "for Dr. Gully." The doctor emphatically denied all knowledge of this transaction but to the public it gave the case, in Mr. Sapsea's phrase, "a dark look," though in fact it had nothing to do with it.

bad witness. She answered in a low voice, after long pauses, and persistently fenced with awkward questions. When such were pressed, we read, "the witness sat for some time in the midst of the silent Court, but made no reply; she sat quietly brushing the tablecloth with her gloved hand, and did not look up." She kept her head throughout, however, and was more than a match for her learned adversaries. Mrs. Bravo, on the other hand, gave her evidence generally "in a calm and composed manner, and in a firm and distinct voice"; but she made to the Coroner an hysterical appeal for protection from the ruthless catechism of Mr. Lewis regarding her former connection with Dr. Gully. That old gentleman produced a very favorable impression. His evidence, entirely voluntary, was given with much frankness and with a due sense of the painful position in which he stood—or rather sat: for to the indignation of the audience, having just recovered from illness, he was allowed, like the female witnesses, a seat. While admitting that Mrs. Bravo's account of their intimacy was "too true, too true," he solemnly swore that he had nothing to do, directly or indirectly, with Charles Bravo's death.

The history of the *liaison* between Dr. Gully and Mrs. Ricardo, as it was forced from these ladies throughout long days of mordant cross-examination—from Mrs. Cox, not without much prevarication and resistance; from Florence Bravo, not without tears and shame—was, briefly, this. In 1872, the year after her husband's death, Mrs. Ricardo formed two connections which were equally to affect her fate: she accepted Mrs. Cox as her companion and Dr. Gully as her lover.

The pair became inseparable. Dr. Gully, who had retired from practice, was constantly in attendance, devoting his whole time to his attractive neighbor; he took a house near her at Streatham, and afterwards at Balham he was allowed the privilege of a latch-key; he accompanied Mrs. Ricardo to divers English watering-places, he went on tour with her to Italy and to

Germany; yet in all this Mrs. Cox saw nothing beyond "gentlemanly familiarity" on his part, and refused to acknowledge that they were lovers. Finally, she was brought to admit that she had seen him kiss her, that the attachment "was the subject of much conversation locally," and that Mrs. Ricardo's family had cast her off because of her infatuation for her assiduous ally. Having gone so far, Mrs. Cox admitted that had there been no Mrs. Gully, "it might have been a match"; and vouchsafed the damaging fact that the couple had arranged to marry so soon as the doctor's wife was dead. As that venerable lady was over ninety, it seemed unlikely to be a long engagement. The net result went to show that Mrs. Cox had lied heartily upon this matter, both at the first inquest and in her statement to the Treasury.

Poor Florence Bravo, who followed her companion in the witness-chair, had, in view of her friend's revelations, a bad time. The spectacle of her martyrdom is not improving, and I do not propose to dwell on it. Suffice it to say that she fought bravely to retain some small rag of reputation and to minimize the extent and character of her fall; but in the end she had to confess that, from the death of her first husband, she had been Dr. Gully's mistress. Ten days after meeting Charles Bravo at Brighton Mrs. Ricardo wrote to "her ancient lover," breaking with him for good and all, giving as her reason the desire to become reconciled to her people. Ten days before the wedding she and Dr. Gully met for the last time. The doctor took his dismissal in good part; "his sole wish was for her happiness"; and it was not unreasonable that at his time of life he should have been willing to retire. They returned to one another their mutual gifts, and so far as the principals were concerned the chapter was finally closed. But Mrs. Cox, as we shall see, showed an unaccountable disposition to turn over the old leaves. Before she accepted Mr. Bravo's proposal Mrs. Ricardo told him "everything" as to her past relations with

Dr. Gully. Bravo seems to have taken the disclosure calmly; he described her candor as noble, and conferred with Mrs. Cox as to the probability of a woman who had once gone wrong "going wrong again," which that experienced matron thought unlikely. He was not, as appears, a sentimental man.[22] A hitch occurring in the ante-nuptial negotiations regarding the lady's proposal to include in the marriage settlement upon herself the furniture, carriages, etc., at The Priory, the prospective bridegroom was exceeding wroth, saying he would rather break off the marriage than not sit on his own chairs. In this dilemma Florence took counsel with her old adviser; they had a brief interview at the lodge, when Dr. Gully told her to agree. "So, in fact, it was Dr. Gully who made the match at last?" was Mr. Gorst's sarcastic comment; but indeed this was nearer the truth than he imagined. Thenceforth they saw each other no more—until the inquest.

Whoever made the match, and whether it was made in Heaven or elsewhere, it was clearly not Mrs. Cox, for though aware of old Mrs. Bravo's disapproval, she urged Charles to communicate to his mother his fiancée's confession, which he refused to do, as it would mean breaking off the marriage. In January 1876 Mr. Bravo received an anonymous letter, charging him with having married Dr. Gully's mistress for money. He was vastly annoyed, says Mrs. Cox, to whom he showed it, and wanted to shoot the doctor, believing him to be its author; but Mrs. Cox, whatever may have been her source of knowledge, was able to assure him that it was not written by that gentleman. In view of the delicate position of the parties, it is not a little surprising to find Mrs. Cox keeping in touch with Dr. Gully, from the honeymoon until the death. The doctor

---

22. When the bride-elect's solicitor congratulated him on his engagement, he replied, "Damn your congratulations; I only want the money!"—*The Balham Mystery*, p. 47.

plainly desired to have no dealings with his former friends, and had instructed his butler not to admit the ladies should they call. Yet on no less than five occasions Mrs. Cox contrived to waylay him upon various pretexts. She spoke to him in the street, at Victoria, at Balham Station, whenever and wherever she got the chance; now asking him to prescribe for Jamaica fever, as she "would probably soon be going" to expose herself to its attack; now for a "treatment" for contingent ague. After the miscarriage in April, she required of him a sleeping draught for Mrs. Bravo, which he agreed to supply, ordering half an ounce of laurel water—*cerasee* is the homeopathic term—and leaving it at Mrs. Cox's house in London, as he wished to have no communication with The Priory, which he regarded as, for him, "forbidden ground."[23] When, the day before the death, the doctors gave up the case as hopeless, Mrs. Bravo bethought her of her old friend, whom she esteemed "the cleverest medical man in the whole world," and sent Mrs. Cox to ask if he could help her husband. Pritchard, the butler, opened the door. "Is the Doctor in? Poor Mr. Bravo is dying," said Mrs. Cox. Pritchard announced the unwelcome visitor. "You shouldn't have let her in," said his master; "I suppose I must see her."[24] The butler adds feelingly, on his own account: "I should not have been sorry if I had never seen her," a sentiment in which surely he was not alone.

To certain curiosities of conduct on the part of Mrs. Cox in connection with her host's illness I have before referred; another example, which to me seems not less significant than

---

23. The phial, unopened, was after the death thrown away by Mrs. Cox at Mrs. Bravo's request, for fear it should be deemed "poison." It had no connection with the case; but the incident was an unfortunate one for Dr. Gully, as inviting suspicion.

24. He prescribed the *arsenicum* and mustard poultice already mentioned.

remarkable, I must find space for. Upon her administration of the mustard, Mr. Bravo was again sick—the first time, you remember, was out of the window, whereby most of the result was lost. On the second occasion he used, copiously, the bedroom hand-basin. Now, Mrs. Cox was plainly a lady who kept her head in a sickroom; she had, as she avers, just learned from himself that he had taken poison; she had, very properly, exhibited an emetic; she was about to summon medical aid— though not the nearest; and she must, in the circumstances, have been aware how vital it was that the vomited matter should be preserved for the doctor's inspection. Yet what says Mary Ann Keeber?

> I held the basin for him. It had not been used before—not for sickness that night. The vomit in the basin looked like food, and was red. *Mrs. Cox told me to take the vomit away*, and I threw it down the sink in the house-maid's room, and washed the basin out.[25]

"I told Mary Ann to empty the basin and bring it back," says Mrs. Cox, "in case it should be wanted again." Cross-examined upon this by the Attorney-General, she gave the following explanation:—

> He had had the mustard and water before he was sick in the basin. It might have been ten minutes after that he was sick in the basin, for the mustard had to be mixed. When he made that statement I thought he had poisoned himself. I did not think he was in a precarious way, because, as he was sick, I smelt I thought chloroform, and I

---

25. *The Balham Mystery*, p. 16.

saw the bottle was empty. I never thought he had taken anything else but chloroform. I gave Keeber instructions to take away the vomit. I gave the emetic to get off his stomach any deleterious matter that might be upon it. I did not save the vomit, so that he might have a clean basin. It did not strike me that as he had told me he had taken poison it would be well for the medical men to see the vomit. There were other basins and receptacles in the room, but I never thought of them. Mr. Bravo had told me he had taken poison, but it did not occur to me that it was important to save the vomit. I had no object in sending the basin away. *Why should I send it away? What object could I have?*[26]

Echo answers, "Why?" But the fact that she did so send it, and thus destroyed most valuable evidence, remains. Again, Mrs. Cox thrice specifically states that Mr. Bravo made to her the famous admission *so soon as she entered his room* and *before* he vomited from the window, and that he *then* screamed for hot water. Mary Ann states: "I went with Mrs. Cox to Mr. Bravo's room, and there I saw him standing by the window vomiting, and he called again for hot water." But she heard nothing of the alleged confession, though present at the moment when it is said to have been made.

Let us recall the text to Mrs. Cox's progressive revelations, which show her to have been, as regards the development of truth, a disciple of Dr. Newman. To Dr. Harrison she said: "I am sure he has taken chloroform"; to Dr. Johnson she reported the words: "I've taken some of *that* poison, but don't tell Florence"; at the first inquest: "He said, as soon as I went to him, he had taken poison"; to the Treasury: "Mrs. Cox, I

---

26. *The Balham Mystery*, p. 34.

have taken poison *for Gully*. Don't tell Florence"; at the second inquest: "Mrs. Cox, I've taken poison *for Dr. Gully*. Don't tell Florence."[27] Against which must be set the solemn oath of the dying man: "Before my God, I have taken nothing but laudanum."

I have only space to note one other point: What were the real relations of the couple during their brief four months of marriage? Upon this matter Mrs. Bravo spake with two voices. To Miss Bell, the day before the death, she remarked: "We have been very, very happy, and Charles has said he has never been so happy in all his life. *We have never had a word to-gether*"—which hardly rhymes with the perpetual quarrels about "that wretch Gully," with his violence, his threats of suicide, and his desire for a separation. In this connection, Mr. Lewis put to her certain letters of the dead man to his wife, written when she was staying with her people or he with his, the last three within a fortnight of his death, in which occur the following phrases:—

> I hold you to be the best of wives. . . . I wish I could sleep away my life till you return. . . . I miss you, my darling wife, dreadfully. When you once come back I will so take care of you that you will never leave me again. . . . I have been thinking all this morning of the sweet old girl I left behind me. . . . You shall find me the best of husbands. . . . I cannot be happy in the absence of the best of wives.

---

27. Mrs. Cox had a last card up her respectable sleeve, which she did not produce until she played it at the second inquest. On the Wednesday, being alone with the patient, he said to her, "Why did you tell them? Does Florence know I poisoned myself?" to which she replied, "*I was obliged to tell them: I could not let you die.*" The obligation did not operate until four hours after she was told that he was dying. She had never mentioned this conversation before, "because I thought he did not wish me."—*The Balham Mystery*, p. 32.

> My only object in life is to make your life happy to you,
> and I hope I have succeeded. . . . I do not believe that any
> love can be greater than mine. . . . My darling Florence,
> without you I am lost. . . . Two of the happiest people in
> the world will meet to-morrow. . . .[28]

"After hearing these letters read," asked Mr. Lewis, "do you
mean to tell the jury that your late husband was always—
'morning, noon, and night'—speaking in disparaging terms of
Dr. Gully?" "I do," replied the witness; "I told others than
Mrs. Cox in his lifetime; I told my mother at Buscot." Mrs.
Campbell, Mrs. Bravo's mother, corroborates this: "She [Flor-
ence] said that he often upbraided her about Dr. Gully, and was
very passionate—like a spoilt child." Her daughter told her
this in January. At the same time Mrs. Bravo was writing to
her mother-in-law: "Charlie and I are as happy as can be, and
*never have an unkind word*." Which and what is one to believe? A distinguished (married) lady novelist of my acquaintance, whom in my ignorance of feminine psychology I ventured
upon this point to consult, assures me that no reliance can be
placed on these passages as representing the true relations of
the wedded pair: the glowing Agapemone of the letters may
have been a factual bear garden. Well, perhaps so, as regards
the letters to third parties whom it was deemed desirable to
blind; but fancy can suggest no reason why a husband should
employ this amorous camouflage in private letters to a wife
with whom he was on the terms described by Mrs. Cox and endorsed by Mrs. Bravo.

As a last instance of these discrepancies I quote a letter from
Charles Bravo to his mother, written on Good Friday, seven
days before his death—the very day, you may remember, the last

---

28. *The Balham Mystery*, p. 47.

"serious quarrel" is said to have arisen between the spouses. He was "very angry" with his wife for resting (on her first day downstairs after her illness!), called her "a selfish pig," said he despised himself for having married her, wished she were dead, was quite determined to go away, and had made up his mind he would no longer live with her: "let her go back to Gully!" Thus the ladies; let us now hear Mr. Bravo:—

THE PRIORY, BALHAM, GOOD FRIDAY.

My Dear Old Granny,—I am sure I am very sorry if I have been negligent in writing. I thought I had written two or three times a week to you or the governor since you left town. However, you shall hear from me more often for the future. We are suffering from horrible weather. My farming operations are at a standstill. My fowls lay as if they were Turks and their eggs the money due on coupons, and my spirits are nothing like what they would be if the sun was visible. Florence is better, but very cross. I went to the library and brought her six volumes of books; three she had read, and three contain the uninspired preachings of an idiot. She has finished a pair of slippers for me in a rage, and is now slanging me for not being able to tell a good book, as you tell good music, by the look. . . . I have bought a splendid lawn tennis [*sic*]. I intend to play with you and Father Joseph. I rode both the cobs the day before yesterday, and I feel very much as if the muscles of my legs were ossifying. I have difficulty in dragging my shooting boots, which I am obliged, *par ordre supérieure*, to wear, in addition to a red flannel garment, which is a cross between a kilt, a sporran, and a pair of bathing drawers, and has as many strings as a harp. Nothing but great firmness on the part of my better half, and an assurance that it "became me," made me put it on. I feel as if I had stays on my stomach.—I am always, dear Granny,

> your loving son,
> Charles.[29]

"Look here, upon this picture, and on this."

In the obscure politics of The Priory one thing is clear: Jane Cannon Cox was a Jacobite—James Gully, not Charles Bravo, claimed her allegiance. Though she had survived the Revolution and retained her office, her heart was with the old régime. Such loyalty as she owed the reigning house would hardly survive her dismissal. Did she do her best to bring about a Restoration? If we accept the evidence of Mrs. Campbell, there must have been some foundation for the tale of Mr. Bravo's retrospective jealousy. It is probable that the resourceful widow saw in this, if suitably magnified and embellished, the means of extricating herself from rather a tight corner. There can be no question which of the two ladies in this drama played "lead." Mrs. Bravo stood in real peril; and being persuaded, as I believe she was, of her husband's suicide, would readily be induced to back her strong-willed confidante in their common danger. If Truth suffered some abrasions in the process, it was done in self-defense. Her faith in her friend must have received a rude shock when she heard that lady's revelations at the inquest. "Now, Mrs. Bravo, do you not feel towards Mrs. Cox the same kindly regard you have always felt?" was Mr. Murphy's last question. "I think she might have spared me many of these painful inquiries to which I have been subjected," was Mrs. Bravo's reply.

---

29. *The Balham Mystery*, p. 7.

The jury, having considered the conundrum propounded for their solution, tendered the following answer:—

> We find that Mr. Charles Delaunay Turner Bravo did not commit suicide; that he did not meet his death by misadventure; that he was willfully murdered by the administration of tartar emetic; *but there is not sufficient evidence to fix the guilt upon any person or persons.*[30]

It will be seen that the jury avoided the usual formula: "by some person or persons *unknown*"—a distinction with a difference.

Florence Bravo is said to have died, heart-broken, within the year. On the facts, in the phrase of her discreet companion, but with more sincerity, I "conscientiously believe" her entitled to share the exculpatory epitaph pronounced on the daughter of Leonato. Ruin—professional, social, and complete— came upon "her ancient lover" by reason of his unhappy connection with the case, although Sir Harry Poland has placed upon record his conviction that Dr. Gully knew nothing about the murder.[31] Mrs. Cox—realizing the aspiration so beautifully expressed by Lady Emily Hornblower in the touching lines—

> Lead us to some sunny isle,
> Yonder in the western deep;

---

30. *The Balham Mystery*, p. 52.

31. "I am as certain as I can be that Dr. Gully had no part in the death of Bravo." And of Mrs. Bravo Sir Harry remarks: "Her conduct generally was consistent with innocence." This, coming from Crown counsel, is of the greatest weight.— *Seventy-two Years at the Bar*, by Ernest Bowen-Rowlands, pp. 131, 135. London: 1924.

> Where the skies for ever smile,
> And the blacks for ever weep—

was by force of circumstance compelled after all to go back to Jamaica, whence her late husband had before departed for a better world, not, it has been whispered, without certain suspicions as to the expediting of his journey. The reluctance of his relict to revisit a scene of such painful association need not surprise us. Some day perhaps, in one of those impracticable writing-desks of the period, built like a small sarcophagus of massive rosewood, lustrously inlaid with mother-of-pearl, will there be found among the papers of that ambiguous widow, written in a ladylike angular hand, the true version of the Bravo tragedy? I wonder.[32]

---

32. In this year of writing [1926], the dramatic quality of the Bravo case inspired the pens of two talented novelists. The interested reader is recommended to peruse for further entertainment: *Not Sufficient Evidence* by Mrs. Victor Rickard (London: Constable & Co., 1926); and *What Really Happened* by Mrs. Belloc Lowndes (London: Hutchinson & Co., n.d. [1926]).

## DR. PRITCHARD REVISITED

*A great reckoning in a little room.*

*—As You Like It*

MY FIRST BOOK, which concerned the life and labors of the late ingenious Dr. Pritchard, was published many years ago.[1] Since then I have written about the centenaries and bicentenaries of divers of my fellow-mortals, but as I shall surely have no occasion to commemorate my own, I should like to seize this minor opportunity, offered by my first-born's attainment of majority, to indulge for a space the pleasant retrospect of parenthood. I am beckoned to this amiable if anile course by the manifest finger of Providence. While I was engaged upon the book, Professor Sir Henry Littlejohn, the well-known occupant of the Chair of Forensic Medicine in the University of Edinburgh, was so obliging as to lend me for reproduction

---

1. *Trial of Dr. Pritchard.* Notable Scottish Trials. Edinburgh: 1906.

certain photographs in his possession illustrative of the case including those of Dr. Pritchard himself, his wife, his mother-in-law, and his mistress-maid, which added greatly to the attractions of my volume. He, Pritchard, had a passion for being photographed, and used to carry about with him for presentation to casual acquaintances packs of his counterfeit presentment, in the handy carte-de-visite form then in vogue. I knew from my preliminary researches that one of those represented a family group, depicting the good physician in the very bosom of domesticity—surrounded, like Mr. Venus, by the trophies of his art; a portrait which he took with him to Edinburgh for his trial, and frequently exhibited to the warders and others, taking pleasure, we are told, in pointing out by name the several members of his flock. Sir Henry's collection, however, apparently contained no copy of this desideratum, or at any rate he could not lay his hands on it at the time. And, behold, one fortunate day, on my chancing to consult upon another matter my friend Professor Harvey Littlejohn, who then worthily filled his father's Chair, he showed me, among sundry interesting articles which belonged to his distinguished predecessor, the veritable photograph of my former quest! The picture is of unique interest and significance: the likeness of a poisoner in amicable association with two of his patients: and as such is well worth preserving for posterity.

I have long had an uneasy feeling that I did not do justice to Dr. Pritchard, either as a man or as a murderer. With regard to the text of my book I have no regrets. It was prepared from a careful and discomfortable collation of the contemporary reports in the *Scotsman, Courant,* and *Glasgow Herald* newspapers; and I was rewarded for my labors by the gratifying opinion of the late Lord Young—who as Solicitor-General conducted the prosecution—that it was the best account he had ever read. The Appendices, too, contain much new and valuable material. But the Introduction is another story. Never having written before for publication, I was naturally diffident, and somewhat shy of my readers; I blushed to figure myself in print—a sensation to which, alas, I have been long a stranger. Hence the conventional and rather timid treatment of what ought to have proved a rousing theme.

I remember once going to lunch with Mr. Henry James at his charming rooms in Cheyne Walk, Chelsea, on an April day of 1915. I recall the windows open to the river, the slow-passing barges, the soft spring sunshine; the gracious atmosphere of amenity that was the peculiar setting of his genius. He greeted me in friendly wise with one hand laid lightly on my shoulder, while enveloping me in a flowing and embroidered robe of welcome; his other hand held a volume of an aspect to me painfully familiar. "I am reading, you see," he sociably observed, "one of your books—'Pritchard.'" "I'm sorry it's that one," I ruefully protested, "for it was my first, and is, I hope, my worst." "Well, well," came the bland rejoinder, "perhaps it *is* . . . less mature than your later work." Thus, all genially and generously, was I let off.

I

I have often wondered that no philosopher has considered the strange affinity between crime and whiskers. The campaign so capably conducted some years ago by Mr. Frank Richardson against what he pleasantly terms "face fittings" did not, I think, invade this region of the hostile province. That most of the homicides of history have been hairy-faced folk, sealed of the tribe of Esau—Cain was certainly unshaven—admits of no dispute, and invites to curious reflection, a subject upon which, luckily for the reader, I lack space to dwell. I shall content myself with reminding him that King James the Sixth and M. Landru were both, though unequally, bearded—James affording, in comparison with the fertile Frenchman, but poor soil; and that the mustaches of the Kaiser and of his subject Oscar Slater each influenced evilly the wearer's fortunes. Of all such unscraped scoundrels Dr. Pritchard may be hailed as king and emperor. To none of them can with more propriety be applied the phrase of Adrian Harley: "You carry matters with too long a beard." In these days of whitewash and psychology it might be plausibly maintained that no man so heavily handicapped with hair could be otherwise than wicked, the umbrageous growth in question, like the fabled Upas Tree of Java, blighting all within its baleful shade. Be that as it may, Dr. Pritchard gloried in his shame; his beard was to him as the apple of an eye. To his daughter Fanny, at her school in Edinburgh, between the deaths of his two victims, he writes: "I hope to be over again soon. . . . I liked all your companions on a single glance. One had very bonny eyes, and looked as if she would like to clip off my little beard, just for the mischief in doing it."[2] And being arrested and consigned to jail upon a double charge of murder, his main regret was "that he could not be favored with a supply of pomatum for the trimming of his beard and hair."[3] Pritchard was almost entirely bald—indeed, as in the case of Mr. Spottletoe, "he seemed to have stopped his hair, by the sudden application of some powerful remedy, in the very act of falling off his head, and to have fastened it irrevocably on his face." The nakedness of the land above, however, was characteristically camouflaged by training long side-wisps—"ribands" is, I believe, the technical term—to festoon the dome.

If any afternoon early in the year 1865 you had chanced, at the consulting hour, to call at No. 131 (now No. 249) Sauchiehall Street, Glasgow; had ascended the steps, and having ad-

2. *Trial*, p. 315.

3. *Glasgow Herald*, 24th April 1865.

mired the brazen legend of the door-plate, rung the bell; you would have been ushered by a trim and comely handmaid into the sanctum of the popular physician. A tall, handsome man of an imposing presence, sandy-fair, with clean-cut, aquiline features and a benevolent brow: yet, for the expert in such signals, a cunning gleam in the fine eyes and a touch of cruelty about the sensitive mouth: rises to receive you with an elaborate and studied courtesy—the perfection, as was reported at the time, of the *suaviter in modo*. Should you be a lady patient, and attractive to boot, it were well that you be on your guard; for certain ugly rumors are afloat, touching the very unprofessional license sometimes taken by the Doctor in similar circumstances. These, surely, must be but calumnies of the ill-favored; you have only to look upon the refined, benignant countenance, to listen to the musical and cultured voice, to note the swift lighting of the winning smile, in order to realize that this is a gentleman without reproach.

And yet how hard is it for even such an one to escape the malice of the froward! Two years before, on 5th May 1863, a regrettable incident, occurring in his house, 11 Berkeley Terrace, Glasgow, gave occasion for the enemy to blaspheme. Mrs. Pritchard, with the younger children and one of the two maids, was out of town; the other, a young girl, kept house for the Doctor. At three in the morning a policeman, noticing the glare of flames in an attic window, rang the bell. Dr. Pritchard, who happened to be up and dressed, opened the door. He explained that he had just been aroused by a smell of fire and was about to summon assistance. The Fire Brigade came, the fire was soon extinguished, for only the servant's bedroom was involved; the girl was found, lying peacefully in her bed, burned to death. She had made no effort to escape, and was assumed to have been suffocated. It was further supposed that, as she lay late reading, she fell asleep, and the curtains caught fire from the gas jet. No sign of the supposititious volume was seen among the debris, nor, more remarkably, could any trace be found of certain articles of jewelry for which Dr. Pritchard claimed compensation under his policy. So, as the Insurance Company refused to pay, the Doctor suffered both in pocket and repute; for not only was he held to have made a fraudulent claim, but there were those who whispered that the girl had been drugged, otherwise she must at the first touch of fire have tried to save herself. Accidents, however, will happen in the best regulated families, and no one who thought they knew the respectable practitioner believed him capable of so dastardly a deed. Verily, urbane manners and an attaching smile are valuable assets. When the day came that Dr. Pritchard must face his trial for slaying with every circumstance of cruelty his devoted wife and mother-in-law, neither the relatives of those ladies nor his proper kinsfolk doubted for a moment his innocence; the son and brother of his victims was the first witness for the defense, and his own brother, by permission, actually sat beside him in the dock! I don't think that nowadays our medical friend would have had so long a run for his money. Such an episode as this "melancholy accident," coupled with his "treatment" of his fairer patients, would damn a Court physician, let alone a family doctor. But in the egregious sixties the risk which these foibles involved was sufficiently "covered" by a devout demeanor—Pritchard, I regret to say, was an Episcopalian—by a command of pious slang, a good address, a sleek silk hat, glossy linen, and the physical advantages above described.

Edward William Pritchard came of a naval stock. Born at Southsea in 1825, he was bred to surgery and the service. As assistant surgeon of H.M.S. *Hecate* he met at Portsmouth in 1850 Miss Mary Jane Taylor, the daughter of a retired Edinburgh silk merchant, then on a visit there. They were married that autumn, the bridegroom going to sea again with his ship and the bride returning to her parents. Next year a practice was found for him at Hunmanby in Yorkshire; he quitted the service, and with his wife settled down ashore. In 1857 he purchased from the German University of Erlangen the diploma of Doctor of Medicine *in absentia*.[4] By 1860, having sold his Yorkshire practice, he broke new medical ground at Glasgow. After the "melancholy accident" of the fire, he left Berkeley Terrace for 22 Royal Crescent, removing thence at Whitsunday, 1864, to a house he bought with borrowed money, in Clarence Place, then one of the divisions of Sauchiehall Street, which was to be the stage of his domestic drama.

Dr. Pritchard's memory did not smell sweet and blossom in the dust of Hunmanby and Filey, which for some years had enjoyed the benefit of his professional attendance. He left behind him, in addition to a heavy crop of debts, the reputation of a man vain, unreliable, and mendacious—the prettiest liar, as was said of him, ever known in those parts; and of a physician reckless, quackish, and unscrupulous—especially where women were concerned. Despite the Doctor's impudent assurance and plausible pushfulness the Glasgow campaign did not at first promise well. His medical brethren repulsed his advances; such learned and scientific bodies as he sought to enter fought shy of him, regarding his vaunted exploits and attainments as equally apocryphal. He even had what is expressively termed "the face" to apply for the vacant Chair of Surgery, producing testimonials from sundry great medical guns, the genuineness of which was open to question. Dr. (afterwards Sir George) Macleod, Crown expert in the Sandyford murder case three years later, got the job and made a better one of it than Pritchard would have done, whose chief qualification for the post was his ability to draw the salary. But with the unlettered and credulous vulgar the Doctor had more success.

---

4. "A venal diploma, which was not registerable; so that he has no legal claim to the title of Doctor."—*Lancet*, 15th July 1865, p. 73.

His vogue as a popular lecturer was great; he held spell-bound round-eyed audiences as he declaimed such sentences as this: "I have plucked the eaglets from their eyries in the deserts of Arabia, and hunted the Nubian lion in the prairies of North America." He froze their middle-class blood with tales of his adventures among the Fiji Islanders, and stirred that stagnant fluid with anecdotes of his friend and old-time comrade-in-arms General Garibaldi. Other cards the Doctor had up his politic and wily sleeve: he worked his Masonic connection for all it was worth —and if, as has been profanely hinted, there is in the mysteries of that craft an element of humbug, it is not surprising to learn that he became a Past-Master. Then, more literally, he dealt out to local stationers copies of his own photograph, which, as a philanthropist, he let them have below cost price. In short, never was there so indefatigable a follower of Gilbert's counsel:—

> If you wish in the world to advance,
> Your merits you're bound to enhance,
>     You must stir it and stump it
>     And blow your own trumpet,
> Or, trust me, you haven't a chance!

By strict attention to these precepts Dr. Pritchard acquired in time an extensive, if not a very exclusive, practice; but the goodwill and respect of the profession were still to seek.

The house in Clarence Place consisted of four stories. In the basement were the kitchen offices and the servants' bedroom; on the street floor, the dining-room to the front, and the consulting-room and pantry to the back; on the first floor, the drawing-room and two bedrooms; and on the top flat, two bedrooms and the nursery. The inhabitants of these apartments were the Doctor and his wife; four of their five children—the eldest, a girl of fourteen, was practically adopted by her grandparents in Edinburgh; two young medical students, boarders and pupils of their learned host; and a cook and a house-nursery maid, the only servants. The lads, Connell and King, respectively joined the establishment in November 1863 and October 1864. The cook, Catherine Lattimer, had been ten years in office; the composite maid, Mary M'Leod, entered the Doctor's service at Whitsunday 1863, to fill the vacancy created in his staff by the "melancholy accident" before described. Her ordeal, as we shall find, was to prove only less fiery than that of her luckless predecessor.

## II

Mrs. Pritchard's health had never given, either to herself or to others, any trouble until the autumn of 1864. A well-favored, robust woman of eight-and-thirty, she had hitherto successfully survived the vicissitudes incidental to fifteen years of matrimony with her unconventional consort; but in the month of October she fell sick, having caught, as she believed, a chill. She suffered from depression and headaches, had frequent attacks of sickness, and was often confined to bed. Her mother, Mrs. Taylor, and her daughter, Fanny, wrote pressing her to go to Edinburgh for rest and change, but the Doctor replied— it was a busy household—"I do not think we could manage without her, unless Dear Grandma could come and take charge while she is away." In the end he yielded, and on 26th November she went to her own folk, for what was to be the last time. "Dear Grandma," as we shall see, in pursuance of her son-in-law's invitation, came later to Glasgow—and her doom. In the security of her parents' home—at No. 1 Lauder Road, in the Grange district—Mrs. Pritchard speedily recovered her health. "Ma is very well, all fat and blooming," wrote Fanny on 5th December to her anxious father; she "has gained

311

three pounds of flesh since she came. We can't keep her any longer, she eats so much!"[5] Christmas approached; the good Doctor was giving "a juvenile party," and could no longer do without his helpmate; so on 22nd December his wife, well and happy, resumed her duties. A fortnight after her return her symptoms reappeared, but more intensely. Everything she ate or drank made her sick, and the constant vomiting soon reduced her to a pitiable state of weakness and distress. "She said it was very strange that she was always well in Edinburgh and ill at home."

On 1st February Mrs. Pritchard's mysterious ailment assumed a new form. The cook heard her vomiting in the pantry after dinner as usual; presently her bedroom bell rang, and Lattimer, going up, found her suffering severely from cramp. "Catherine," she cried, "I have lost my senses; I never was so bad as this before!" Dr. Pritchard was called, and exhibited spirits and water. The attack, which lasted half an hour, left her much exhausted. On the 6th Dr. Cowan, Mrs. Pritchard's cousin and a retired medical man, who lived in the Northern Club, Edinburgh, received from Dr. Pritchard a letter stating that he was becoming anxious about his wife's health, and would like another opinion. So Dr. Cowan went to Glasgow on the 7th, saw the lady, and prescribed a mustard poultice and small quantities of champagne. On his return to Edinburgh next day he called on Mrs. Taylor, urging her to go to Glasgow to nurse her daughter, who, he considered, in so large and understaffed a household, was not getting proper attention. The night he left, Mrs. Pritchard had a second and more alarming attack of cramp. At midnight the cook, hearing her cries, went up, and found her in great agony. She said the Doctor had given her chloroform, but she did not blame him. "I want to see Dr. Gairdner," she cried; "fetch Dr.

5. *Trial*, p. 311.

Gairdner!"[6] Her husband, who was in attendance, making no objection, M'Leod was sent to summon Dr. Gairdner forthwith. When between 12 and 1 a.m. that gentleman reached the house he was met by Dr. Pritchard, who said the patient had for some weeks suffered from inability to retain food. He, Dr. Gairdner, had never seen her before; she was in a state of violent mental excitement, with spasms of the hands. Her husband expressed the opinion that it was a case of catalepsy[7]; Dr. Gairdner saw that she was drunk, and said so. His colleague then explained that Dr. Cowan had prescribed stimulants; this Dr. Gairdner said was "very bad treatment"; he forbade her being given any more until he saw her again. He called next day, found her easier, and ordered a simple diet, with no stimulants or medicine whatever. Dr. Gairdner was a consulting physician; there was a doctor in the house, and when that practitioner left for him a message that Mrs. Pritchard was better and he need not call again, his connection with the case ceased. But Dr. Gairdner was not satisfied; he was puzzled by the case, which presented no symptoms of gastric fever, offered by Pritchard as an alternative diagnosis. So he wrote to the lady's brother, Dr. Michael Taylor, Penrith, an old college friend, expressing his doubts as to her treatment and strongly advising her removal to her brother's house and care. Dr. Taylor wrote to his brother-in-law accordingly, but Pritchard, Pharaoh-like, hardened his heart and would not let her go.[8]

---

6. Dr., afterwards Sir, William Tennant Gairdner, K.C.B., then Professor of Medicine in Glasgow University, and residing at No. 21 Blythswood Square.

7. Dr. Gairdner, in cross-examination, admitted that Dr. Pritchard was not "a model of accuracy, wisdom, and caution in applying names to things." Indeed, so happy-go-lucky was his diagnosis of disease as to recall the schoolboy's rendering of *pax in bello*: freedom from indigestion; which certainly was not the case with Mrs. Pritchard.

8. It was my privilege, forty years later, to discuss the case with Sir William Gairdner himself. He told me that at the time he had no suspicion that Pritchard

The day after she received Dr. Cowan's report of her daughter's condition Mrs. Taylor went to Glasgow. She found her confined to bed and suffering from continued vomiting, varied by occasional cramp. Though perhaps a mere coincidence, it is a suggestive fact that after Mrs. Taylor's arrival she herself prepared in the sickroom all the invalid's meals. She assumed charge of the house, gave the maids their orders, and shared her daughter's bed, to the exclusion of the lawful occupant, who was relegated to a spare room on the first floor. On the 13th, two days later, some tapioca was wanted for Mrs. Pritchard. One of the children brought it from the grocer's in a paper bag, which was handed to M'Leod, who left it on the lobby table, where it lay unguarded till it was taken down to the kitchen by somebody and given to the cook; she made a breakfastcupful, which M'Leod took up to Mrs. Taylor in the dining-room. That lady, tasting it, became so sick that she said she must have got the same illness as her daughter! No more was used, and the bag remained in the kitchen press till required to bear witness at the trial.

On the 16th there was a change in the kitchen department: Catherine Lattimer resigned, and was succeeded by Mary Patterson. She did not, however, leave town, and on Friday, the 24th, she called to ask for the invalid. "Well, Catherine," said Mrs. Taylor in reply to her inquiry, "I don't understand her illness; she is one day better and two worse." This, the last day of her life, was spent by Mrs. Taylor, a strong, healthy woman for her seventy years, in attending as usual upon her daughter. In the evening she came down to tea with the family in the dining-room, about seven she was in the kitchen speaking to the cook, she afterwards wrote some letters in the consulting-room, sent M'Leod out to buy sausages for her supper, and at

---

was willfully poisoning his wife, but thought her the victim of what he termed the "harum-scarum" methods of that rash and irresponsible practitioner.

nine o'clock walked upstairs to her daughter's room for the night. Half an hour later the bedroom bell rang violently, and M'Leod, answering it, saw the old lady sitting in a chair, crying out for hot water to make her sick. Mrs. Pritchard bade her bring the Doctor, but that man of medicine was engaged with a patient at the moment, and could not come. Again the bell rang for more hot water; at a third ring M'Leod, returning, found Mrs. Taylor insensible in the chair, with her head hanging down upon her breast. When the Doctor came up he and M'Leod lifted her on to the bed beside her daughter.

At half-past ten Dr. James Paterson, Professor of Midwifery, who lived at No. 6 Windsor Place—195 yards distant from Pritchard's door, as he afterwards told the jury—received a message in consequence of which he went to his neighbor's house. Dr. Pritchard met him in the lobby and gave such an account of the seizure as affords a capital example of that lack of "accuracy, wisdom, and caution in applying names to things" of which we have already heard. His mother-in-law, he said, had suddenly been taken ill while writing a letter in the consulting-room, had fallen off her chair upon the floor, and had been carried upstairs to her bedroom! This attack he attributed to some bitter beer which she and her daughter drank, with the result that both were sick. Dr. Paterson expressed surprise that either Bass or Allsopp's should produce such effects. Dr. Pritchard then told him that Mrs. Taylor "was in the habit of taking a drop," adding that Mrs. Pritchard "had been very poorly for a long time past with gastric fever." Being thus advised of the "facts" of the case, Dr. Paterson was ready to see the patient.

> We then went upstairs to the bedroom. On entering, I observed Mrs. Taylor on the outside of the bed next to me. She was lying on her right side with all her clothes on, and on her head a cap with a small artificial flower. She

had all the appearance of having had a sudden seizure. Mrs. Pritchard, in her nightdress, with her hair very much disheveled, was in the same bed, but underneath the bed-clothes, and sitting up immediately beyond her mother.[9]

Dr. Paterson examined Mrs. Taylor; she presented no appearance of an alcoholic subject, and he expressed his conviction that she was under the influence of some powerful narcotic, probably opium. His colleague then explained that the old lady was in the habit of taking Battley's Sedative Solution—a preparation of opium—of which she had lately bought a half-pound bottle, and that "he had no doubt she had taken a good swig at it." Dr. Paterson said she was dying, and nothing they could do would be of any use; but Pritchard might try mustard poultices and a turpentine injection, which he did. A degree of consciousness ensuing, her son-in-law clapped the old lady on the back and said, "You are getting better, darling." The other shook his head: "Never in this world." At 11:30 p.m. Dr. Paterson went home. Shortly before 1 a.m. an invitation came for him to return, which he declined, as he could do no more.

The passing of Mrs. Taylor is thus described by her disconsolate relative in his Diary:—

> 25 Saturday.—About 1 a.m. this morning, passing away calmly—peacefully—and the features retaining a life-like character—so finely drawn was the transition that it would be impossible to determine with decision the moment when life may be said to be departed.[10]

It was but a fortnight before that she had come, a hale and hearty woman, to that house of death. She was laid out by

9. *Trial*, p. 138.

10. Ibid., p. 307.

the cook and a charwoman named Mrs. Nabb. In the pocket of her dress they found her bottle of Battley. As the women were about their nameless offices, Dr. Pritchard entered the room and asked for the bottle, which he said (falsely) M'Leod had told him they had found. "Good heavens!" he cried, raising his hands and eyes, "has she taken all that since Monday?" He added that she ought not to have sent "a girl like that" for it,[11] but should have consulted him; and he charged them to say nothing about the matter, as "it would not do for a man in his position to be spoken of: it might lead to trouble." It did.

### III

On Saturday, 25th February, Mr. Michael Taylor, the husband of the dead lady, came from Edinburgh in response to his son-in-law's telegram. Dr. Pritchard sent him to Dr. Paterson for the death certificate, which that gentleman refused to grant; so Pritchard himself certified the cause of death as follows: "Paralysis, 12 *hours*. Apoplexy, 1 hour"! On Thursday, 2nd March, he had the further satisfaction to record in his Diary: "Buried Mrs. Taylor, poor Dear Grandma, in Grange Cemetery, fifty yards from entrance, to the left—Next to the Lover's Loan."

Now Dr. Paterson, for reasons which will presently appear, was even less satisfied with the consultation at Clarence Place than Dr. Gairdner had been on an earlier occasion, and when despite his refusal to Mr. Taylor he received from the District Registrar on 2nd March a blank form to fill up, he wrote to that official as follows:—

---

11. M'Leod got a five-ounce bottle filled for Mrs. Taylor at a local chemist's on 20th February.—*Trial*, pp. 90, 206.

6 WINDSOR PLACE, 4TH MARCH 1865.

Dear Sir,—I am surprised that I am called on to certify *the cause of death* in this case. I only saw the person for a few minutes a very short period before her death. She seemed to be under some narcotic, but Dr. Pritchard, who was present from the first moment of the illness until death occurred, and which happened in his own house, may certify the cause. The death was certainly sudden, unexpected, and to me mysterious.—I am, dear Sir, yours faithfully,

James Paterson, M.D.

To Mr. James Struthers, Registrar.[12]

The Registrar would seem to have been subject to the Pritchard spell, for not only did he pay no attention to this suggestive note, but he destroyed it. The causes moving Dr. Paterson to take the step were, as he later explained, three in number: "My first motive or object was to do what was in my power to save Mrs. Pritchard's life; second, *to guard my professional reputation;* and lastly, if possible, to detect the poisoner." On the night of her mother's death he had been greatly struck by the appearance of that lady herself, whose symptoms to his skilled eye "betokened that she was under the depressing influence of antimony." On Wednesday, 1st March, he met Pritchard accidentally in the street; the Doctor said he was going to Edinburgh next day to bury his mother-in-law, and would be obliged if he (Dr. Paterson) would then visit his wife. Dr. Paterson did so, and received from the patient such an account of her illness as to confirm his former opinion. He said

---

12. *Trial*, pp. 149, 331.

nothing whatever to put her on her guard, but prescribed some powders and left the house.[13] On Sunday, 5th March, Pritchard called upon him and said that his wife was much relieved by the treatment. Her case was not discussed: each had his private reasons for avoiding so delicate a topic.

Since his mother-in-law's death Dr. Pritchard had resumed his offices in the sickroom, either giving the invalid with his own hand, or sending her by another, all that she ate or drank. On the evening of the 13th he gave M'Leod a piece of soft cheese for her mistress's supper. That lady took a little and asked the girl to taste it, which she did and found it "hot, like pepper"; it burned her throat and produced thirst. The residue was taken down to the pantry, and next morning Patterson, the cook, ate a small piece. It had a bitter taste and burned her throat; she became sick and vomited frequently, suffering internal pain, and had to go to bed for five hours. On the 15th the Doctor sent by M'Leod to his wife a jug of chamomile tea. Mrs. Pritchard drank of it and immediately vomited. That night, between 10 and 11, he asked the cook to make some egg-flip for her mistress, giving her an unbroken egg and telling her to beat it up very smooth in a "porter glass"—which I take to be a soda tumbler. This she did in the pantry, the Doctor watching the operation. When it was ready, he said he would bring her some sugar and she could add hot water. He then went into the dining-room (where was the sugar basin), next into the consulting-room (where were more mordant flavorings), and from thence into the pantry, with two lumps of loaf sugar which he dropped into the glass, remarking that he would add whisky when it (the egg-flip) "came upstairs." While she was putting in hot water in the kitchen Patterson swallowed a spoonful of the mixture

---

13. Why, in view of his "conviction," did he not secure for chemical analysis a specimen of the patient's urine, a measure to which Dr. Pritchard could have taken no exception?

and commented to M'Leod on its horrible taste. It produced a bitter, burning sensation in her throat; she was immediately sick and continued so till 4 a.m. Despite these untoward happenings the flip was duly exhibited by the Doctor to the patient, who, having drunk a wineglassful, vomited forthwith.

Friday, 17th March, was the last day of Mrs. Pritchard's four months' martyrdom. Between 12 and 1 p.m. her bedroom bell rang three times. It was M'Leod's duty to answer it, but at the third ring the cook went up to see what was wrong. She knew the Doctor was at home, saw the consulting-room door ajar, and tried to open it, but it resisted her touch. She turned to go upstairs, when, looking back, she saw the Doctor come out followed by M'Leod. "How is Mrs. Pritchard now?" he blandly inquired, and they all went up to see. Mrs. Pritchard had another attack of cramp, so the Doctor gave her "something out of a porter glass." At 5 p.m. her bell rang violently. M'Leod, going up, found Mrs. Pritchard in her nightdress on the drawing-room landing. Her mind was wandering, for, pointing to the floor, she cried: "There is my poor mother dead again!" M'Leod summoned Patterson; between them they got her back to bed and called the Doctor, in whose care they left her. At 7:45 p.m. Dr. Pritchard visited Dr. Paterson and asked him to come and see his wife. They went together to the bedroom. Dr. Paterson was much struck by her terribly altered appearance. Her expression was wild, and her eyes fiery red and sunken. She told him she had been vomiting, but Pritchard said that was not so: she was only raving. She complained of great thirst, and Pritchard poured out water for her to drink, remarking, "Here is some nice cold water, darling." Dr. Paterson expressed surprise at her alarming condition, and her husband said she had not slept for five nights. Dr. Paterson then prescribed a simple sleeping draught, and asked Pritchard to make it up himself so as to save time; but that physician said *he kept no drugs in the house* except chloroform and Battley's Solution! So Dr.

Paterson went his way. That night, in pursuance of his virtuous practice, Dr. Pritchard slept with his wife, M'Leod lying on
a couch at the bedfoot. At 1 a.m. the girl was aroused by her
master, who told her to go down and make a mustard poultice;
when she returned with it, accompanied by the cook, her mistress was beyond the aid of poultices. The Doctor, however, insisted that it be applied. The cook refused. "There is no use
putting mustard on a dead body," said she. "Is she dead, Patterson?" he cried. "Doctor," justly rejoined the cook, "you
should know better than I." "Come back, come back, my darling Mary Jane!" wailed the distracted husband. "Do not leave
your dear Edward." But Mary Jane had passed into more merciful keeping. Leaving the body to the attention of the maids, the
Doctor went down to the consulting-room to write certain letters connected with his loss, and to make in his Diary the following entry relative to that lamentable event:—

> 18 Saturday.—Died here at 1 a.m. Mary Jane, my own
> beloved wife, aged 38 years—no torment surrounded her
> bedside—but like a calm peaceful lamb of God, passed
> Minnie away. May God and Jesus, Holy Gh.—one in
> three—welcome Minnie. Prayer on prayer till mine be
> o'er, everlasting love. Save us, Lord, for thy dear Son.[14]

One of these letters, which were of a more practical cast,
bore reference to the overdraft of his bank account, as to which
he was being pressed. On his return from posting them he
summoned the cook to tell her that his wife had walked down
the street with him and kissed him on the cheek, bidding him

---

14. *Trial*, p. 308.—The Doctor was not always in so grave a mood. Breaking the sad
news next day to a lady friend, he said he had called in no less than three doctors
to attend his wife, and yet she died; "a case," he pleasantly commented, *"of too
many cooks."*

take care of the children. Consoled by this ghostly benediction the good physician retired to rest.

Monday, 20th March, was a busy day for the Doctor. In view of the success which attended his diagnosis of Mrs. Taylor's case, he had no difficulty in certifying her daughter's death: "Gastric Fever. Two Months." She was to be buried beside her mother in the Grange Cemetery, and the arrangements completed, her husband traveled with the body to Edinburgh, where it was deposited in the house of her doubly afflicted father, whence the funeral was to take place on the ensuing Thursday. There occurred an incident which can only be equaled in horror by the grim imaginings of a Webster or a Tourneur. Dr. Pritchard had the coffin unscrewed, so that he might look for the last time upon his dead wife's face; which being done, he "exhibited a great deal of feeling," and in the very presence of the old man whom he had bereft of both wife and daughter, tearfully kissed the cold lips. History records three infamous false kisses, namely, that of Judas; that with which King James the First and Sixth sped the fallen favorite Somerset to his fate; and lastly, and not least, this given in such fearful circumstances by Dr. Pritchard to his dead victim. Here, I think, the hideous hypocrisy of the man achieved its supreme effect; though further choice examples were, as we shall find, produced by him under the intensive culture of the condemned cell.

IV

That morning's post brought to the office of Mr. William Hart, the Procurator-Fiscal[15] of Lanarkshire, an anonymous letter in the following terms:—

---

15. The official in Scotland charged with the cognition of matters criminal, as is in England the coroner and his jury.

GLASGOW, MARCH 18TH, 1865.

Sir,—Dr. Pritchard's mother-in-law died suddenly and unexpectedly about three weeks ago in his house, Sauchiehall Street, Glasgow, under circumstances at least very suspicious. His wife died to-day, also suddenly and unexpectedly and under circumstances equally suspicious. We think it right to draw your attention to the above, as the proper person to take action in the matter and see justice done.—Yours, &c.,

Amor Justitiæ.

W. Hart, Esq.[16]

There can be little doubt that this was written as the result of Dr. Paterson's "confidential consultation" with certain medical friends "as to the nature of the two mysterious cases."[17] None but he had the requisite cause of knowledge, the terms "sudden" and "unexpected" occur in both letters, and use of the plural "we" suggests joint action. Be the fact as it may, the Fiscal was more swift to mark iniquity than the complaisant Registrar had been upon his earlier hint, and as the result of sundry inquiries as to the Doctor's doings, a warrant was issued for his arrest on suspicion of causing the death of his wife. That sanguine physician returned to Glasgow that evening in a first-class compartment and with an easy mind. As was his affable wont, he conversed with a chance fellow-traveler, to whom he presented one of his own photographs, and bidding him a courteous adieu when the train reached Queen Street,

---

16. *Trial*, p. 33.

17. Ibid., p. 333.

alighted in his usual stately fashion. He did not expect anyone to meet him; but Superintendent M'Call of the Glasgow City Police was awaiting his arrival, and at the pressing invitation of that functionary, Dr. Pritchard accompanied him to the North Prison. "Previous to retiring to rest," we read, "and before the room was vacated by the officers, the Doctor engaged in prayer."[18] Doubtless he audibly petitioned for the forgiveness of his enemies, persecutors, and slanderers, and for the turning of their hearts.

The development of the case for the prosecution proceeded amain. The members of the Doctor's household were seen and precognosced, the secrets of the consulting-room laid bare, and his accounts for drugs examined. On the 21st, at No. 1 Lauder Road, Edinburgh, Drs. Maclagan and Littlejohn made a post-mortem examination of Mrs. Pritchard's body, which presented no appearance of recent morbid action, and nothing at all capable of accounting for death. Certain organs were therefore removed for chemical analysis. On the 22nd the prisoner was judicially examined before Sir Archibald Alison, Sheriff of Lanarkshire, and the historian of Europe,[19] and emitted a declaration on the charge of murdering his wife by poison. He gave her, he declared, no medicines whatever during her illness, trusting Nature to right itself; he never gave her antimony, except when in October he applied it externally to her neck for a swollen gland, and some years earlier gave it once, internally, for inflammation of the eyelids; there was a "considerable quantity" of that drug in his repositories, as he used it extensively in his practice. "I never administered anti-

---

18. *Glasgow Herald*, 24th April 1865.

19. It is, for us, unfortunate that the autobiography of the learned Sheriff (*Some Account of My Life and Writings*, Edinburgh: 1883) stops in 1862. His references to the M'Lachlan case of that year are of great interest, and one would have welcomed his reminiscences of Pritchard.

mony internally to her on any occasion, nor any other substance calculated to injure or destroy life." The investigation having disclosed the unusual relations which subsisted between the Doctor and his housemaid, M'Leod was apprehended as being concerned in the murder, but after two days' examination before the Sheriff she was released—to testify against her master and seducer. The analysis disclosed the presence of antimony in all the organs tested, as well as in the bed and body linen of the dead lady. The authorities then decided to exhume the remains of Mrs. Taylor, which was done, with results similar to those obtained in the case of her daughter. So on 21st April the prisoner again appeared before the Sheriff on the fresh charge of murdering his mother-in-law by poison. He declared that he was in no way accessory to Mrs. Taylor's death. "I never administered poison to her. I did and do believe she died from paralysis and apoplexy"; and he refused to answer any further questions. But although things looked black enough for the Doctor, they failed to disturb the atmosphere of holy calm by which he was environed and sustained. Stern governors, harsh warders, and insensitive policemen alike felt the charm of his benign and mild demeanor. His belief in his "innocence" was infectious; even the official heart —that obdurate organ—was touched by the meekness with which he bore unjust suspicion, while to his relatives and friends, as I have said, he was a blameless victim of the Blind Goddess.

In turning over the files of old newspapers chronicling the case one is struck by the latitude allowed to Pressmen of that day. Every step of the investigation is reported with a frankness now impossible to conceive in an affair *sub judice*; results of post-mortem and analysis are published; all, and more than witnesses are prepared to swear, with comments on their characters and personal appearance, is cheerfully set forth for the entertainment of the public; while divers ingenious theories are propounded as to the manner in which the crimes were committed, and the nature of the accused's defense. But these engaging freedoms were pretermitted so soon as Messrs. Galbraith & Maclay, Writers, Glasgow, were instructed to act for the prisoner. I remember the late Sir David Brand, Sheriff of Ayr, to whom, as one of the few survivors of those concerned, I dedicated my account of the case—he was junior counsel for the defense—telling me that when Mr. Galbraith accompanied Dr. Pritchard to Edinburgh for the trial, that gentleman took a gloomy view of the chances of an acquittal. But his client was more optimistic and bade the man of law be of good cheer. "Keep up your heart," said he; "we will return to Glasgow together." The Doctor's prognosis, as had happened before in other cases, was, as regards his own, at fault.

The trial began on Monday, 3rd July 1865, before the High Court of Justiciary. The great John Inglis, who as Dean of Faculty had eight years earlier saved at that bar the life of Madeleine Smith—winning literally by a neck—presided as Lord Justice-Clerk. Lord Advocate Moncreiff, who had prosecuted the fortunate fair one, was to have discharged a similar duty on this occasion also, but as on the eve of the trial he was called to London upon official business, the Crown case fell to be conducted by the Solicitor-General, Mr. (afterwards Lord) Young, assisted by Mr. (afterwards Lord) Gifford and Mr. (afterwards Sheriff) Crichton. The accused's interests were in the able hands of Mr. (afterwards Lord) Rutherfurd-Clark, Mr. (afterwards Lord) Watson, and Mr. Brand. In the multitude of counselors there may be wisdom, but even so great a galaxy of legal talent could not make of the Pritchard case what connoisseurs of crime call a "good" trial. The contest was too one-sided: the forces of the Crown had it all their own way, and in the defense there was but little fight. One misses the flash and report of interchanged shots, the explosions of opposed artillery, the intermittent rumble of judicial guns by which the well-fought fields of Blythswood Square and of Ardlamont are distinguished in the annals of forensic warfare. It lacks alike the thrilling moments of the Sandyford murder case, and the many problems presented by the slaying of Miss Gilchrist. Still, there *is* one unsolved mystery: the motive for the crimes: upon which the reader may exercise his wits.

As I have elsewhere printed the evidence in full, I shall confine myself to noting one or two points of interest. Here doctors do not differ: this is the only great poisoning trial known to me where no medical evidence was offered for the defense—which relied, for what it was worth, upon the cross-examination of the Crown experts—and where the case for the prosecution was not, in this respect, seriously challenged. There could be no question that the death of Mrs. Pritchard was due to the administration of tartar emetic in small doses over a prolonged period; her body was impregnated with that poison—from the liver and intestines alone ten grains were recovered; and as no one could conceivably kill themselves in that manner, and as her husband and physician denied giving her medicinally any antimony whatever, it followed that she was willfully done to death. The cause of Mrs. Taylor's death was more complex and difficult to determine. Antimony was found in her body, antimony and *aconite* were found in her bottle of Battley[20]; and the Crown doctors were clear that her

---

20. Sir Henry Littlejohn used to tell his students, in his own inimitable way, how, when the Crown experts were wondering precisely what poison had been added to the Battley bottle, he put his finger in the mixture and tasting it, at once felt the characteristic tingling and numbness of the gums which enabled him to exclaim dramatically, "Aconite!"—the presence of that subtle vegetable poison being afterwards established.

death was due to the combined action of antimony, aconite, and opium. The defense, however, sought to maintain that she might have died from the opium alone, which she took knowingly and voluntarily, and that if so, whoever put into her medicine bottle the two other poisons was not guilty of her death. But this distinction was too fine for the jury. She had been used for years to taking opium in increasing quantities, and the amount consumed by her from her last bottle could have been taken with impunity. It was neither by accident nor to no purpose that antimony and aconite found their way into her accustomed remedy.

Dr. Pritchard got his drugs from two different Glasgow chemists. His purchases during the period in question are instructive. These are the accounts:—

(I)

1864

Sept. 19 —10 grains Strychnine.

Nov.  4 —1/2 oz. Tinct. Conii.

" 16 —1 oz. Laudanum.

      —1 oz. *Tartar Emetic.*

" 24 —1 oz. Tinct. Aconite.

Dec.  8 —1 oz. Fleming's Tincture Aconite.

" 9 —1 oz. Tinct. Conii Maculat.

1865

Feb.  4 —1 oz. Tinct. Conii.

Feb.  7 —1 oz. *Tart. Antimon.*

      —1 oz. Tinct. Aconite.

" 9 —1 oz. Tinct. Aconite.

" 11 —2 oz. Tincture of Digitalis.

" 18 —2 oz. Tinct. Conii.[21]

---

21. *Trial*, p. 157.

(II)

1865

| | | |
|---|---|---|
| 18th February | —Two ounces Solution Morphia. | |
| | —One ounce Fleming's Tincture of Aconite. | |
| 8th March | —Solution of Atropine one dram, one gr. to dram. | |
| 9th " | —Solution of Atropine one dram, two grs. to dram. | |
| 13th " | —1/2 ounce of Fleming's Tincture of Aconite. | |
| 14th " | —Solution of Atropine one dram, two grs. to dram. | |
| 16th " | —Solution of Atropine one dram, five grs. to dram.[22] | |

Even to the lay reader, if he takes the trouble to compare the dates with those in the foregoing narration, the result will appear both striking and suggestive. It was contended for the accused that these articles were but the necessary weapons of his armory, employed by him in his daily battle with disease and death on behalf of his suffering fellow-creatures. To this view there were upon the proof two objections: no ordinary physician in general practice was ever known to require such quantities of deadly poisons; and the defense offered no reason for their acquisition, nor any account of their disposal.[23] There were found in the consulting-room, among other toxicological

---

22. *Trial*, p. 159.

23. Two of the Doctor's patients, called for the defense, stated that he had attended them for ear trouble; one he treated with iodine, the other with glycerine and strychnia. As explaining his wholesale purchases of tartar emetic, conium, aconite, and atropine, this hardly fills the bill.

curiosities, a wooden box containing a mixture of fifteen grains of arsenic and tartar emetic in equal proportions; an empty wine bottle with ten drops of a solution of corrosive sublimate remaining; and between forty and fifty bottles and packets of medicines, some harmless, some lethal. Yet Dr. Pritchard told Dr. Paterson he kept no drugs in the house!

It is plain that, having thus ample means, he had, as relative and medical attendant, every opportunity of administration; but with only two poisoned articles of food taken by the patient could his association directly be established. In the unused portion of tapioca antimony was discovered to the amount of five grains to the pound, but there was no proof that it had been, in a double sense, "doctored" by him. The incidents to which I refer were those occurring respectively on 13th, 14th, and 15th March, namely, that of the cheese and that of the egg-flip. For the defense, a great deal was made of the difficulty of adding the white powder of antimony to a piece of yellow cheese; but, as was pointed out by the Justice-Clerk in his charge to the jury, a *solution* of tartar emetic might easily have been employed. With regard to the egg-flip, it was argued that the amount of antimony dusted on two lumps of sugar could not have produced in the cook the severe sickness which followed her taking a teaspoonful, and that if it did so, the wine-glassful drunk by Mrs. Pritchard must have killed her on the spot. But the lady's constitution had been habituated for months to the effects of antimony: the cook's was virgin soil.

In this connection I cannot refrain quoting from the cross-examination of Dr. Littlejohn a passage which has always appealed to me as characteristic of that nimble-witted expert. The Professor having stated in reply to the Solicitor-General that tartar emetic could be exhibited in egg-flip "with great facility," and that a sufficient dose, not to kill but to keep up illness, could be given "quite easily" on a lump of sugar, Mr. Rutherfurd-Clark began as follows:—

Do I understand you to say that if two pieces of sugar were put into a cup of egg-flip, enough of antimony can be conveyed by dusting over the sugar with tartar emetic, so that a teaspoonful of the egg-flip could produce the effects mentioned?—It is quite possible. Egg-flip being a thick mucous substance, it would sustain mechanically a considerable quantity. You observe I am not speaking of the egg alone, but of the beat-up egg with hot water poured upon it.

Suppose egg-flip is made in the ordinary manner, can you convey into the cup as much antimony upon two pieces of sugar as, taking a spoonful of the liquid, would produce the effect you have heard?—I think it is quite possible.

Have you made any experiments to try it?—I have made no direct experiments to try it.

Have you made any indirect experiments?—I have not.

You have made no experiments at all?—We doctors are continually making experiments.

But I mean experiments for this purpose?—I have made no experiments with direct reference to this case.

Then this is mere theory?—Grounded on my experience of this drug . . . I may say that I am intimately acquainted with tartar emetic, and I hold I am entitled to answer the question in the way I have done.[24]

No doubt the Professor was right; but I think that in order to produce the "horrible taste" referred to by the cook, there must have been in that tumbler a poison other than antimony, for in the Bravo case of 1876 tartar emetic in solution was demonstrated to be tasteless. At all events the jury were

---

24. *Trial*, p. 200.—Sir Henry did me the favor to read the proof sheets of his evidence.

satisfied that Dr. Pritchard had contributed to the brew something more recondite than sugar.

V

In the kennel of "dirty dogs" called Pritchard, the scurviest, to my mind, was the particular cur that instructed the line of defense, namely, that if crimes in fact there were, Mary M'Leod committed them. This girl, when fifteen years of age, had been seduced by her master, in the summer of 1863, at No. 22 Royal Crescent, while his wife and children were in the country. In May 1864, as the result of their intimacy, she found herself with child, and the Doctor performed upon her an illegal operation which produced a miscarriage. The connection was continued until Mrs. Pritchard's death. Now it is an amazing fact, testified to by the girl herself in the box and by Pritchard in the confession published after his suspension, that his wife was aware of this intrigue, and according to him, "sought to cover my wickedness and folly." Nay, more: M'Leod swears that upon one occasion the guilty pair were actually surprised by Mrs. Pritchard in one of the bedrooms, and that in consequence she "wanted to go away"; but her mistress would not let her, saying she herself would speak to the Doctor, who, she justly observed, "was a nasty, dirty man."[25] The lady, as appears, could beat the Doctor at a diagnosis. To her mid-Victorian mind, a public scandal doubtless seemed more shocking than a private wrong.

It was only after repeated questioning by counsel and on the

---

25. It was the disclosure to the police by Mrs. Nabb, the charwoman, of how Mary had told her that Mrs. Pritchard "discovered the Doctor and her in circumstances which need not be further adverted to," coupled with her having remarked at divers times, "in a boasting spirit," that she would succeed her mistress, which led to M'Leod's apprehension.—*Glasgow Evening Citizen*, 23rd March 1865.

solemn warning of the Justice-Clerk that if she did not answer she would be sent to prison, that M'Leod was brought to admit that Pritchard had promised her marriage. "He said that when Mrs. Pritchard died, if she died before him, and I was alive, he would marry me."[26] This admission had an important bearing on the case: the Crown holding that it furnished a reason for the prisoner's suppression of his wife; the defense, that it supplied the maid with a motive to murder her mistress.

At the time of the trial Mary M'Leod was sixteen. "In stature she is slightly below the middle height of women, and is of a slender and rather delicate make. She is red-haired, with a pale, not unhandsome, freckled face, and speaks with a Highland accent."[27] No one who has studied the character of Dr. Pritchard can for a moment believe him, though capable of most things, likely to have married in any circumstances this wretched girl. His "promise" was but the current small change of the seducer; she had been his mistress for over a year, and no Freudian complication could impel so vain, ambitious, and crafty a rogue to ruin himself, socially and professionally, by *marrying* his own housemaid. He had nothing to fear from his wife, whose faith in him survived the revelation of his baseness. No; I expect that he had merely tired of the poor woman, was bored by her devotion, and found her continued existence incompatible with the free pursuit of his lawless pastimes. It may be that he saw his way to a more attractive match, for he was hugely popular with the opposite sex.

In the matter of Mrs. Taylor's murder the pecuniary motive alleged by the Crown was even less convincing: a liferent interest under her settlement to the extent of two-thirds, in a sum of £2500, until his children came of age. There was no proof

---

26. *Trial*, p. 106.

27. *Glasgow Evening Citizen, supra.*—She was a native of Islay. The photograph of her reproduced in the *Trial* indicates a disposition decidedly dour.

that he knew the terms of her will, and if he did, I doubt if he would have deemed the game worth the candle. His bank account was overdrawn, he had raised money on his life-policy, and borrowed £500 from Mrs. Taylor, who appears to have been an ideal mother-in-law; but although his financial position was unsound, the old lady, of whom he was said to be the idol, would willingly have helped him further. My belief is that she had conceived and given birth to some suspicions touching the strange features of her daughter's illness, and would thus have proved a dangerous witness in the event of any inquiry into the circumstances of Mrs. Pritchard's death. It is certain that she had discovered his dallyings with the maid, for the Doctor tells us in his confession that Mrs. Taylor, the day before her death, "caught Mary M'Leod and myself in the consulting-room," which seems to have been their grisly trysting-place. The mother-in-law may have shown less complaisance than did the wife upon a like occasion, and this probably was what turned the balance of her fate. Be that as it may, the assassin struck swiftly and at once; there was no time for the delicate finesse which attended the destruction of his other victim. But, with regard to this question of motive, surely the crimes of Pritchard are just a manifestation of the criminal intellect, which, as Dickens has so wisely said, "its own professed students perpetually misread, because they persist in trying to reconcile it with the average intellect of average men, instead of identifying it as a horrible wonder apart."[28]

The position of Dr. Paterson calls for a passing word. The key-note of that gentleman's conduct is sounded by himself in his second reason for writing to the Registrar: "to guard my professional reputation." He was called in professionally to Mrs. Taylor, and found her dying of a narcotic poison; at the same time he formed the opinion that her daughter was being

---

28. *The Mystery of Edwin Drood*, chapter xx.

poisoned with antimony. He was later twice called in professionally to Mrs. Pritchard, when his previous judgment was confirmed. Now it is sufficiently obvious to the reader of his evidence at the trial and of his subsequent apologia,[29] that Dr. Paterson had what is termed in Scotland "a good conceit of himself," and that he held his primary duty to be the protection of his own interests. He maintained that by refusing to certify the death of Mrs. Taylor he did everything possible to save Mrs. Pritchard's life. But it is difficult to accept this view. He says that having been called in for consultation, "it would be a breach of the etiquette of my profession" to go back uninvited to see a patient whom he believed was being murdered. Nay, more; that had he done so, the defense might have alleged that it was *he* who administered the antimony which he was so sure would be found in her body! He breathed no word of his suspicions either to Pritchard or to old Mr. Taylor; nor did he communicate his uneasiness to Dr. Michael Taylor, as Dr. Gairdner had done, by letter. He gave to Mrs. Pritchard, *when he saw her alone*, no warning of any kind, not the least hint that someone was practicing upon her with poison, and that her life was threatened; while his manner to Pritchard cannot have been such as to alarm that wary and astute practitioner, who evidently thought that he had hoodwinked his colleague. "The immediate consequence would have been most assuredly an action for heavy and ruinous damages!" he writes; and bitterly concludes that it would have been better for him to have been "an ignoramus in my profession," who thought Mrs. Pritchard's complaint "gastric fever," or was "puzzled" by her case, or believed that she was "drunk." This smacks somewhat of that "malignant professional jealousy" of which Dr. Paterson deemed himself the victim at the hands of "Edinburgh graduates." The whole matter was dealt with at

29. See his letter to the newspaper Press, 11th July 1865.—*Trial*, pp. 330–334.

the time from the medical standpoint, in two sensibly written articles,[30] in which it is well observed:—

> There were clearly two things, either of which he could have done. He might have given Pritchard to understand that he rejected the theory of gastric fever, and that he suspected antimonial poisoning, without charging anyone in particular, or he might have expressed an intention or wish to consult with the professional men who had already seen Mrs. Pritchard.

Either of these courses, if adopted, would probably have scared the murderer from his prey. And upon the famous "etiquette" passage the writer further remarks:—

> He has done a yet more grievous wrong to the whole profession in throwing the burden of the blame due to his cowardice and want of judgment upon an alleged etiquette which does not exist.

Some charitable folk sought to excuse Dr. Paterson by suggesting that his celebrated diagnosis was retrospective, and depended on the result of the chemical analysis; that his dislike and distrust of Pritchard—of which, in the box, he made no secret—led him to think the case suspicious; and that by a mental process such as enabled George the Fourth to fancy he had been at Waterloo, the doctor came to believe that he had "spotted" antimony from the first. He claims to have consulted *at the time* certain medical friends unnamed: one would like to know what he said to them. The last word on the subject is the stern rebuke administered by the Justice-Clerk in his charge to the jury:—

---

30. *Lancet*, 1865, ii. 69 and 95.

I care not for professional etiquette or professional rule. There is a rule of life, and a consideration that is far higher than these—and that is, the duty that every right-minded man owes to his neighbor to prevent the destruction of human life in this world, and in that duty I cannot but say Dr. Paterson failed.[31]

## VI

The Solicitor-General had, relatively, an easy task. The fact that these ladies did not die of gastric fever and of apoplexy, as respectively alleged and certified by the accused, but of poison, was not disputed. Suicide and accident were equally out of the question, and antimony was not administered medicinally. "There was a murderer in that house practicing the dreadful art of slow poisoning from the end of December to the middle of March." It could not have been done by the children, the boy-boarders, or either of the cooks—the poisoning began before the one came and continued after the other left. They were forced to the conclusion that these crimes were committed either by the prisoner or by M'Leod. "It was a murder"—that of Mrs. Pritchard—"in which you almost detect a doctor's finger." It was effected by gradual poisoning—"poisoning carried on so as not to kill but to weaken; leaving off for a day and then resuming again; the victim one day better, two days worse." Could a servant girl of sixteen have done that under the very eye of a medical man, the husband of the victim, who was in close attendance upon her? Could such a girl have had, in the case of Mrs. Taylor, the knowledge and skill to introduce into her medicine the antimony and aconite found in the

---

31. *Trial*, p. 283.

bottle? The prisoner alone had the means, the opportunity, the ability, and the motive (the last, by the way, was the only weak strand in the rope which the learned Solicitor so competently spun for the prisoner's neck); and his lies to the doctors and others, his false certificates and declarations, the whole facts of the case, left no doubt as to his guilt. And indeed, looking back with counsel over the evidence, one realizes that it was mainly out of his own mouth that the Doctor was condemned.

Mr. Rutherfurd-Clark began his address to the jury with the sound proposition that if the accused were guilty, "he is the foulest criminal that ever lived." The physician became the destroyer and used his art of healing to sap the foundations of life. To the one victim he was bound by the most tender of human ties; of the other he was the idol: it was a cold-blooded, deliberate murder of these trusting and loving women. Offenses such as these must be proved by over-whelming evidence, for the mind of man could hardly conceive of a wretch so devoid of human feeling as to perpetrate such frightful crimes. Yet here there was nothing but suspicion. M'Leod's story of their relations was not corroborated. If the prisoner ever spoke to her of marriage it must have been in jest; but though that could have been for him no motive, it might well have supplied a motive to someone else. That he slew Mrs. Taylor in order to obtain a chance of succession was equally incredible. No article of food which the Crown alleged to be poisoned reached these ladies without passing through other hands than his; and it was remarkable that in every instance the person who administered it, and who carried away what was left, was Mary M'Leod. The Crown said it was the act either of the prisoner or of M'Leod, and that it was unlikely that a girl of sixteen had the skill to do it; but they must prove that it was not M'Leod before they could bring home the charge to the prisoner. It was highly significant that the Solicitor-General did not venture to ask her whether she put anything in the food. Mrs. Taylor died from an overdose of her own opium; knowing this, the prisoner, humanely enough, to spare his father-in-law's feelings, ascribed her death to apoplexy—"the real cause would indeed be painful for a husband to hear." Dr. Paterson's evidence was quite unreliable, colored as it was by his intense animus against the prisoner. Here was a medical man—"fearful of his purse, fearful of his person, fearful of his reputation"—who took no step whatever to stop a murder which he was convinced was being perpetrated! Why should the prisoner have thought his wife's symptoms due to poison when neither Dr. Cowan nor Dr. Gairdner suspected foul play? Why, if guilty, did he call in three other physicians? He was proved to have lived on the most affectionate terms with both ladies. He slept with his wife throughout her illness, she died in his arms, he had her coffin opened that he might kiss her for the last time. Was he upon mere suspicion to be held guilty of such unparalleled wickedness?

> A more cold-blooded, a more frightful, a more dreadful atrocity could not be supposed. It is impossible that evidence of probability, upon which the whole case of the Crown hangs, can ever justify you in believing that he was capable of committing the crime, and of the hideous hypocrisy which he is said to have manifested. Suppose such a case: one would almost believe the thunderbolt of the Almighty would have stricken down the man who could have done it.[32]

The charge of the Lord Justice-Clerk, as I have elsewhere said, "was in the highest degree careful, complete, and exhaustive, abounding in subtle insight into special points of the case untouched by those who had previously dealt with it, and

---

32. *Trial*, p. 263.—The prisoner, we learn, was more affected by the speech for the defense than by that for the prosecution; which is not surprising.

was in every way worthy of so great a judge." There could be no mistaking, however, that in his Lordship's judgment the Crown had proved their case. As to abridge would be to spoil it, I shall give but a single sample. The prosecutor maintained that the prisoner committed the murders; the defense, that they were committed by M'Leod:—

> Gentlemen, that is a very painful position for you to be placed in. If it be necessary that you decide absolutely between the two, it must be done. At the same time the prisoner's counsel did not seem sufficiently alive, in considering this point, to the possibility that both might be implicated, and if that were so, I suppose we should have little doubt as to which was the master and which the servant; and that, although the one might be the active hand that administered the poison, if two were concerned, you could have very little doubt who prepared it and who set on the other. And in fact, if you should arrive at that conclusion, every article that the prisoner's counsel alluded to for the purpose of showing the guilt of Mary M'Leod would be an article of evidence to implicate the prisoner at the bar.[33]

But his Lordship made it plain that, while M'Leod might well have been employed in the poisoning, she had, in his view, no guilty knowledge of the fact.

After a decent interval of fifty-five minutes the jury unanimously returned the only possible verdict; and the Justice-Clerk, observing that no reasonable being could have the slightest doubt of his guilt, sentenced the prisoner to death. Courteous to the last, that remarkable man bowed severally to Judge and jury before passing from the public gaze.

---

33. *Trial*, p. 291.

Three times have I, sitting in the hushed High Court, heard pronounced that last dread sentence of the law. The first was upon Jessie King, the Edinburgh baby-farmer; who stifled her pitiful charges for their exiguous "premiums"; the second was upon John Watson Laurie, who brained and buried on the flanks of Goatfell, in Arran, an English tourist for a pound or two and the contents of a Gladstone bag; the third was upon Oscar Slater, who may or may not have slain with a hammer in Glasgow a venerable old lady for her jewelry. But when, as sometimes happens, I stray into the Justiciary Court-room, dim and deserted in vacance time, it is none of these that fancy shows me in the empty dock. No; in the shadows of that lofty chamber two other figures occupy, for me, the narrow seat within the bar. One, a beautiful girl, in a brown silk dress and a small chip bonnet trimmed with white ribbons, her hair arranged in the Eugénie style, and in her lavender-gloved fingers a silver-tipped smelling-bottle and a little cambric handkerchief, who smiles brightly and confidently upon a phantom jury. The other, a gentleman-like personage of forty, pale but respectable, bearded but benignant, attired in deepest mourning, who, craped hat in black-gloved hand, bows gravely to the Bench as he hearkens to the words of doom.

## VII

The last days of Dr. Pritchard provided an edifying spectacle. He posed as a misjudged martyr, read diligently in his Bible, and wasted much precious time upon the transcription of texts, more or less relevant to his situation and neatly written on slips of paper, which, in default of the usual photographic souvenirs, he distributed to all and sundry. In view of his quenchless thirst for popularity it must have been disappointing for him to find that not a finger was raised to obtain a reprieve. The "genuine philanthropist" who, unmindful of the sufferings of the victim, waxes eloquent over the murderer's cruel fate, was for once reduced to silence: not even cranks could champion Dr. Pritchard. Meanwhile that ill-used gentleman, unwearied in well-doing, desired to cleanse his bosom of such perilous stuff as accumulates in the best of consciences. He admitted that he had murdered his wife in collaboration with M'Leod, who knowingly gave her poisoned food. As nobody believed this, he was moved to make a second "confession"; he killed his wife with chloroform, M'Leod still holding the candle; but he declared—"before God, as a dying man, and in the presence of my spiritual adviser"—that he was innocent of Mrs. Taylor's blood. He put aconite in the bottle *after her death*, "in order to prove death by misadventure." In a third and final statement, "made in the presence of an all-seeing God and of the Rev. J. Watson Reid," he admitted the perpetration of both murders "in the way brought out in the evidence," and acquitted M'Leod of any knowledge of, or participation in, the crimes. These he attributed to "a species of terrible madness and the use of ardent spirits." Even at the last, and in the face of Providence and its depute, the Doctor could not tell the truth.

In view of the complexity of his spiritual state, over and above the advice of those whom he terms "my own immediate faith-professors"—clergy of the Scottish Episcopal Church—the penitent patient called into consultation two great Presbyterian doctors: Andrew Bonar and Norman Macleod. Never had these famous physicians of the soul been confronted with a case so difficult. Excerpts from an unpublished diary of Dr. Macleod[34] show how strenuously that good man strove with the sinner to induce him to clear the girl he had falsely accused. "I told him I did not believe one word he said, and that his crimes were almost unexampled. He was sitting on his bed.

---

34. *Scotsman*, 1st June 1912.

He threw himself back, stretching out his hands, and said, 'Do you know, Dr. Macleod, I now understand how Jesus suffered from the unbelief of men in His Word.' " The reverend doctor, properly horrified, "expressed himself strongly" and burst into tears; whereupon the other fell on his knees and began to pray aloud. "There was an unreality in his prayers." After days of godly wrestling, Dr. Macleod brought him to confess his guilt. Dr. Bonar also notes in his diary his experiences of this singular convert, who had invoked his ghostly counsel and advice.[35] On bidding him farewell the latter airily remarked, "I will meet you in Heaven." Dr. Bonar, turning round, sternly replied, "Sir, I shall meet you at the Judgment Seat!"

Dr. Pritchard's last letter was addressed, the day before his death, to his brother-in-law, Dr. Michael Taylor—with whom, by the way, during his wife's illness he had been in the habit of corresponding with greater frequency than good faith:—

27TH JULY 1865.

Farewell, brother, I die in twenty-four hours from this. Romans viii, 34 to 39 verses.

Mary Jane, Darling Mother, and you, I will meet, as you said the last time you spoke to me, in happier circumstances. Bless you and yours, prays the dying penitent,

Edward William Pritchard.[36]

It would be for so vain a man not the least part of his punishment that his admiring relatives at long length knew him as he was.

Next morning, about eight o'clock, on Glasgow Green,

---

35. *Diary and Letters*, p. 250. London: 1894.

36. *Trial*, p. 44.

before a great multitude of spectators, with the professional assistance of Calcraft, Dr. Pritchard departed for his own place. A shower had fallen in the night, "which gave rise to apprehensions that the morning might be wet, but fortunately the rain wore off." The subject of the ceremony proposed to address the crowd from the scaffold; this the authorities would not permit, and with his passion for the platform he must have deplored the neglected opportunity: it was the last public execution in Glasgow.

The final scene is thus described by Dr. Macleod in a letter to his wife:—

> Please do not excite yourself when you see by the papers that I have been with Pritchard to the last. I thought it rather cowardly to let Oldham[37] do this work alone when we had shared the previous portion of it. So I offered to go, and I am glad I did. I saw it all from first to last; was with him in his cell, and walked at his back till he reached the scaffold. As to his behavior, strange to say, no patriot dying for his country, no martyr dying for his faith, could have behaved with greater calmness, dignity, and solemnity! . . . He marched to the scaffold with a deadly pale face but erect head, *as if he marched to the sound of music.* He stood upright and steady as a bronze statue, with the cap over his face and the rope round his neck. When the drop fell, all was quiet. Marvelous and complex character! Think of a man so firm as to say, smiling, to Oldham, "I am glad you have come with your gown and bands"![38]

37. The Rev. R. S. Oldham, incumbent of St. Mary's Episcopal Church, Renfield Street, of which Dr. Pritchard was an unworthy member.

38. *Memoir of Norman Macleod, D.D.,* ii. 185. London: 1876.

His body was buried within the precincts of the prison, but this world was not yet rid of Dr. Pritchard. Equally remarkable in life as in death, it was his strange fate to undergo a premature resurrection. Forty-five years after being laid in the grave to await his summons to the Great Assize, his bones were dug up and his skull furnished matter for the scientific article.[39] How Sir Thomas Browne would have welcomed the occasion! In 1910 the old Justiciary Buildings in Jail Square were pulled down to make way for a more modern structure. In the course of these operations the courtyard, in which were interred the bodies of executed criminals, was excavated, and the remains of divers malefactors, including those of Dr. Pritchard, were exhumed. "The skull was in a good state of preservation, the teeth and the lower and upper jaws being almost intact. The clothing which deceased wore at his execution, consisting of a surtout coat, vest, and trousers, was thrown up, along with the bones of his legs, arms, and other parts of the skeleton. Some shreds of undergarments were also found, and a pair of elastic-sided boots was the last relic to be unearthed. The coffin containing the remains was very brittle, and broke in pieces when the shovels of the workmen struck the soil."[40] These "relics" were afterwards reburied.

> For he who lives more lives than one
> More deaths than one must die.

---

39. "Note on the Skull of Dr. Pritchard," by Geo. H. Edington, M.D. *Glasgow Medical Journal*: February 1912.

40. *Dundee Advertiser*, 24th November 1910.

# THE ARRAN MURDER

T H E   I S L E   O F   Arran, as most readers know, lies in the estuary of the Clyde, between the pleasant shores of Carrick and Kintyre. To the north, beyond the Kyles of Bute, are the sealochs, moors, and mountains of Argyll; southward the Craig of Ailsa stands sentinel in the wider Firth. The first prospect of the island, whether from the Ayrshire coast or from the deck of some passing vessel in the fairway, is unforgettable—the majestic outline of the serrated peaks soaring out of the sea to pierce the rain clouds too often wreathed about their summits, the sunlight gleaming on their granite flanks, wet from some recent shower, and over all, austere and solitary, the great gray cone of Goatfell, "the mountain of the winds." Amid these formidable giants are many glens, some bare and savage as themselves, others domesticated as it were by the kindly uses of man; while at their feet lie certain bays whose yellow sands, beloved by generations of children, are, alas! no "undiscovered country" to the excursionist.

At the time of which we write, the moral and physical

atmosphere of the island was above reproach; wickedness and manufactories were alike unknown. The larger villages boasted each its own constable, who embodied the law in some peaceful cottage, incongruously labeled "Police Station"; but these officers led a life of ease and dignity among the blameless lieges, being only called upon to exercise their functions now and then on the person of an obstreperous tripper. Yet this fortunate isle was to become the scene of a crime, characterized at a later stage as "unprecedented and incredibly atrocious."

On the forenoon of Friday, 12th July 1889, the once famous Clyde steamer *Ivanhoe*, in the course of her daily run to Arran from the upper reaches of the Firth, called at Rothesay, the "capital" of Bute. Among the passengers who then joined the vessel was a party from Glenburn Hydropathic, including a young Englishman named Edwin Robert Rose, a clerk in the employment of a Brixton builder, then spending his fortnight's holiday in Scotland. He was thirty-two years of age, of light build, five feet seven in height, of athletic, active habits, and in the best of health and spirits. On the sail to Arran he struck up an acquaintance with a fellow-passenger, a young man who gave his name as Annandale, and they landed together at Brodick for an hour or so until the steamer's return from Whiting Bay. Apparently they had decided to take lodgings in the village, for shortly after the steamer's arrival Annandale presented himself at the house of Mrs. Walker, Invercloy, and inquired for rooms. Invercloy is the name of the village, Brodick that of the district. It was then the Glasgow Fair week, and the limited accommodation available was taxed to its utmost limits. Mrs. Walker, however, was able to offer a room with one bed, in a wooden structure adjoining her house, having a separate entrance from the outside. Annandale agreed to take it for a week, stating that he came from Tighnabruaich, and that his room would be shared by a friend who could not remain longer than the following Wednesday. It was arranged that they should occupy the room next day, and that Annandale was to take his meals there, while Rose got his at Mrs. Woolley's tea-shop in the village. They returned together to Rothesay that afternoon, and Annandale accompanied Rose to the Hydropathic, where the latter introduced him to some of his friends.

Two of these named Mickel and Thom, who also intended spending the week-end at Brodick, left for Arran by the *Ivan-hoe* on Saturday, the 13th, and were joined on board by Rose and Annandale. Mickel and Thom were unable to find rooms, and slept on a friend's yacht in the bay. From the Saturday to Monday the four men saw a good deal of each other, walking and boating together, and occasionally meeting at meals in Woolley's shop. Mr. Mickel formed an unfavorable opinion of Annandale, who struck him as singularly silent and uncommunicative, and as he could neither find out who that young man was nor where he came from, Mickel more than once strongly advised Rose to get rid of him, even if he had to leave his lodgings, and in particular not to climb Goatfell in his company, as he had proposed to do. Rose promised accordingly, and at half-past three in the afternoon of Monday, 15th July, Mr. Mickel and his friend left by the *Ivanhoe*, Rose and Annandale being on the pier to see them off.

Both Mickel and Thom spoke highly of Rose as a young fellow of agreeable manners, very frank and open, and "ready to take up with strangers." So far as they knew he seemed to have plenty of money. He had a watch and chain, and carried a pocket-book, containing a return half-ticket to London, and his luggage consisted of a black-leather Gladstone bag. His wardrobe included a chocolate and brown striped tennis-jacket, a gray felt hat, and a white serge yachting cap.

Mrs. Walker saw nothing further of her lodgers that day, as, from the situation of their room, they could go out and in without her knowledge. At eleven o'clock on the Tuesday morning she knocked at their door. Getting no answer, she entered and found that the visitors had vanished, together with the two bags which they had brought with them when they came. The room appeared to have been occupied overnight by two persons. A straw hat, a pair of slippers, a waterproof, and a tennis racket had been left behind. Such incidents are probably not unknown to Arran landladies, and the worst that Mrs. Walker anticipated was the loss of her rent. She did not report the matter to the police.

Rose's holiday expired on Thursday, 18th July, on which day his brother went to the station in London to meet him. His relatives, alarmed at his non-arrival, telegraphed to the Reverend Mr. Goodman, the son of Rose's employer, who was staying at Glenburn Hydropathic, from whom they learned that Rose had gone to Arran with an acquaintance a few days before, and had not returned. On Saturday, the 27th, Rose's brother, accompanied by the Chief Constable of Bute, arrived at Brodick. They ascertained that, in spite of Mickel's warning, the missing man had gone up Goatfell on the Monday afternoon with the mysterious Annandale, who had been seen to leave Brodick alone next morning by the early steamer, and it was believed that Rose had never left the island.

On Sunday, the 28th, a search was organized, every able man willingly taking his share of the work, and various parties began systematically to beat the district. No one unacquainted with the nature of the ground can form any idea of the difficulties attending their efforts. Upon the north and west Goatfell is bounded by a congregation of jagged mountain ridges and fantastic peaks, with deep shadowy glens and grim ravines, the bleak sides of which are furrowed by innumerable gullies and abrupt watercourses—a scene in its awful solitude and grandeur so wild, dreary, and desolate as hardly to be matched in Britain. Day after day the search was continued among the barren screes and boulder-strewn corries, day after day the weary searchers returned unsuccessful to their homes, nor till the evening of the following Sunday, 4th August, was the object of their quest attained.

That day the search party, consisting of upwards of two hundred persons, was divided into three portions, one of which was scouring the east shoulder of Goatfell, at the head of Glen Sannox. Francis Logan, a Corrie fisherman, being high up on the mountain-side, near a place named Coire-na-fuhren, noticed an offensive odor which he traced to a large boulder some distance further up the slope. Built up about its face was a heap of smaller rocks and stones, with pieces of turf and heather inserted between the clefts. On examining this structure more closely, Logan saw among the stones part of a human arm. He at once raised a shout, and Sergeant Munro with others of the search party, including the lost man's brother, were quickly on the spot. When the stones, forty-two in number, were removed, in a cavity beneath the boulder was seen the dead body of a man. The screen of stones which had concealed it, the largest being over a hundred-weight, was obviously the work of human hands. Dr. Gilmour, Linlithgow, a summer visitor at Corrie, was sent for as the nearest medical man, and until his arrival the body, which was guarded by the police, remained untouched. When the doctor reached the boulder about eight o'clock he first examined the position of the body, which lay at full length upon its face, and was fully clothed, the skirt of the jacket being turned back over the head, probably to conceal its ghastly appearance while the stones were piled around it. The body was then lifted from beneath the boulder, and having been identified by Mr. Rose as that of his missing brother, a thorough examination was made by Dr. Gilmour. Nothing was found upon the body; all the pockets were empty, and one of them was turned inside out. On examining the head and face, Dr. Gilmour found both "fearfully and terribly smashed." Practically the whole of the face and left side of the head was destroyed and in an advanced stage of decomposition, but the body otherwise was uninjured, excepting a fracture of the top of the left shoulder-blade.

While those who found the body were awaiting the doctor's arrival, a search of the surrounding ground was made. Above the boulder the hill slopes steeply upward to the ridge, at an angle of about forty-five degrees, on the line of a deep gully and watercourse, often dry in summer, but in which there was then a small stream. The ground is composed of slabs of granite, rough heather, sand, and gravel, strewn with boulders and loose stones. The following articles, afterwards identified as Rose's property, were found higher up the gully at various distances from the boulder: a walking-stick, lying head downwards, as if dropped; a waterproof, split in two pieces, "huddled together in a dub, as if they had been trampled upon"; a knife, pencil, and button; and a cap, folded in four, with a large heavy stone on the top of and almost completely concealing it, in the center of the bed of the stream. On one side of the gully, above where the cap was found, was a clear drop of nineteen feet, while on the other side, lower down, above where the knife and pencil were found, was a similar fall of thirty-two feet.

About nine o'clock the body was placed in a box and taken to the coach-house of Corrie Hotel, where a post-mortem examination was made next day by Dr. Gilmour and Dr. Fullarton of Lamlash, after which it was buried in the ancient and picturesque burying-ground of Sannox, at the entrance to the glen. On 27th September the body was exhumed by warrant of the Sheriff, to enable Sir Henry (then Dr.) Littlejohn and Dr. Fullarton to examine more particularly the condition of the internal organs. The conclusion arrived at in the various medical reports as to the injuries which caused death were, that these had been produced by direct violence of repeated blows on the left side of the head, inflicted with some heavy, blunt instrument.

We shall now see what, so far as ascertained, were the movements of the mysterious Annandale on the day of the murder.

From the sea-level at the old inn of Brodick—now used in connection with the estate—on the north side of the bay, the way to Goatfell lies through the grounds of Brodick Castle, past the Kennels, and through the woods to the open moor, whence the climber has a clear view of the task before him. Two relatives of Mrs. Walker, who knew her lodgers by sight, returning from Goatfell that afternoon, met Annandale and Rose in the Castle grounds about four o'clock. One of them noticed that Rose was wearing a watch-chain. Shortly thereafter the Reverend Mr. Hind, with two other visitors from Lamlash, who had left Brodick about three o'clock to climb the fell, were overtaken on the open hill beyond the Castle woods by two young men. One of these (afterwards identified by a photograph as Rose) walked with the party for about half an hour. The other kept steadily some yards ahead, and spoke to no one. Rose mentioned that he came from London, and had been staying at Rothesay. A shower coming on, Mr. Hind's party took shelter behind a boulder, but the others, who had waterproofs, continued the ascent. The party could see them going up in front, and when they themselves gained the top about six o'clock, they saw Rose and his companion standing upon the further edge of the plateau from the point at which they reached it. The view from the summit is one of the most extensive and magnificent in Scotland. After enjoying the prospect for about a quarter of an hour Mr. Hind's party descended the mountain by the way they came, reaching Brodick in time for the 8:30 steamer to Lamlash. They saw no more of the young men on the way down, and wondered what had become of them. Two brothers named Francis were photographing on the hill that day; one sat down to rest, while the other went on. After the first reached the top he was joined by his brother, following the two young men, walking in single file. Rose had some conversation with the brothers about the scenery. When they left the summit at six twenty-five they saw these young men standing on a boulder, with their backs to Ailsa Craig, and pointing in the direction of Glen Sannox, as if discussing the way down. This is the last that was seen of Rose alive. The brothers, we may here anticipate, at the trial identified the prisoner as his companion.

There are two recognized routes in descending Goatfell— the direct and comparatively easy one to Brodick, which is that usually taken; and the much longer and more arduous descent by "The Saddle," the lofty ridge connecting Goatfell with its giant neighbor Cir-Mhor, and forming the head of the two great glens of Rosa and Sannox, which run almost at right-angles from each other. A third way, rarely taken by anyone before this case occurred, save by shepherds or others familiar with the hills, is to go straight down into Glen Sannox from the ridge of North Goatfell by the wild and lonely gully of Coire-na-fuhren. By either of these last routes the climber, having descended into Glen Sannox, follows that glen east-ward to its entrance at Sannox Bay, three and a half miles from the ridge, returning to Brodick by the coast road and the village of Corrie, a further distance of seven and a half miles.

At half-past nine o'clock that Monday evening a shepherd named Mackenzie was talking to two servant girls near the old burying-ground of Sannox, when he saw a man coming out of the glen and going in the direction of Corrie. Mackenzie remarked at the time that the man was "awful tired and worn-out like, and seemed to have had a heavy day's traveling on the hills." This is the first that was seen of Rose's late com-panion after they were left together upon the mountaintop shortly before half-past six. A few minutes after ten o'clock a visitor standing at the bar of Corrie Hotel was accosted by a stranger, who asked the visitor to order a drink for him, which he could not get himself as it was after closing time. The barmaid supplied him with some spirits in a bottle, which he took away with him, remarking that he had to walk the six miles to Brodick. He was afterwards identified by his impromptu host.

Next morning (Tuesday, 16th July), Mary Robertson, who had been staying in Invercloy, went to Brodick pier at seven o'clock to take the early steamer to Ardrossan. Between the village and the pier she overtook a man, whom she later identified, carrying two bags, one black, the other brown, on his way to the boat. It happened that on the Saturday before the murder Mickel and Thom had introduced Rose and Annandale to a friend named Gilmour. By a curious chance, Mr. Gilmour was returning to Glasgow that morning, and on going on board the *Scotia* at Brodick pier the first person he saw was Annandale, wearing a gray felt hat. They traveled to Greenock together, and Mr. Gilmour offered to help Annandale to carry his luggage. He noticed particularly the black leather bag, which his companion took into the compartment with him when they left the steamer at Ardrossan. This, so far as the evidence goes, was the last that was seen of Rose's bag.

On Saturday, 6th July, ten days earlier, a young man, whose card bore the name of "John Annandale," had taken a room for a fortnight in the house of Mrs. Currie, in Iona Place, Port Bannatyne, Rothesay. His luggage consisted of a brown leatherbag. On Friday, the 12th, he told his landlady that he was going to Arran for a few days, and left, wearing a straw hat and taking the brown bag with him. On the afternoon of Tuesday, 16th July, he reappeared at Port Bannatyne, wearing a gray felt hat and carrying a paper parcel containing, as his landlady afterwards found, a white serge yachting cap and a chocolate and brown striped tennis jacket. These articles he wore during the remainder of his stay. He talked "quite pleasantly" to Mrs. Currie about his visit to Arran, saying that he had been up Goatfell and had enjoyed himself. His time expiring on Saturday, the 20th, he asked her to have his bill and dinner ready at one o'clock. He went out, however, in the forenoon and never returned; all that Mrs. Currie got for his fortnight's board and lodging was the yachting cap and a pair of tennis shoes, which were afterwards identified as Rose's property.

Even as Mrs. Prig, on a certain historic occasion, boldly expressed her disbelief in the existence of the immortal Mrs. Harris, so may the discerning reader have had his own misgivings regarding the genuineness of Mr. Annandale. These may now be justified by the statement that this name had been temporarily adopted, for what reason does not appear, by a man named John Watson Laurie, twenty-five years of age, employed as a patternmaker at Springburn Works, Glasgow. Since 8th June of that year he had been living in lodgings at 106 North Frederick Street there, until he went to Rothesay on 6th July. While at Rothesay he met an acquaintance named Aitken, who knew him as Laurie. To him, Laurie pointed out Rose as a gentleman with whom he was going to Arran. Aitken saw him again on Saturday, the 20th, when Laurie was leaving Rothesay for Glasgow. He was then wearing a yachting cap which struck Aitken as very like the one he had seen Rose wear. Aitken asked, "How did you and your friend get on at Brodick?" to which Laurie replied, "Oh, very well." He returned to his Glasgow lodgings and resumed his work as usual on 22nd July. He mentioned to a fellow-lodger that he had a return-half ticket to London. On Wednesday, 31st July, Aitken met him accidentally in Hope Street. That week the fact of Rose's disappearance had been published in the Glasgow newspapers, and Aitken accosted Laurie with the startling question, "What do you know about the Arran mystery?" Laurie "hummed and hawed"; and Aitken said, "Dear me, have you not been reading the papers? Was not Rose the name of the gentleman with whom you went to Brodick?" Laurie said it could not be the same man, as his Mr. Rose had returned with him and had since gone to Leeds. Aitken then strongly advised him to communicate what he knew to the authorities, and asked him whose cap he was wearing when they last met at Rothesay. Laurie replied, "Surely you don't think me a . . ." and did not complete the sentence. He excused himself for leaving Aitken at the moment, as he saw someone approaching whom apparently he wished to avoid, but at Aitken's request he agreed to meet him at his office that evening at six o'clock to give him further particulars. Laurie did not fulfill the engagement, and Aitken never saw him again. Four days later Rose's body was found, and Aitken, so soon as he learned the fact, gave information to the police.

Evidently realizing that Glasgow was now no place for one in his peculiar circumstances, Laurie that day applied to the foreman at the Springburn Works for his wages, saying that he was leaving to be a traveler in the grain trade. He also informed a fellow-worker that he was going to Leith as an engineer, that he had a return-half ticket to London, and that he had been spending his holiday at Brodick with a friend whom, he euphemistically added, "he had left in Arran." The same day he sold his patternmaker's tools to a broker in the Commercial Road for twenty-five shillings, and disappeared from Glasgow. His landlady there, more fortunate than those who had enjoyed his patronage at Brodick and Port Bannatyne, received on 3rd August a letter from him, posted at Hamilton, enclosing a remittance for rent due. "There are some people trying to get me into trouble," he wrote, "and I think you should give them no information at all. I will prove to them how they are mistaken before very long." She afterwards communicated with the police, and delivered to them certain articles which Laurie had left in his room.

Laurie was next heard of at Liverpool, where, on Tuesday, 6th August, he took lodgings at 10 Greek Street, paying a week's rent in advance. On the morning of Thursday, the 8th, however, he informed his landlady that he was leaving that day, as he had got a situation in Manchester as a traveler in the cotton trade. He left behind him a box he had brought from Glasgow which, when taken possession of later by the authorities, was found to contain some white shirts, identified as Rose's property, having the name of "John W. Laurie" impressed thereon with a stamp, also found in the box. It does not appear from the evidence led at the trial why Laurie left Liverpool so suddenly, but the *Liverpool Courier* that day published the fact of his identity with "Annandale," together with an account of his recent movements, which plainly showed that the police were upon his track.

Since the discovery of the body, the Glasgow newspapers had been full of "The Arran Murder," and the hunt for the perpetrator had been followed with keen interest, so when the *North British Daily Mail* received and published a letter from the wanted man, the local excitement was intense. This letter was dated 10th August, and bore the Liverpool post-mark. "I rather smile," he wrote, "when I read that my arrest is hourly expected. If things go as I have designed them I will soon have arrived at that country from whose bourne no traveler returns, and since there has been so much said about me, it is only right that the public should know what are the real circumstances. . . . As regards Mr. Rose, poor fellow, no one who knows me will believe for one moment that I had any complicity in his death. . . . We went to the top of Goatfell, where I left him in the company of two men who came from Loch Ranza and were going to Brodick." He admitted that he himself returned by way of Corrie, and had been in the hotel there about ten o'clock.

The renewed outburst of newspaper articles and correspondence produced by the publication of this letter drew a further protest from the fugitive. In a second communication, dated 27th August and bearing to have been posted at Aberdeen, addressed to the *Glasgow Herald*, he complained of the "many absurd and mad things" appearing about himself in the papers, which he felt it his duty to correct. "Although I am entirely guiltless of the crime I am so much wanted for," he wrote, "yet I can recognize that I am a ruined man in any case, so it is far from my intention to give myself up. . . . When I saw from an evening paper that Mr. Rose had not returned to his lodgings, I began to arrange for my departure, for I had told so many about him. Seemingly, there was a motive for doing away with poor Rose; it was not to secure his valuables. Mr. Rose was, to all appearances, worse off than myself; indeed, he assured me that he had spent so much on his tour that he had barely sufficient to last till he got home. He wore an old Geneva watch with no gold albert attached, and I am sure that no one saw him wear a ring on his tour. . . . As I am not inclined to say any more, I hope this will be the last the public will hear of me." Both letters were signed "John W. Laurie," and were proved to be in his handwriting.

It is difficult to see what induced Laurie to write these letters. He seems to have lost his head at finding himself the subject of so much of the popular attention which, that August, was divided between himself, Mrs. Maybrick, then on her trial at Liverpool, and "Jack the Ripper," whose mysterious crimes were horrifying humanity. Be that as it may, the first letter enabled the police to get the box left by him at Liverpool; but they considered that the posting of the second at Aberdeen was intended as a blind, and that Laurie had returned to his old haunts, as he was reported to have been seen at Uddingston and also at Coatbridge. How much money Rose actually had upon him at the time of his death was never proved, but at least there must have been enough to enable his murderer so successfully to elude the vigilance of the police during the five weeks which elapsed between his absconding and apprehension.

On Tuesday, 3rd September, a man entered the railway

station at Ferniegair, which is the first out of Hamilton on the Lesmahagow branch of the Caledonian line. He was about to take a ticket, when he saw a police constable on the platform; he at once left the station and made for the Carlisle road. The constable followed, as the man resembled Laurie, whom he had previously known. Laurie, for it was he, realizing that he was being shadowed, began to run; crossing a field and the railway, he reached the Lanark road, and running along it till he came to a wood called the "Quarry Plantation," near Bog Colliery, about three miles from Hamilton, was lost sight of by his pursuer. The constable, who had been joined by some of the workmen from the colliery, got them to surround the wood, which he himself began to search, and presently found Laurie lying under a bush, with an open razor beside him and a superficial wound in his throat. His hand had been less certain than at Coire-na-fuhren. He was then arrested, and having received the usual caution said, "I robbed the man, but I did not murder him." On the following day the prisoner was taken to Rothesay, where he was examined before the Sheriff on the charge of murdering Rose, upon which he was duly committed for trial, and was removed to Greenock prison. There on the 11th he was further examined before the Sheriff. In his first declaration the prisoner admitted his identity, adding, "I have nothing to say to the charge in the meantime." In his second, being shown the cap, waterproof, and other things found near the boulder, he declared, "I wish to say nothing about any of these articles."

The trial of John Watson Laurie for the murder of Edwin Rose took place before the High Court of Justiciary at Edinburgh on Friday, the 8th, and Saturday, the 9th of November 1889. So greatly had the public interest been excited and sustained by the unusual and mysterious character of the crime, the circumstances in which the body was found; and the subsequent hue and cry after the murderer, that long before the opening of the doors the entrance to the Court was besieged by a crowd, estimated by the *Scotsman* of the day to consist of about two thousand people. Specially stringent regulations, however, had been made regarding admission to the Courtroom, and only a privileged few were able to witness the proceedings when the Lord Justice-Clerk (Lord Kingsburgh) took his seat at ten o'clock. There appeared for the Crown the Solicitor-General, Mr. (afterwards Lord) Stormonth-Darling, assisted by Mr. Graham Murray (later Lord Dunedin) and Mr. Dugald M'Kechnie, Advocates-Depute; the counsel for the defense were the Dean of Faculty, Mr. John Blair Balfour (the late Lord Kinross), and Mr. Scott Dickson.

According to the theory of the prosecution, Laurie, who was familiar with the locality, having induced Rose to descend by Coire-na-fuhren, struck him down by a blow with a stone upon the left side of the head, delivered from above and behind, as they clambered down the steep incline; then, as he lay on the ground, his face and head were furiously battered so as to prevent recognition, the injury to the top of the shoulder-blade being caused by a blow which missed the head and struck the top of the shoulder. Laurie had thereafter rifled the body and buried it beneath the boulder, close to which the deed was done. Why he did not also conceal in the same hiding-place the cap and other articles found in the gully the Crown failed to explain. Possibly he overlooked them until he had finished building up the turf and stone dike about the body, when even he may have hesitated to reopen the cavity, preferring to place the cap under the large stone in the stream where it was found, and let the rest take their chance of discovery. The waterproof was split up the back into two pieces. No reason was given for this, but it looks as if it had been thus torn from the body (for Rose when last seen alive was wearing it) and then rolled up and trampled into the pool. The stick, knife, pencil, and button were either dropped, unnoticed by Laurie, during the assault, or thrown away by him after he had searched the pockets of his victim.

The theory of the defense was that all the injuries to the body were produced simultaneously as the result of a fall over one or other of the steep rocks before referred to, further up the gully. On the left side, above the place where the cap was found, as already mentioned, was the nineteen-feet drop, 156 yards beyond the boulder; the thirty-two-feet drop was on the other side, forty yards lower down, above where the knife and pencil were found. The former fall was that favored by the defense. There was no indication on the body or clothes of its having been dragged from thence down to the boulder, which, looking to the nature of the ground, must, if done, have left unmistakable signs of the process. Indeed, the only injury to these, apart from the head, was that of the shoulder-blade, with corresponding damage to the flesh, the clothing, and the waterproof. If killed further up the gully, the body of Rose must therefore have been carried down to the boulder. The prisoner in his letter to the *Mail* had stated that he left Rose on the top of the mountain with two men from Loch Ranza, and the defense maintained that Laurie never saw him again, alive or dead. Even if the death were the result of an accidental fall, the robbing and elaborate burial of the body and the folding and concealment of the cap proved the presence of another person, and the defense could do no more than deny, with the prisoner, that these acts were the work of his hands. The unlikelihood of any third party finding and robbing the dead body, and thereafter running the needless and fearful risk of burying it, is obvious, while the suggestion of the learned Dean that the stone (which, by the way, weighed between seven and eight pounds) might have been carried down by a freshet, was negatived by the witnesses who saw its position upon the folded cap.

On the first day of the trial the prosecution was mainly concerned to prove that Rose met his death by murder; on the second, they sought to establish the prisoner's connection with the crime. The members of the search party who had seen the body found, one and all denied that the descent was dangerous or specially difficult, or that a man going down by the left side of the gully, which was the natural way, would have any occasion to go near the steep rocks at all. In cross-examining the police witnesses, the Dean elicited the curious fact that, after the post-mortem examination on 5th August, the boots removed from the body were taken to the shore at Corrie and there buried below high-water mark. The constable who had done this was severely pressed by the Dean as to his reason for so disposing of them, the Dean holding that their condition as regards nails and heels was most important with reference to the question at issue, but the witness could give no more satisfactory answer than that he had been ordered by his superior officer "to put them out of sight." It has been said that the object of this irregular act was to prevent the dead man's spirit from "walking," which, if true, would seem to imply some deficiency of humor on the part of the authorities.

The medical evidence as to the cause of death was the real battle-ground of the case. The skilled witnesses for the Crown were Drs. Gilmour and Fullarton, who saw the body at the boulder and performed the post-mortem examination, and Sir Henry (then Dr.) Littlejohn, who examined the body later, on its exhumation. Into the ghastly details of the injuries to the head and face it is unnecessary here to enter; it is sufficient to say that the three medical witnesses concurred in stating that these had been produced by direct violence, in the manner alleged by the prosecution. The limbs and extremities were free from fractures and dislocations, and there was no indication of blood either upon the body or clothes. The injured parts were horribly decayed, and the fact that the highest of the cervical vertebrae was lying loose when first seen by Dr. Gilmour was attributed by that gentleman to the advanced decomposition of the neck. The whole of the upper jaw was detached in one piece. These injuries, in his opinion, must have been due to repeated impacts, whether by blows or falls. All the injuries were confined to the left side; and in the case of a sheer fall the injuries to the face would not, he said, be present. Dr. Fullarton stated that the extent and severity of the fractures were the result of repeated blows with a blunt instrument; he had never seen a head so smashed except by a machinery accident. The injury to the shoulder confirmed his view, for any conscious person falling would have had his hands before him, and the injuries, which in this case were all localized on one spot, would have been different. He thought the first blow had been given while the man was standing, and the others when he was on the ground. Dr. Littlejohn stated that the condition of the cranium as seen by him was at once suggestive of direct violence by blows. A heavy stone in the hand would be an instrument likely to have caused the injuries. The severity of the bruises would stop hemorrhage, and the absence of hemorrhage would account for the speedy decomposition. The detachment of the cervical vertebra, as described in the first medical report, might be consistent either with dislocation or decay of the tissues. A fall would not have inflicted such localized violence without producing severe injuries to the extremities and to the internal organs of the abdomen, which in this case were intact and uninjured, and the latter remarkably well preserved. He had considerable experience of falls from heights such as the Dean Bridge and the Castle Rock, Edinburgh, but he never saw injuries like these so caused. A fall of such severity must have implicated the liver, the condition of which was normal, and there would also be other injuries not present in this case.

The medical experts for the defense were Sir Patrick (then Dr.) Heron Watson and Drs. M'Gillivray and Alexis Thomson, none of whom had the advantage of seeing the body. They were therefore called to give their opinion solely upon the medical reports and evidence adduced for the Crown. Dr. Heron Watson stated that the injuries which he had heard described were, in his view, more consistent with a fall than with repeated blows, and he considered that they had been produced instantaneously. All the probabilities were in favor of a fall upon the vertex. The vertebrae of the neck were probably broken, and there would be little bleeding, which, in the case of blows, would have been copious. The fact that the liver was not ruptured did not affect his opinion. He described, as the result of certain grisly experiments, the difficulty of fracturing the human skull by blows, so as to produce the extensive smashing present in that case. He suggested that Rose had slipped on the slope, and, turning round before he reached the edge, fell over the cliff headlong, backwards and leftwards. If the head alighted on a granite boulder on which there was a nodule of some size, this would account for the injuries to the face and shoulder. The other two medical witnesses for the defense concurred generally in the opinion of Dr. Heron Watson as against that of the Crown doctors.

With regard to the conflict of medical testimony, it is noteworthy that upon cross-examination neither side absolutely negatived the possibility of the other's theory; and it occurs to the lay mind that perhaps, as Mr. Mantalini remarked in another connection, they may "both be right and neither wrong," in the sense that Laurie may have first pushed Rose over the rocks, and, having stunned him, then completed the deed with a stone.

The several chapters of the story which has here been briefly told were elicited from the various witnesses. The identity of the prisoner and "Annandale" was clearly established; the property of the dead man found in his possession was duly identified by relatives and friends; and his movements, as well before as after the murder, were traced beyond all manner of doubt. It was proved that to go from the top of Goatfell to the boulder took half an hour, and that to walk at an ordinary pace from the boulder to Corrie Hotel took an hour and forty minutes, while the prisoner had spent four hours upon the way. In addition to their medical men the defense called only four witnesses: one, an Italian fisherman, to give expert evidence as a guide regarding the dangerous character of the descent by Coirena-fuhren; another, a girl who had known Laurie at Rothesay, to say that she found him "chatty and agreeable" on his return from the excursion to Arran. It appeared, however, on cross-examination, that the guide, who had only been three years in the island, had never been in Glen Sannox till after the body was found; while the girl admitted that on her asking Laurie how long he had taken to climb Goatfell he avoided the question and made no reply. The other two witnesses called were the servant girls who had been with Mackenzie at Sannox burying-ground. They did not remember Mackenzie's remark as to the man, but admitted that it might have been made.

At a quarter past five on the second day of the trial the Solicitor-General rose to address the jury on behalf of the Crown. After drawing their attention to the exceptional features of the case, he remarked that if this was a murder, it was undoubtedly one of a peculiarly atrocious character. The salient facts of the case were these: Two young men went up the hill together. Only one came down. The other was found, after an interval of weeks, with his body horribly mutilated, hidden away among the rocks of the hillside, and all his portable property removed. The survivor was seen within a few hours of the time when the death of his friend must have been accomplished. He returned to the place from which they both started, and gave no sign or hint of anything having happened to his friend, or that he had not returned with him. The next morning he left Arran and resumed his ordinary occupation, which he continued until the hue and cry arose. Then he fled, and when he was about to be arrested, attempted to cut his throat. The Solicitor-General then reviewed the evidence led for the Crown bearing upon the movements of the prisoner, from his arrival at Rothesay under a false name and his subsequent association with Rose until his return to their Brodick lodgings alone. Laurie spent the night in the room which he and his friend had shared, and left next morning by the first available steamer, before the people of the house could see him, without paying his bill, and leaving the room in such a state as would suggest that it had been occupied by two persons. When he left, he obliterated every trace of Rose except the tennis racket, which, as it bore Rose's name, would have been awkward to take with him. He returned to Rothesay wearing Rose's hat and carrying other property of his in a parcel, while certain things which also had belonged to Rose were found in the trunk left by the prisoner at Liverpool. The watch and chain and pocket-book, which Rose was known to have upon him, were missing, and though they did not know how much money he had in his possession, it must have been sufficient to pay his way during the remainder of his holiday. The question was: Whose hand rifled the pockets and put the body under the boulder? He thought they would have little difficulty in coming to the conclusion that the prisoner was with Rose down to the end. The suggestion of the defense that these two parted on the top of the mountain was excluded by the facts of the case. If, then, the prisoner robbed and buried the body, was his the hand that caused the death? The supposition that Rose's death was the result of an accident, and that the robbery and secretion of the body was the work of the prisoner, was so inherently, so wildly improbable that, even apart from the medical evidence, the jury must hesitate to give it credence. If such were indeed the fact, it indicated a depravity of mind but little removed from that which led to murder. The Solicitor-General then discussed the nature of the *locus* and the character of the injuries to the body, and examined the conflict of medical testimony. The prisoner's own behavior, he said, afforded the readiest solution of what had really happened. He asked them to apply to it the ordinary standard of human conduct, and to say if any man could have so acted who was not the murderer of Rose. As to motive, the prisoner probably expected to get more by the murder than he actually got, but having done it, he had to go through with it. Finally, counsel submitted that the prosecution had established beyond reasonable doubt that the prisoner at the bar was guilty of the crime with which he was charged.

The Dean of Faculty then addressed the jury for the defense. He agreed with the prosecutor that if the case were true, this was a murder unprecedented and incredibly atrocious. If so, the onus of proof was all the heavier upon the Crown. Every probability, he might say every possibility, was against it. Even if they came to the conclusion that murder had been committed, of which he hoped to show there was no evidence, they must consider whether there was sufficient proof that the murder was committed by Laurie. They would bear in mind that suspicion was not proof. Before they could arrive at a verdict of "Guilty," they must be clear in their minds upon these points. He then described the injuries to the body, and pointed out that there were no signs of any struggle or of the body having been dragged, nor was it suggested that any instrument had been found in the neighborhood to which the infliction of the injuries could be attributed. All these were upon the left side. No right-handed man would have attacked Rose upon that side, and it was not suggested that the prisoner was left-handed. He argued that the fractures of the skull and the injury to the shoulder, involving as it did the clothing, together with the severance of the highest joint of the backbone, all supported the theory of the defense. Near the spot they had two declivities such as would bring about these results if a man fell over either of them. He did not know where the Crown said the murder was committed. If at the boulder, how came the various things at the places where they were found? Concealment could not have been the object, for they were left lying perfectly open, and their position was much more consistent with Rose's pitching over the rock and the things flying in all directions. His first point against the Crown was that they had failed to prove a murder, and that the probability on the medical testimony was that the injuries were due to causes other than willful infliction of violence. With regard to the prisoner's conduct, the Dean remarked that there was nothing in Laurie having called himself "Annandale" when he went to Rothesay; he was not then aware of Rose's existence, and he was seen and known as Laurie there by other persons. Their meeting was casual, and the visit to Brodick in company was, in the circumstances, quite natural. Laurie could then have had no murderous design. The reticence of the prisoner, as described by some of the witnesses, was due to his suffering from toothache. There was no evidence that Rose and Laurie were ever together in this world again from the time they were seen on the top of Goatfell. Whoever removed the body, the jury would understand that their verdict must not proceed upon the suggestion of the Solicitor-General that it was the theory of the defense that the prisoner had done so. No one knew by whom it was done, but at those Fair holidays there were plenty of other people on the island who might have robbed the body and put it where it was found. That the prisoner alone and unaided could have lifted, carried, and piled the heavy stones upon it was most unlikely; two men would be required to do that. When Laurie arrived at Corrie Hotel he had no appearance of being a red-handed murderer, but if the Crown case were true there must have been some traces of the deed upon him. He left the island next day, and it was proved that he improperly took away with him some things belonging to Rose. He made no secret of it, for he wore these things at Rothesay among people who knew them both. If this were a charge of theft, these circumstances might be important; but what connection had they with the murder of Rose? Not one article which Rose had with him on the day of his death had been traced to the prisoner. If he had murdered his friend would he have gone back among people who had seen them both together, and afterwards have quietly returned to his work? Not until Aitken showed that he suspected him did Laurie realize that, having been seen with Rose in Arran, he might himself be held responsible for his disappearance. If he had expected this charge he would not have waited till 31st July before leaving Glasgow. He would realize later that his disappearance then had only tended further to compromise him, so he continued in hiding, and when about to be captured he attempted to cut his throat. When he said, "I robbed the man, but I did not murder him," it was certainly not a confession that he had rifled the body, but had reference to the things which he had taken away from the lodgings. In conclusion, the Dean maintained that the Crown had failed to prove, first, that there was any murder, and, secondly, if there had been, that Laurie was the murderer. He asked the jury to return a verdict which would acquit the prisoner of that most terrible and appalling charge.

At twenty minutes to nine o'clock the Lord Justice-Clerk began his charge to the jury. His Lordship described the case as one of the most remarkable that had ever come before a Court of Justice. Both the theories which had been set up presented points almost inconceivable to the ordinary mind. As this was a case of purely circumstantical evidence, he proposed in the first place to go over the facts as to which there was no doubt. His Lordship then reviewed the evidence as to the movements of Rose and Laurie till they were last seen together on the top of the mountain. It was proved that the deceased was then wearing his watch-chain, and they also knew that he had in his pocket-book a return-half ticket to London. It was quite certain that neither of them descended by the same way as they came up. They took a route which, though not the ordinary one, was proved not to be dangerous to any person taking reasonable care. Now, on the way down Rose unquestionably met his death by violence of some kind, and after death his body was carefully hidden by someone under the boulder. If he died by falling over one or other of the rocks further up the gully, it must have been a work of great labor and difficulty to bring the body down to the boulder and conceal it with the stones. His cap was found folded up, with a heavy stone placed upon it, his waterproof, cut in two, was rolled together near the burn, his pockets were rifled, his watch, money, and return ticket were gone. All that must have happened within a few hours of a summer evening. The prisoner was seen coming out of the glen at half-past nine, and again at Corrie Hotel about ten o'clock. He returned to Brodick, and, without any intimation to the people of the place, left the next morning, taking with him Rose's bag, and wearing his gray felt hat. On his return to Rothesay the prisoner was seen wearing Rose's tennis jacket and yachting cap. His Lordship then referred to the incident of the prisoner's conversation with the witness Aitken, to the fact that Laurie had stated to others that he had a return-half ticket to London, to the circumstances of his flight to Liverpool with a box containing property proved to have belonged to Rose, to the letters which he addressed to the newspapers, and finally, to his apprehension and attempted suicide. These were facts about which there could be no doubt, and the Crown said they all pointed to the prisoner as having committed the crime with which he was charged. The defense was that the death of Rose did not take place in presence of Laurie, that they, having gone up Goatfell together, did not descend together, although the one met his death on the way by Glen Sannox to Corrie, and the other reached Corrie by way of

Glen Sannox. Laurie must have been surprised to find that his friend did not return to their lodgings, but the effect which Rose's non-arrival had upon him was, that without saying a word to anyone, he went off with his own and Rose's luggage. The defense maintained that Rose had fallen over one of the rocks at a considerable distance from the boulder, and that it would have been impossible for one man to have brought the body down and buried it. His Lordship was afraid there were two views as to that, for the Crown's contention was that Rose was done to death by blows with a stone, which could have happened close to the boulder. The Dean had asked if Rose was killed there, how came the various articles to be found below the rocks further up the gully? Again his Lordship was afraid that if Rose in fact was killed at the boulder, the person who put him to death might so have disposed of the articles as to suggest that Rose had fallen over a precipice. His Lordship pointed out that the hiding of the cap and the cutting-up of the waterproof must have been done by a human hand after Rose's death. The defense being that Laurie and Rose were never seen together after they left the top of the hill, it was extremely remarkable that the prisoner did not reach Corrie Hotel till ten, while the witnesses who left the top at the same time reached Brodick before half-past eight. The jury must consider if they could reconcile all these facts with the idea that Laurie was not present at Rose's death. If he was, there was no escape from the conclusion that his was the hand that folded the cap, cut off the waterproof, and hid the body; and then they would have to consider could these acts possibly have been done by a man who had witnessed a terrible and accidental death. With regard to Laurie's possession of a return ticket to London, it was in evidence that Rose had such a ticket in his pocket-book. It had been urged for the defense that the prisoner openly wore the coat and hats of Rose, and that no person anxious to conceal a crime would have done so, but it was his duty to point out that such rashness on the part of criminals often formed the very threads of the web of justice. They must take the whole facts of the case together, and say whether it led to a conclusion that was reasonable and just. His Lordship then reviewed the medical evidence, and observed that those who saw all the details and examined them were necessarily in a better position to give their evidence and opinions than those who merely based their statements upon evidence which they heard. It was not the province of the jury to decide between the medical opinions, but to find what, taking the whole facts and incidents along with that evidence, was the most probable cause of death. If they came to the conclusion that the prisoner was present and that his hand buried the body, that would tend very much against the theory of the defense. The case was purely one of facts, and it was the jury who had the responsibility and duty of coming to a conclusion on those facts which would commend itself to their consciences as reasonable and experienced men.

At a quarter to ten, on the conclusion of the Judge's charge, the jury retired to consider their verdict, and after an absence of forty minutes they returned to Court, when the Foreman announced that their verdict was "Guilty, by a majority." It was afterwards ascertained that the verdict was arrived at by a majority of one, eight voting for Guilty and seven for Not Proven. So soon as the Lord Justice-Clerk had pronounced sentence of death the prisoner, who stood up to receive judgment, turned round in the dock and, facing the crowded benches, said in a clear, firm voice, "Ladies and gentlemen, I am innocent of this charge!" His Lordship at once intimated that the prisoner could not be allowed to make a speech. Laurie was then removed to the cells below, and the Court rose at twenty minutes to eleven o'clock.

No one who witnessed the closing act of this famous trial can forget the impressive character of the scene. Without, in the black November night, a great crowd silently awaited the issue of life or death. The lofty, dimly-lighted Court-room, the candles glimmering in the shadows of the Bench, the imposing presence of the Justice-Clerk in his robes of scarlet and white, the tiers of tense, expectant faces, and in the dock the cause and object of it all, that calm, commonplace, respectable figure, the callous and brutal murderer whom Justice had tardily unmasked.

On Monday, the 11th, the convict was conveyed from Edinburgh to Greenock, where the sentence was to be executed on 30th November. This was a distinction which the magistrates and citizens of that town viewed with anything but satisfaction, for since its creation as a burgh of barony in 1675, only four executions had taken place there, the last being in 1834, and it was hoped and expected that the sentence would be carried out in Edinburgh.

A movement was at once set on foot in the Coatbridge district, where Laurie's relatives were well known and respected, to obtain a commutation of the death sentence. Various meetings were held, and a petition to Lord Lothian, the Scottish Secretary, was adopted. Apart from the stereotyped objections to the verdict common to such documents, the petitioners stated that there had been, and then was, insanity in the convict's family; that he himself had shown from infancy decided symptoms of mental aberration, which accounted for the extraordinary and eccentric character of his conduct both prior and subsequent to the 15th of July; and that the petitioners were prepared to adduce proof of such aberration if required. This petition, which was widely signed in Glasgow and the West of Scotland, was duly dispatched to Dover House on Friday, 22nd November. Meanwhile, pending the result of this application, the Greenock magistrates proceeded to make the necessary arrangements for carrying out the sentence, and thriftily borrowed the Glasgow scaffold. Laurie, who still maintained the cool and calm demeanor which he had preserved throughout the trial, was said to be confident that his life would be spared.

On Saturday, the 23rd, on the appointment of Lord Lothian, the convict was visited by Sir Arthur Mitchell, K.C.B., Dr. Yellowlees, of Glasgow Royal Asylum, and Professor (afterwards Sir William) Gairdner, of Glasgow University, with a view to examining and reporting upon his mental condition. It was stated in the newspapers at the time that Laurie had himself written a letter to Lord Lothian to the effect that Rose was killed in his presence by an accidental fall from a rock, and that his (Laurie's) subsequent actions arose from his dread that he would be charged with murder, and, owing to the absence of witnesses, might be unable to prove his innocence. This was at least a more plausible explanation than that afforded by the defense at the trial; but it is understood that the line of argument then taken was the prisoner's deliberate choice, and was adopted by his counsel at his own request.

On Thursday, the 28th, two days before that fixed for the execution, the local authorities were informed by telegraph that in consequence of the Medical Commission having reported that the convict was of unsound mind, the Secretary for Scotland had felt justified in recommending a respite. The terms of the commissioners' report were not disclosed.

The death sentence having been formally commuted to penal servitude for life, Laurie was removed on 2nd December to Perth Penitentiary, the scaffold was returned to Glasgow, and the Greenock magistrates were left to pay the bill.

The *Glasgow Herald* of 3rd December 1889 published an interesting account of the unfavorable impression made by Laurie upon those who were in close contact with him during his confinement, from which the following passage may be quoted: "His references to Rose were not marked by any exhibition of sympathy for that unfortunate gentleman. On the contrary he spoke of him as a vain, proud man, always boastful of his money, and desirous of making his hearers believe that he was wealthy. The significance of Laurie's comment upon this point is striking; with singular callousness he added that Rose had not very much after all."

Four years elapsed before public attention was again directed to the Arran murderer. On 24th July 1893 Laurie, who had been removed to Peterhead Convict Prison, made a bold bid for freedom. He was employed as a carpenter, his behavior had been exemplary, and, having a good voice, he was, as a newspaper reporter records, "the mainstay of the Presbyterian choir, leading the praise with great enthusiasm." But the old Adam was not wholly eradicated. That morning a gang of convicts under a civil guard was early at work upon an addition which was being made to the warders' houses outside the prison walls, and Laurie was carrying planks for the scaffolding. There was a dense sea fog; so, seizing his opportunity, he leapt a fence and made for the public road. He was then seen by the civil guard, but before the latter could fire the fugitive had disappeared in the fog. An alarm was instantly raised, and guard and warders started in pursuit. One warder, mounted on a bicycle, speedily overtook the running man. He struggled violently, but other warders arriving on the scene, he was quickly handcuffed and marched back to prison. On the way, says our reporter, "Laurie characterized his captors in language wholly inconsistent with the ecclesiastical office which he fills." Human nature was too strong for the precentor.

In 1909, on the completion of twenty years of his sentence, echoes of the old story were heard in the Press, and persistent rumors were circulated that the convict was about to be released. But on 28th April 1910 Laurie was removed from Peterhead to Perth Criminal Asylum, where he died on 4th October 1930, forty-one years from the date of his first imprisonment.

In the ancient burying-ground of Sannox, briers and brambles have striven to conceal the granite boulder which, with a somewhat painful propriety, marks the resting-place of Edwin Rose; and year by year the tourists visiting that beautiful and lonely spot leave, with better intention than taste, their calling-cards upon the stone.

# THE ARDLAMONT MYSTERY

*It is so difficult for a clever man not to be too clever.*

—MISS BRADDON: *Birds of Prey*

IN JULY 1893 I was admitted, after due examination, a member of the Society of Writers to His Majesty's Signet, and as such became qualified to follow the profession of the law. In August, feeling that I had earned my holiday, I set forth for Brodick in the Isle of Arran—that delectable land to whose charms I had in early years succumbed and to which in the autumn of my age I continue faithful. There, towards the middle of the month, I read in the Glasgow newspapers an account of a fatal gunshot accident at Ardlamont House, Argyllshire, within sight of my fortunate isle, involving the death of a lad of twenty, Cecil Hambrough. Such an incident of the sporting season was not so rare as to cause any sensation save among those immediately concerned, and none could have foreseen that the names of Ardlamont and Hambrough were presently to resound throughout the English-speaking world. But by the end of the month one learned that there was more in the case than met the eye. It appeared that the dead boy's life had been, a day or two before his death, insured for no less than £20,000, and that this sum was claimed by his friend and host, Mr. Monson, the shooting tenant of Ardlamont, under an assignation (assignment) in favor of that gentleman's wife. Whereupon the authorities, who hitherto had been strangely supine as regards the circumstances of the tragedy, sat up and began to take notice. The Procurator-Fiscal of the county at Inveraray, the official responsible for the initial steps in matters criminal, at length looked into the affair; and as the result of his belated perquisitions Monson was arrested on a charge of murder.

The subsequent trial was, with the single exception of the historic case of Oscar Slater, the outstanding murder trial of my generation. When, in December, the proceedings began I chanced to be at a loose end, not then having commenced practice. So during those ten momentous days I was daily to be seen in the seat appropriated to the Society in the High Court of Justiciary at Edinburgh, an enthralled spectator of the thrilling drama. I recall that, fearful of losing my place on those besieged benches, I sat from dewy morn till stuffy afternoon; sustained morally by excitement, and physically fortified by the chocolate and digestive biscuits of which I carried a supply. Well, it is a wonderful thing to be young; nowadays my enthusiasm for criminal trials falls short of the sacrifice of lunch. Each evening, after I got home from Court and had supplemented the shortcomings of my exiguous midday meal, I started to cut out that day's evidence, as excellently reported in the contemporary Press, and pasted it into a large scrap-book. That volume is now before me, embellished by pictures from all the illustrated papers within the compass of my purse, and forms a high tribute to my youthful industry. Never before in Scotland had any trial been reported on so elaborate a scale. Over a hundred Pressmen were engaged, including twenty-one descriptive writers, fifteen artists, and seventy reporters. The *Scotsman* figures, for example, show the magnitude of the undertaking: the report of the trial extended to 173 columns, or roughly 20 columns a day. The descriptive matter contained 52,000 words, and the verbatim report 346,000. So you see that already I had my work "cut out" for me! For the other newspapers, the total number of words telegraphed from Edinburgh in connection with the case was 1,860,000.

How vividly the opening sentence of the *Scotsman's* report evokes for me the memory of that stirring time: "Stormy wintry weather ushered in the morning of this great trial." That was on Tuesday, 2nd December 1893—a good old-fashioned winter, such as we never see in these degenerate days—the climate, like other British institutions, being, in Mrs. Marston's dolorous phrase, "not what it was." Every available inch of space was occupied, and the audience was of a type more usual in the stalls of the Lyceum Theatre than in the austere auditorium of the High Court. When the trapdoor in front of the dock was raised, and the prisoner, between two policemen, came up the narrow stair from the cells below, all eyes were fixed upon him. Slim, well-groomed, and boyish-looking for his three-and-thirty years, with clean-cut, aquiline features, pale complexion, yellow hair, and strange shifty eyes, he remained throughout his long ordeal cool, collected, and intelligently attentive to the evidence, with a ready smile for anything ludicrous or amusing. Once only was his composure shaken: when, on the ninth day of the trial, the Solicitor-General completed his masterly reconstruction of the alleged attempt to drown young Hambrough the night before he met his death. At that point the prisoner obviously became restless, and asked to be allowed to go below; but after a brief adjournment he resumed his place and listened with his usual unruffled calmness to the remainder of the Crown speech.

Miss Mary Cameron, R.S.W., who, as the only lady artist employed—she represented the *Oban Times*—was a conspicuous figure in Court, told me that from the beginning of the case, each morning on entering the dock the prisoner greeted her with a smile, which she suitably acknowledged, until he sent her one day a note, inviting her to tea in the cells at the customary afternoon interval. This, as they had not been introduced, she deemed a liberty, and the acquaintance went no further. It is surprising that she should have been so squeamish, because, from her passion for depicting bull-fights, she was familiarly known as "Bloody Mary." The special correspondent of the *Pall Mall Gazette* has recorded an incident which throws a curious light on the mentality of the accused:—

> The jurors filed out to consider the verdict; and as we all thrilled at the drama of their fateful departure, Monson stood up, stretched himself, and turned round to me and Walter Evans who sat next me. We were astonished to find he was smiling broadly, and you can imagine how our amazement grew at the remark he addressed to us. Pointing to the hard form from which he had risen, Monson said: "Why am I like a railway engine? Because I've got a tender behind."
>
> So he felt the tenseness of the situation rather less than the hardened reporters who, accustomed to those criminal trials, confined their concern in the verdict to preparing for a smart despatch of it over the wires to London. It was a horrible piece of bathos, this stale and feeble joke at such a moment; but what a lightning flash

it was in its illumination of the inner consciousness of the man at so terrific a crisis in his life![1]

I

Seafarers on the Firth of Clyde—that admirable estuary—following the Royal Route to Ardrishaig so long familiar to the old *Columba*, after negotiating the "Narrows" of the Kyles of Bute, round Ardlamont Point to enter the fair waters of Loch Fyne. Above Ardlamont Bay stands Ardlamont House, conspicuous amid the greenery of its woods, a stately old-world mansion, white-harled, with spreading wings, long the seat of the ancient and honorable family of Lamont of Cowal. At the date in question the house was unoccupied, and the estate was offered for sale by the law agents of the proprietor, Major Lamont, at the price of £85,000. But the former glories of Ardlamont were about temporarily to be revived. Word came that some grand English folk had taken for the season the house and shootings; and the neighboring village of Tighnabruaich, where were shops, a bank, and an hotel, rejoiced in the prospect of their patronage. How far these hopes were justified will presently appear; at least the advent of the strangers secured for the district an unlooked-for and unenviable notoriety, which it enjoys even unto this day.

Of Alfred John Monson, the protagonist of our drama, the trial tells us little, beyond his exploits as a financial wizard. But five years afterwards, Monson having been sentenced to a like period of years' penal servitude in connection with some of his later activities, an enterprising journal obtained from Mrs. Monson, doubtless, as Trapbois would say, for a consideration,

---

1 *Some Piquant People*, by Lincoln Springfield, p. 101. London: 1924.

and published in a series of articles, an account of his antecedents and singular career which gave its readers exceptionally good value for their money.[2]

The account is presumably correct, seeing that Monson, on the expiry of his sentence, does not seem to have challenged its accuracy in the law courts, as he was wont to do when he deemed himself traduced. A man of good family and high connections—he could claim kinship with Lord Houghton and Lord Crewe, and his uncle was our ambassador at Paris—educated at Rugby and Oxford, Monson began life with every prospect of success. When a young Government official, he married at Cape Town, in 1881, Miss Agnes Maud Day, the daughter of a Yorkshire colliery owner. Tiring of South Africa, he threw up his appointment and brought his young wife back to England, where he found employment as a tutor. But the teaching profession had few charms for one of his bold and ambitious nature. Perennially hard up, he was ever hankering after money, "and for money," says his wife, "he was prepared to sacrifice everything." In 1886 he took over the lease of a large place, Cheyney Court. No sooner had he insured this mansion against fire than it was burnt down. Such accidents will happen in the best regulated families.

About 1889, Monson made the acquaintance of Major Dudley Hambrough, to whom he was introduced by one Tottenham, a financial expert and their mutual friend. The Major, though a life tenant of the Hambrough estates, with a rental of £4000 a year, had borrowed upon them up to the hilt and was in a chronic state of impecuniosity. In 1885 he had mortgaged his life interest with the Eagle Insurance Company for £37,000; by 1890 he had failed to pay the interest due, and the Company had foreclosed, thus becoming the absolute owners of the Major's life interest. Tottenham was financing the Major

---

2. *To-Day*, 23rd July, 6th, 13th, 20th, and 27th August 1898.

with a view to effecting a rearrangement of the foreclosed mortgage. Major Hambrough destined his son and heir, Cecil, for the Army, and it was ostensibly to further this end that Monson was introduced to him as an army tutor, though what were his qualifications for the post does not appear. It was arranged that Cecil should live with Monson and be coached by him, that gentleman receiving £300 a year for his services, payable at such time as the Major's finances should permit. But much greater than his interest in his pupil's progress was the tutor's infatuation for the Hambrough estates. "Waking or sleeping," says our authority, "Monson's thoughts were concerned with the Hambrough estates"; and his whole energies were bent on carrying through that scheme which Tottenham had failed to accomplish: the purchase of Major Hambrough's life interest from the Eagle Insurance Company.

In 1890 we find Monson, his wife, his two children, their governess, and his new pupil established at The Woodlands, near Harrogate, after an agricultural interlude at Gaddesley Farm, which had resulted in his arrest for fraud in connection with a bill of sale, when, after trial, he was acquitted. In Yorkshire, according to his wife, Monson gave little dinners to the élite of the district, largely overdrew his bank account, ran up big bills at the hostelries where he stabled his hunters, and figured prominently, to their ultimate loss, in the books of the local tradesmen. He was wont to boast that he never cultivated the acquaintance of anyone of whom he could not make use, "and he was so alive to the help derived from the family name that he used to say he could stock a five-floored warehouse on the strength of it."

Harrogate having become too hot for him, the next move was to Riseley Hall, Yorkshire, the eleventh home of Monson since his marriage, where, although he had now been adjudicated bankrupt, he took the field in style. Butler, coachman, several maidservants, and sundry outdoor hands were engaged;

there was a governess for the children, and a tutor for Cecil at £150 a year. Mrs. Monson describes the home life as "unbearable." Monson could drink hard, but liquor had no effect upon him, and he used his own immunity to prey upon the weakness of others. His guests were "a peculiarly unpleasant crew," and the tutor did not turn out well. "There was any amount of drinking and revelry." Cecil once had occasion to protect Mrs. Monson from her husband's violence; but as a rule the boy was completely dominated by Monson and did whatever that gentleman desired. "Hambrough trusted Monson," says his wife; "but Monson never trusted anybody." At Riseley Hall they remained from 1892 until the fatal flitting to Ardlamont. On the subject of the tragedy that terminated their tenancy of Ardlamont House Mrs. Monson is naturally reticent; but we shall hear from her again as to the subsequent adventures of her lord and master after his acquittal at Edinburgh of the terrible charge of murdering his pupil.

II

It is, of course, impossible in the space at my disposal to follow in any detail the windings of the financial labyrinth wherein by the machinations of Monson the Hambroughs, father and son, became involved. The evidence is fully set forth in Mr. Sheriff More's excellent report of the trial, wherein it may be conveniently digested.[3] I give but an imperfect outline. Mortgages to the amount of £16,000 were taken from them, and bills were granted by the Major for £5000. That gentleman, finding that these securities were being used by Monson for his

---

3. *Trial of A. J. Monson.* Edited by John W. More. Notable British Trials series. Edinburgh: 1908. See also Adam's *Judiciary Reports*, 1893–1895, i. 114–312: H. M. Advocate *v.* Monson and Another.

own purposes, began to distrust his ingenious adviser. The purchase of the Major's life interest from the Eagle for £40,000 —the grand aim and object of Monson's financial jugglery— broke down, because he insisted that he would be a party to no arrangement *"which does not make me personally the absolute owner of Major Hambrough's life interest."* Had this been effected, Monson, when the boy attained majority and could concur in disentailing the estates, would have been master of the situation. His own share, in the event of success, was to be £11,000. It may be noted that the proposed scheme did not involve the insurance of Cecil Hambrough's life.

Now, the Major had arranged that his son should join the Hampshire Militia, in which were many friends of his family, and he was greatly annoyed to find that Monson had put the boy into the Yorkshire Militia instead, directly contrary to the father's express commands. His parents did everything in their power to induce Cecil to leave Monson and return to them; but Monson, like Pharaoh and the Israelites, would not let him go. Whatever the hold he had over the boy, unquestionably it was a strong one. In answer to the father's repeated appeals, the tutor once wrote: "Sir,—In reply to your letter, I beg to say that *I am not your son's keeper*"—a phrase which has, in view of the later happenings, an ominous association. By the beginning of 1893 the Monson *ménage* depended for its sole source of maintenance upon the weekly doles of the philanthropic Tottenham. As an instance of the straits to which the establishment was reduced, we find Mrs. Monson bringing an action against Cecil for £800 for board and lodging due. The suit was undefended; and as a result of this friendly move, the judgment thus obtained was sold to Tottenham for £240 in cash.

In these stringent pecuniary circumstances and as an undischarged bankrupt—liabilities £56,000; assets £600—it is surprising to find Mr. Monson negotiating for a lease of the house and shootings of Ardlamont at a rent of £450 for the season. He himself, being bankrupt, could not be a party to the lease, and Cecil, too, was disqualified by reason of his minority; but Monson told the agents that one Mr. Jerningham, whom he described as the boy's guardian and trustee, would, as a responsible man of substance, sign along with Cecil. The agents agreed and the transaction was completed.

At the trial the Crown put into the box a gentleman bearing the regal name of Adolphus Frederick James Jerningham, who stated that his whole means consisted of a small income derived from his marriage settlement. He and Monson were both recipients of the bounty of Tottenham—also baptismally distinguished by the resounding names of Beresford Loftus, ex-officer in the Turkish army, then carrying on business as a moneylender, under the style of Kempton & Co. in the City of London. Mr. Jerningham says he was asked by Monson to become "a kind of trustee for young Hambrough," but that was his sole title to the office, for he heard no more about it. When the Solicitor-General put into his hand the lease of Ardlamont, which bore to be signed by Cecil and himself, the witness said that he had *only seen it once before*, a week ago, when he came to Edinburgh for the trial! The Solicitor-General then proposed to ask him whether his signature to that deed was genuine; whereupon Mr. Comrie Thomson, for the defense, objected to the question, as tending to prove the accused guilty of forgery, a crime with which he was not charged. After long debate the Court, following precedent in the case of *Pritchard*, held that the question was incompetent, forgery not being libeled in the indictment. I find in the apologia—or rather, vindication—published by Monson after his acquittal, this explanation of how the signature came to be adhibited: "Jerningham was not available at the time, and therefore his name was signed under a distinct authority given by him, and without any fraudulent intention whatever."[4] But there is no word of this in the evidence of Jerningham, and the effect was certainly to defraud the proprietor of his rent.

This impecunious gentleman was the "capitalist" put forward by Monson as an intending purchaser of Major Hambrough's life interest when the negotiations were resumed in the spring of 1893! Another offer to the insurance company was from a London solicitor, Mr. Price, in behalf of the Major, and it was proposed to take the title in the name of his friend Dr. Hambleton, as trustee for Cecil. Where Monson and Jerningham were to find the money does not appear; but the directors, being satisfied of the stability and good faith of the Major's representatives, gave the contract to them, and on 6th April 1893, as the Solicitor-General begged the jury to keep in mind, it was finally settled that Monson was not to be the purchaser of that life interest after which he had so long and ardently lusted. The game, so far as he was concerned, was, in that regard, definitely up.

### III

To escape from the bailiffs and duns that beset Riseley Hall and to enjoy the free air of Ardlamont implied divers outlays, for railway fares are not to be had without cash. Once again the gallant ex-officer of Baker Pasha stepped into the financial breach, and funds were forthcoming sufficient to effect the flitting. But the household linen had to be left in pawn at the laundry, as they lacked the means to pay the washerwoman! Once established as tenants of the great house, however, Credit resumed her beneficent sway and everything necessary

---

4. *The Ardlamont Mystery Solved*, by A. J. Monson (to which is appended Scott's Diary), p. 11. London: Marlo & Co., Publishers, 27 Bouverie Street, E.C. (1894).

was to be had for the asking. A suitable household staff was engaged, including, if you please, a butler; and the Royal Hotel at Tighnabruaich was privileged to enjoy the custom of the family in respect of household stores and liquor. There were carriages and gamekeepers and guns; yea, even a steam yacht was hired; so here was every prospect of an ideal holiday, luxurious, if expensive—particularly to the providers of the material elements. Cecil was to join the party so soon as his regimental training was completed, and some of his brother officers—he was now a lieutenant in the Yorkshire Militia—were invited for the forthcoming festival of the Twelfth.

Meanwhile the restless and scheming mind of Monson, not content with the placid pleasures of a country gentleman's life, was busy upon another project. On 10th July—exactly one month before Cecil Hambrough met his death—Monson sent to the Edinburgh office of the Scottish Provident Institution a proposal for a £50,000 policy on the boy's life, to be taken out in the name of Mrs. Monson. The reason alleged for requiring this huge insurance was stated to be: "to cover advances made and liabilities in connection with the Hambrough estates." Cecil passed the doctors and the proposal was accepted, *subject to Mrs. Monson being able to satisfy the Company that she had an insurable interest in the boy's life to the value of* £50,000. Monson then wrote that he was making other arrangements; a policy for only £10,000 would be required. But the smaller sum was subject to the same condition, which was equally impossible of fulfillment, so the matter dropped. On 18th July he had a shot at the Liverpool and London and Globe Company: a similar proposal for £50,000 on Cecil's life in favor of Agnes Maud Monson, to cover the advances and liabilities aforesaid. But here again he was met by the same difficulty: you must show a legal insurable interest. Monson repeated his move; as, in order to secure Mrs. Monson, other means were to be adopted, only £26,000 was now necessary; and to satisfy the directors he enclosed a letter by Cecil to the manager: "Ardlamont House, 31st July 1893. Dear Sir,—I am requested by Mrs. Agnes Monson to write and inform you that *she has an interest in my life to the extent of* £26,000. I have given her an undertaking under which I agree to pay to her this sum after my attaining twenty-one, *if I should live until then.*" The proposal was declined.

Undismayed by these successive failures, for the third time Monson tried again, with the luck proverbially attending that adventure. On 2nd August he called at the Glasgow office of the Mutual Assurance Company of New York. There was now a complete change of program. Monson informed the manager that he was the trustee and guardian of young Hambrough, who was coming into a fortune of £200,000; that he (Cecil) was about to buy the Ardlamont estate, that Mrs. Monson was advancing £20,000 to secure the purchase, and that the boy's life was to be insured for £20,000 to cover that advance. Monson said that the transaction must be carried through by 8th August, as the purchase of Ardlamont was to be completed on that date. The same afternoon he brought Cecil to the office; the boy was medically examined, and signed a proposal for two policies on his own life for £10,000 each. On 8th August Monson again called at the office, paid the premium, £194, 3s. 4d., with a check drawn by Mrs. Monson on the Royal Bank, Tignabruaich, and got delivery of the policies.

How came Mrs. Monson, into whose bank account only £15 had hitherto been paid and who was unable to pay her laundry bill, to be in a position to draw this large check? On the 7th Monson had written to the bank agent, enclosing a check by Tottenham, in favor of Cecil Hambrough and endorsed by him, for £250. As a matter of fact this check was afterwards dishonored and the bank had to stand the loss. How came Tottenham to send this check? *On 23rd July*—note the date—Monson had written to that financial sorcerer that he had just returned from Edinburgh, where he had seen Messrs. J. & F. Anderson, W.S., the solicitors for Major Lamont, as to the purchase of the estate by Cecil. They, the agents, had agreed to accept £48,000 for the property, and required a deposit of £250, on the contract being signed by Mrs. Monson. "I have told C. that the price is £50,000—£1000 each for division; thus he will have to raise £13,000 to enable him to complete next year," *i.e.* when he came of age. On the 24th Tottenham replied: "You seem to have made a good bargain *re* Ardlamont. Cecil had better write me a letter requesting me to pay the £250 deposit." As a conscientious historian it is my painful duty to admit that in the letter of 23rd July to "Dear Tot"— as Monson familiarly addressed his correspondent—there was not one word of truth. These false statements were made, despite the proverb touching honor among "financial agents," for the sole purpose of defrauding his friend and benefactor out of the money to pay the premium. But, as we have seen, "Dear Tot," though he rose to the £1000 fly, detected the hook in time.

On that busy and important 8th of August we find Monson, having secured possession of the policies, actually going to Edinburgh and calling upon the Lamont law agents. Mr. W. H. Murray, W.S., the partner whom he interviewed, stated in the witness-box that Monson then said he was commissioned by Cecil Hambrough to offer £60,000 for the Ardlamont estate. Mr. Murray replied that his price was £85,000, so there was no use discussing the subject further. As a matter of fact he had since sold the property for £70,000. Monson's proposition was that he should find the deposit and secure himself by insuring the boy's life, the settlement to take place on his attaining his majority. Mr. Murray added, by the way, that he had never got the shooting rent, and that an action raised against Jerningham for its recovery under the lease had been abandoned as hopeless.

When Monson got delivery of the policies, he handed to the

manager a letter from Cecil Hambrough, dated 7th August, in which the boy wrote: "Will you kindly deliver my two insurance policies of £10,000 each to Mr. and Mrs. Monson as I have assigned the policies to Mrs. Agnes Maud Monson for proper considerations received. *Mrs. Monson will, therefore, be the person to whom the insurance is payable in the event of my death.*" Three days later he was dead. On the same date, to make assurance doubly sure, Monson took from the boy another letter in the following terms:—

ARDLAMONT HOUSE, ARGYLLSHIRE,
AUGUST 7TH/93.

Dear Mrs. Monson,

If you will pay the premiums on the two policies of Assurance of my life of £10,000 each with the Mutual Life Assurance Company of New York, I am willing that you should hold the Policies as security for all monies due to you from me, & as security against all liabilities incurred by you on my behalf, & *in the event of my death occurring before the repayment of these monies* you will be the sole beneficiary of these Policies, & I have given notice to the Mutual Assurance Company of New York that you are the person to whom the insurance is payable, & they have accepted that notice.

Yours sincerely,
W. D. C. Hambrough.

To Mrs. Agnes Maud Monson
Ardlamont House.

Whether or not this letter be the spontaneous production of a boy of twenty is for the reader to judge. Of the legal effect of the purported assignation or assignment of the policies to Mrs. Monson there will be more to say in the sequel.

## IV

We now approach what, for me, has ever seemed the real Ardlamont Mystery: the presence there of the man called Scott. Our first glimpse of this illusive personality is obtained on that same red-letter day, the 8th of August, which Monson had so profitably spent in Glasgow and in Edinburgh. Returning to his country seat by steamer from Princes Pier, Greenock, Monson met on board Mr. Donald, a Paisley shipbuilder, from whom the steam yacht *Alert* had been hired for the pleasure of the house-party, after the new tenants came to Ardlamont in May. On 22nd July Monson had written to this gentleman, agreeing to purchase the yacht for £1200, and adding: "I shall not be able to forward you a check before *10th August*," his reason being that he had to settle by that date with the agents for the purchase of Ardlamont! On the steamer Monson was talking to a man whom he described to Mr. Donald as "a person from the estate office, who was going to see Mr. Hambrough." As the steamer was nearing Kames Pier, where passengers for Ardlamont disembark, Monson, who, as is the habit of Clyde voyagers, had been below—"looking at the engines" is the technical term—came on deck, and said to Mr. Donald, "Where is that fellow?" The stranger had, appropriately, vanished. What happened, as appears, was that, obviously having heard the name Tighnabruaich in connection with Ardlamont, the unknown had got out there, it being the pier before Kames. Monson drove back in his dogcart, picked up the too-previous emigrant, and returned with him to Ardlamont House.

The next we hear of the mysterious guest is from Miss Hiron, the governess, who recalled the arrival of Monson and his friend on Tuesday, 8th August. "I first saw him [Scott] about eight o'clock that evening at dinner. The dinner party consisted of Mr. and Mrs. Monson, myself, and Scott. Cecil Hambrough was out fishing that evening." Contrary to the custom of the house, Scott did not dress for dinner; he looked delicate and was very quiet. He did not join the ladies in the drawing-room afterwards. She understood he had come "on some business." She would not describe him as a gentleman. "I should think he was a Londoner; he dropped his 'h's'." To others, Monson stated that the visitor was an engineer, called in by Cecil Hambrough, as "an independent man," to overhaul in his behalf the boilers of the recently-purchased yacht, then lying unpaid for at Kames.

Next day, Wednesday, 9th August, is the first of the two crucial dates in the case, and how Monson and Scott improved the time is of supreme importance. Scott breakfasted with the family; in the forenoon he and his host had a bathe; he was present at lunch, at tea, and at dinner. One would have thought that opportunity would have been taken to inspect the boilers, but they never went near the yacht. Now, in June Monson had hired for the season from one M'Kellar, a boat-hirer of Tignabruaich, a rowing-boat, which Cecil Hambrough regularly used for fishing. *It had no plug-hole.* At ten o'clock that morning Monson and Scott—Cecil did not come down to breakfast till eleven—called at the offices and asked M'Nicol, the estate joiner, for the loan of his boat *for two nights.* "Monson said his own [M'Kellar's] was not extra safe." Permission being given, they went to Ardlamont Ferry, where the boat was lying, and brought her round to Ardlamont Bay. There was a plug-hole in this boat, closed with a cork. After lunch—still unconscionably neglecting the boilers—Monson and Scott took the children out in the boat which that morning he had said was dangerous, for a row in the bay. Cecil and Mrs. Monson were then walking on the high ground above Ardlamont Point. After the children were landed, the nurse saw Monson go up to the house, leaving Scott alone in the boat; twenty minutes later he took off his shoes and stockings, came out of the boat, and pulled it ashore, when he was rejoined by Monson. The Crown alleged that this was the time when there was cut in that boat a plug-hole of which we shall hear again. At dinner somebody suggested that they should go a-fishing. So Monson, Cecil, and the superfluous engineer left the house some time after ten o'clock. The two first entered the boat, Scott remaining on the shore. The most gentle reader will be surprised to find that, instead of using the new boat, M'Nicol's, expressly borrowed for that purpose, they put off in M'Kellar's boat, which, whether or not it had been before "unsafe," was certainly so now, unless that newly-fashioned plug-hole were securely closed. It, the hole, would be covered by the large net which they took with them for splash-net fishing and which filled the bottom of the boat. In the deepening dusk the two friends pulled out upon the dark waters of the bay, while the watcher waited on the beach. Monson was a strong swimmer; Cecil could not swim a stroke. If an accident should happen it would go hard with the boy. Happily, in case of need, help was at hand, for there, by the other boat, stood the enigmatic engineer.

When at a later stage this strange adventure was the subject of investigation, of the three persons participating one was dead, one had fled, and the third, in his judicial declaration, gave the following account of the occurrence:—

> Hambrough took off his coat and rowed, while I busied myself preparing the nets. While occupied with the nets, suddenly there was a bump, and the boat tilted, and I fell over the side. At the same time the boat capsized, and

for a minute or two I was entangled in the nets. Immediately on getting clear I called out for Hambrough, and then saw him sitting on the rock, laughing. The boat had struck the side of this rock and tilted over, which, with the load, and piled up as it was with nets, she could easily do. Hambrough, I knew, could not swim, so I told him to wait while I swam ashore and fetched another boat which was there. The sea was a little rough and the night was dark. The distance I had to swim would be between 200 and 300 yards.

Having safely landed, Monson says he saw Scott, "a man who was staying in the house at the time," and bade him run and fetch a lamp. It was then so dark that he [Monson] could find neither the plug nor the plug-hole in the other boat; but the tide was rising, so he decided to risk it, and without waiting for the lamp, pulled off and picked up Hambrough. They then recovered the first boat and the nets which were floating about 20 yards away. "So far from attempting on that evening to take young Hambrough's life, I consider that I saved it." They all returned to the house, and after drinks in the smoking-room Monson went to bed, leaving the others together. As to the fresh plug-hole in M'Kellar's boat, Hambrough made it himself, because he found it a bother to empty her of water after he had been splash-net fishing. Asked as to the identity of Scott, Monson declined to answer.

John Wright, the butler, at the trial stated that when the three gentlemen went out fishing on the night in question he was told to sit up for them. About one o'clock in the morning one of them—Hambrough as he thought—but the passage was dark—came back for the smoking-room lamp, saying that the boat had sunk and they had had to swim ashore. In half an hour they all came in and, after changing, went into the smoking-room, where witness left them when he went to bed at two, having first collected the clothes of Monson and Hambrough, which were soaking.

The other evidence relating to this matter stands thus. Next day M'Nicol and M'Kellar, learning of the mishap, came to look after their respective boats. These lay together on the beach, M'Kellar's being overturned, with a jacket rolled up under the seat. Both witnesses examined the newly-made plug-hole; it was an inch and a half in diameter, obviously cut with a knife; of unusual form and in an unusual place: too far up the side and too far from the keel. The boat was otherwise undamaged, and showed no sign of having been in contact with a rock. Near it M'Nicol afterwards found a clasp knife, which was proved not to be that usually carried by Hambrough. The Crown surveyor stated that he had searched for, and failed to find, in Ardlamont Bay any rocks below the low-water mark, and divers local witnesses, well acquainted with the bay, negatived the existence of any such rocks.

I have been thus particular in setting forth the evidence upon this branch of the case because it must be kept in mind, if the allegation of the Crown be well founded, that the original scheme was to murder Cecil Hambrough that night by *drowning*; the shooting of him next day being an afterthought, necessitated by the failure of the first plot. The Solicitor-General maintained that what had happened was this: providentially, the boat filled with water much sooner than Monson expected; both men were thrown into the sea, but so near the shore that Hambrough was able to reach land in safety, without the plan which had been devised being effectually accomplished. In the story which Monson published after the trial, he gives substantially the same account of the incident as that contained in his judicial declaration already quoted,[5] and has

5. *The Ardlamont Mystery Solved*, pp. 17–19.

nothing to say in reply to the criticisms of that version so cogently made by the learned Solicitor-General.

## V

The morning of Thursday, 10th August, broke dark, wet, and stormy over the house of Ardlamont. Yet despite wind and rain, and notwithstanding the trying experience of the previous night as well as the late hour of their going to rest, the inmates were up and about by 6 a.m. Mrs. Monson, with the children and governess, set out to catch at Kames Pier the early steamer for Glasgow, where they proposed to spend the day shopping and getting the children's hair cut. Of the house-party there remained the sporting host, the so-lately insured youth, and the strangely ineffective marine engineer.

The first we hear of their doings is from the butler, who at 7 o'clock gave Cecil a glass of milk and a biscuit in the dining-room. Lamont, the second keeper, tells us that at the same hour Monson came to his house at the offices, instructing him to go and tell the head keeper, M'Intyre, that he would be wanted at 10 o'clock, "as the gentlemen were going out." Witness usually kept the guns. *"Mr. Monson asked me for Mr. Hambrough's 20-bore gun, saying that Mr. Hambrough wanted it."* Having given it to him, witness went off to deliver the message to M'Intyre, who lived two miles distant from the mansion house. About 9 o'clock James Dunn, a visitor on holiday, then living in the schoolhouse on the Ardlamont estate, was looking out of the window when he saw Monson and Hambrough, whom he knew by sight, accompanied by a stranger, cross the road and walk towards the plantation behind the mansion house on the north. He lost sight of them as they entered the wood; Hambrough went off to the right, Monson and the stranger to the left. Three minutes later witness heard a shot. That shot ended Cecil Hambrough's life. The only other gun out that morning—the engineer was un-armed—was a 12-bore gun, with which admittedly Monson was accustomed to shoot. Normally, therefore, Cecil would be carrying his own short 20-bore boy's weapon, Monson his cus-tomary 12-bore gun.

The next that was seen of any of the party was by Car-michael, the ploughman, who, while standing at the stables, saw Monson, carrying two guns, and Scott, carrying some rabbits, come from the direction of the wood and make straight for the house, *without speaking to him*. Ten minutes later they returned without the guns and told him that Hambrough had shot himself. Shortly after 9 o'clock the butler saw Monson and Scott in the dining-room; Monson said that Hambrough had shot himself and was quite dead. The three then left the house, and at the stables Monson informed Carmichael and Whyte, the gardener, of what had happened. He bade them come and bring the body to the house. Guided by Monson they reached the spot where the dead lad lay. The body was on its back, upon the top of a turf dike or sunk fence, below which ran a ditch overgrown with grass and bracken. The face of the fence was four feet deep; the ground above was level. The body lay about two feet from the edge. It was wrapped in a rug and taken to the house in a farm cart. That forenoon, in consequence of what they had heard as to the alleged original position of the body, Whyte and Lamont examined the ground. On the spot where the head had lain they found two pieces of bone, and 2 feet away *a 12-bore cartridge wad*, stained with blood. The herbage in the ditch was undisturbed; they saw no signs of blood there, neither any appearance of a body having lain therein nor of two persons having lifted it.

Scott's version of the story we were not allowed, at the trial, to hear, as by absconding from justice he rendered his hearsay evidence inadmissible. Monson's account, in his written statement, furnished next day by request to the police, is as follows:—

> I, Alfred John Monson, of Ardlamont House, gentleman, aged thirty-two, say with reference to the sudden death of Windsor Dudley Cecil Hambrough, that about 6:30 a.m. on the morning of 10th August I went out shooting in company with Mr. Hambrough and Mr. Scott. Mr. Hambrough was in perfect health and spirits. I and Hambrough alone had guns. I shot three rabbits, which Mr. Scott was carrying. When we entered the cover by the house Hambrough took the right side, walking on the top of the sunk fence. I was walking on the left side, and Scott was following behind. Just as we got to the end of the cover I heard a shot fired. I waited a minute or so, and then called out and asked what he had shot. There was no reply. I walked towards the corner of the cover in the direction of the shot with Mr. Scott. I called "Hambrough!" several times, and there was no reply. *I then saw Hambrough lying at the bottom of the sunk fence on his left side, with his gun beside him. We lifted him up, and he was quite dead. I then called out to the men at the stables.* Three or four men came, and Mr. Hambrough was conveyed to the house. I think the time would be 7:30 a.m.

How far this statement is supported by the other evidence the reader will judge.

In April 1894, the year following the trial, the evanescent engineer, emerging from his retreat in the circumstances aftermentioned, contributed to the *Pall Mall Gazette* a series of articles, entitled "The Truth Out At Last. By Scott (The Missing Man)," from which, upon the crucial point as to the position of the body when discovered, I now quote, for what they are worth, these words:—

> We had not proceeded far when I heard a single shot. I came to the end of the wood, and there I saw Mr. Monson ahead of me, going towards the direction of the shot. He was carrying his gun on his shoulder.
>
> We turned in the direction Mr. Hambrough should be walking in and had not gone more than fifteen to twenty yards when—what did I see? That which I can never forget. The apparently lifeless body of Cecil Hambrough. Mr. Monson was by his side immediately and lifted up his head to ascertain if the poor fellow was dead. He called him by his name, Cecil, but the lips and eyes made no response.
>
> I am not a soldier or a doctor, and the sight of this fine young gentleman lying dead before me almost took away my scared senses. *I am told I helped to lift him up, and if I was asked to, I have no doubt I assisted to the best of my ability.* But if my life was staked upon my answer I could not tell with any minuteness what did or did not happen, or what was not said during the few seconds we were standing by the lifeless body of Cecil Hambrough, a few hours ago the bright, handsome fellow who made fun of my timidity. Run to the house and get assistance was the only thing to do, and we lost no time in doing it.

It is regrettable, seeing that his memory is in all other respects so clear, that it should fail him upon this vital question: whether or not the body was lifted from the ditch, as alleged by Monson. As to no time being lost in summoning aid, well, we have heard Carmichael and the other witnesses. Nobody was, in fact, told one word about the accident until the guns were deposited in the smoking-room and the cartridges of both withdrawn.

At 11:30 Dr. Macmillan of Tighnabruaich, called in by a message from Ardlamont, arrived at the house. He was received by Monson and Mr. Steven, the factor. The latter took him to the bedroom where the body of the dead boy had been laid. He found behind the right ear a wound involving the scalp and bone. It was smooth behind, jagged and irregular in front, and wider in front than at the back. Obviously, it was a gunshot wound, but the doctor had never actually seen before a gunshot wound in the head. From the hole in the skull he "fancied the charge would be in the head." He then joined Monson, Steven, and another gentleman, introduced to him as "Mr. Scott," at lunch. Mr. Scott mentioned that he had an important engagement that day in Glasgow, and must leave by the first available steamer. "At luncheon," says the doctor, "the subject of the death and how it occurred was pretty much avoided, but Mr. Monson remarked that had it happened in England there would have been a coroner's inquest, and *he supposed there would be nothing of that kind in Scotland?*" The doctor explained that there would be a private inquiry by the Procurator-Fiscal; but as this was an accident, there would probably be no postmortem. After lunch Dr. Macmillan took, for the Fiscal's information, a note of Monson's account of the affair. He said he was 50 yards away when the shot was fired. He and Scott had not gone very far along the sunk fence until they found the body lying in the ditch, with the gun beside it. The doctor then took a separate statement from Scott, which at the trial was objected to and was not permitted to be read. Dr. Macmillan having expressed a desire to inspect the *locus* of the accident, he and the factor were taken to the spot by Monson, who pointed to two places in the ditch as those from which, alternatively, he thought he had lifted the body. They saw no traces of blood at either, nor any marks of a man having fallen there; the brackens were unbroken. "To tell you the truth, Mr. Steven," said Monson, "I don't know where we lifted him from, but we lifted him." The doctor then departed to prepare his report.

At 2 o'clock that afternoon Constable M'Calman, being on Tighnabruaich Pier, had heard of the accident at Ardlamont. Scott was there, waiting for the steamer; and the policeman, who knew him as one of the house-party, asked why he was not staying for the inquiry. He said he could not do so, and M'Calman took down his address in case his evidence should be required: the Central Station Hotel, Glasgow. Thence-forth nothing more was seen of Mr. Scott, though much was heard of him, and he was presently to become the best-sought-for man in Britain.

## VI

On 10th August Monson telegraphed to Tottenham—not to the bereaved parents: "Cecil had serious gun accident. Come up at once." He also wired to Dr. Hambleton, who told the Hambroughs. They left for the North forthwith, telegraphing to Monson to wire to Newcastle how Cecil was and the nature of the injury. No telegram met them there; and at Glasgow the Major first learned from an evening paper that his son was killed. On Saturday, the 12th, Major and Mrs. Hambrough reached Ardlamont. Next morning Monson took them to see the place where the boy met his death. The Major remarked to his wife that there was no sign of a heavy body having lain in the ditch. Cecil, by the way, was six feet in height and heavily-built. Monson's report to the parents of how the accident occurred is sufficiently remarkable to warrant quotation. Major Hambrough states:—

When I asked him how the thing happened he told me that Cecil had been getting over a dike, and had fallen and shot himself. He said that Mrs. Monson was going to Glasgow on business early in the morning, and that Cecil got up to see her off, and that after doing so he went down to the shore to tell the men at the yacht to get up steam. While they were doing this Cecil had taken his gun and gone for a stroll.

THE SOLICITOR-GENERAL.—Did Monson say where he himself was or what he had done?

WITNESS.—He said that he was out for a walk before breakfast in the meadow, and that he heard a shot.

THE SOLICITOR-GENERAL.—Did he say whether or not he had been shooting with Cecil?

WITNESS.—*I understood him to say distinctly that Cecil was the only one who had a gun.*

The Major learned further that his son had been accompanied by a man named Scott, who, said Monson, was so affected by the affair that he could not remain in the house, and had returned to Glasgow. "He [Monson] said he was an engineer who lived in Glasgow, and that I could see him there on my way back to England." On the Monday, as he was passing through Glasgow, the Major made inquiries for Scott at the hotel, but failed to find him. When he reported this result to Monson, that gentleman said: "I have made a mistake as to where he [Scott] lives; he is still at Tignabruaich," which it was then too late to verify. Major Hambrough's attempt to interview Dr. Macmillan was equally unsuccessful: Monson said "the doctor had got tired of waiting and had left." So Monson accompanied the bereaved parents on their sad journey home to Ventnor, in the Isle of Wight, where on Thursday, the 17th, the body was buried in St. Catherine's Churchyard. At Ventnor Monson gave the Major, for the first time, some account of the insurances upon his late son's life. He said that, but for that unlucky accident, a policy with the Scottish Provident for £50,000 would have been carried through! He made no mention of the £20,000 effected with the Mutual Assurance Company two days before the death. The sole completed policy, he said, was one for £400, which was held by Mrs. Monson. The astute reader will perceive that these statements fall something short of "the truth, the whole truth, and nothing but the truth."

On Saturday, the 12th, in response to a telegram from Monson, came also to Ardlamont Mr. Beresford Loftus Tottenham. "I had been out of pocket by advancing money to the establishment for some time," says that philanthropic financier, "and I said to Monson I wished I had never heard the name of Hambrough." Monson replied that it would be all right, as he would recoup Tottenham when the policies were paid. Tottenham asked to see the assignation (assignment) which Cecil had granted, of which he took a copy on the notepaper of the steamer *Iona*, on their way to Glasgow. "I told Monson, I thought that under Scots law the assignment was good; he was under a contrary impression." On Monday, the 21st, having returned to Scotland after the funeral, Monson, still accompanied by Tottenham, called on Mr. M'Lean, the district manager of the Mutual in Glasgow, "to talk over the claim." Mr. M'Lean expressed surprise that the death had not been intimated to the Company; he had read of it first in the newspapers. Monson explained that he had sent a telegram, which must have gone astray. The manager told him that the death certificate by Dr. Macmillan was not enough; they required evidence of the death from the Procurator-Fiscal. So on Wednesday, the 23rd, Mr. M'Lean and his secretary went to Inveraray to interview that functionary. At Tighnabruaich they were joined by Monson and Tottenham, who proceeded with them on the *Lord of the Isles* to Inveraray. There Monson met upon the open pier the Procurator-Fiscal, who says that at that time there was in the official mind no suspicion whatever that young Hambrough's death was other than accidental. "He [Monson] told me there were two friends behind him on the boat—insurance men—who wanted to see me." The Fiscal said he understood that the boy's life was not insured; "Monson stated that Major Hambrough had insured his son's life, but that he had not been aware of it; he said the amount was £15,000." This statement came as a surprise to the Fiscal; he was further surprised to learn in his office from Mr. M'Lean about the insurances for £20,000. This unlooked-for communication completely altered the Fiscal's view of the matter, and he asked Monson to send, so soon as he got home, the 20-bore gun and the amberite (smokeless) cartridges referred to by Dr. Macmillan in his report as the instruments of death. Monson promised to send them by the next day's steamer; but as he failed to do so, the Fiscal, who was becoming ever more dissatisfied with the business, went personally to Tighnabruaich, where, on 24th August, he at last began really to inquire into the matter. From Lamont, the keeper, he learned, among other interesting facts, that *there were no amberite cartridges for the 20-bore*—only for the 12-bore gun. Monson called at the hotel that evening, but the Fiscal declined to see him. On the 26th Monson wrote to the Fiscal, saying that he had been in Glasgow looking for Scott, but could not find him. "I had nothing to do with the engaging of him," he writes, "and know nothing of him. He came here the day before the accident happened, and left the day on which it happened between 2 and 3 o'clock." Monson's inquiries were supplemented by those of the police authorities throughout the kingdom; but of the eloping engineer it had to be said, with De Quincey's famous connoisseur: *Non est inventus.*

## VII

On 25th August, Dr. Macmillan, whose knowledge of the case had been considerably increased since the pleasant luncheon party at Ardlamont on the 10th, withdrew the reports which he had formerly made to the Fiscal and to the Insurance Company as to the cause of death.

> I implicitly accepted the statement of the witnesses Monson and Scott [he writes] that the injuries to Hambrough were due to an accidental shot from his own gun, *a short-barreled 20-bore boy's weapon, charged with amberite.* The apparently entire absence of motive made the bent of my inquiry not so much how could this injury most likely be produced, as how could the deceased have done it accidentally. It now transpires that there were no amberite cartridges for this diameter of gun, and that I too hastily came to the conclusion or theory advanced at the end of my former report. Having handled and tried the gun (the 12-bore) now in the possession of the Procurator-Fiscal, I am convinced the injuries were not caused in the way I thought possible.

Meanwhile the fact that the Fiscal was in residence at the Royal Hotel, Tighnabruaich, and was daily examining witnesses, must have suggested to Monson that though the dead boy was buried, the question how Cecil Hambrough met his death was very much alive and it behoved him to prepare for the worst. Messrs. Davidson & Syme, W.S., Edinburgh, a legal firm of high repute, were retained by the Hon. Mrs. Monson in her son's interest, and on 25th August Mr. John Blair, the senior partner, went to Ardlamont to consult with his client. Obviously the first thing to be done was to get in touch with Scott, and Monson furnished Mr. Blair with information for framing an advertisement to that end: "Edward Scott, engineer, who was at Ardlamont, Argyllshire, on 9th and 10th August 1893, is urgently requested to communicate with," etc. Now, three days earlier, on the 22nd, Monson had written with his own hand for instruction of the police, who were equally anxious to find Scott: "I am informed that Edward Scott started business as an engineer in Glasgow, and that he failed; that he was afterwards working in connection with yachts; and that he was well known in Greenock." And when in Glasgow on the 24th Monson told Mr. M'Lean, of the Mutual, "that all he knew about Scott was that he came from Stockton-on-Tees and that *it was Hambrough who employed him.*" Mr. Blair had to admit, in cross-examination, that these additional "facts" were not disclosed to him by his client. The advertisement was repeatedly inserted in the Press of the United Kingdom, America, and Canada, but without result.

The Fiscal's investigation being completed and his report communicated to the Crown authorities in Edinburgh, a warrant was issued for the arrest of Monson, which was duly effected by the Chief Constable of Argyllshire on 30th August. He was taken to Inveraray, where next day he was judicially examined by the Sheriff-Substitute of the county, emitted the declaration before mentioned, and was committed upon the charge of murder for trial in due course of law. Two constables were appointed to watch the place where the body was found, in order to prevent any possible interference, and these officers remained alternately on duty until 5th October. On the day of the arrest the police searched Ardlamont House, took possession of the two guns, together with several bundles of cartridges, respectively applicable thereto. Behind the door of a press in Cecil Hambrough's bedroom was found the jacket he was wearing when he was shot, in the pocket of which were 19 cartridges: 18 *for the 20-bore gun* and one for the 12-bore. All these were taken to Inveraray for production at the trial.

Mention has been made of certain of Cecil's brother officers being bidden to Ardlamont for the Twelfth. On 11th August there duly arrived, in pursuance of this invitation, Captain White and Lieutenants Massey and Strangeways, of the 3rd West Yorkshire Militia; a Mr. Manfield, who "had taken a gun in the shooting," joined the party a few days later. These gentlemen were shocked to hear of the accident and wished to leave at once; but Monson invited them to stay on and shoot, which they did, though not until his return from the funeral at Ventnor. The shooting was continued till the 31st, when it was stopped by the proprietor as the rent due on 1st August had not been paid, and on that date the party broke up, the guests going their several ways. There had been shooting enough for that season at Ardlamont.

On 4th September, Dr. (afterwards Professor Sir Henry) Littlejohn, then surgeon of police and lecturer on medical jurisprudence at Surgeons' Hall, Edinburgh, as instructed by the Crown Agent and accompanied by Dr. Macmillan, went to Ventnor for the purpose of making a post-mortem examination of Cecil Hambrough's remains. The body, which was generally well preserved, was disinterred, and before it was examined certain photographs of the wound were taken. The two medical men later embodied in a report, dated 13th September 1893, the results of their examination. It is, of course, expressed in technical terms, bewildering to the layman, but the following description of the injuries may be quoted:—

> This wound was of a triangular shape, the base of the triangle being towards the face, while the apex was situated about an inch below and slightly in advance of the occipital protuberance. Its extreme length was $3\frac{1}{2}$ inches. At its base it had a width of $2\frac{1}{2}$ inches. At its middle it measured 2 inches, whence it tapered off posteriorly. The right ear was mutilated—a portion of its external

surface being awanting, leaving a lacerated surface measuring from above downwards $1\frac{1}{2}$ inches, and leaving the upper part of the ear and its lobe below intact.

On no part of these surfaces was there any appearance of blackening or scorching from gunpowder. On dissection, the skull presented a localized shattered appearance corresponding to the injuries to the skin and tissues. From the brain, which otherwise was uninjured, four metallic fragments resembling shot were removed and preserved. The rest of the body was uninjured. The great vessels were empty, and generally throughout the body there was an absence of blood. The conclusion arrived at was that the deceased died from shock, the result of a gunshot injury of the skull and brain, and of subsequent loss of blood. We shall hear more of these matters when we come to the trial.

## VIII

After long and careful consideration of the precognitions or statements of the witnesses taken by the Procurator-Fiscal, the law officers of the Crown decided to make a further charge against the prisoner. Monson, it will be recalled, had been arrested for murder by shooting; he was now also to be charged with attempted murder by drowning. Accordingly, on 30th October, the prisoner was brought again before the Sheriff-Substitute and emitted on this new charge another declaration, in which he gave his account of the boating mishap as above described. Two questions only were asked him by the Sheriff: "Were the nets used that night at all?" *Answer:* "I have no further answer to give." "Is Scott, to whom you have referred, really called Davis, and do you know him?" *Answer:* "I have already said that I have no further answer to give to this charge."

This brings us to the vexed question of the identity of Scott, picturesquely termed in the newspapers of the day "The Missing Man." Although the police had not succeeded in securing the person of the fugitive, they had at length, with considerable trouble, been able to unveil his personality; and on 6th November was posted the first official bill containing his description. From this bill it appears that he was a bookmaker's clerk, whose home was at 35 Sutherland Street, Pimlico; that his real name was Edward Sweeney, *alias* Edward Davis, *alias* Edward Scott; and that he was known in racing circles as "Ted Davis" or "Long Ted." His description was as follows:—

> Age about 30; height about 5 feet 10 inches, thin build, broad shoulders; complexion pale, inclined to be sallow; eyes, full, steel-gray, high cheek bones, long thin face, sharp chin, dark wavy hair, brown mustache (may be shaven off); carries his shoulders well back, head slightly forward, suffers from asthma, has a habit of putting his right hand to his side when coughing, in delicate health; dresses well, and generally wears a low hard felt hat.

"Long Ted" made no response to this official invitation to come forward and clear himself of complicity in the alleged crimes, so on 1st December a reward of £200 was offered for such information as would lead to his apprehension. This also failed to produce any result.

The difficulty with which the Crown authorities were faced was this: they had a body of evidence clearly establishing the identity of Edward Sweeney in London; they had a dozen witnesses to swear to the identity of Edward Scott at Ardlamont; but, in the continued and regrettable absence of the original, how was it to be proved that both sets of witnesses spoke to the same man? The obvious way was to obtain a photograph of the undoubted Sweeney, and show it to those who had seen him as Scott; but "Long Ted" seems to have been shy of the camera, and such was not then to be had. By a singular irony of chance, no sooner had the indictment been served upon the prisoner, containing a list of productions to be used against him, than the police became possessed of an excellent photograph of Edward Sweeney, which, had it been secured in time, would have settled the question in five minutes. But as, according to our generous practice, nothing can be produced against a prisoner of which he has not been given due warning in his indictment, the acquisition came too late to be of use. Despite this misfortune for the prosecution, however, the evidence led at the trial left no reasonable doubt as to the identity of Scott with Sweeney.

## IX

Not until Tuesday, 12th December 1893, four months after the fatal shot rang out that stormy morning in the Ardlamont woods, were the forces of the Crown ready to take the field. The trial was held within the historic High Court of Justiciary at Edinburgh. The presiding Judge was the Lord Justice-Clerk, Lord Kingsburgh (Sir J. H. A. Macdonald), eminent as an authority on criminal law. The prosecution was conducted by the Solicitor-General (Alexander Asher, Q.C., M.P.), assisted by R. U. Strachan, J. A. Reid, and J. Campbell Lorimer, Advocates-Depute. The defense was in the capable hands of John Comrie Thomson, Q.C., Sheriff of Forfar; John Wilson (afterwards Lord Ashmore) and William Findlay, advocates, were his juniors.

No counsel of those times could touch Comrie Thomson with a jury. His handsome face and figure, his silver hair and golden voice, his persuasive manner, his perfect courtesy to the most hostile witness, and above all his profound knowledge of human nature, not always in its most admirable aspects, combined to make him the best jury pleader of his day. If he cut rather less ice with the Bench, that did not matter, so long as few jurymen could withstand his spell. There were then no "Ladies of the Jury"; if there had been, he could confidently have counted on their vote and interest. Asher was a counsel of another type. Equally personable and distinguished in his own so diverse style; of dignified and imposing presence; admittedly the greater lawyer, but lacking the personal and peculiar charm that was the note of Comrie Thomson's advocacy; there surrounded him an aura of aloofness and austerity in marked contrast with the genial warmth of feeling diffused by his friendly rival. Thus, while I was wont to listen to Mr. Asher with respectful admiration, not unmingled with awe, I used, as an idle apprentice, to run away from the office as often as I could to hear Comrie Thomson in a proof or jury trial. Such was the advocate by whom the accused had the good fortune to be defended. It was his last big case, for a few years later he met with an accident from which he never recovered; but no other counsel then at the Scots Bar could have handled it with more ability or to better effect, securing with such odds against him a modified acquittal. The whole burden of the prosecution rested on the stately shoulders of the Solicitor-General, for it was no secret that the Crown team, apart from his leadership, was not conspicuous for strength. Yet throughout the long ten days of battle he bore the brunt with tireless energy, and his speech for the prosecution is the most powerful and impressive that I have ever heard. Unlike another famous address for the Crown to which, in the same Court and in similar circumstances, I was years afterwards to listen, it was scrupulously fair and just.

The indictment, which was at the instance of the Right Hon. John Blair Balfour, Her Majesty's Advocate, charged Monson and Scott—as for convenience I shall continue to call him—with two crimes: (1) that, having formed the design of drowning Cecil Hambrough, they bored a hole in a boat, and on 9th August induced Cecil to embark therein; and that Monson, while the boat was in deep water in Ardlamont Bay, removed the plug, sunk the boat, and thus attempted to murder Hambrough; and (2), that on 10th August, in a wood near Ardlamont House, Monson and Scott did shoot the boy, and thus murdered him. Annexed to the indictment was a list of 266 productions and of 110 witnesses for the Crown. The prisoner being placed at the bar, and the diet called against him and his associate, Scott, of whose absence everybody in Court was aware, the Macer was ordered to call his name in the Parliament Hall, and having done so, reported, not surprisingly, that there was no answer. Whereupon the Solicitor-General moved for sentence of outlawry against Edward Sweeney, *alias* Davis, *alias* Scott, which was formally pronounced by the Lord Justice-Clerk. The prisoner having pleaded Not Guilty, a jury was empaneled and the trial proceeded.

As there is according to our law and custom no opening address for the prosecution, in a case of such extent and complexity the jury might well feel overwhelmed by the mere mass of evidence which they were called upon unaided to digest. Pundits actuarial and financial; medico-legal and shooting experts; gamekeepers, boatmen, and servants; bookmakers, detectives, and a choice assortment of police officers, succeeded each other in the witness-box to help solve the manifold riddles with which the Ardlamont Mystery bristled. It is impracticable here to follow in detail the testimony of so great a cloud of witnesses. The reader is now, I hope, possessed of the main outlines of the case, and I shall therefore confine myself to the more salient features of the evidence, lest he should be in danger of not being able to see the wood for the trees. The metaphor is appropriate, for the forensic fight waxed fiercest in the plantation; but some of the trees will call for separate notice. Unlike Mrs. Monson, I do not propose to incur further "liabilities in connection with the Hambrough estates," and of the alleged attempted drowning I have already said enough. The real question at issue may, I think, briefly be considered under three heads: (1) With which gun was Cecil Hambrough shooting when he was shot? (2) Did he die "in his tracks" on the dike, or was he lifted from the ditch? and (3) Did Monson stand to gain or lose by the death? And over and above these, the queerest business of all: What was Scott doing at Ardlamont? Before tackling the major problems, let us have a crack at this subsidiary conundrum.

## X

Mr. and Mrs. Keen, of 35 Sutherland Street, Pimlico, had as lodgers for two years prior to October 1893 a family who called themselves Davis: father, mother, daughter, and two sons, Edward and George. Letters and telegrams used to come addressed to E. and to G. "Sweeney"; these were claimed by the Davis sons. The elder was known as "Ted." He frequented race meetings. On 7th August he told his landlady he was "going to the North" and left, presumably to do so. She never saw him again. His relatives flitted in October, when the hue and cry was at its height. The description of "Ted" which they, the Keens, were able to give was incorporated in the police bills.

George Sweeney, hall porter at the Westminster Palace Hotel, stated that his family used the name Davis in connection with his brother's business as a bookmaker. Edward was, physically, very delicate. The last time witness saw him was in the middle of September 1893, when he (Edward) called at the hotel and spoke to him in the hall for half an hour. He then told witness he thought he would go a voyage to Australia for his health. On 20th August George himself went on holiday, curiously enough, to Scotland, where he stayed with friends at Helensburgh on the Firth of Clyde. He was reluctant to admit this visit, but was compelled by the Court to answer. His brother was not in Helensburgh while he was there.

George Smith, tailor, Eton, stated that in July of that year he received from Edward Davis an order for clothing to the value of £23. 9s. which, when completed, he sent as instructed to 35 Sutherland Street, half on 27th July and the rest on 4th August. Davis introduced a friend, "George Hunt," whom witness now identified as George Sweeney—George seems to have shared his brother's partiality for an *alias*. After delivery of the first parcel he wrote: "Clothes to hand. Glad to say they fit very well. I shall not be going North for fully a week, so when ready please forward." That letter was signed "George Hunt"; he paid the bill.

Four sporting characters—Robertson, a spirit merchant; King, a solicitor's clerk; and two gentlemen of no specific profession, Law and West—stated that they knew Monson as associated for purposes of betting with a bookmaker named Sidney Russell and his clerk Ted Davis. *Three of them were introduced to Davis by Monson himself.* King was present when Davis visited Russell in August, as after mentioned. With this exception, none of them had seen Davis in his customary haunts since the affair at Ardlamont; he had disappeared.

Sidney Russell, turf commission agent, stated that Ted Davis had been his clerk for the last two years. Witness knew Monson and had seen him a dozen times with Davis in connection with betting: at the Grand Buffet, Charing Cross, at the Ship in Parliament Street, at the Mitre in Chancery Lane, and at the Hotel Metropole. On 16th August Davis called at his house while King was there. At this point the witness was removed, and the Solicitor-General intimated that he proposed to ask him a question which, if answered, would involve the repetition of a statement made by Davis. That statement could not be direct evidence in the case; but it would prove the identity of Sweeney or Davis with the fugitive Scott. After citing divers authorities, the learned Solicitor submitted that the evidence was admissible. Mr. Comrie Thomson strongly objected to its admission. Hearsay evidence could only be accepted if the person to whom it related was dead or insane. There was no evidence that Davis was one or the other. The Lord Justice-Clerk thought that to admit such secondary evidence would be a dangerous principle. If the Crown were unable to produce Sweeney they must abide by the consequences. The question was disallowed. Witness, recalled, said that when Davis came to his house on 16th August he remained a quarter of an hour. Witness had not previously seen him since 25th July. He never set eyes on him again and did not know what had become of him.

The Solicitor-General was equally unfortunate in a further effort to establish the identity of Davis with Scott, when he proposed to ask Wright, the butler, whether he had seen in the hands of the police a certain photograph, the original of which he recognized? Mr. Comrie Thomson objected, as the photograph was not and could not competently be produced. The objection was sustained. Verily, in these, as in other rulings of the Court, the luck was all against the Crown.

Let us now hear the truth of the matter, as disclosed by Mr. Monson himself after his acquittal. I have collected from his book the passages in this connection.[6]

> In the first place I must explain the presence of Scott. He arrived at Ardlamont on the evening of August the 8th. *Cecil and I being in Glasgow on the 7th*, we returned on the 8th ... and traveled to Greenock in company with Mr. Donald, the builder of the yacht *Alert*. Whilst on the

---

6. *The Ardlamont Mystery Solved*, pp. 16, 19, 33, 47.

steamer I met Scott, with whom I was having some conversation when Mr. Donald came up and spoke to me.

Instead of discussing the boilers, which were the alleged occasion of Scott's coming, Monson told Donald that he was "a person from the estate office, *who was going to see Mr. Hambrough*"! It does not appear from the evidence that Cecil was with Monson that day in Glasgow.

The yacht was to have come round by 10 o'clock [on the morning of the fatal day], when Scott was to have gone on board.

There is in the evidence no word of such an arrangement being made, and most certainly the yacht remained at Kames.

I answered one or two other questions [by the Fiscal]; that I was unaware of Scott's address, and had had no communication from him since he left Ardlamont; in fact I had never any correspondence with him whatever, and did not know anything concerning him *beyond what I had heard from Hambrough.*

There is no evidence that Cecil was aware of Scott's existence till he was brought by Monson to Ardlamont, and we have heard what the several witnesses swore as to Monson's close association with Davis.

Inspectors Brockwell and Greet, who were searching for Scott, according to Monson,

... appear to have formed the opinion that Edward Scott was the same person as Edward Sweeney.... Personally, I never heard the name of Sweeney until some time after my arrest. It is not necessary for me to give the public particulars of the shocking blunders that have been made by the police; it will suffice my purpose to say that if they had pursued a different course to what they did, instead of so hastily jumping at false conclusions, they would undoubtedly have found the man who was at Ardlamont under the name of Edward Scott. Previous to his coming to Ardlamont I had only seen the man about three times in my life, although some evidence was given at the trial about my having had bets with Edward Davis. The evidence was quite untrue.

Whether or not this explanation "solves" the mystery of Scott's visit to Ardlamont is a matter of opinion.

We have also the advantage of knowing what was Scott's own version, as communicated by him in April 1894 to the *Pall Mall Gazette*. It is regrettable to find that he contradicts his friend Mr. Monson in every particular. Edward Sweeney tells us that he used the name Davis for professional purposes. From May 1893 Monson had been his patron and client, and their transactions on the turf were to their mutual satisfaction.

During the latter part of July Mr. Monson invited me to come to visit him at Ardlamont, and his invitation and the promised welcome were so kindly insisted upon that it was out of the question to refuse. I accepted the offer, and it was arranged that I should set out for Scotland about the 7th or 8th of August, when Mr. Monson hoped to be in Glasgow, where we could meet and journey on to Ardlamont together. . . . *Here let me at once state that at this time I did not know of the existence of Mr. Hambrough, and had never seen or heard of that young gentleman.*

Monson, alone, met him in Glasgow, and on the way to Ardlamont remarked:—

> "Look here, old fellow, it will never do to introduce you to my wife as Ted Davis, the bookmaker, so you must not mind if I say you are something else, for I feel sure she would make a fuss about it. Not that she herself would care, but you know that some people are funny about the turf, and think anyone connected with it must be a wrong 'un."[7]

So, to safeguard Mrs. Monson's susceptibilities, Ted Davis was to be introduced as Mr. Scott, "the engineer about the engines of the yacht *Alert*."

> Mr. Hambrough did not appear at dinner, and though I understood he was staying in the house, *I had at this time never seen him*, and did not know but what he was a guest similar to myself, and it never crossed my mind that he was the real owner and that Monson was his tutor. . . . I subsequently ascertained that Mr. Hambrough was away fishing that evening and did not return until very late that night—past midnight.

Scott is corroborated by the governess as to Cecil's absence. Next morning he was introduced to the boy by Monson: "Mr. Scott—Mr. Hambrough." There is an old play of Philip Massinger with the attaching title: *Believe as You List*. We will leave it at that.

Mr. Comrie Thomson ridiculed to the jury the suggestion that Scott was there for any sinister purpose, and maintained

---

7. Why should Monson invite this bookmaker to join the house-party, to which Cecil's brother-officers were bidden for the Twelfth?

that his disappearance was the greatest misfortune that could have befallen the defense. But the question is: Why did he flee and hide himself *before there was any question of foul play?* And why, if all were fair and above board, did Monson so persistently lie, even to his own law agent, concerning his knowledge of the stranger? The Solicitor-General argued that Scott was a party to the drowning plot; that his was the hand that cut the plug-hole; that he was on the shore beside the second boat in case his accomplice should need assistance; and that next day, knowing what had really happened in the wood, his nerve failed him and instead of staying to support his friend's story, he absconded—remaining, as we know, in concealment until the trial was safely over. The observations of the Lord Justice-Clerk upon this matter suffered a disadvantage from which we are exempt: that the identity of Scott with Davis had not been established. His Lordship was of opinion that Scott could have no conceivable interest in Hambrough's death, and if the Crown theory were correct must have been there as a hired assassin; a view for which in his judgment there was no basis. "No doubt his presence there is mysterious in many ways, but, gentlemen, it is for the Crown to solve the mystery." Had his Lordship allowed us to hear what Davis said to Sidney Russell on 16th August, peradventure it would have lightened our darkness.

## XI

The reader will remember that there were only two guns: a heavy 12-bore, commonly carried by Monson; and a short 20-bore, specially got for Cecil's use. For the first were cartridges of ordinary black powder, with No. 5 shot; for the second, cartridges of amberite, a smokeless powder, with No. 6 shot. It is indisputable that the fatal shot was fired from the former weapon—the pellets in the brain were No. 5 shot, and the blood-stained wad found near the head was that of a 12-bore cartridge. Both guns were removed by Monson at the time, taken back to the house, and cartridges from each extracted, all before any alarm was given. On the morning of the death Monson admittedly asked for and obtained from Lamont, the keeper, the 20-bore, saying, "Mr. Hambrough wanted it." Dr. Macmillan, having heard the accounts of Lamont, Monson, and Scott, in his first report states that the injury was caused by "a short 20-bore gun." And in his amended report he says: *"I implicitly accepted the statements of the witnesses Monson and Scott that the injuries to Hambrough were due to an accidental shot from his own gun, a short-barreled boy's weapon, charged with amberite."*

The first person to be told anything of the alleged change of guns was Lamont. "It was," says the keeper, *"about a fortnight after he had been examined by the Fiscal* that Monson first spoke to me about a change of guns . . . and said that when he came down with the 20-bore that morning, Hambrough had out the 12-bore on the front lawn to try the amberite cartridges."[8]

Mr. Steven, the factor, stated that on the night when Monson was under police surveillance in the house he said, when he came back from the keeper with the 20-bore, Hambrough had lifted the 12-bore and taken it with him. "Mr. Hambrough, Monson said, kept the 12-bore all morning, while he, Monson, kept the gun he got from the keeper, that is the 20-bore gun." Monson also said that he had fired one shot in the field before they entered the wood, and killed a rabbit, which he left lying, intending to pick it up on the way back. With reference to this incident Monson in his book remarks:

---

8. Why did not Monson tell this to the Fiscal when that official asked him to send the 20-bore gun and amberite cartridges?

"When I gave this statement to my law agent, Mr. Blair, he went to look for the rabbit, and found it there, or rather what was left of it."[9] It is curious if it did not occur to so astute and experienced a solicitor as Mr. Blair that in the remains of that rabbit lay the solution of the Ardlamont Mystery, for a brief post-mortem examination would have shown *whether it was killed by No. 5 or by No. 6 shot*. Perhaps he deemed it wiser to let dead rabbits—like sleeping dogs—lie. Mr. Steven, who was present, also saw the residue of the rabbit. Scott, too, in his "story" confirms the shooting of this rabbit by Monson, which impressed him as "the first I had seen killed in my life."

The only other point in this connection is the fact that in the pocket of the dead boy's jacket were found 18 cartridges for the 20-bore gun and one for the 12-bore. Mr. Comrie Thomson, in his speech for the defense, thus dealt with this significant fact:—

> It is essential to bear in mind that this discovery was made on 30th August. That jacket had been within the power of Monson ever since the time of the accident. If he were addressing you now, instead of me, he would tell you this, that he had been instructed to send to Inveraray the jacket and certain cartridges in the house, without any distinction, and that day, before it was taken away, he had, in order to facilitate matters, put a certain quantity of cartridges into the jacket for facility of carriage to Inveraray.

This explanation was characterized by the learned counsel as "perfectly rational and natural," and presumably the jury agreed with him. But Mr. Steven had stated in his evidence that on the day of the accident "I did not examine the pockets

---

9. *The Ardlamont Mystery Solved*, p. 20.

of Mr. Hambrough's jacket; I felt cartridges in the pocket from the outside only." So there were assuredly *some* cartridges in the pocket before Mr. Monson so considerately "facilitated matters."

## XII

It is out of the question here—for I am writing merely a chapter, not a book, about the Monson case—to deal adequately with the great body of testimony given by medical and shooting experts, which forms the bulk of the evidence adduced. The conflicting opinions of the skilled witnesses respectively called for the Crown and defense must, to be appreciated, be studied at large in the report of the trial. I can but shortly summarize the rival theories. The medico-legal experts for the prosecution were specialists of the highest eminence in their profession. Dr. (later Sir Henry) Littlejohn; Dr. (afterwards Sir Patrick) Heron Watson; Dr. Joseph Bell, the famous prototype of Sherlock Holmes, and Dr. Macdonald Brown, Lecturer on Anatomy in Surgeons' Hall, were all, professionally, favorites. Dr. Macmillan of Tighnabruaich also ran. For the defense were Dr. Matthew Hay, Professor of Medical Jurisprudence at the University of Aberdeen, and Dr. Woodrow Saunders, assistant to the Professor of Clinical Medicine in Edinburgh University. The shooting experts were, for the Crown, James Macnaughton, gunmaker, Edinburgh; for the accused, Tom Speedy, the well-known shooting agent, and George Andre, manager of the Clyde Powder Mills.

Everybody agreed that the fatal shot was fired from behind—from the left rear; a glancing shot, part of the charge striking the right side of the head, and the rest flying off past the ear. The line of fire was horizontal and slightly upwards. As to the wound itself there was no question, for it was described in the post-mortem reports, shown in several photographs taken at Ventnor on the exhumation, and the head itself—a ghastly "production"—was brought to Edinburgh for the trial. Both sides had made elaborate experiments with the actual gun and cartridges; and the results, as regards blackening and singeing or scorching at close range, and the spreading of the shot at various distances, were shown on the pieces of cardboard and wooden targets respectively produced for Crown and defense. They also practiced upon divers heads, human and equine, for which the late owners had no further use. But the boldest experiment of all was that of gallant Tom Speedy, who, in his scientific zeal, fired sundry times through his wife's hair—a "hair-raising" feat, which at least demonstrated the lady's confidence in her husband's marksmanship.

It was established by the Crown medical evidence that the boy bled to death from laceration of the large vein in the brain called the lateral sinus. The head lay in a hollow, in a pool of blood; Whyte, the gardener, says: "There was about a kitchen-bowlful of blood in the pool beneath the head. I saw no other blood." When on 12th September, a month after the death, Dr. Littlejohn visited the *locus*, he observed distinctly a circular staining of the turf at the place where the head had lain. Portions of the stained grass were removed, and on chemical examination proved to be blood-stained. There was no blood upon the boy's clothing, except one small spot on the collar of his jacket. None of those who at the time looked specially for marks of blood in the ditch saw any sign of such. The clothes of Monson and Scott were admittedly free from blood. Upon these facts the Crown doctors were of opinion that Cecil Hambrough died where he lay upon the top of the dike, and that he had not been lifted from the ditch. A further factor in their judgment was the presence near the head of the two pieces of bone detached from the skull and of the blood-stained wad, before referred to. On the other hand, the defense experts held that the flow of blood would be slow, that the wound was plugged by the wad, and that it and the pieces of bone were detached when the body was lifted from the ditch and laid down upon the dike.

The theory of the Crown, to which all its experts subscribed, was this: In a line drawn from the head of the body, assuming it to be standing upright, in a northerly direction were successively three trees, a rowan, a beech, and a lime. These were grooved and furrowed by pellet marks, plainly caused by the same shot. It was found that by standing at a point 22 feet south of the rowan tree and 9 feet from the body, at a gap in the whins, on a slightly lower level than the top of the dike, a person firing at where the head would be would produce by the shot precisely such an effect upon the line of trees. The defense experts maintained that these pellet marks were older than the date in question, and that the whole wood was so riddled with shot that no reliance could be placed upon any particular marks. The three trees, by the way, were uprooted, brought to Edinburgh, and "lodged in process." The Crown said that the injuries to the head were caused by merely the outmost pellets of the charge striking it; the defense, that the charge struck the head *en balle* in an oblique direction and was immediately deflected. It will be recalled that four pellets only were found in the brain. Hambrough's head showed no signs either of blackening or of scorching. As the result of many experiments made by Mr. Macnaughton before the Crown medical experts, it was found that up to 3 feet blackening and scorching were produced with all the powders used. In no instance at a greater distance were blackening and scorching present. Under 3 feet, the injuries produced were dissimilar from those in the case of the deceased. Experiments made at 9 feet presented the closest similarity to those injuries. At any distance under 3 feet the head was shattered. For these reasons they held it impossible for the injuries to have been caused by the hand of the deceased. The Crown case, therefore, was that Cecil Hambrough was shot by the accused from behind, at a distance of 9 feet in the line indicated by the three trees.

I recall a quaint incident in connection with Dr. Littlejohn's evidence. That expert had brought with him in a black hand-bag, for purposes of demonstration, a skull. As he was leaving the witness-box, the suave voice of Comrie Thomson called to him: "Stay, Dr. Littlejohn, stay! You have forgotten your head." "You are very right, sir," briskly rejoined the witness, seizing the bag from the corner of the bench where he had laid it; "I can't afford to lose my head!"

For the defense, Professor Hay, who had examined the *locus*, disputed the correspondence of the pellet marks on the trees in the alleged line of fire. If Hambrough, when shot, were walking towards the rowan he would have fallen forward on his face; whereas he lay on his back, with his head towards the rowan and his feet towards the gap in the whins. The inference was that the shot came from the direction of the rowan, rather than from the whins. Witness was not surprised at the absence of blood in the ditch, the bleeding from a gun-shot wound being very slow. Having criticized the supposed line of fire, witness was of opinion that the injury could have been inflicted by the gun held in the boy's own hand. There were innumerable positions permitting of the gun being so held as to cause it; he produced photographs showing some of these. The deceased might have tripped on the dike, or slipped on the wet grass, or jumped from the dike to the ditch. In his judgment, looking to the nature of the injuries and from experiments made by him, the distance from which the shot was fired was about 3 feet. He considered the absence of stray pellet wounds around the main wound of the very greatest importance. A charge of small shot leaves a gun with the pellets in compact mass, but these immediately begin to spread. From experiments made, he was satisfied it was impossible that the shot in this case was fired from a distance of 9 feet. Separate pellet wounds began about 4 feet and went on increasing at greater distances. At 9 feet there was a large area of dispersion and a great number of pellet wounds around the central wound. With amberite powder there was no scorching at 2 or 3 feet, and only such blackening as could be readily removed. Blood might have washed away any blackening. Dr. Woodrow Saunders concurred as to the results of these experiments.

Tom Speedy stated that, from his long experience, he had no doubt that the injuries were self-inflicted. He thought that Hambrough stumbled and threw the gun from him, and that it caught on something as it fell. He put the distance at not more than 2 feet. He had known cases of gun accidents where the shot entered the crown of the head, the back of the neck, the sole of the foot, and the palm of the hand. Referring to the injuries in the present case, Mr. Comrie Thomson asked: "Do you think it possible that only four pellets striking the head could have produced all that?" To which the witness emphatically replied: "Downright balderdash; it could never do it."[10] George Andre, gunpowder manufacturer, stated that with amberite at 5 feet there was no discoloration; at 1 foot slight discoloration, but no singeing. Even at 6 inches there was no singeing. Had the deceased dropped his gun, it might go off with the shock of the fall. Colonel Tillard, late of the Madras Staff Corps, stated that he deemed it his duty to volunteer to give his evidence. He was out with a gun in 1871, and turning to call his servant, slipped and fell backwards. He was shot from the front, horizontally, through the flap of the ear— a glancing shot, furrowing the flesh and scraping the bone of the skull. Cross-examined, his eyebrows and eyelashes were

---

10. It was currently reported by Dame Gossip that there were in fact several other pellets in the wound, and that someone had judiciously extracted these with a tooth-pick before the body left Ardlamont.

scorched and his ear was blackened; that lasted some months. Re-examined, he was using ordinary black powder.

So the net result of the skilled evidence for the defense came to this: that with a gun, as with Providence, nothing is impossible. Here, however, the probabilities, in relation to the other facts and circumstances of the case as disclosed upon the evidence, fell to be considered by the jury.

## XIII

There remains the last question: What effect had Cecil Hambrough's death upon the financial position of Monson? The defense maintained that, for him, it meant disaster. Had the boy lived to attain majority, there would have been ample money for everybody. Upon his life depended the pecuniary assistance of Tottenham, requisite for the continued running of "the show"—in that gentleman's pleasant phrase. Was it likely that Monson was such a fool as to slay the golden goose? With respect to the assignation to Mrs. Monson of the policies on the boy's life for £20,000, it was argued that Monson well knew that it was not worth the paper it was written on. "I told Monson," said Tottenham, "I thought that under Scots law the assignment was good; he was under a contrary impression." This is the only evidence as to the state of Monson's knowledge. Yet the fact remains that Monson *did* take from Cecil the assignment and caused him to write to the Company that he had done so. And immediately after the funeral, Tottenham, acting for Mrs. Monson, intimated to the Company a claim under the policies, having arranged with Monson that if and when the money were paid he was to get £4000 commission! In cross-examination, Tottenham represented this as merely an attempt to "bluff" the insurance people. Then, on 28th August, just before Monson's arrest, Mrs. Monson wrote, manifestly at her husband's dictation, a letter to her banker at Tigh-nabruaich, enclosing for collection one policy for £10,000 and instructing him to obtain payment thereof from the Glasgow office, and to pay the amount to the credit of her account—according to the defense, a further instance of "bluffing."

How can one explain all this, except on the assumption of Monson's ignorance that an assignation by a minor was invalid? If he did know, the whole business becomes Gilbertian. It is an established fact that the cleverest rogues often have, fortunately for their fellows, a blind spot; this may have been Monson's.

On the other hand, the Crown maintained that in this regard his actings amply demonstrated his belief that he had so arranged matters that by his victim's death the time had come for him to reap the profits of his villainy.


## XIV


On 21st December, being the ninth day of the trial, the Solicitor-General delivered his memorable address to the jury; the next and last day was occupied by Mr. Comrie Thomson's splendid speech for the defense and by the elaborate, careful, ultra-cautelous charge of the Lord Justice-Clerk. I do not propose to offer these the indignity of abridgment; to be appreciated they must be read in full. I am sure that had a verdict been taken on the conclusion of the speech for the Crown there could only have been one result, so cogent, nay, overwhelming, was the force of the presentment. Then followed Comrie Thomson, contesting each foot of the ground, plausible, persuasive, with an explanation for everything suspicious, enveloping the plainest facts in an atmosphere of fog—a great performance. Never shall I forget the effect of his opening reference to the historic speech of John Inglis, delivered in that Court in defense of Madeleine Smith:—

Gentlemen, I remember more than five-and-thirty years ago sitting in one of these benches and hearing an advocate, who afterwards became a great Judge, standing where I now stand, pleading for a woman who was sitting in that dock charged with the crime of murder. He opened his address to the jury in words which have since become historical, but I repeat them to you now because of their great truth and wonderful simplicity. "Gentlemen," he said, "the charge against the prisoner is murder, and the punishment of murder is death; and that simple statement is sufficient to suggest to you the awful nature of the occasion which brings you and me face to face."

And the dramatic quality of his peroration was equally notable:—

Gentlemen, we are all liable to make mistakes. I pray you make no mistake in this terribly serious matter. The result of your verdict is final, irreparable. What would any of you think if some day, it may be soon, this mystery is entirely unraveled, and it is demonstrated that this man was innocent, while your verdict has sent him to his death? He will not go unpunished if he is guilty. There is One in Whose hands he is, Who is infallible and Omniscient. "I will repay, vengeance is mine, saith the Lord."[11]

---

11. Year by year, on each anniversary of the death, the following notice appeared in *The Times* and *Glasgow Herald* newspapers: "In loving memory of our dear son, Windsor Dudley Cecil Hambrough, found shot dead in a wood at Ardlamont, Argyllshire, August 10th, 1893, in his 21st year. 'Vengeance is mine; I will repay, saith the Lord.'"

The Lord Justice-Clerk, if I may say so, seemed over-anxious that, in a case of circumstantial evidence such as this, the jury should not be led to jump to conclusions. So obviously was his Lordship oppressed by the burden of his task, so beset was he by its doubts and difficulties, there is little wonder that the jury, in the expressive vernacular of to-day, "got the wind up."

> Gentlemen, you have got a path to go on in this case in which you must see your way. You must not either walk through darkness at any point of it, nor leap over anything that you meet in it. It must be a straight path, and a path on which you have light. If you have light which takes you to the end of that path so that you can give a verdict for the prosecution, then you must do it manfully, and you must not allow yourselves to be stopped, though Pity, with uplifted hands, stand pleading and entreating that you shall not go on. On the other hand, if there is any darkness or dimness on that path which you cannot clear away, you cannot go on to the end. If there is any obstruction on that path you have to stop there. The prisoner is entitled to that. And, lastly, if you yourselves do not see your way along that path without passing through darkness, or dimness, or other obstruction, *you must not allow yourselves to be urged forward along that path blindly by any Demon pushing you from behind*, telling you that the prisoner is a bad man, a liar, and a cheat, and that, therefore, you should send him to his doom. You must keep yourselves free from that.

One wondered at the time how the Solicitor-General relished this allusion to *vis a tergo*.

His Lordship having finished his charge, the jury retired to consider their verdict, and after an absence of 73 minutes returned to Court with the result of their deliberations: Not Proven on both charges. The finding was stated in the Press to be unanimous. Through the thronged benches ran a muffled murmur—was it surprise, or satisfaction, or mere relief from the tension of the crisis? The prisoner, smiling, stood up in the dock, a free man; his two junior counsel shook hands with him on the happy issue of the deadly duel. Comrie Thomson left the Court without looking at his late client. The Court then rose.

It is, or ought to be, luciferous to know the considered judgment of a Judge upon a trial tried by himself. In the Monson case we have this illumination. Lord Kingsburgh's strangely disappointing volume of reminiscences, which should have been so much better than it is, gives us his own views of the Ardlamont Mystery.

> During my experience of the Bench in the High Court of Justiciary, it fell to me to preside at the trial of A. J. Monson for murder, the longest and most protracted inquiry since I joined the profession. I went through nine days of anxiety, such as I have never experienced before or since. The case was one which so bristled with points, that one had to watch its course from moment to moment, and to take scrupulous care lest the jury should be misled by feelings aroused by the disclosure of the evil character of the accused. So dominant was the anxiety, that morning after morning I awoke long before my usual time, and lay in a dull perspiration, turning things over and over, endeavoring to weigh them and determine their weight in the balance. Never before had I gone through an experience the least like it, and I am well pleased that I have never had a similar experience since. It was all the more trying because I felt quite unable to form a determined opinion in my own mind. The way

never seemed to me clear. In the end I was able to feel that I had done my best to put the case in a fair light before the jury, and can freely say that the verdict they returned was that which in all the circumstances was the safe one.[12]

Had the scales of justice been held by a Judge less prone to perspiration, with a firmer grasp of the proven facts of the case, and a greater capacity to make up his mind as to their significance and value, the verdict, if less "safe," might possibly have been by some deemed sounder. It were curious to speculate what would have happened had the case been handled by a different Judge. Lord Young, for instance, would have left the jury in no doubt as to what was his own opinion.

That Monson did not resent the omission of his senior counsel to congratulate him on his acquittal appears from the fact that he wrote to him next day a letter of thanks, which I am fortunate to possess and print herewith. It has not hitherto been published; and as it throws a very remarkable light upon the psychology of the writer, who had just emerged from the most fearful ordeal to which a human being can be subjected, I think it instructive for the reader to see. It is dated from the lodgings occupied by Mrs. Monson during the trial.

5 CAMBRIDGE STREET,
EDINBURGH, DEC. 23/93.

Dear Mr. Thompson [sic],

I feel anxious to express my gratitude to you for the able and powerful speech which you addressed to the jury on my behalf yesterday. I regret very much that I am

---

12. *Life Jottings of an Old Edinburgh Citizen*, by Sir J. H. A. Macdonald, P. C., K.C.B., Lord Justice-Clerk, pp. 462–463. Edinburgh: 1915.

unable to thank you personally before leaving Edinburgh, because I feel that I cannot properly convey my thanks in writing. After the very able speech made by the Solicitor-General I quite realized that you had a most difficult and responsible duty, to destroy the web which the Solicitor-General had wove in his speech of nearly six hours' duration. I am quite satisfied that you did your utmost in my defense, and I fully appreciated that the close of your address was so impressively pathetic that the jury were visibly affected to such an extent that the case for the Crown was so shaken as to render it impossible for the jury to find a verdict of Guilty.

I am leaving for Scarbro' but expect to be in Edinburgh again soon, when I hope I may have the opportunity of thanking you in person.

I remain,
Yours truly,
A. J. Monson.

To Comrie Thompson [*sic*], Esqre.

The curious detachment of the writer, as of a reporter contrasting the relative merits of the two speeches, and his apparent insensitiveness to "the awful nature of the occasion" which led to his writing, will strike with wonder the least observant reader.

## X V

As a general rule, when the curtain falls upon the last act of such a judicial drama as that of which we have been, at a remove, spectators, the protagonist vanishes from public view—

either at the instance of the hangman, if convicted, or of his own motion, should he be acquitted. Either way he becomes but a memory and a name, unless he be unearthed by some crimino-logically minded resurrectionist like myself. To that rule this strange case is an exception. No sooner was the late prisoner secure in the privilege of privacy, than by reason of his fresh activities the Press continued to find in his affairs abundant "copy." It was presently announced that Mr. Monson would give in Prince's Hall, Piccadilly, under the direction of one Mr. Morritt, of whom we shall hear again, a series of lectures on the Ardlamont Mystery. The subject was topical and popular; once more the personality of Monson proved a good draw. The first part of the entertainment, ventriloquial and conjuring, being over, Mr. Morritt informed the audience that he had just received from Monson a telegram stating that the star performer would not appear. Whereupon the audience demanded back their money, which was given them, and they departed in dudgeon no wiser than they came.

Doubtless Mr. Monson had other things to think about, for he had applied to the Court of Queen's Bench for an injunction against Madame Tussaud, to restrain that lady from exhibiting in her well-known establishment in Baker Street a portrait model of himself. The case came before Justices Mathew and Collins. "Mr. Monson arrived early, and took his seat at the solicitors' table in front of his counsel"—it must have seemed quite like old times. It was alleged that the effigy was dressed in the very clothes worn by Monson at the time of the "accident," that it was equipped with the actual gun which caused the death, and that, adding insult to injury, it was exhibited in the Chamber of Horrors, an extra sixpence being charged to see it. Tottenham, as appears, had disposed of these interesting mementoes to Madame Tussaud in consideration of a payment of £100. Counsel for that lady admitted that the scene of the tragedy was staged in the invidious Chamber, but denied that

Monson was represented as an actor therein. His figure was indeed placed near its door; but upon his right were the Archbishop of Canterbury and the Pope of Rome; on his left, Queen Victoria and the Prince and Princess of Wales, so that the model was exhibited in a place of honor and the original had suffered nothing by such association. The Court granted the injunction, with leave to appeal. Subsequently the appeal was heard in the House of Lords by Lord Halsbury and Lord Justices Lopes and Davey, Mr. Finlay, Q.C., appearing for the appellant and Mr. Coleridge, Q.C., for the respondent. Mr. Finlay narrated the transaction with Tottenham, and said that a check for £50 had been sent to Monson on account. He returned the check and refused to sanction the agreement entered into on his behalf. Madame Tussaud declined to accept the check, and exhibited the figure as arranged. Judgment was given for Madame Tussaud, their Lordships holding that, from the correspondence between the parties, it appeared that there had been willingness by Monson to have the model exhibited for a consideration. They therefore set aside the injunction; and the figure, which had been temporarily removed pending the appeal, was reinstated amid its august companions. In view of this decision it is probable that Monson, putting his pride and the proceeds in his pocket, cashed the check.[13]

Then, duly heralded by puffs preliminary, appeared "Monson's Book"—*The Ardlamont Mystery Solved*—which proved to be a pamphlet of 72 pages, containing the author's criticisms of the Scots system of criminal procedure, of which he represented himself to be the victim, and his own version of the story of Cecil Hambrough's death. It is disappointing to find that it throws no fresh light upon that mysterious happening and merely reiterates—with variations either unsupported

13. The proceedings in Monson v. Tussaud Ltd., on 16th, 18th, 19th, 23rd, 24th, 29th January 1894, are reported in 1 Q.B. 671.

or contradicted by the evidence—the case for the defense as stated at the trial. The "Book" had a bad Press; it was unkindly described as a catch-penny pamphlet, and the *Daily Chronicle* succinctly termed the "solution" rubbish. But although the newspapers declined seriously to notice the arguments of the author, his controversial gauntlet was taken up by the Rev. Evelyn Burnaby, author of *Memories of Famous Trials* and brother of the celebrated Colonel Fred Burnaby of *Ride to Khiva* fame. This gentleman, who had a praiseworthy practice of attending criminal trials, was present at Edinburgh and took notes of the evidence.[14] He examines the "solution" in detail, and he also is struck "with the strange and manifest inconsistencies of several statements contained therein if compared with the sworn testimony of witnesses who gave evidence at the High Court of Justiciary in Edinburgh." I cannot here follow the reverend and learned author through his refutation of Monson's special pleading; suffice it that, to me, he seems to have much the better of the argument.

Possibly roused to emulation of his late associate's literary achievement, Mr. Sweeney or Davis—whom for convenience of reference I shall continue to call Scott—emerged from his retirement, after certain pecuniary negotiations with the *Pall Mall Gazette* had been satisfactorily concluded. Before availing itself of the new contributor's material, that journal communicated with Scotland Yard and forwarded three statutory declarations to establish the identity of "The Missing Man." Had this occurred a few months earlier, what an amazing sensation it would have caused! But now the authorities had no use for Scott and the matter was quietly allowed to drop. "With the consent of his solicitor," says Mr. Lincoln

---

14. *The Ardlamont Mystery: a Reply to Mr. Monson's Pamphlet.* By Evelyn Burnaby, M.A., S.C.L., Oxon, brother of the late Colonel Fred Burnaby. Price Sixpence. H. A. Ives, Pier Street, Ventnor, I.W.: 1894. Pp. 31.

Springfield, "we endeavored to stage the arrest of Sweeney in the *Pall Mall Gazette* offices . . . but Scotland Yard declined to accept our treasure trove."[15] From the account which Scott published in the *Pall Mall Gazette* I have already quoted: he adds nothing to our knowledge of what happened at Ardlamont. I note that he makes no reference to the plug-hole: for the rest, he is content to concur with the version of his former friend.

> My readers will say, Why was I not at the trial to tell the jury this? But do not forget I never had the chance given me. I awoke one morning to find myself charged with murder, and had I gone to Scotland I should have been popped straight into a cell, and without a chance to speak; have been put in the dock, where my mouth would have been closed, and where I could not speak of what I saw and knew, but should have had to stand and listen to other people, who knew nothing whatever about the occurrence, deliberately giving all sorts of versions and opinions of what they knew nothing about, with the manly and charitable intention of convicting me of murder—innocent or not.

Rather a strange view, this, of the Crown witnesses' duty to their oath. He left Ardlamont "because neither Mr. Monson nor myself had anything to fear"; Dr. Macmillan said he was not wanted (?), and in the lamentable circumstances it was natural and respectful to relieve his host and hostess of his presence. He did not give his permanent address, lest it should furnish "cause of chatter to every busybody," by revealing his real occupation and assumed name. On reaching Glasgow he decided to get back to business and forget the "unpleasant recollection" of his visit to Ardlamont. He stayed in

---

15. *Some Piquant People, supra,* p. 108.

London until he read in the newspapers: "Warrant granted for arrest of Scott."

> I am a moral coward; I must confess it. I must also lack much reasoning power in the hour of danger, for I had but one idea, and that was flight.

He shaved off his mustache, donned his shabbiest suit, and with a bag labeled "Mr. White, passenger to Newcastle," vanished into space. He went to Bradford, thence to Halifax, whence with a first-class ticket to Newcastle and the labeled bag he continued his travels. But at the first station he got out of the train, having changed his clothes *en route*, and walked back to Halifax, where he lived quietly in the lodgings of an old lady, who "was firmly of the opinion that Scott had done away with Mr. Hambrough and would be brought to justice, and, she hoped, hanged!" Fearing that his published description might lead her to suspect the identity of her lodger, he sent himself a telegram, summoning him to his mother's deathbed, and set out for Birmingham, *en route* for Holyhead and Ireland, with a view to adding his personal troubles to those of that distressful country.

> I was already on the gangway [of the Irish boat], when, waiting on the deck to receive me, not five yards off, stood a London detective, scrutinizing every passenger by the strong glare of the electric light. I knew him, and he knew Ted Davis intimately. To pass him was to surrender myself; to go back was impossible, the narrow gangway between the quay and the steamer being crowded both behind and before me with the steady stream passing on board. A few more paces and I should be by his side under the light, whereas I had not yet passed from the shadow. What could I do? How could I get back or

save myself? A splash, a scream; I had dropped my bag into the water between the boat and the shore, and in the rush to discover the cause the officer was pushed aside as I passed on board. Abandoning my intended trip, I left the boat by another gangway, striking for the open country as fast as my legs would carry me.

Luckily his money was in his pocket; he bought a pony and trap, wrote to a firm advertising for an agent, and set up as an itinerant vendor of jewelry. But the police were again upon his trail; so once more he fled on foot, and dodged about various North of England towns, doing odd jobs, such as painting. For six weeks he was laid up with a bad attack of asthma. Somebody lent him a copy of *The Ardlamont Mystery Solved*, to which (although I have not yet dealt with it) is appended what purports to be "Scott's Diary"—a palpable fiction. This is the only crow Scott has to pick with his old patron:—

> I cannot understand, after all I have suffered through adopting at his instigation the name he suggested, why he should have done me the injustice of allowing this absurd and fictitious diary to be published in my name. . . . I never saw it, wrote it, or had any hand in it. It was not written by my consent or knowledge, and does not contain a word of truth.

When he recovered from his illness Scott went to London, got in touch with the *Pall Mall Gazette*, and is most grateful to that journal for restoring to him his peace of mind and freedom.

On 4th May 1894 there was presented to the Lords Commissioners of Justiciary at Edinburgh a petition by Edward Sweeney, Commission Agent, 66 Meadow Road, Clapham, stating that he was now prepared to stand his trial and praying for recall of the sentence of outlawry, pronounced against him on 12th December. The Court ordered the petition to be intimated to the Lord Advocate; but when on 21st May the case was called, there was no appearance for the Crown. The Lord Justice-Clerk, having commented adversely on the fact, in which observations Lords Adams and Wellwood concurred, the Court granted the prayer of the petition and recalled the sentence of outlawry.[16] So Scott, in his turn, was now free to follow his own devices.

### XVI

Meanwhile Mr. Monson continued to extend his experience of the law by prosecuting at the West Riding Assizes for theft his former benefactor, Mr. Beresford Loftus Tottenham. It appeared that prior to the Ardlamont flitting the Monsons, desirous of making inaccessible to their creditors the furniture at their Yorkshire seat, Riseley Hall, near Ripley, removed it to Leeds and there stored it in the name of "John Kempton," which, as the reader may recall, was the financier's *nom de guerre*. Monson averred that "Dear Tot," taking base advantage of the difficulties in which, by reason of Hambrough's untimely death, he became involved, sold the furniture, estimated as worth £700, and appropriated the proceeds—"the oof from the sticks," in Monson's light-hearted phrase—to his own use. It is characteristic that the furniture had been purchased on the hire system and was not paid for. Tottenham's case was that Monson had swindled him out of several hundreds of pounds, that the furniture was his sole security, and that he honestly believed that, partly to recoup himself, he had

---

16. Petition, Edward Sweeney, for Recall of Outlawry. Adam's *Justiciary Reports*, 1893–1895, i. 392.

a right to deal with it. The jury returned a verdict of Guilty, and Mr. Justice Henn Collins sentenced the prisoner to three months' hard labor.

Meanwhile Major Hambrough, as administrator of the estate of his son Cecil, was suing the Mutual Life Assurance Company of New York for recovery of the £20,000 for which the boy's life had been insured. The case was tried in the Queen's Bench by the Lord Chief Justice and a special jury, who, after a three days' hearing, found for the defendants, on the grounds that the policies were obtained upon statements false, fraudulent, and material, and that Monson was the party substantially effecting the insurance on young Hambrough's life. In effect the finding was that, in the words of the Judge, Cecil Hambrough was mere putty in the hands of the man who acted as his guardian and was afterwards tried for his murder, and that by Monson's own hand and lips, or by those of the unhappy lad who had become his creature, lies were told to the Company, which was thus persuaded to enter into a bargain it would never have made had the truth been known. Judgment was given accordingly. Major Hambrough appealed, and his appeal was dismissed with costs. The Master of the Rolls (Lord Esher), in giving judgment, endorsed the Lord Chief Justice's reference to Cecil as putty in Monson's hands. "A greater mass of impudent falsehoods had never been told. The statements were infamous lies, and upon them these policies were issued. Monson was clearly acting for Cecil throughout; the boy was under his influence, and had been, so to speak, mesmerized into signing the false statements in the proposal which his tyrant had written for him."[17]

Undismayed by this judicial anathema, Mrs. Monson had a

---

17. For a report of Hambrough *v.* The Mutual Life Assurance Company of New York, 5th and 25th January 1895, see 72 *Law Times*, 140.

sporting shot at the policies. In the Probate Court she applied to Mr. Justice Jeune for a subpœna against Messrs. Davidson & Syme, W.S., the agents for the defense at the trial, commanding them to bring into Court the famous assignation in her favor, contained in the letter written to her by Cecil Hambrough on 7th August. His Lordship, being informed by counsel that a writ had been issued, granted the application. We hear no more of the matter: probably, in Tottenham's phrase, it was but a further instance of "bluff."

Once again in the Queen's Bench we find the Lord Chief Justice and a special jury occupied with the affairs of Mr. Monson. That versatile and tireless litigant had raised an action against Madame Tussaud for libel, in respect of the exhibition of his figure as aforesaid; the defendant denied that the exhibition was libelous and pleaded that the effigy was exhibited by the plaintiff's consent. Mr. Coleridge, Q.C., appeared for Monson, Mr. Murphy, Q.C., for Madame. Monson, examined, stated that Tottenham stole the clothes and the gun from his rooms and sold them to Tussaud unknown to him. He refused to give a sitting for the wax model, and insisted on the return of the check. He had visited the exhibition and found the figure was placed between those of Mrs. Maybrick, the murderess, and Pigott, the forger. The suggestion plainly was that he was a criminal of like fashion with them. He claimed substantial damages for the daily torture which he and his family suffered from the exhibition of his effigy. Cross-examined, his portrait appeared on the cover of his pamphlet without his authority. He admitted having signed a contract with Morritt for a lecturing tour at £125 a week. He had repudiated that contract, as he shrank from the publicity involved. The defendant called Beresford Loftus Tottenham, who came into Court in charge of a warder. He stated that the proposal to sell the gun and clothes to Tussaud proceeded from Monson himself. Witness thought that unless he took the initiative,

"Monson would get ahead of him." He therefore conveyed the things to Tussaud and made the bargain, to which Monson afterwards declined to agree, solely on the ground that the price was "ridiculously low." Monson actually accompanied him in a cab when he carried the clothes to Tussaud, and waited for him in an hotel close by while the negotiations were in progress. When he came out, the plaintiff had disappeared: "It was not odd—for Monson." Referring to his own conviction, witness said there had been a lot of hard swearing: "I shall prosecute Mr. and Mrs. Monson as soon as I get out." The learned Judge in summing up said that the plain meaning of the exhibition was: "This is Monson, the man who was tried for the murder of Cecil Hambrough, against whom a verdict of Not Proven only was passed." If it meant that, it was clearly libelous. The question of damages was a very different one. His Lordship, having reviewed the history of Monson's connection with Hambrough and Ardlamont, remarked of the insurance business that the whole story reeked of fraud. The jury returned a verdict for the plaintiff, with one farthing damages. The *Scotsman*, in a leading article on the case, observed:—

> There is a Portuguese coin called a maravedi, a shovelful of which are said to make up a penny. A maravedi would have been a more accurate estimate of the solatium due in this case; but a farthing is near enough for practical purposes. Thus are the rights vindicated of decent people to be protected against being publicly pilloried alongside of notorious murderers and thieves, and Monson himself recompensed handsomely for his own personal wrong.

## XVII

Escaping for the moment from the dusty desert of the law courts, we find the year 1895 opening for Mr. Monson on a more cheerful note. On 25th April there appeared in the *Edinburgh Evening Dispatch* a letter from that indefatigable correspondent, challenging Mr. Morritt, "the well-known hypnotist," to try his "hand" on the writer, with a view to clearing up the mystery in which the affair of Ardlamont was still involved. "I see that Mr. Morritt is advertised to appear at the Operetta House in Edinburgh on Monday next," he writes; "and *as I shall be in Edinburgh at the same time*, I am willing to afford him an opportunity of publicly testing his theories." The challenge was accepted. Replying in the *Dispatch* on 29th April, Morritt undertook to extract from Monson, while in trance, all he knew about the Ardlamont mystery, "whether he is willing or not."

It happened that in the afternoon of the great day on which all our doubts and difficulties were to be hypnotically dispelled, I was walking along Princes Street when I saw, accompanied by a stranger to me, the unforgettable face and figure of Monson, which I had studied throughout the ten days of his trial. As of old, he was excellently arrayed and wore a silk hat. The couple, chatting amicably, walked westward and then turned up the Lothian Road. I followed them, entranced as by an enchanter's spell, until they vanished through the swing-doors of a public-house. Nowadays, at all costs, I would have entered too; but I was younger then, and lacked courage. That evening found me at the Operetta House, where I saw the sorcerer resuscitate a man whom, unconscious, he had brought from London in a box. Morritt—he was, of course, the stranger I had seen with Monson that day—then announced that *if Mr. Monson was in the building* he would have pleasure in accepting his challenge. Whereupon Monson rose from his place in the dress circle and intimated his willingness to submit himself to the experiment. The séance was fixed for 9 o'clock the next night. I attended betimes; but the result was frankly disappointing. Monson appeared to succumb to the arts of the operator, through whom sundry questions were put to him by members of the audience: such as, "Did you murder Mr. Hambrough?" to which the patient answered "No"; and "How was Cecil Hambrough killed?" to which he replied, "I don't know." A skeptical voice from the gallery called out: "Stick a pin in him!" and from my place at the end of the circle overlooking the stage I distinctly saw a smile flicker across the face of the unconscious subject. So hard is it to suppress a sense of humor, even when in a trance. Another doubter asked whether Mr. Monson was paid for the sitting, to which Mr. Morritt solemnly rejoined "that he had taken an oath that there was no agreement with Monson for coming there." He believed the gentleman had come forward voluntarily, to prove his innocence of the alleged crime. But as I went home after the show was over I shook my head: that friendly call at the public-house seemed to me suggestive.

Strangely enough, I find from the *Westminster Gazette* that this very week Mr. Charles Morritt, "the well-known hypnotist," was summoned at Bow Street for selling spirits without a license in the Eden Theatre, where he was then running a show! The defendant telegraphed from Edinburgh that he had hypnotized there several persons whom he dared not leave until they recovered from their trance, but Sir John Bridge imposed a penalty of £20.

## XVIII

The reader may remember the check for £250, obtained by Monson from Tottenham on pretense of paying an imaginary deposit in connection with the pretended purchase of Ard-lamont, but applied by him to pay the premiums of the two policies on Cecil Hambrough's life. The check was endorsed by Cecil and handed to Mrs. Monson, who paid it into her bank account and then drew a check in favor of the Insurance Company. Tottenham stopped his check, but not until the Bank had allowed her to draw against it.

In these circumstances the Royal Bank of Scotland brought an action against Tottenham to recover the £250. The case was heard in the Queen's Bench before Mr. Justice Wills, sitting without a jury—Mr. Willis, Q.C., for the plaintiffs; Mr. Chan-nell, Q.C., for the defendant. The defense denied that the endorsement of the check was genuine. For the Bank, two of Hambrough's brother-officers and Mr. Gurrin, the eminent handwriting expert, stated that they had no doubt that the en-dorsement was written by Lieut. Hambrough. Mr. Ker, the lo-cal manager of the Bank at Tighnabruaich, having described the transaction, Mrs. Agnes Maud Monson was examined. She said that she saw Cecil endorse the check; he handed it to her and she sent it to the Bank. On 11th August she learned from Mr. Ker that the check had been returned unpaid. Mr. Tottenham was at Ardlamont at the time, and when she told him, he said he would pay it in a few days "and would call at the Bank of England to verify the signature." Cross-examined, she denied that the whole matter was untrue from beginning to end. Mr. Tottenham then gave his version. He drew the check solely for the purpose of paying the deposit. He received no consideration for the check and stopped it on the advice of his solicitor. He did not afterwards promise to pay the check. He was now satisfied that the endorsement was genuine. Having heard counsel, the learned Judge said it was impossible to ac-cept the defendant's story. The defendant must have known that the check would be paid into Mrs. Monson's account, and if it were made available by Mrs. Monson for another purpose than that defendant intended, that could not affect the Bank's title to it. He therefore gave judgment for the plaintiffs, with costs. On an application for a new trial, the defendant's appeal was dismissed.[18] But that was not to be the last heard of the famous check.

On Saturday, 18th January 1896, a gentleman, known locally as Alfred John Wyvill, was arrested at Douglas, Isle of Man, upon a charge of perjury. Mr. Wyvill had been living with his family at Balla Brooie, near Douglas. In December that mansion had been unfortunately destroyed by fire, and Mr. Wyvill lodged a claim for £500 worth of jewelry which he had thereby lost, the same having been insured with the Birkenhead Insurance Company, through the agency of their Douglas representative, whose name, appropriately enough, was Scott.[19] The Company uncharitably refused to pay, and Mr. Wyvill instructed a Manx solicitor to take proceedings. But the man of law, who had attended the Tussaud trial, recognized in his proposed client the notorious Mr. Monson, and declined to act for him.

The prisoner was brought to England in custody, and in due course made his appearance at Leeds Police Court. The charge against him was that at the trial of Tottenham for stealing his furniture he swore on his oath that a certain letter produced for the defense was not the letter sent by him to Tottenham, but was in part a forgery. This was the letter written to "Dear Tot" on 23rd July, giving his account of an apocryphal interview with Messrs. J. & F. Anderson regarding the purchase of Ardlamont, whereby Tottenham was induced to send the £250 check. Upon that evidence the complainant was sentenced to three months' imprisonment. Beresford Loftus Tottenham, called, recounted his relations with Monson during the last three or four years. Monson suggested the furniture at

18. 4th July 1894.

19. 2 Q.B. 715.

Riseley Hall as security for the £250; afterwards witness sold the furniture for his debt, but it only realized about £100, and Monson prosecuted him for fraudulently disposing of it. The letter in question was wholly in Monson's handwriting; witness had never written anything in it or procured anyone to do so. Cross-examined, he had done business under various names. His full name was Beresford Patrick Stewart Crichton Lofthouse Tottenham. Q.—"Then are you ashamed of your name?" A.—"I am not. It is a very good name. Crichton-Lofthouse-Tottenham is my surname; it is a treble name. I cannot help it." (Laughter.) The letter in question had been used in five unsuccessful actions. Asked whether there was not a warrant out against him for failing to account for money for which he was a trustee, witness replied: "I hope not. I have not heard of it." After the evidence of a handwriting expert, Mr. Mellor, for Mr. Monson, argued that no case had been made out against his client. The learned Stipendiary agreed with him and dismissed the case. "The result was received with expressions of surprise from various parts of the Court. Monson walked out of the dock with a smile on his features." The next time he left the dock, as we shall see, Mr. Monson had less cause for satisfaction.

## XIX

Mr. Lincoln Springfield, in his entertaining book from which I have already quoted, gives us an account of his acquaintance with a brilliant, charming, and handsome young man, named Owen Macdonnell Callan, son of Phil Callan, a respectable Irish M.P.[20] Artist, journalist, sometime private secretary to General Boulanger, and decorated with the Legion of Honour,

20. *Some Piquant People*, p. 86 *et seq.*

his was a graceful and attractive figure of that nickel-silver age, the nineties. Mr. Springfield put him up for his own club. Later, he was dismayed to find that, in addition to his other accomplishments, this engaging youth was a swindler, a blackmailer, and a would-be murderer for money. What first opened his eyes to the defects of his former protégé was Callan's conviction at the Old Bailey for a singularly bad case of blackmail, of which Mr. Justice Grantham, in sentencing the versatile lad to three years' penal servitude, observed that it was one of the worst he had ever known.

"Now," says Mr. Springfield, "we are to meet again the sinister figures of young Owen Callan and Alfred John Monson, and curiously enough they would seem to have had certain mutual associates."[21] Some two years after he had served his time, Callan got hold of a young man named Hubert Birkin, who was to succeed to great wealth on the death of his grandfather. In December 1897 Callan introduced Birkin to a moneylender of Piccadilly, whom Mr. Springfield refers to as Z. This benefactor of youth agreed to allow him £400 a year for ten years, or until the death of his grandfather, in return for which Birkin gave a *post obit* for £50,000. His life was also insured by Z for £50,000. The premium was very heavy, for Birkin was what is technically known as a "bad life," by reason of his addiction to drink and drugs. In June 1898 another premium of £1000 would fall to be paid. In March Z wrote to the Insurance Company, asking whether there would be an extra premium if Birkin went abroad for the benefit of his health? and was told, No, so long as he did not go farther south than the 35th parallel north latitude. Whereupon, accompanied by Callan as his secretary, Birkin set forth for Tangier, just within the permitted parallel. There they put up at the Hotel Bristol, and during this healthful holiday Callan kept his employer

---

21. *Some Piquant People*, p. 176.

well supplied with liquor and cocaine. At midnight on 19th May Callan invited Birkin to look out from the hotel window at the lights of the harbor, and while doing so, hit him a violent blow on the back of the head with a life-preserver, with which he had thoughtfully provided himself before leaving England. The lad closed with the murderer, who then tried to throw him over the balcony; but after a fierce struggle he freed himself from his grasp and fled from the room, Callan firing four revolver-shots after his quarry and hitting him in the head, but not fatally. Birkin believed that the murder plot had been hatched in London. Callan, arrested for attempted murder, was tried at Gibraltar, convicted, and sentenced to ten years' penal servitude. Mr. Springfield adds:—

> The evidence disclosed the startling fact that Callan had been visited at Tangier by an employee of Z. One began to pry very inquisitively into this affair; and who should prove to be among the business acquaintances of Z but Alfred John Monson, of the Ardlamont case.
>
> Monson, it appears, was carrying on business as "an insurance and financial agent" in Shaftesbury Avenue, under names that varied from time to time. He was acting, in fact, as a tout for several money-lenders— some of them of the very worst class—and with his public school and Oxford education, and his good birth and connections, he was steering to these moneylenders many a youth about town who had large reversionary interests to sell or pawn. Z was one of the men to whom Monson took some of his needy young acquaintances.[22]

The *Daily Mail* having called attention to the circumstance that Monson was a business associate of Z, the holder of the

---

22. *Some Piquant People*, p. 178.

policies in question, Monson threatened an action of damages for libel. "But before he could do anything," says Mr. Springfield, "the police butted in and arrested Monson, together with a notorious Jermyn Street alien moneylender calling himself Victor Honour, and another man, on a charge of having defrauded the Norwich Union Life Office a year or two earlier."

## X X

Of Mr. Monson's last public appearance, so far as my research extends, an authoritative report is furnished in the Central Criminal Court Session Papers, 1898,[23] and full accounts of the proceedings are to be found in the contemporary Press. On 1st July 1898, before Sir John Bridge, at Bow Street, Alfred John Monson, *alias* Wyvill, *alias* Hobson; Victor Honour, *alias* John Milton, William Shakespeare, Dent, or Urbanowski—he seems to have had a pretty taste in pseudonyms; and Robert Ives Metcalfe, were charged with conspiring to defraud the Norwich Union Life Insurance Society, while Honour was further charged with aiding and abetting to procure the forgery of a promissory note. It was alleged that Monson for some time past had been acting as a kind of tout or jackal for Honour, and assisted him in carrying out his nefarious schemes.

The story, as unfolded by Mr. Avory for the prosecution, is one of the most amazing ever told in a law court. Honour, a middle-aged Israelite, sealed of the tribe of Fagin, drove the trade of a moneylender under several striking names and at various good addresses. His specialty was to induce young men, who had fallen into his clutches, to forge the signatures of their relations on bills of exchange or promissory notes, by which documents Honour was enabled to blackmail the rela-

---

23. Vol. cxxviii. pp. 893–921.

tives to any extent he pleased. One of his victims was Percival Edward Norgate, the son of a country rector. This youth was first inveigled into forging his parents' names to divers promissory notes, and was later induced to forge another in his mother's name, to redeem the former notes. This one was payable to Urbanowski, who as a matter of fact was Honour's cook-housekeeper! Having thus got young Norgate securely in the toils, and having repeatedly "tapped" his unhappy parents, who paid up in order to avoid their son's exposure and disgrace, Honour suggested that Percival, who had a reversionary interest contingent on his surviving his father and mother, should insure his life and assign the policy to him (Honour); he would then hear no more about the forgeries. The youth agreed, and signed a proposal for £200; but the form sent to the Insurance Company was for £2000, and though bearing to be written by Norgate, was actually filled up and signed in his name by somebody else! The "Private Friend," on whose confidential report as to the proposer's admirable health and habits the Company relied, was alleged to be Mr. Monson. Now, the trouble was that this young man's health and habits rendered him utterly uninsurable; so the ingenious syndicate procured a robust representative named Stanley Hobson—who probably was the man who signed the proposal—to impersonate Norgate at the medical examination. Hobson thereafter disappeared; and when the assignment of the policy to Honour was required, it was unfortunately found that Norgate's writing was quite different from that in the proposal form. Honour therefore furnished him with a copy of the false signature, and bade him take it home and *practice imitating it till he was perfect*! Honour next issued a writ against Mrs. Norgate for £120, the amount of the forged note. Monson then called upon the Rev. Mr. Norgate, saying that he was Hobson's brother, and was anxious to arrange "the dispute" which had arisen. He was prepared to find £100 to settle with Honour, if Mr. Norgate would put up £300 or £400. The matter was eventually compromised by the Norgates paying £210 and getting back the forged note. In the end young Norgate went to the Insurance Company and made a clean breast of the whole business. Whereupon the conspirators were arrested.

After a four days' hearing, Sir John Bridge committed the three prisoners for trial, refusing bail in the cases of Honour and Monson. During the examination of one of the Insurance Company's officials an interesting passage occurred. Witness had been informed by Metcalfe that a lady was going to pay the premium on young Norgate's life:—

> Q.—Did he say who the lady was?
>
> A.—Madame Urbanowski. It was to be a "worldwide" policy.
>
> Q.—What does that mean?
>
> A.—It means that the person insuring may go anywhere.
>
> MR. AVORY.—I see. *Tangier*, or anywhere else? (Sensation.)

On 29th July 1898, in the Central Criminal Court, before Mr. Justice Lawrence, began the two days' trial of the three impostors. Mr. C. W. Mathews and Mr. Horace Avory prosecuted; Mr. Marshall Hall, Q.C., with Mr. Bodkin and a junior, defended Honour; Mr. Rawlinson, Q.C., defended Monson; and Mr. H. C. Richards, Q.C., defended Metcalfe. Young Norgate and his parents, the insurance officials, the doctor who passed the spurious Percival as a "good life," sundry solicitors, the real brother of Hobson, Monson's landladies, and Detective-Inspector Arrow (who had handled the case with an ability commended by the Judge, and had apprehended the prisoners), were all examined and "crossed" at length. But not even the wonder-working Marshall Hall could do anything with such material. The several counsel addressed the jury, his Lordship summed up, and in fifteen minutes the jury returned a verdict of Guilty against all accused, but strongly recommended Metcalfe, who was the tool of Honour and Monson, to mercy. Mr. Richards, in his behalf, stated that he had a wife and seven children, had never been in trouble before, and in his eagerness for business had committed this fault. Mr. Mathews agreed; but as regards the two other prisoners, he pointed out that Monson had acted in a similar way in other cases, and that part of Honour's business had been to get young men into his hands and induce them to commit forgery, which could be used as a means of extorting money from their parents. His Lordship sentenced Honour and Monson to five years' penal servitude each, and Metcalfe to eighteen months' hard labor.

The *Scotsman*, in a leading article on the case, remarked of the accused, in the historic words of the great Lord Braxfield: "Ye're a verra clever chiel, man, but ye wad be nane the waur o' a hangin'."

## XXI

No sooner was Monson under lock and key than the weekly journal to which I have referred began its revelations, based, as alleged, on the disclosures of his wife. *To-Day* opens the series with the following sensational statement:—

> The public may be interested to learn that Monson has commenced a suit for divorce against his wife. The petition was filed last month. It is alleged that Mrs. Monson was guilty of infidelity in the year 1891 with a person unknown, and later in the year with another person. The other person is both known and remembered; *it is the late Cecil Hambrough*. Since the death of the late Cecil

Hambrough at Ardlamont, and that famous trial which resulted in the unsatisfactory verdict of Not Proven, Monson has had two children by his wife. He will, therefore, have to show that he bases his petition on information which did not come into his possession until some years after Ardlamont.[24]

This statement is sufficiently startling, and invites to curious reflection.

The Honour-Monson case being then *sub judice*, our authority wisely waited for the verdict before proceeding with its narrative; but on the pronouncement of the sentence it returned to the charge in four consecutive articles. From the account of Monson's pre-Ardlamont period I have already quoted, and it were weary work to follow him again down the devious and shady ways wherein, according to his wife, she was forced to accompany her adventurous spouse, until he fell, not without Honour, in the financial fight. It is no edifying itinerary, and we have heard enough of his versatile activities and of the disadvantages which these entailed upon those with whom he had to do.

It is pleasant to be able to close this romance of roguery upon a brighter note. Some readers of the foregoing narration may, on its perusal, have formed of the chief actor's character an unfavorable impression. If so, in as far as his connection with Ardlamont is concerned, I am happily in a position to dispel it. Sheriff More's *Trial of A. J. Monson* was published in March 1908. I find in the *Academy* of 10th April 1909 a belated review of the book with the familiar heading: "The Ardlamont Mystery Solved." That vigorous weekly was then, if I remember aright, under the able editorship of Lord Alfred Douglas; and the two and a half columns of this notice suggest,

---

24. *To-Day*, 23rd July 1898.

to anyone acquainted with his forthright and forceful style, that it emanates from his trenchant pen. Further, there is internal evidence for the attribution. After recalling the facts of the case, the reviewer proceeds:—

> We began the book languidly, we got interested, we became absorbed, we read it breathlessly to the end: the verdict of Not Proven. We rubbed our eyes and read it all through again carefully and judicially, and with ever-increasing amazement and horror. For there is no mystery, no ambiguity, no possible room for doubt in the mind of any man with brains and a heart; Alfred Monson was innocent of the charges brought against him, and not only was he innocent, but the case against him of the prosecution was scarcely even a superficially plausible case. We defy any honest man to read this book through and come to any other conclusion. . . .
>
> The verdict of the jury was a cowardly and wicked verdict, given as a cowardly and wicked concession to the unfair prejudice raised against Monson in the viler section of the Press. An English jury would have unhesitatingly acquitted Monson. . . .
>
> The writer of this article is a Scotsman, and proud of it; he bears a surname which is known and honored all over Scotland, and he says deliberately that the verdict in the Monson case was a disgrace to Scotland, a disgrace to Scottish justice and fair play, and a disgrace to humanity. . . .
>
> His family behaved as families are apt to behave on this kind of occasion: a few of its members believed in his innocence, and proceeded nobly to give expression to their belief by referring to him with bated breath as "poor Alfred," by refraining from asking him to their houses "for fear that he might meet somebody who

might be rude to him," by effectually preventing him
from taking any steps to rehabilitate himself on the
ground that "it would only make more scandal," by giving him "good advice," and by keeping him as short of
money as was possible consistently with not allowing
him and his wife and children to die of starvation; the
other members of his family frankly spoke of him as a
murderer, and as is the amiable wont of hostile members
of a family, were more virulent about him, even than
outsiders. A man who gets into any sort of trouble may
generally be recommended to pray to God to save him
from his family. . . .

If these be not the authentic accents of Lord Alfred, I am
the more deceived. Deprived of any chance of honest employment, denounced as "Monson the murderer," small wonder,
says the writer, that he took to dishonest courses and was sentenced to a term of penal servitude for fraud. "We do not know
the details of this case; we should not be surprised to learn that
he was unjustly convicted owing to the prejudice which had
been excited against him." Well, *we* know the details of the
case, and that here, at least, the writer is mistaken. Referring
to Monson's pamphlet, he concludes:—

There is no photograph of Monson in the book, but
we have seen one taken at the time of his trial. He was
then thirty-three years of age, and we confess that as we
looked at the presentment of his gay and gallant good
looks (he had a singularly beautiful and attractive face)
and considered the horrible brutal tragedy of his life,
we were uncomfortably moved. We are informed that he
died shortly after his release from prison, but our authority on this point is dubious, and it may be that he is still
alive. If he is dead, and we hope for his own sake that he

is, let this article serve as a tardy reparation offered to the memory of one of the most piteous victims of man's inhumanity to man who ever turned a face brave, undaunted and debonair to the pack of howling dogs that hounded him down.

All which shows the truth of the old saying that to every question there are two sides.

### NOTE.—THE BIRKIN-CALLAN CASE

A full and first-hand account of this astounding affair is given by Mr. Herbert Marshall, the doyen of private inquiry agents, in his volume of reminiscences entitled: *Memories of a Private Detective* (London: 1924). In the spring of 1898 Mr. Marshall received instructions from the Insurance Company with whom young Birkin's life was insured, only one premium having been paid, to go to Tangier and find out who was at the bottom of the murderous and well-nigh fatal attack that had been made upon him by Callan. He did so; and there learned the following facts:—

On arriving at the Bristol they [Birkin and Callan] were given a large double room in the front of the house. This room overlooked a sloping space where the Moorish guard of the town slept at night. Owing to the sloping of Tangier the distance from the windows of this room to the ground was very slight. A few nights after their arrival Callan received a cable from London.

After reading it he at once complained to Secconi [the landlord] that this front room was too noisy, and in consequence their room was changed to the back of the hotel. Their new room had two windows with balconies, the rails of which rose knee-high, and from the windows to the ground was a terrific drop into a paved courtyard.

After dinner, when they had retired to their room, he induced Birkin on some pretext to step out of the French window on to one of the small balconies. No sooner had he done so than Callan hit him a terrific blow on the head with a life-preserver, and then, springing on him, attempted to push him over the rail. Birkin, however, fell backwards and, eluding Callan, rushed to the door shrieking for help.

Callan struck him eight more blows, but Birkin rushed downstairs with Callan in pursuit. The blows were so heavy that one side of the life-preserver was nearly flattened. The murderer seized Birkin on a landing and drawing a five-chambered revolver placed it against his forehead. The revolver missed fire. After a struggle, Callan then tried to shoot Birkin in the chest, but again the revolver missed. By this time Birkin's cries had roused the hotel and people were rushing in all directions.

A third time Callan placed the revolver to Birkin's jaw and pulled the trigger. This time the revolver went off, and the bullet passed clean through the unfortunate man's face and buried itself in the door of Secconi's office, where it remains to this day. Birkin fell and Callan was overpowered and taken to the British Consul, who ordered him to be detained in custody.

Marshall found Birkin physically and mentally in a parlous state. His lower jaw was almost shot away; he said that "they" would finish him, and he besought Marshall with tears to save him; he was in fact a nervous wreck. Marshall was authorized by the British Minister to take charge of him and to collect evidence for the forthcoming trial of Callan at Gibraltar. "I knew the members of the gang were in Tangier," he says, "and that they would leave no stone unturned to bring about the deaths both of Birkin and myself." He refused the offer of a guard, but never went abroad without a loaded revolver in his pocket. Riding through the market-place one day he was approached by a snake-charmer, who suddenly flung at him a poisonous adder. "Driving my spurs into my horse I made him rear, and the danger missed me by a hair's breadth." Twice when out on horseback—he never went afoot—he was fired at from an ambush and narrowly escaped being killed. He was warned by anonymous letters that unless he left Tangier forthwith he would never do so alive.

Meanwhile Birkin's health had grown worse, and his doctor said that if he did not return to England he would surely die. So it was arranged with the authorities that Marshall should take him home and bring him back in time for the trial. The tale of how he and his charge eluded the machinations of the gang, by whom they were shadowed until they reached safety at Gibraltar, would make the fortune of a detective novelist, so thrilling the adventures of the pursued, so sinister the devices of the pursuers. Finally, Birkin was safely delivered to his family in Nottingham.

Callan had left with a friend in London a dispatch-box containing his credentials from the gang, which would have proved their undoing. This, at his request, was recovered by the criminal authorities and forwarded to him at Gibraltar. But the box had been already borrowed by the gang, who paid the holder £500 for the loan, abstracted the incriminating papers, and left their tool to stand the racket.

When the time came for Marshall to take Birkin back for the trial, the principal witness had disappeared. With infinite trouble Marshall traced him to a village in North Wales, where he was under the care and custody of the local doctor, who maintained that the patient was totally unfit to travel and if taken to the trial would lose his reason. Marshall consulted the Home Secretary, and was advised that the doctor should go in Birkin's stead and testify to his wounds and condition. But the doctor, approached to this end, flatly refused to go; so the resourceful detective kidnapped him and took him to Gibraltar by force! The unwilling witness made the best of a bad job and gave the required evidence at the trial. As his wealthy employers had let him down, Callan had to conduct his own defense, which, Marshall says, he did magnificently; but the facts were too strong for him, and being convicted, he got ten years.

> Throughout the trial two or three members of the gang passed the days in a rowing-boat in the bay near the Spanish shore. One day the Judge mentioned them by name. I was interested to see the lawyer who was watching the case for them leave the court hurriedly, hasten to the Water Port, embark in a boat and row hurriedly to their craft. After a vigorous confabulation, the gang were rowed to the Spanish shore, where they landed and appeared no more.

It would have been instructive to have known the names of the baffled speculators. One regrets that no other member of the syndicate shared the scapegoat's fate. Unlike De Quincey, who in an admirable essay considered murder as a fine art, these gentlemen regarded it as a business proposition.

# THE SLATER CASE

*THE COURT, in charge. The learned counsel is right in his position, and if he can shew precisely at what moment it was done, and that the prisoner was not there when he did it, and if so he could not do it. We cannot divest ourselves of common sense in courts of justice.*

*—Arabiniana, or Remains of Mr. Serjeant Arabin*

WITH NONE OF my cases have I been so long and intimately associated as with that of Oscar Slater. I often wished to edit a trial at which I had been present; one where I was familiar with the *locus* and circumstances of the crime, and knew personally some of those engaged in the proceedings. These conditions being fulfilled when I sat from 3rd to 6th May 1909 in the High Court of Justiciary at Edinburgh, in due course I produced a complete report of the trial. But I did not then anticipate that five years later I should be called upon to deal in a new edition with an official inquiry into certain fresh

465

facts, held in Glasgow by the Sheriff of Lanarkshire in 1914. Still less could I have conceived it possible that I should live to see, and chronicle in a third and definitive edition, the amazing sequel, when in July 1928 the appeal of Oscar Slater against his nineteen-year-old sentence was sustained and his conviction quashed by the Scottish Court of Criminal Appeal. Nay, more, that at the hearing in the appeal I myself should be called as a witness. Had anyone told me *that*, twenty years before at the trial, I should have deemed him certifiable.

Looking back across those years to-day, it is sad to note how few of the actors in the original drama survive. The learned Judge who pronounced the prisoner's doom; the Lord Advocate to whose masterful handling of the case he owed his condemnation; counsel and agent for the defense; the medical experts; the local authorities who, in a very real sense, got up the case against him—all have been called before a higher tribunal. Doubtless in the wilds of Glasgow some hardy veterans yet wag beard or bonnet as, with legitimate pride, to rather bored descendants they boast how they who speak were witnesses at the famous trial.

There are gaps also in the ranks of those who afterwards concerned themselves in this strange business. Sheriff Gardner Millar, who presided at the Glasgow inquiry, is no more. Gone are Detective-Lieutenant Trench, that fearless officer, whose career was ruined and his heart broken in the effort to right what he believed to be a grievous wrong; William Park, perfervid Scot and indefatigable journalist, who wore himself out in striving to have the case reopened, and died just before success crowned his endeavors; "and lastly (without wrong last to be named)," as John Webster has it, Sir Arthur Conan Doyle, that paladin of lost causes and champion of forlorn hopes, who spared neither time nor money nor energy in his conflict with the embattled forces of the Circumlocution Office, and happily lived to win the well-fought fight. These, too, have passed; and one whose privilege it was in some measure to share in their labors will ever hold them in brave remembrance.

I feel as if, in these depressing circumstances, I ought to apologize for my own protracted existence. But instead of doing so I propose to recall, for such as have patience to attend my reminiscences, the memory of those stirring times, in the hope that a generation which knew not Joseph may find it all as interesting as I did. For material, I have an embarrassment of riches. The shorthand writers' notes of evidence, both at the trial at Edinburgh and at the extradition proceedings in New York; the Government White Paper, containing the official report of the inquiry at Glasgow; countless documents, original or copies, relating to the various phases of the affair; two huge volumes of Press cuttings, the harvest of twenty years; and the several editions of my book. But as in this respect I am strong, so shall I be merciful, and a bird's-eye view of this formidable monument to my zeal and industry is all that the gentlest reader has to fear.

## 1908

### I

I well remember that Christmastide of 1908, when the news of the Glasgow murder was the sensation of the hour. Nowadays one's morning paper teems with murders, assassinations, and the daily toll of deaths exacted by our motor Juggernauts. It was otherwise in the peaceful times of which I write, when wanton and savage slaying was yet a thing to shudder at, exciting horror and dismay.

At seven o'clock on the evening of Monday, 21st December, an old lady, living alone with one servant in a comfortable flat in a well-to-do Glasgow street, was brutally butchered on her dining-room hearth-rug, during the temporary absence of the maid to buy an evening paper. The victim was Miss Marion Gilchrist, eighty-three years of age, a person of reserved and solitary habits, only remarkable in respect that she possessed some £3000 worth of jewels, which she kept hidden among her dresses in a wardrobe. The servant was Helen Lambie, twenty-one years of age, who had been in her service for three years. Miss Gilchrist was morbidly afraid of robbers; her door, in addition to the normal protections of lock and chain, was furnished with double bolts and two patent locks, opened by separate keys; and she had arranged with her neighbors in the flat below that should she at any time require assistance, she would knock three times upon the floor.

That night as Mr. Adams, the neighbor, was sitting with his sisters in his dining-room, they heard a noise from above: a heavy fall, followed by three sharp knocks. He at once went upstairs to see what was wrong. He rang three times but received no answer, and heard within a sound as of someone chopping sticks. He returned to his own house, but the noises continuing—"the ceiling was like to crack"—he went up again and had his hand on the bell when the maid came back with the paper. Learning what had passed, she suggested the noise was caused by the clothes-pulley in the kitchen falling down! She opened the door and made for the kitchen across the lobby, Adams remaining on the mat. As she did so, there emerged from the bedroom door a man, who passed behind her and approached Adams "quite pleasantly"—he thought he was a visitor; but on reaching the landing the man rushed downstairs, slamming the street door after him. Lambie then went into the kitchen and next into the bedroom; not until Adams said: "Where is your mistress?" did she enter the dining-room. Hearing her scream, Adams joined her, and was horrified to see the body of the old lady lying in front of the fire-place with a rug over her head. It was plain that she had been assaulted, and Adams ran down to the street, but the man had vanished. He met a constable with whom he returned to the house. On lifting the rug it was seen that Miss Gilchrist had been attacked with hideous ferocity, her head and face being smashed to pulp. Adams then summoned his own doctor, who lived across the street and whose name also was Adams. Dr. Adams, having examined the body, saw that life was extinct and rang up the police. We shall hear later his opinion as to how the deed was done. Meanwhile Lambie had left the house in order to tell Miss Birrell, a cousin of the dead lady, what had happened.

Detectives arrived; they found that the fire-place was splashed with blood and the wooden lid of the coal-scuttle blood-stained and broken. There were no signs of a struggle. Near the head stood a chair on which the old lady had been sitting; an open magazine, with her spectacles folded on it, lay upon the table. In the bedroom the gas had been lighted by the murderer, who had left behind him, appropriately, a box of "Runaway" matches. On the toilet-table were a diamond and two other gem rings, a gold watch and chain, and a gold bracelet. These lay openly in a glass dish, untouched by this singular robber. But Lambie declared that a diamond crescent brooch was missing. The treasures of the wardrobe were unrifled. A small dispatch-box, in which the deceased kept her private papers, had been broken open, and the contents were scattered on the bedroom floor. If he had committed murder in order to get the jewels, it is strange that the assassin should devote some of his few and precious minutes to examining the old lady's documents; but this undoubtedly he did.

## II

Two people had an opportunity of seeing the murderer: Lambie and Adams. On the night of the murder Lambie told two detectives that she would not be able to identify the man; Adams was short-sighted and had not on his glasses at the time. Despite these disadvantages, the police were able, on the information supplied by them, to publish in the next day's papers the following description of the wanted man:—

> A man between twenty-five and thirty years of age, 5 feet 8 or 9 inches in height, slim build, dark hair, clean shaven; dressed in light gray overcoat, and dark cloth cap. Cannot be further described.

On Wednesday, the 23rd, however, they were so fortunate as to be in a position to amplify this description. A little message girl of fourteen, Mary Barrowman, said that while passing along West Princes Street that night she saw a man run down the steps from 15 Queen's Terrace, where Miss Gilchrist lived. He collided with her, and ran on in the direction of West Cumberland Street, down which he turned and vanished from her view. Although she had but a momentary glimpse of the fugitive, at seven o'clock on a dark and rainy December night, in a street indifferently lighted, the result of her fleeting observation was much more detailed and distinct than that of Lambie and Adams, whose opportunity of seeing the man was infinitely better.

> The man wanted is about twenty-eight or thirty years of age, tall and thin, with his face shaved clear of all hair, while a distinctive feature is that his nose is slightly turned to one side. The witness thinks the twist is to the right side. He wore one of the popular round tweed hats known as Donegal hats, and a fawn-colored overcoat, which might have been a waterproof, also dark trousers, and brown boots.

This new description was published in the two o'clock editions of the Glasgow evening papers on Friday, the 25th. From these disparate descriptions the police very rightly inferred that they related to *two* different men; and that day was issued from headquarters, to police forces only, a notice containing both, in which it was stated that "the servant met the man *first* described leaving the house, and about the same time another man, *second* described, was seen descending the steps leading to the house, and running away." Officers were specially cautioned not to confound these two men. We shall see that, when it suited their theory, this is precisely what the authorities themselves unblushingly did. As a matter of fact the individual—Slater—whom, despite discrepancies, these descriptions were by the Procrustean methods of the Glasgow police made to fit, was then thirty-nine, of medium height, heavily-built, conspicuously broad-shouldered and deep-chested, with a short black mustache and a nose, though aquiline, untwisted. But the most obvious thing about him, which would strike even a casual observer, was that he was patently and unmistakably *a foreigner*. Yet neither Adams, Lambie, nor Barrowman noticed this. We shall find that on the night of the murder Lambie was alleged to have told Miss Birrell that she knew the man, and actually named him! Further, it was believed and averred that Barrowman was not there at all! Certainly Adams did not see her when he followed the man immediately to the street. These matters were the subject of future inquiry.

### III

The description of the missing brooch issued by the police met with more success. On Friday, the 25th, Allan M'Lean, a cycle dealer, called at the Central Police Station, and stated that a German Jew, whom he knew only as "Oscar," had been trying to dispose of a pawnticket for a diamond brooch resembling that said to have been appropriated by the murderer. He accompanied a detective to St. George's Road and pointed out No. 69, a common stair, as the place of "Oscar's" abode. Inquiries made in the stair showed that Slater, under the name of "Anderson," occupied a house on the third flat. Accordingly, at midnight steps were taken to arrest him on suspicion; but the bird had flown: "Anderson," accompanied by a lady friend and attended by no less than seven trunks and several packages, had left that very night for Liverpool. Here was a priceless clue; so, abandoning the view hitherto held officially: that *the murderer was personally known to his victim*, they decided that Slater was the wanted man. But a great disappointment awaited them. The brooch was readily traced to a pawnshop in Sauchiehall Street; but, alas, it appeared that the brooch had been in continuous pledge since 18th November, over a month before the murder! Nay, more; when it was shown to Lambie she rejected it at once: the missing brooch was set with a single row of stones; the pawned one, with three rows.

It is to be borne in mind that apart from the brooch clue, which thus completely failed them, the police had nothing whatever to connect Slater with the crime, and that but for M'Lean's mare's nest he would never even have been suspected. He had made no secret of his intention to leave Glasgow, so soon as he could get someone to take over his flat; one Rogers, a London friend, had found there two accommodating ladies willing to do so; they arrived in Glasgow that morning, and Slater left the same night. The order of his going was in nowise secret; his purpose to return to America was known to his friends and others; and he registered as "Oscar Slater, Glasgow" when he arrived at the North Western Hotel, Liverpool. Surely a strange proceeding, this, for a murderer fleeing from the gallows! But it might have struck the police as equally remarkable that the murderer should have been perambulating Glasgow for five days after the deed in the effort to dispose of a pawnticket for a diamond brooch, at the very time when the newspapers were full of the brooch stolen from the dead woman's house. This should really have been the end of the case, so far as Slater was concerned; but the authorities, like Pharaoh in another connection, refused to let him go. A £200 reward was offered for his apprehension, and the following instructions were cabled to the New York police:—

> Arrest Otto Sando second cabin *Lusitania* wanted in connection with the murder of Marion Gilchrist at Glasgow. He has a twisted nose. Search him and the woman who is his traveling companion for pawntickets.

Antoine, his mistress, with reference to the change of name, at the trial explained that they wished to conceal their movements from his wife. On a previous visit to America they had traveled as "Mr. and Mrs. A. George." In London and Glasgow, years before the murder, he called himself "Adolf Anderson." Plainly, in the matter of names, the accused was of counsel with Juliet.

And here, before the *Lusitania* reaches New York, it may be convenient to see who Slater really was. His name was Oscar Leschziner, which, being beyond the compass of English speech, he simplified as above mentioned. He was a Jew, born in Germany, and had left his native country to avoid military service. In London he became a bookmaker's clerk, and then a bookmaker. He afterwards lived in Glasgow and in Edinburgh. He had married in the former city in 1902 one May Curtis; but the marriage proved a failure, and for the last five years he had been living with Antoine, a young Frenchwoman whom he met in London. They lived on the Continent and in New York, finally returning to England. He specialized in the running of social clubs, the sociability of which consisted in gambling, and was an expert in games of chance. The police maintained that he had other and more despicable means of livelihood, but of that there is no proof. In November 1908 he removed his establishment to Glasgow, furnishing upon the installment system a flat in St. George's Road. They had one servant, Catherine Smalz, a German. The door-plate bore the name "Anderson," and he was ostensibly a dentist; but whatever operations were therein conducted had no reference to the practice of that dread profession. Some of his visiting-cards bore the designation: "Dealer in Diamonds and precious Stones," which, in relation to Miss Gilchrist's collection, was for him an unfortunate coincidence. His time was spent in divers billiard-rooms and gambling-houses, notably the Sloper Club in India Street, of which he was a member. He had several friends, mostly of his own nationality, and although his course of life was certainly neither reputable nor regular, he had never been in what is technically termed "trouble"; and even to this day there is not a tittle of evidence to disprove his reiterated and constant statement that he never so much as heard of the existence either of Miss Gilchrist or her jewels.

## IV

The brooch clue having broken down and the "flight from justice" being, as we shall find, equally fallacious, one would have thought that the Glasgow police would now desist from the pursuit of Slater and follow up the most material fact that Lambie had said she recognized the man she saw in the lobby. But they were loath to admit their mistake, and it was decided to risk sending Adams, Lambie, and Barrowman to New York, in the hope that they might see their way to identify Slater. As a fair and equitable preliminary to their task they were shown a photograph of him, so that they would know the man they were going so far to see. Anything more subversive of the ends of justice could hardly be imagined. The two girls were well drilled for their important parts as identifying witnesses. Lambie afterwards told how her statement was taken more times than she could number; Barrowman said she was examined every day for a fortnight. No wonder that they both swore at the trial that during the voyage, on which they occupied the same cabin, they never once referred to the subject of their quest: doubtless there was nothing more to be said about the matter.

## 1909

### I

The *Lusitania* reached New York on 2nd January. Slater and his companion were arrested, and on him was found the pawn-ticket for his diamond brooch. It does not appear that the New York police were advised that the brooch clue had been long exploded. The three identifiers did not arrive until the 25th. Next day, while Lambie and Barrowman, in charge of Inspector Pyper of Glasgow, were waiting in the corridor outside the Commissioner's room in which the extradition proceedings were in progress, Slater was brought along between two United States marshals, to one of whom he was handcuffed. Both girls exclaimed: "That's the man!" Whether they really meant the man they had seen on the night of the murder, and not the man whose photograph they were shown by the police, is another question. In these favorable circumstances it is hardly surprising that they were able to pick out "the man" in Court. In reply to the Commissioner, Lambie said that she recognized him not by his face—"I never saw his face," *i.e.* the murderer's—but by his walk. Yet at the trial she was afterwards to swear: "I *did* see his face"; and being asked why she did not say so in America, rudely retorted: "I am saying it now." When Mr. Gordon Miller, the able American barrister who acted as counsel for Slater, asked her for what purpose she and Barrowman were posted in the corridor, she impertinently replied: "That's my business and none of yours." But despite her impudence and prevarication Mr. Miller got from her a most important admission. At the trial, the vital question of how the murderer obtained access to that carefully-guarded, double-locked house was—though the reader will scarcely credit it—lost sight of by everybody and was never raised at all. But Mr. Miller saw the point and put it. Lambie's answer was highly significant: "*Miss Gilchrist must have opened the door.*"

When Lambie left the house that night she closed the street door. It was open when she returned. This could be done, in answer to a ring, by a handle within the house door. Miss Gilchrist's invariable custom, if alone in the house, was in such circumstances to look over the banisters—the staircase is wide, open, and well-lighted—and if the bell-ringer were a stranger to her, or someone she did not wish to see, to retreat into her house, and shut and bar the door. Slater, as I have said, was a strange-looking man of markedly foreign aspect, the last sort of person whom the old lady would voluntarily have admitted. The inference is plain: *the visitor was known to Miss Gilchrist*, otherwise, without two false keys (which no one ever suggested), it was virtually impossible for him to have got into the house.

Barrowman stated that Slater was "something" like the man; later, that he was "very" like him. Adams would not go further than that Slater "resembled" him. Against the advice of his legal advisers, who were confident that his extradition would be refused, Slater, on the adjournment of the proceedings, decided to resist no longer, but to go back to Glasgow and face the music. So everyone concerned sailed for home: the witnesses in the *Baltic*; Antoine, now released, in the *Campania*; and the Glasgow detectives, with Slater and his seven trunks, direct for the Clyde in the *Columbia*.

## II

In Glasgow the prisoner's baggage was unsealed and opened. The contents were mainly wearing apparel, and despite the haste connected with a "flight from justice," the packing had been done with extraordinary care. There were no fewer than seven dress suits; but the only garments which the police deemed relevant to the charge were a soft felt hat, two cloth caps, and a light waterproof. A small tin tack hammer which, as afterwards appeared, Slater had bought with other household tools on a card for 2s. 6d., was taken possession of as "the weapon" with which the fearful injuries had been inflicted.

Meanwhile the Glasgow police had been besieged by people claiming to have seen "the man." From among these were chosen as witnesses twelve persons who had observed a suspicious-looking stranger hanging about West Princes Street and staring up at Miss Gilchrist's windows for weeks before the murder. None of these knew Slater by sight, none described the stranger as of foreign aspect, and the only one to whom the watcher spoke said distinctly that he was not a foreigner. (Even at the time of the appeal, twenty years later, Slater still spoke broken English with a strong German accent, and had lost nothing of his foreign aspect.) The recollection of these eye-witnesses having been duly refreshed by exhibition to them of a photograph of the suspect, the original was put up before them for "identification." A swarthy German Jew, patently and unmistakably an alien, was placed among eleven Scotsmen: nine Glasgow policemen and two railwaymen: totally different from Slater in type and appearance. In such circumstances the task of the witnesses was unattended by serious difficulty; they all picked out "the man" at once. One of the police officers, asked in cross-examination at the trial whether it would not be fairer to an accused if he were placed among men more or less like him, naïvely replied: "It might be the fairest way, but it is not the practice in Glasgow"! We shall hear presently how some of these identifying witnesses justified the faith that was in them.

The evidence of one of them caused much official heart-burning. Agnes Brown, a young lady of education and intelligence—she was a school teacher—had informed the police that on the night of the murder, being at the corner of West Cumberland Street, she saw *two* men running away from the scene of the crime. One was dressed in a gray coat, the other in a blue Melton overcoat with a velvet collar. The police, thinking that the gray-coated fugitive would prove to be the Adams-Lambie-Barrowman gentleman, took her sworn deposition and sent it, along with others, to America. But, alas, when confronted with Slater in Glasgow, Miss Brown picked him out as the wearer of the *blue overcoat*! Further, she did not see Barrowman, who, if really there, must have been equally visible; and worst of all, her fugitives ran away in a direction opposite to that taken by Barrowman's. This would never do. If her evidence were accepted, it would conflict with that of the others, besides bringing in *two* men, which did not now suit the official book. So that although the name "Agnes Brown, teacher, 48 Grant Street, Glasgow," is No. 46 in the list of witnesses for the prosecution and she had definitely identified the accused as "the man," the Lord Advocate was too wise to call her and she was quietly dropped. She was, of course, no use to the defense, for she was prepared to fit the blue coat on the accused's broad shoulders.

Another lady witness by whom confusion was made worse confounded was Mrs. Liddell, a married sister of Adams, who, reaching her brother's door that night at five minutes to seven, saw a man leaning against the railings, and having a special animus against loiterers, stared at him "almost rudely." She identified the accused as "the man." To the annoyance of the police, she described him as wearing a brown tweed cap and a long, heavy brown tweed overcoat, with a tweed collar, having a peculiar hem. It was emphatically not the waterproof produced. We have seen that the Adams-Lambie man was dressed differently from Barrowman's and Agnes Brown's; so Mrs. Liddell's thick brown top-coat was, as the Princess Ida remarked to Lady Blanche in another connection, "Superfluous, yet not Needful."

The man must have been a quick-change artist, to appear in such variety of costume; respectively, at 6:55 (Mrs. Liddell), 7:10 (Adams, Lambie, and Barrowman), and 7:12 (Agnes Brown). But this was far from exhausting the resources of his wardrobe. Mrs. M'Haffie lived with her three daughters in a house opposite Miss Gilchrist's. They all identified the accused as the watcher, whom they had often seen prowling up and down the street. The mother dressed him in a light overcoat, not a waterproof, check trousers, spats, and a black bowler hat. The young ladies concurred with their mama. Unfortunately, the seven trunks contained none of these vestments; curious that the accused, when making a holocaust of his raiment before leaving for America, should have spared only the waterproof in which he did the deed. One of the damsels, to whom "the man" had spoken, said that she noticed no accent and did not think him a foreigner. In the case of two of the other witnesses who claimed the accused, differently garbed, as the watcher, Slater at the trial had a perfect alibi; so they, at least, identified the wrong man. One of them affords a typical example of the value of this sort of evidence. Having asked the accused to turn round in the dock, the witness, in answer to the Lord Advocate, emphatically said: "Yes; I am certain that is the man." Cross-examined as to how he could be so positive as to a man whose back only he had seen but once, at a distance of 13 yards, at 9:15 on a dark December night? witness replied: "Oh, I will not swear in fact, but I am certain that he is the man I saw. But I will not swear!"

## III

The case for the prosecution being now as armiferous as the Glasgow authorities could make it, on Monday, 3rd May 1909, the battle was joined in the High Court of Justiciary at Edinburgh, the forces of the Crown being led by the Lord Advocate (Mr. Alexander Ure, K.C., afterwards Lord Strathclyde), and those of the defense by Mr. (later Sheriff) M'Clure. Lord Guthrie was judge of the lists. As I have already written three accounts of the trial and the next of the evidence is easily available, I do not here propose to do more than make some comments on its conduct.

It should be borne in mind that prior to seeing "the man," none of the identifying witnesses had ever seen Slater, none noticed that he was a foreigner; those who had dealings with him both in Glasgow and in Liverpool said they saw at once that he was an alien; and all the identifiers were first shown his photograph.

Lambie and Barrowman had now been brought into line, the former adopting the latter's Donegal hat and waterproof in lieu of her own original gray overcoat and dark cap. As an instance of Lambie's mental and moral capacity—no pun is intended—she now maintained that she saw the man's face, which hitherto she had denied doing; that he walked down the stair deliberately, while Adams swore he went down "like greased lightning"; that she was standing on the door-mat beside Adams, who swore she was well into the lobby; and that being asked what enabled her to identify so positively the waterproof produced as the actual coat the man was wearing, she sharply replied: "That *is* the coat!" The memory of Mary Barrowman had been strengthened by repeated examinations and her experiences in New York. She was now able to swear, in reply to the Lord Advocate's last dramatic question: "Look at the prisoner; is that the man?": "Yes; that is the man who knocked against me that night." In cross-examination, she said the man approached and passed her running at top speed, with his hat pulled down over his eyes. Let the interested reader test the truth of little Mary's evidence for himself, by getting someone to tear past him at night in a dark street, near a gas lamp; if he is able to see as much as she says she did, I will be the first to congratulate him on his powers of, well—let us say, observation. Adams was, as ever, perfectly fair: he thought the prisoner "resembled" the man. "It is too serious a charge for me to say from a passing glance."

So anxious was Mrs. Liddell to be accurate that she even caused the prisoner to assume in the dock the attitude of the watcher by the railings; and having closely studied him, said she was "afraid" he was "the man." The Lord Advocate had forgotten to put to her that the watcher wore a heavy tweed overcoat. Reminded of this by Mr. M'Clure, the witness said it was a thick cloth coat, not a waterproof: "I have stuck to that all along, and I will stick to it still." Which rather suggests that someone had been trying to improve her recollection. She admitted that when she saw Slater at the police station parade she was very much surprised by his robust appearance: the watcher looked a delicate man. Doubtless Slater's physique was improved by the double sea voyage.

Among the witnesses adduced to prove the "flight from justice" was the girl at the turnstile of Kelvinbridge subway, who through her small ticket window saw a man fly down the stair at about 7:45, flinging her a penny as he fled. The prisoner was "the man." The Lord Advocate made great play with this witness, whose opportunity of observation was more restricted even than Barrowman's. But when we know that among the Crown precognitions was that of Duncan MacBrayne, shop-man at the grocer's with whom Slater dealt, who had informed the police that he saw him standing calmly at the door of his abode at 8:15 on the night of the crime, within an hour of its commission, we wonder why the name of MacBrayne is not to be found among the 98 witnesses cited for the prosecution. And our surprise is increased by the fact that on his picking out Slater at the "line-up" in the police station, the suspect greeted him with the words: "Oh, you are the man in the big shop in Sauchiehall Street!" thus affording the sole indis-putable identification in the case. Despite the singular neglect of his testimony by the Crown, MacBrayne was not born to blush unseen. We shall hear from him again.

## IV

Another regrettable omission from the Crown list of witnesses was the name of Dr. John Adams, 1 Queen's Crescent, the first medical man to see the body. This gentleman, contrary to in-variable practice, was not called at the trial. In his view the injuries to the head were caused by blows from the back leg of a heavy mahogany chair upon which before the attack the old lady had been sitting, the assailant, while wielding it, stamping on the body and thus fracturing the ribs, as was at the post-mortem found to have been done. We shall learn the ground of Dr. Adams's opinion when we reach the appeal, twenty years after.

In the judgment of Professor Glaister, chief medical expert for the Crown, who with Dr. Galt, the casualty surgeon, made a post-mortem examination of the body, the hammer produced could, in the hand of a strong man and forcibly wielded—plus kneeling on the chest—have produced the injuries. To do so, between 20 and 40 blows would be required, inflicted with lightning rapidity. The assailant's clothing must have been bespattered with blood; his hands could not escape, nor could the weapon. It was the most brutally smashed head witness had ever seen. Dr. Galt concurred. The smashing was most extensive. The hammer could have done it, but he admitted he would have expected a heavier weapon. Not under 50 or 60 blows must have been struck: probably a good many more. Professor Harvey Littlejohn, who along with Professor Glaister had examined certain articles for blood-stains, concurred with his colleague in the result, as reported by them. They were unable to affirm that the stains on the waterproof were those of human blood, neither were they in a position to state positively that they found red blood corpuscles on the head of the hammer. It is significant that the Lord Advocate put no question to Professor Littlejohn as to the likelihood of the hammer being the weapon. This may be due to the fact, of which the Professor afterwards informed me, that he had, when consulted, expressed his strong opinion that the hammer had nothing to do with the case.

Why did the Crown experts not take off the metal head of the hammer? I am advised that if that hammer were indeed the weapon, there *must* have been blood-stains beneath the flanges on the soft white wood shaft. Nay, more; that if ever there were any, they are there still. Perhaps some future scientist may settle the question yet, for the hammer is preserved in the Justiciary Office.

The two medical experts for the defense, Dr. Aitchison Robertson and Dr. Veitch, stated that they could discover neither on the hammer nor on the waterproof the least trace of blood. Both considered the hammer a most unlikely instrument; beating and thrusting with a heavy poker or crow-bar would, in their opinion, be much more likely to produce such shocking results. Then why not the stout chair leg?

V

The evidence for the accused's alibi was as good as could be expected from one of his Bohemian habits. The deed was done between 7 and 7:10 p.m. At 6:12 from the Central Station he sent a telegram in his own handwriting to London for his watch, which was being repaired; at 6:30, remarking to his friend Rattman that he was going home to dinner, he left Johnston's billiard-rooms in Renfield Street, a considerable distance from the scene of the murder. He is proved to have been then wearing a waterproof and a bowler hat; yet at 6:55 Mrs. Liddell sees him at the railings in a heavy brown tweed overcoat and a brown tweed cap. Antoine and Smalz stated that he was home as usual to dinner at 7, and *pace* the Lord Advocate, there is nothing to show that they were perjured.

The girl at the subway—"the last witness to see the murderer," as his Lordship dramatically put it—said the accused rushed headlong past her peep-hole at 7:45. Mr. Ure in his speech drew a lurid picture of the murderer, hugging the bloody hammer, fleeing from the scene of his crime into the bowels of Glasgow, "to be taken by a train to some remote part of the city." And all the time there was recorded in the Crown precognitions lying on the table beside him, had he cared to look at it, the statement of MacBrayne: that at 8:15 Slater was standing, cool and unperturbed, at the outer door of his own house.

The Lord Advocate put no questions to Antoine; but he drastically cross-examined Smalz, and extracted from her the admission that Madame received gentlemen in the evening and frequented music-halls. From the witness Cameron was secured the hearsay evidence that he "had it" the accused lived upon his mistress. The deadly but illegitimate use made of this by Mr. Ure will shortly be apparent. On the credit side of the account, Cameron testified to Slater having posted in his presence on the afternoon of the crime a £5 note to his parents in Germany as a Christmas gift. A small point; but a curious thing for a murderer to do within an hour of the deed. The accused, though most anxious to give evidence, was not allowed to do so. This point came up again at the appeal.

But as my goal yet lies twenty years ahead, I have no time to linger longer over the evidence, and must say a word as to that vehement piece of sophistical rhetoric, the speech for the Crown.

## VI

The force and effect of the Lord Advocate's address to the jury none who heard it is likely to forget. Contrary to the tradition of his office, it was a powerful appeal for a conviction, and suffered the further disadvantage of containing several misstatements of fact. I remember after the trial discussing it with Sir Edward Marshall Hall, and expressing my amazement at Mr. Ure's astonishing feat of speaking for two hours on so vexed a question without written note or reference to any document. "That," said Sir Edward dryly, "may account for its manifold inaccuracies." Mr. E. C. Palmer, who under the pseudonym of "The Pilgrim" published, in September 1927, in the *Daily News* the remarkable series of articles on the case which so largely contributed to the success of the agitation for its reopening, in his masterly analysis of the Lord Advocate's speech has noted no less than five-and-twenty erroneous statements and false inferences from the evidence. Prior to publication he invited his Lordship's comments; his Lordship replied that he had no observations to make. Lord Strathclyde had the courage of the opinions of Mr. Ure.

I cannot follow Mr. Palmer on his expository pilgrimage, but one or two of his most signal instances, which I myself had noted, call for brief mention. I was struck at the time, as I listened spellbound to the Lord Advocate's eloquence, by the famous phrase: "We shall see in the sequel how it was that the prisoner came to know that she [Miss Gilchrist] was possessed of these jewels." I had been in Court every day, I had heard all the witnesses; how came I to have missed this paramount, this vital evidence? Anxiously I awaited the promised revelation. It never came. His Lordship said not another word on the subject; but doubtless the jury took the will for the deed. The speech opened with a psychological "howler":—

> Up to yesterday afternoon I should have thought that there was one serious difficulty which confronted you— the difficulty of conceiving that there was in existence a human being capable of doing such a dastardly deed. Gentlemen, that difficulty, I think, was removed when we heard from the lips of one who seemingly knew the prisoner better than anyone else, that he had followed a life which descends to the very lowest depths of human degradation, for by the universal judgment of mankind, the man who lives upon the proceeds of prostitution has sunk to the lowest depths, and all moral sense has been destroyed and has ceased to exist. That difficulty removed, I say without hesitation that the man in the dock is capable of having committed this dastardly outrage.

Oscar Wilde has well observed that the fact that a man is a poisoner is nothing against his prose; and it does not follow that because a man lives an immoral life he is capable of murder. The most damning of Mr. Ure's errors, and one which he repeated and rubbed in, was that Slater fled from Glasgow on Christmas Eve because "his *name* and his description and all the rest of it" were published in that day's newspapers. All that was published that afternoon was, as we have seen, Barrowman's description of "the man"; Slater's name was not mentioned in print until he was half-way across the Atlantic! Of his Lordship's sins of omission, one notes the suppression of the evidence of MacBrayne and of Agnes Brown; of that proving Slater to have traveled with Liverpool, not with London tickets; the absence of any reference as to how the murderer got into the house, and to the suggestive fact that being after jewels—"the motive for the crime is as plain as daylight"—the thief, instead of seizing the valuable jewelry exposed to his view on the toilet-table, broke open the dispatch-box and examined Miss Gilchrist's private papers.

The Lord Advocate told the jury that from the facts proved they could draw seven "priceless inferences." These, on examination, seem to be scarcely so inestimable as he represented. For example, that the murder was coolly and deliberately planned by a clever, cold-blooded, expert performer, who had familiarized himself with the ways and habits of the inmates; that the murderer brought his weapon and took it away with him; and that he was on the hunt for jewels, but did not know where they were kept, never having been in the house before. The character of the attack, however, in its wholly unnecessary violence and brutality is scantly suggestive of a professional burglar, who rarely kills except in self-defense. As for the "skilled eye," daily employed by him in watching the house for "the supreme moment" when the old lady was left alone and unprotected, his Lordship failed to explain why the ten minutes' nightly absence of the maid for the evening paper was chosen in preference to her half-day out twice a week. Finally, "the prisoner is hopelessly unable to produce a single witness who saw that he was anywhere else than at the scene of the murder that night," which is rather hard upon the two women who swore they did.

## VII

Mr. M'Clure put up a good fight for his client, but there is no disguising the fact that for so heavy a charge he was rather a light horseman. Although his experience of the criminal bar was limited, he had plenty of pluck; he stood up stoutly to his formidable adversary, cross-examined effectively, and made a capital speech, less rhetorically brilliant but much more soundly reasoned than that of his great opponent. The jury, stunned by the drums and tramplings of the Lord Advocate, looked to the learned Judge for guidance to a happy issue out of all their afflictions. Unfortunately, Lord Guthrie had fallen to some extent under the dominating spell cast upon them. His Lordship not only homologated the errors of the prosecutor, but introduced some new ones of his own. These matters were fully dealt with at the hearing in the appeal, so we may leave them now.

The jury took an hour and ten minutes to consider their verdict, which was one of Guilty. The vote was: for Guilty, 9; for Not Proven, 5; and for Not Guilty, 1. Amid a scene rendered inexpressibly painful by the prisoner's passionate protestations of innocence, the Judge passed sentence of death and the four days' trial was over.

## VIII

The execution was appointed to take place in Glasgow on 27th May. Much dissatisfaction with the verdict was shown by the Press, and the general opinion—apart from those concerned in the prosecution—was that at the most one of Not Proven was all that the evidence warranted. The curious psychology of the public mind, which before a word of the evidence was heard had been made up as to the accused's guilt, produced a strong reaction in favor of his innocence, and a petition for commutation of the death penalty was signed by over 20,000 persons. This, together with a very able memorial on the facts of the case, prepared by the prisoner's legal advisers, was forwarded to the Secretary for Scotland. Not until the eve of the execution was there any news from London. At 7 p.m. on the 25th the Lord Provost received a telegram from Whitehall, intimating a respite; and next morning came an official letter stating that the sentence had been commuted to penal servitude for life. Questions were asked in the House of Commons as to the grounds for granting the reprieve, but the Lord Advocate refused to be drawn.

So Slater went to Peterhead; and the £200 reward for his conviction was thus divided: Mary Barrowman, £100; Forsyth, of the Cunard office at Liverpool (who thought Slater "somewhat nervous" when taking his ticket—though he was able to joke about not being "Sandow, the Strong Man"), £40; M'Lean, the cycle dealer (who furnished the false clue of the diamond brooch—and who ought rather to have been fined in that amount), £40; and Gordon Henderson, manager of the Motor Club in India Street (who said that Slater, "excited a little," at 9:45 on the night of the crime, attired in "a fawn-colored overcoat and a round *felt* hat which we call a Donegal hat," called at the club and asked him to cash a check), £20. This was the evidence upon which the Lord Advocate described the accused as "gasping and panting for money" on the night of the murder; but his Lordship did not remind the jury that Slater had got that afternoon the last advance of £30 upon his diamond brooch, and thus was in no urgent need of cash. Why Lambie, who had told more stories than anybody else, got nothing does not appear.

## 1914

### I

The events leading up to and culminating in the Gilbertian inquiry of 1914 may be briefly stated. My report of the trial was published in 1910. The unusual circumstances of the conviction attracted the notice, among other authorities, of my friend Andrew Lang, who wrote to me, having read the book, that upon such evidence "a cat would scarcely be whipped for stealing cream." And in reviewing it he remarked: "One thing is clear: a legal case of the highest importance may be accepted as proved, in face of discrepancies of testimony which would leave a ghost story without a chance of acceptance by scientific minds." Other experts interested in the subject were Sir Arthur Conan Doyle and Sir Herbert Stephen, the eminent jurist, both of whom by word and deed never rested from their labors to expose what they deemed a gross miscarriage of justice. Sir Herbert wrote to *The Times* that in his judgment the evidence entirely failed to warrant the conviction, and urged the necessity for a Scottish Court of Criminal Appeal. Marshall Hall put a question in the House; but the Scottish Secretary declined to discuss the matter. Sir Arthur Conan Doyle then published his booklet based upon my report, in which he applied to the problems presented by the case the expert methods of Mr. Sherlock Holmes. He made the new and suggestive point that the murderer was not after jewels, but some document, such as a will. So the controversial ball was kept rolling, and public interest in the subject was not allowed to fade.

An important development occurred in March 1914. Mr. David Cook, Writer, Glasgow, presented to the Secretary for Scotland statements and documents in support of an inquiry into the case. The points upon which these bore were:—

1. Did any witness to the identification on the night of the murder name a person other than Oscar Slater?
2. Were the police aware that such was the case? If so, why was the evidence not forthcoming at the trial?
3. Did Slater fly from justice?
4. Were the police in possession of information that Slater had disclosed his name at the North-Western Hotel, Liverpool, stating where he came from, and that he was traveling by the *Lusitania*?
5. Did one of the witnesses make a mistake as to the date on which she stated she was in West Princes Street (Queen's Terrace)?

The first and last questions relate respectively to the evidence of Lambie and Barrowman.

Yielding to the popular demand which was strongly expressed in the Press, the Scottish Secretary announced that he had appointed Mr. Gardner Millar, Sheriff of Lanarkshire, to hold an inquiry and to report. *The Times*, in a strong leading article, observed that in the interests of justice such an investigation was long overdue, and protested against the restrictions imposed. These were that the proceedings should be held in secret; that no one was to be present but the Commissioner and his clerk; that the witnesses, who could come or not as they liked, *were not to be examined upon oath*; and it was specially ordered that the inquiry "*should in no way relate to the conduct of the trial*"! A more excellent means of finding How-Not-To-Do-It could hardly have been devised by the Circumlocution Office itself. Though Slater was not represented, the Sheriff gratefully acknowledged the "assistance" he received from the Procurator-Fiscal and the Chief Constable of Glasgow. These gentlemen being the officials responsible for the original prosecution, it is not uncharitable to suppose that their interests lay in sustaining the conviction. As Sir Arthur wrote at the time to the *Daily Mail*: "The police are as much on trial as Slater. If the methods of the police are not to be investigated the inquiry is futile." He proved a true prophet.

## II

The spirit that so far successfully had troubled the official waters was that of John Thomson Trench, sometime Detective-Lieutenant in the City of Glasgow Police Force. He joined the Force as a constable in 1893, was from time to time promoted, and in 1912 received his commission as Lieutenant of Police. He also obtained the coveted distinction of King's Medallist, in reward of his exemplary and meritorious services, an honor for which he was recommended by his commanding officer, the Chief Constable of Glasgow. In the course of his twenty-one years' duty he deservedly enjoyed the confidence of his superiors, the regard of his colleagues, and the respect of the public; and he was generally held in high esteem as a trustworthy, capable, and efficient officer. Yet despite this fair and honorable record, he was in 1914 dismissed with ignominy from the Force, his well-earned pension forfeited, his career destroyed, and his reputation ruined. And all because he tried to rescue from prison a man whom he believed to have been wrongfully convicted. Verily, in his case virtue was its own reward.

Mr. Trench was from the first convinced that the police were on the wrong track in endeavoring to fix upon Slater the guilt of Miss Gilchrist's murder. He averred that on the very night of the crime Lambie had named another man, known to her, as the murderer whom she saw leaving the house. But as Trench's superiors preferred to follow up the brooch clue, which led—fallaciously, as we have seen—to Slater, he could do nothing further in what he believed to be the right direction. The subsequent conviction of Slater was always regarded by Trench as unwarranted by the evidence, and the lesson he learned in the Broughty Ferry murder case of 1912, to which I shall presently refer, confirmed his distrust of identification based on personal impressions. He refreshed his memory as to the half-forgotten facts, and in the light of his recent experience was more than ever satisfied that there had been a miscarriage of justice. But his official duty was plain: Slater must be left in Peterhead for life. The matter gave his conscience no rest—he was a man before he was a detective; and as he knew it was hopeless to move his chiefs, he took counsel with Mr. David Cook, a well-known and experienced Glasgow lawyer, as to what he ought to do. Mr. Cook believed his tale and advised him in the interests of justice to tell it. But Trench, dreading the consequences to himself of any disclosure by him touching the secrets of the prison-house, was unwilling to act without some guarantee of immunity from the wrath of his superiors. Dr. Devon, one of H.M. Prison Commissioners for Scotland, was approached; he wrote on the subject to Mr. M'Kinnon Wood, the Scottish Secretary, who, on 13th February 1914, replied: "If the constable mentioned in your letter will send me a written statement of the evidence in his possession of which he spoke to you, I will give this matter my best consideration." This letter was naturally regarded by Trench as authorizing him to give the information; so the statement was sent to the Minister, with two results: the appointment of the abortive commission and, in due season, the dismissal and disgrace of Trench.

Now the eminence of Lieutenant Trench had caused his aid in difficult cases to be sought for outwith the bounds of Glasgow; and when, in November 1912, the Broughty Ferry police were faced by the inexplicable murder of Miss Milne, they called him in as a consultant. The crime presented certain features strongly reminiscent of the Glasgow murder. Miss Milne was an eccentric old lady, living alone in a well-protected house; the murderer must have been admitted by his victim; and her head, like Miss Gilchrist's, was horribly smashed, the superfluous ferocity of the attack showing that the assailant was determined to "mak siccar"—as Lord Guthrie reminded the jury in the Slater trial: "Dead men (and dead women) tell no tales"; and the disinterested conduct of the robber, in leaving seven diamond rings on the dead woman's fingers and her gold watch and chain lying on her toilet-table.

A dozen witnesses, who had seen the supposed murderer, entered for the One Hundred Pounds stakes offered to such as should secure the conviction of the thief of life—for he had stolen nothing else. The reward bill was broadcast everywhere and bore fruit so far afield as Maidstone, where the local police had then in custody a Canadian named Warner, who had defrauded an innkeeper in respect of board and lodging. He was photographed and the result sent to Scotland, when six of the witnesses definitely identified him as "the man." They were taken to Maidstone, and at the customary parade in the prison picked out the original of the photograph with beautiful unanimity, the prisoner bitterly exclaiming—with perfect truth and justice: "It's not fair; it's a farce!" A warrant for his arrest was granted, and Trench went South to execute it. At Dundee, Warner was again paraded for behoof of twenty-two fresh witnesses, when, as was stated in the Press, he was identified by twelve. Be that as it may, the original six were quite positive as to his identity. Precognitions (statements) of 100 witnesses were sent to the Crown authorities in Edinburgh with a view to framing an indictment against the accused, and everything was in train for a first-class, sensational murder trial.

But, alas, that busybody, Lieutenant Trench, had become satisfied, despite the dense cloud of witnesses, that the accused had no connection whatever with the crime. The man had been on the tramp in Holland and Belgium; he could furnish no addresses, having slept out of doors; but he did recall that about the date of the murder he had pawned in Antwerp his waistcoat for a franc. Trench went to Antwerp, found the pawnshop, and redeemed the waistcoat, which had been pledged by the accused there the day after the murder! Whereupon Warner was set at liberty, and the six identifying witnesses—less fortunate than their Glasgow forerunners—had to whistle for the reward. It is a further curious coincidence that Slater's tribulations began, as those of Warner ended—in a pawnshop.

### III

In reply to a question in the House, the Scottish Secretary undertook to lay on the table the statement of evidence taken at the Glasgow inquiry, and in due course this was printed in the form of a Government White Paper, which is reprinted in the second and third editions of my report of the trial. Trench stated that in view of information supplied by Lambie, Superintendent Douglas and two detectives went to the house of A. B. the day after the murder, in order to take his statement. Who that gentleman was and what he said to the officers we are not told, for the Sheriff explains in a note: "The letters A. B. are substituted for the name throughout. Certain passages in the statement relating to A. B. have been omitted, and these omissions are marked by asterisks." So generously is the White Paper besprinkled with these irritating spots that it seems to have suffered a sort of editorial measles. Two days after the murder Trench was instructed by the Chief Superintendent to interview Miss Birrell, a niece of the dead lady, and take her precognition (statement), which he did. Here it is:—

> My mother was a sister of the deceased. Miss Gilchrist was not on good terms with her relations. Few, if any,

visited her. . . . I can never forget the night of the murder. Miss Gilchrist's servant, Nellie Lambie, came to my door about 7:15. She was excited. She pulled the bell violently. On the door being opened she rushed into the house and exclaimed: "Oh, Miss Birrell, Miss Birrell, Miss Gilchrist has been murdered, she is lying dead in the dining-room, and oh Miss Birrell, I saw the man who did it!" I replied: "My God, Nellie, this is awful. Who was it? Do you know him?" Nellie replied. "Oh, Miss Birrell, I think it was A. B. I am sure that it was A. B." I said to her: "My God, Nellie, don't say that. . . . Unless you are very sure of it, Nellie, don't say that." She again repeated to me that she was sure it was A. B. . . .

Trench delivered this statement to Superintendent Orr, who remarked: "This is the first real clue we have got." Subsequently, Trench was informed "that A. B. had nothing to do with it," and was instructed to go and warn Miss Birrell not to repeat Lambie's words, which he accordingly did.

Both Miss Birrell and Lambie ("not upon oath," like The Bantam in *Richard Feverel*) denied that the statements attributed to them by Trench were ever made; and his superior officers also denied that he was sent to Miss Birrell or reported the result to them. The alleged precognition was not on the official file. (One can conceive how that may have happened.) But it was otherwise clearly proved that Lambie *did* bring to Miss Birrell the news of the murder; that two police officers *did* interview that lady next day and took from her a statement; and that Trench *did* visit her for the like purpose. Chief-Inspector Cameron, moreover, corroborated Trench as to the latter's mission, and stated *that Trench told him at the time* "that Miss Birrell had said to him that the girl Lambie had said to her on the night of the murder that the man who passed her in the lobby was like A. B."; and that Trench further told him (Cameron) that he had reported the matter to his superiors, who said it had been cleared up. It is proved by the evidence of three of the police chiefs *that the movements of A. B. were strictly inquired into after the murder*. Why? If neither Trench, nor Miss Birrell, nor Lambie had mentioned his name, what reason was there for these inquiries? And why was not a word of all this said at the trial, when the witnesses were on oath and could have been cross-examined? There are too many "asterisks" about the whole business. It is incredible that an officer of Trench's character and record can have invented the story; but if he did so, Cameron proves that he told his tale before anyone concerned had heard the name of Slater mentioned in connection with the crime.

It was fully established by the evidence of railway and hotel witnesses that Slater traveled with Liverpool tickets and registered in his own name. "We passed on all this information to the Procurator-Fiscal," said Superintendent Orr, who had charge of the case; but these facts, unhappily for the accused, were not "passed on" to the jury, who were led to believe that Slater traveled with *London* tickets. Upon the question as to whether or not Barrowman could have been where she said she was when she saw "the man," many new witnesses were heard. The net result was that little Mary had told as many different stories as Lambie, and it was left at that. Agnes Brown was now allowed to give her account of how, at the same time and place, she saw *two* men running away in the *opposite* direction from that taken by Mary's runaway. Had this lady been called at the trial, the jury would have had to choose between her evidence and that of Barrowman, which were mutually destructive. Then MacBrayne was at length permitted to tell his tale. Put into the witness-box, he would have confounded the girl at the turnstile and discounted the evidence of Gordon Henderson; neither could the Lord Advocate have alleged:

"We know nothing of the man's movements until a quarter to ten at night, when he appears, excited, at the Motor Club." Further, as I have said, MacBrayne would have spoiled his Lordship's dramatic picture of the terror-stricken murderer seeking refuge in the underground.

In reporting to the Minister the result of the inquiry, the Sheriff explains the procedure adopted. He first of all communicated with the Chief Constable and the Procurator-Fiscal, and had several interviews with them, when they promised him "every assistance." The method pursued was this:—

> The only persons present were the witness, Mr. Andrew Sandilands, my clerk, and myself. I put questions to the witnesses and dictated the purport of the answers to Mr. Sandilands, who took it down in longhand. At the conclusion of the statement it was read over to the witness and signed by him as being true.
>
> With regard to the manner of those making statement, I think it is enough to say that Miss Birrell and Miss Brown seemed to me to be very intelligent, careful, and trustworthy witnesses. Mrs. Gillon [Lambie, who had married since the trial], Miss Mary Barrowman, and Mr. MacBrayne seemed to be honest and anxious to tell the truth.

Upon the matter and manner of Lieutenant Trench's evidence the Sheriff has no observations, nor does he make mention of the mysterious gentleman whose identity is veiled under the letters A. B. It seems a pity that with so much professed anxiety for truth we should not have had more of that inestimable virtue. The reception accorded by the Press to the White Paper, issued on 27th June 1914, was cold. The Slater case was already so rich in riddles that the fresh ones now raised but added to its existing perplexities. The only people who were pleased were the police. Questioned in the House as to what he proposed to do about it, the Scottish Secretary replied that after careful consideration of the whole matter he proposed to do nothing.

## IV

Nemesis was now free to strike and the blow fell swiftly. Trench's chiefs had never forgiven him for the disloyalty to his caste shown by him in the matter of Warner's waistcoat, whereby he spoilt a fine case of circumstantial evidence. The time had come when, in the vulgar phrase, they could get some of their own back. On 14th July he was suspended from duty; on 14th September he was dismissed from the Glasgow Police Force. The charge of which he was found guilty was this: "Communicating to a person who is not a member of Glasgow Police Force, namely, Mr. David Cook, Writer, Glasgow, information which he [Detective-Lieutenant Trench] had acquired in the performance of his duty, and copies of documents from the official records in the case of Oscar Slater." Trench's appeal to the Scottish Secretary, reminding the Minister that the information had been supplied at his request and, as was understood, under his protection, met with no response.

When the Great War obliterated all minor wrongs, Mr. Trench, who had formerly served in the Black Watch, enlisted in the Royal Scots Fusiliers, and was sent to Stirling, where his work as drill instructor proved invaluable to the regiment. He was later appointed Provost-Sergeant of Stirling and attached to the Brigade Office. Thus, though the Glasgow police had no use for him, his country was still glad of his services.

## 1915

But even in the national crisis the Glasgow authorities had not forgotten their private and parochial spite. On the eve of the regiment leaving for Gallipoli, Provost-Sergeant Trench was arrested in Stirling on a charge of reset, *i.e.* receiving stolen goods, and on the same day Mr. Cook was arrested in Glasgow upon the like charge. The alleged offense was said to have been committed on 19th January 1914; the prisoners were apprehended on 13th May 1915; and they were not brought to trial till 17th August 1915! The charge arose out of the recovery by them, through an intermediary, of articles of jewelry stolen from a Glasgow shop, the loss of which was covered by insurance. So grateful was the Insurance Company for the skill and promptitude with which the jewels had been recovered, that they actually wrote to the Chief Constable, thanking him for "the good offices of Detective Trench," and suggesting that that officer should receive a reward! This was the reward he received.

At the trial in Edinburgh, the Judge (Lord Justice-Clerk Scott Dickson) told the jury that it was clearly proved that Trench had acted throughout with the knowledge of his chiefs, and also with innocent, nay, meritorious intent. His Lordship accordingly directed the jury to acquit both prisoners of the charge laid against them. This they did, and amid the applause of the auditors the accused were discharged. The trial may may be cited as *The Devil's Law-Case*.

Trench, rejoining his regiment, served in Egypt and in France till the end of the war. He died on the fourth anniversary of his arrest. Mr. Cook survived only two years longer the attentions of the Glasgow police. For epitaph, each deserves the congratulation of the Psalmist: "For they intended mischief against thee: and imagined such a device as they were not able to perform."

## 1925

The ten years' silence was broken by Slater himself. He managed to get smuggled out of Peterhead a letter addressed to Sir Arthur Conan Doyle. To obviate the objections of authority, it was written on a scrap of glazed paper and conveyed out of prison by the mouth of a discharged prisoner. In it the convict begged Sir Arthur to make one more effort to effect his freedom: he had served the fifteen years commonly the measure of a life-sentence. So Sir Arthur wrote to Sir John Gilmour, Secretary of State for Scotland, begging him to look personally into Slater's case, "which is likely to live in the annals of criminology"—another instance of Sir Arthur's gift of prophecy. Sir Herbert Stephen wrote an article in which he maintained "that no English judge would have allowed the case to go to a jury," and no bench of magistrates in England "would upon such evidence have ordered the destruction of a terrier alleged to have been guilty of biting somebody." After the usual official delay, Sir John intimated that he did not feel justified in interfering with the sentence. So Slater was plainly doomed to die in Peterhead.

## 1927

In July of this year William Park, the Glasgow journalist who had made a special study of the subject, published the result of his researches in a book, entitled *The Truth About Oscar Slater*. This, the first shot fired in the final battle with the forces of the Crown, registered a distinct hit. The *Morning Post* of 1st August contained, in addition to a powerful leading article on the case, a long review of the book by Edgar Wallace, which drew the attention of the general reader to the manifold mysteries with which it bristled. Of Lambie and the man in the

501

hall he writes: "Obviously she knew him; as obviously, to my mind, the murderer was in the house when she left." And of the weapon: "Nothing was said about the bloodstained chair, because it did not fit the case that had been manufactured against Slater. No questions were asked Lambie that were in any way inconvenient to the prosecution." The *Solicitor's Journal* took up the matter and urged the necessity for further investigation; other journals followed suit, and one was reminded of the brave old days of the newspaper war over the trial at Edinburgh and the Glasgow inquiry.

But pride of place in this regard belongs to the *Daily News*, which, not satisfied with urging like its contemporaries the need for investigation, determined to investigate the matter at first hand and at its own expense. Mr. Palmer was dispatched to Scotland as its representative, with full powers to go into the whole business upon the spot. I had the pleasure to meet and confer with this gentleman, to whose activities and acumen Slater very largely owed his freedom. The series of articles contributed by him to his journal, written over the pen-name of "The Pilgrim" with admirable force and clearness, are brilliant examples of journalistic efficiency. They were published daily from 16th September to 19th October, and the editor, in his summing up of the matter, observed: "We do not think that anyone can have read our special correspondent's deadly analysis day by day of the evidence in the Oscar Slater case without being convinced that this unfortunate man is really the victim of a scandalous miscarriage of justice."

The *Daily News* was not to have it all its own way. On 23rd October the *Empire News* published an interview with Lambie, which was claimed to be the most dramatic development ever recorded in a criminal case. In this she admits that she knew the man in the hall as one who was in the habit of visiting her mistress; she told the police, who said it was nonsense, and persuaded her she was mistaken. *The man was not unlike Slater*, but was better dressed and of a higher social station. A broadcast appeal to come forward and make her statement on oath left Lambie cold. She had married a man named Gillon, with whom she had emigrated to America. As she had already told so many stories I cannot see why she should have hesitated to vouch for this one, which personally I believe to be her nearest approach to truth. Meanwhile the *Daily News*, not to be outdone by the enterprise of its contemporary, had unearthed Barrowman, no longer a little girl but a middle-aged matron, from somewhere in Glasgow. She now said that she never meant more than that Slater was *like* the man, but was bullied into saying he *was* the man by the Procurator-Fiscal, in whose office she had to rehearse her evidence every day for a fortnight! Her signed statement was published in the *Daily News* on 5th November.

The reminiscences of Lambie and Barrowman were not without effect in high quarters. In reply to the old, old question: What was the Scottish Secretary going to do about it? Sir John Gilmour on the 10th gave a new and original answer: "Oscar Slater has now completed more than eighteen and a half years of his sentence, and I have felt justified in deciding to authorize his release on license." This generous gesture met with a poor return. Public opinion, as expressed in editorials and correspondence, uncharitably held that the release was an ingenious attempt to silence the demand for further investigation, now more insistent than ever before. Be that as it may, the chief end was attained: on 14th November 1927 the gates of Peterhead were opened and Slater was set free. There is no need to sentimentalize over the situation; the event is sufficiently remarkable to speak for itself.

While Slater retired into such privacy as insatiable reporters would permit him to enjoy, Sir Arthur Conan Doyle, not content with this partial victory, had sent to members of the House of Commons a circular letter, setting forth the facts of the case and urging the need for a public inquiry. Questioned in the House, the Secretary replied that the Government proposed to remit the whole matter to the new Scottish Court of Criminal Appeal, provided Parliament would pass a short Act giving retrospective effect to that statute. This was duly done, and everything now depended on the decision of the Scots judicial tribunal. At long last Slater's case would receive a fair and impartial hearing and a righteous judgement.

## 1928

### I

But before that consummation could be attained Slater's legal advisers had to sift the accumulated evidence of twenty years. Old witnesses had to be traced, old papers sought for; new material made available, fresh facts and circumstances assembled and coordinated—such a task as no other appellant has ever been called upon to face. Of these labors I myself saw something and marveled at the patience, perseverance, and ability with which they were performed. For the important duty of leading counsel in so extraordinary a cause no better choice could have been made than Mr. Craigie Aitchison, K.C., the most eminent and resourceful advocate then at the Scots Bar. Upon his experienced shoulders lay the chief burden of the appeal, in the bearing of which he was loyally assisted by Mr. J. C. Watson and Mr. J. L. Clyde, advocates, who proved themselves worthy of their calling. These gentlemen were instructed by Messrs. Norman Macpherson & Dunlop, S.S.C., Edinburgh. William Park, though not officially connected with the appeal, did yeoman service in its preparation. As I have said, unhappily he died before the successful issue to which his zeal so largely contributed.

The requisite preliminary procedure being at length completed, the first hearing of the Appeal of Oscar Slater against His Majesty's Advocate was called in the High Court of Justiciary at Edinburgh on 8th June 1928 and lasted for two days —for me a memorable occasion, recalling my old yet vivid recollections of the original trial. It was my fortune to accompany Sir Arthur Conan Doyle daily throughout the proceedings; next to the appellant himself none of the auditors was more keenly interested in the result. Slater declined to sit beside his counsel and agents in the well of the Court, preferring a place in the crowded public benches, from which with painful eagerness he strove to follow the technicalities of the proceedings. His former position in the dock was now filled by an army of Pressmen, rivaling in variety and strength that assembled on the same field in 1893 for the great battle of Ardlamont. The Judges were the Lord Justice-General (Lord Clyde), the Lord Justice-Clerk (Lord Alness), and Lords Sands, Blackburn, and Fleming. Counsel for the Crown were the Lord Advocate (the Right Hon. William Watson, K.C.) and Mr. Alexander Maitland, Advocate-Depute.

Mr. Aitchison said his application was for leave to lead further evidence and to recover certain documents. He proposed to call the appellant and to recall Helen Lambie, if she could be found. Every effort had been made to find her, but so far without success. He was going to ask the aid of the Crown to get her, as he was informed that she was in hiding. He proposed to call her former mistress, whom she had told that Miss Gilchrist said she was going to be murdered. She also told this lady that no one could get into the house in her absence except by a pre-arranged signal. A week after the crime she told the same lady that she would not know the man again, and denied that she had said anything about a signal. He wished to put in the deposition of MacBrayne, who was now dead; also the evidence at the inquiry of nine people who saw Slater between his leaving Glasgow and his sailing from Liverpool, and who said they saw nothing suspicious in his manner. As regards the alleged identification in New York, he proposed to call Slater's American counsel and agent, and the United States marshal who had him in custody. (These three gentlemen had come to Edinburgh for the purpose.) With respect to the weapon, the late Dr. John Adams, the first medical man to see the body, had expressed a most decided opinion that the injuries were inflicted with the leg of a chair. The name of Dr. Adams was not in the Crown list, and there was no recorded case of homicide in which the Crown had not called the doctor who first saw the body. His opinion could be proved by his widow and by Mr. William Roughead, with whom he had discussed the matter at the time. It was understood that Professor Littlejohn had declined to support the Crown theory of the hammer, and his report was called for. Lastly, he wished to call Sir Bernard Spilsbury, who held a very strong opinion that the hammer had nothing to do with the case, based upon the views of Dr. Adams, the description of the injuries, and actual photographs of the head.

The Court asked that a written list of the names and addresses of the proposed witnesses be submitted, and this Mr. Aitchison undertook to have prepared forthwith.

The Lord Advocate said there must be no attempt to retry the case. Only new evidence could be allowed, and mere expert opinion was inadmissible. He opposed the calling of the appellant and the production of the documents called for; also the New York identification evidence, which had been fully gone into at the trial. Professor Littlejohn made no formal report. He did not object to the Liverpool evidence.

The decision of the Court was this: they would allow the evidence of Lambie and of her former mistress, also that of Mr. Pinckley, the United States marshal; but not that of Slater's American lawyers. With respect to the medical question, they would allow the evidence of Mrs. Adams and of Mr. Roughead, but not that of Sir Bernard Spilsbury. They would allow the deposition of MacBrayne and the statements of the Liverpool witnesses. They refused to allow the evidence of the appellant to be received. For the rest, they made no order. The proceedings were then adjourned to 9th July.

## II

When Slater realized that after all he was not to be allowed to give evidence, he was neither to hold nor to bind. He set off to Glasgow where, without consulting his legal advisers, he told the reporters, who were speedily on his track, that he intended to withdraw the appeal. This announcement, published in the Press on 14th June, caused consternation to everyone concerned. Fortunately, that same day Slater was persuaded to listen to reason, and the announcement was in its turn withdrawn. But the appellant had taken the unprecedented and improper step of writing personally to the Lord Justice-General, and it was a question whether in these circumstances Mr. Aitchison would retain his brief. The affair blew over, as the incident was admittedly due solely to the appellant's acute disappointment with the Court's decision.

It should be remembered that the grievance was one of twenty years' standing. Slater was most unwillingly kept out of the witness-box at the trial by his counsel because of the attack upon his character made by the Lord Advocate in cross-examining his witnesses, and he had been refused a hearing at the Glasgow inquiry. I may add that having attended the consultations with Mr. Aitchison pending the appeal, at which Slater was present, I can attest his abiding anxiety to give evidence in his own behalf, which he never doubted he would at length be permitted to do.

## III

When the Court met on 9th July the new evidence was first led. Lambie, having preferred the seclusion of her home in Peoria, Illinois, to the publicity of the High Court, was not forthcoming; and in her regrettable absence, her former mistress could not competently be examined. It fell, the evidence, into four sections: (1) Dr. Adams's theory of the weapon, (2) the testimony of MacBrayne, (3) that as to the openness of Slater's movements in Liverpool, and (4) that relating to the "identification" in the corridor at New York.

Mrs. Adams stated that she remembered her husband being called to Miss Gilchrist's house on the night of the murder. He told her that in his opinion it (the murder) was done by a chair; he expressed surprise at not being cited as a witness at the trial. William Roughead stated that he edited the report of the trial. While writing the book, he was informed that Dr. Adams held a certain view as to the manner in which the deed was done, and in February 1910 he had an interview with that gentleman by appointment and discussed the matter with him. Witness made notes at the time of Dr. Adams's views, which he incorporated in the Introduction to his report. The passage referred to was as follows:—

> Close to the head, and facing it, stood an ordinary chair. Having examined the body and ascertained that life was extinct, Dr. Adams's attention was attracted by the condition of this chair. He observed that the left back leg, farthest from the head, was soaked with blood, and that the *inner* aspect of each front leg was spotted with blood. The back leg, in his opinion, had evidently been in contact with the wounds. With this instrument, in his view, the injuries to the head had been inflicted. In addition to the appearance of the chair, he inferred that it had been

so used from the character of the injuries, the comparatively small quantity of blood near the head, and the restricted area of the blood-stains. In the opinion of Dr. Adams, the assault was committed by a few heavy, swinging blows from the back leg of this chair, the assailant, while wielding it, stamping upon the body, and thereby fracturing the ribs. The hands of the assailant would thus be clean, and the seat of the chair would be interposed between his person and the spurting blood at the moment of impact.

Witness produced two letters written to him by Dr. Adams, one approving the references to his views contained in the page proofs of the Introduction sent him for revisal; the other acknowledging a copy of the book as published. Witness described a further interview had by him with Dr. Adams in March 1911, when that gentleman, having then read the report of the trial, adhered to his original opinion. Cross-examined by the Lord Advocate, his impression was that Dr. Adams had not at the time communicated his views to either the Crown or the defense. The chair was shown in a photograph in the first edition of his book, facing page 182. It was that upon which Miss Gilchrist had apparently been sitting. The back leg was described by Dr. Adams as actually "dripping" with blood. The examination made of the head by the doctor was visual; he did not discuss the injuries in a technical way with witness, but demonstrated with a chair how he thought the blows had been struck. Reexamined by Mr. Aitchison, Dr. Adams had all the relevant facts before him and had read the reports of the post-mortem.

Duncan Lee, clerk in the Crown Office, produced the depositions of Adams, Lambie, and Barrowman, which were sent to America; also that of Superintendent Orr, as to Slater's having signed the hotel register in his own name. Andrew Sandilands, clerk to the late Sheriff Gardner Millar, produced the signed statement of MacBrayne, taken at the Glasgow inquiry. Only he himself, the witness, and the Sheriff were present. Superintendent Duckworth of the Liverpool police stated that he forwarded to the Glasgow authorities before the trial all the information obtained regarding Slater's movements in Liverpool, as to which witness produced the statements of thirteen witnesses taken by him. (Of these witnesses one only, Forsyth, who got the reward, was called at the trial!) John Pinckley, assistant chief-deputy-marshal for the Southern District of New York, stated that at the extradition proceedings there he was instructed to convey Slater from the Tombs Prison to the Commissioner's Court. Slater was handcuffed to his left arm. In the corridor they passed a group, including Lambie and Barrowman, and Mr. Fox, attorney for the British authorities in the extradition proceedings. He heard Mr. Fox say: "Is that the man?" or "That's the man!"

IV

On the conclusion of the new evidence Mr. Aitchison explained to the Court that everything possible had been done to procure the attendance of Lambie. A representative had been sent to America to induce her to come, but she declined to do so, and there was no machinery by which she could be brought. The evidence which depended upon her presence could therefore not be led. He then proceeded to address the Court upon the whole matter. It was obvious, he said, that so far as the appeal rested on fact, the crucial question was that of identification. He maintained that the evidence as to that was altogether insufficient as a basis for a verdict in a case of murder. After dealing with the discrepancies and contradictions of the evidence relating to "the watcher," he reviewed that of the three vital witnesses: Adams, Lambie, and Barrowman. Lambie knew the man who passed her in the hall, otherwise why did she not challenge him, and why did she show no anxiety as to her aged mistress? In New York she was an untruthful and insolent witness; in Edinburgh, false and unscrupulous. Her "identification" in the corridor was a travesty. Having commended the fairness of Adams's evidence, he criticized that of Barrowman, showing the different accounts of "the man's" appearance given by her in Glasgow, in New York, and at Edinburgh. As regards the value these girls attached to the virtue of an oath, he instanced their sworn testimony that during the voyage to New York they never talked about the case. There could be no doubt that had the evidence of MacBrayne been before the jury, the Crown would not have secured a conviction. He (counsel) would rather not characterize the action of the Crown in failing to call him as a witness. All suspicions as to Slater's movements in Liverpool were now disproved; that information was in the possession of the Crown at the trial, and it also was withheld from the jury. Commenting on the failure to call Dr. Adams, whose evidence, he argued, for all they knew might have turned the scale in the accused's favor, he admitted it was only now available at second hand, but their Lordships would not assume it could not have been corroborated by expert testimony, had he been allowed to call it. There was no excuse for the failure of the Crown to call Dr. Adams. Mr. Aitchison then exhaustively examined the alleged identification by Adams, Lambie, and Barrowman. If Lambie were negligible and Adams inconclusive, they were left with Barrowman as to this crucial point; and in view of the notorious liability to mistake in this class of evidence, he submitted that was not sufficient. As to the alibi, it was never fairly put before the jury. The failure to call MacBrayne would alone entitle the appellant to succeed. It was the best identification in the case, and his non-calling, unless inadvertent, was a fraud

511

both on the accused and on the jury. He next considered the attack made by the Lord Advocate upon the accused's character, which struck at the very root of the criminal administration in Scotland; and his searching review of his Lordship's address to the jury was even more damaging than the analysis of "The Pilgrim." Turning to Lord Guthrie's charge, the jury were told that the accused "maintained himself by the ruin of men and on the ruin of women," of which there was no proof; the evidence was that he was a gambler and kept a mistress. Again: "We do not know where he was born, who his parents are, or where he was brought up"—matters no more relevant to a charge of murder than the birthplace, et cetera, of the jury. But the most vital thing Lord Guthrie said was this:—

> A man of that kind has not the presumption of innocence in his favor which is a form in the case of every man, but a reality in the case of the ordinary man. Not only is every man presumed to be innocent, but the ordinary man, in a case of brutal ferocity like the present, has a strong presumption in his favor.

That direction was supported neither by principle nor by authority, and could not be justified. Finally, he submitted that individually the grounds of appeal were strong; but collectively they were overwhelming. To quash the conviction would be an act of simple justice to the appellant. The Court then rose.

## V

The Lord Advocate's reply for the Crown struck one as rather half-hearted—it lacked the glowing sense of conviction which informed Mr. Aitchison's masterly address. His Lordship's position was invidious; he had no previous connection with the case, and yet must accept responsibility for, and seek to condone, the deeds and misdeeds of the prosecution. With regard to the new evidence, he could find no trace of any statement by, or communication from, Dr. Adams made to the Crown. His theory would not have stood the test of cross-examination. As to the corridor incident and the Liverpool evidence, Slater knew all that at the time, and could have informed his law agent. His Lordship was unable to say why MacBrayne was not on the Crown list; he had no reason to believe that the then Lord Advocate knew anything about the matter. As for the identification, there was plenty of evidence; the jury had Adams, Lambie, and Barrowman, and they were entitled to believe any of the three. It was supported by that relating to the watcher. No objection was taken at the trial to the Lord Advocate's questions as to the accused's mode of life. The opening of the speech for the prosecution was merely a dramatic one; the point was quite fairly put later in the address. With respect to the exceptions taken to the Judge's charge, their Lordships had heard only isolated phrases; the jury heard the whole. Taking all the passages together they, the jury, could not be held to have been misled.

The remainder of the address took the form of a discussion, the Lord Advocate having to reply to a running fire of commentary from the Bench. Thus did his Lordship dispose in two hours of a case which had taken Mr. Aitchison, a master of verbal economy, fourteen hours to state. The Court adjourned.

## VI

The Court disposed of the appeal in twenty-five minutes. On 20th July the Lord Justice-General pronounced judgment. The findings were unanimous. Except in the final result, these were a disappointment to the appellant's supporters. The questions for the Court's decision were: (1) Whether the jury's verdict was unreasonable or unsupported by evidence; (2) whether any new facts had been disclosed material to the issue; (3) whether the appellant had suffered prejudice by nondisclosure of evidence known to the Crown; and (4) whether the verdict was vitiated in respect of misdirection by the presiding Judge? On the first three heads the appeal failed; on the fourth, the Court held that the conviction must be quashed, which was accordingly done. And so ended the twenty years' contention.

Now it was obvious from the debate that some of their Lordships were much impressed by the arguments of Mr. Aitchison. For example, the Lord Justice-Clerk observed that the use made by the Lord Advocate (Ure) of evidence as to the accused's mode of life was "unjustifiable"; and of the evidence of MacBrayne, that "its importance was surely undeniable." Yet the judgment dismisses it, with the rest of the new evidence, as "immaterial." Their Lordships admit the case to be "one of great difficulty," and characterize Mr. Aitchison's criticisms of the identity evidence as "most formidable"; so it would seem that the unanimous result was arrived at by a compromise.

There is neither use nor satisfaction in going over again the old ground. As Sir Arthur remarked of the decision: "It is done now, and we must be thankful for what we have got." Such also was the sentiment expressed by Mrs. Gillon, *née* Lambie, when informed at Peoria of the result of the appeal: "I am glad it is all over." I have no doubt that here at least she spoke the truth.

## VII

But the Secretary of State for Scotland was not yet in a position to echo the voice from Peoria. When questioned in the House on 23rd July as to the Government's intentions with regard to compensating the successful appellant, he replied that "the person concerned" might put forward a claim. Whereupon "the person" indignantly wrote to the Press that so far as he, Oscar Slater, was concerned, "there will never be a bill for compensation sent in." Questioned again as to this, the answer of the Secretary was that one must not believe all one reads in the papers. On 4th August the Minister wrote personally to "the person," offering him £6000 "in consequence of your wrongful conviction in May 1909 and subsequent imprisonment," and asking whether he wished payment to be made direct or into his bank account. Without consulting his legal advisers Slater, with his wonted impulsiveness, accepted the Government's offer and the money was duly paid. Had the settlement of this transaction been carried through by his law agents, it is likely that he would have obtained a larger payment. In any case, the unseemly situation which arose regarding the costs of the appeal would have been avoided.

The matter stood thus: Sir Arthur had generously guaranteed expenses up to £1000; £750 had been raised by public subscription, so there remained a balance of £250 to be met. This Slater steadfastly refused to pay, doubtless holding that, in the grim words of Mr. Kipling, he had already "paid in full." Probably Government intended £5000 for solatium and £1000 for costs, but the matter was effected in so unbusinesslike a manner that this was not stipulated. Be that as it may, when Slater recovered from a certain newspaper, which had libeled him, damages of £250, this sum was promptly arrested by Sir Arthur's lawyer. Slater waxed exceeding wroth, but Sir Arthur got the cash.

## VIII

Of the many mysteries presented by the Slater case not the least strange is the fact that the Glasgow police never thought of applying to it those finger-print tests which are a commonplace in such investigations. These had been officially in use for six years, though not a word was said about them at the trial or elsewhere. The circumstances afforded peculiar facilities for the exercise of the art. The murderer had handled the matchbox, the gas-bracket, the dispatch-box and its contents; there was thus ample provision for its application. Nay, more; I happen to have a "close-up" photograph of the fire-place in Miss Gilchrist's room, taken at the time and showing the blood-splashed grate and fender, together with the famous chair, on the back of which is plainly to be seen the imprint of what appears to be a bloody hand. I said so in my last Introduction; it interested Sheriff Wilton, K.C., who is an authority on the subject; and in a couple of articles contributed by him to the *Glasgow Herald* (26th and 27th December 1933), entitled: "Conviction by Fingerprints," the learned author mentions the case. He says he had shown my photograph to divers other experts, who were clearly of opinion that the mark was that of a right hand, holding the chair from behind. Unfortunately, it is on too small a scale to serve any useful purpose.

As regards the remanent problems of the case and the possibility of their ultimate solution, Sir Arthur Conan Doyle, in his last letter to me, written shortly before his passing, stated his opinion thus: "I think when A. B. dies a flood of evidence may come out. I think, also, when Helen Lambie dies she may leave a full confession. Only along these lines do I see any hope of clearing the mystery." Should Sir Arthur once again prove a true prophet, and if I can manage to survive the keepers of the secret, I may yet have a fifth and final word to say about the Slater case.

# THE MERRETT MYSTERY

*I know that death hath ten thousand several doors*
*For men to make their exits; and 'tis found*
*They go on such strange geometrical hinges,*
*You may open them both ways.*

*The Duchess of Malfi,* Act IV. sc. 2

ON THE EVENING of Wednesday, 17th March 1926, I happened to be dining with friends in Buckingham Terrace, in the West End of Edinburgh. No sooner were we seated at table than my hostess, aware of my perennial interest in matters criminal, portentously announced that there had been a murder in the Terrace that morning! Such an incident occurring in so respectable a residential quarter was appetizing indeed. Although I myself lived in the immediate vicinage I had heard nothing about it, and naturally asked on what authority the statement was made. The news, I was told, had been delivered at the door by an errand boy, in supplement to his usual

517

"messages." It was to the effect that a lady had just been found shot in her flat at No. 31, and that the police were in possession of the house. But the boy, in the optimistic enthusiasm of his youth, had, it appeared, overstated the fact. According to the subsequent official version, it was a case of attempted suicide; the victim still survived and was then in the Royal Infirmary, although her recovery was not expected. Finally, the question seemed settled by an obituary notice, published by her relatives in the *Scotsman* on 2nd April, which read as follows:—"MERRETT.—At Edinburgh, on the 1st inst., Bertha Merrett, third daughter of the late W. H. Milner, of Manchester. (By accident.)"

To which of these three attributions—that of the message boy, of the police, or of the family—Mrs. Merrett's death was actually due formed well-nigh a year later the subject of a protracted investigation, whereof it is my present purpose to furnish some account. I may mention that I attended the trial; and should I be able to arouse in the reader any of the interest with which I heard this most remarkable and exceptional case, I shall not have written in vain.

I

Mrs. Merrett at the date of her untimely end, howsoever brought about, was in her fifty-sixth year. Her father was a well-to-do wine merchant in Manchester. Her eldest sister was the wife of Mr. Walter Penn, an artist. Some twenty years before, while on a voyage to Egypt with her sister, Bertha Milner met an electrical engineer named John Alfred Merrett, then on his way to New Zealand. They became engaged, and subsequently she went out to him there to be married. The only child of the marriage, John Donald Merrett, was born in North Island on 17th August 1908. Thereafter they moved to St. Petersburg, where Merrett pursued his calling. The climate did not suit the child, so Mrs. Merrett took him to Switzerland, leaving her husband in Russia. Then came the Great War; and Mrs. Merrett devoted herself to Red Cross and kindred activities. When the war was over she returned to New Zealand, settling in South Island, where the boy was sent to school. Her husband had disappeared; she believed him to have been killed in the Russian Revolution, but he was afterwards said to be alive in India. Be that as it may, the sole care of the boy now devolved on her. That she was devotedly attached to her son above the common way of mothers; that she lived, worked, and planned for him alone, clearly appeared from the testimony of her friends and relations. In 1924, when he was sixteen, she brought him back to England to finish his education. A clever, well-grown lad of engaging manners, she destined him for the diplomatic service, and entered him at Malvern College, she herself taking up house at Reading. He remained at Malvern for a year. His work was described as brilliant, but unhappily for the anxious mother, his conduct was less satisfactory. So, on the advice of a scholastic friend acquainted with the circumstances, she decided not to send the lad to Oxford as she had purposed. It was deemed wiser that he should attend Edinburgh University, a non-resident college, and that she should take a house for them both in that city, where she could keep him under her own eye. So mother and son came to Scotland at Christmastide 1925, which they spent at Melrose Hydropathic; thence to Edinburgh, where they took rooms first at No. 7 Mayfield Road, removing thereafter to a boarding-house at Nos. 33 and 35 Palmerston Place.

Meanwhile Mrs. Merrett had been looking about for a furnished house; she found what she required at No. 31 Buckingham Terrace, a "converted" mansion, in which she took the first flat for four months, at a rent of £50, paying £25 in advance. On Wednesday, 10th March 1926, she entered upon her fatal tenancy. The flat, which had been the drawing-room floor of the original house, consisted of a sitting-room and bedroom to the front, and a bedroom, kitchen, and bathroom to the back. Between these was a hall, containing presses and a coal-cellar. In the modern fashion, the architect had made no provision for servants' accommodation, and after some difficulty Mrs. Merrett engaged a daily maid, who attended between 9 a.m. and noon. She was to begin her duties on 10th March. A young married woman living apart from her husband, her name was Henrietta Sutherland.

During her brief sojourn in Edinburgh Mrs. Merrett made several friends. Some of these I happened to know, and they all spoke in praise of her personal charm and manifold accomplishments. Cultured, musical, intelligent; a keen bridge-player and in general a social acquisition, it was obvious that her real object in life was her boy's welfare. Her oldest friend, who had known her for thirty years—the lady to whom she was writing at the very moment she received her injury and whom I also knew—paid a warm tribute to her character and gifts. At the trial another old friend testified: "Everything she did, she did to perfection"; and her sister said of her in the witness-box: "She was a splendid woman." Further, Mrs. Merrett had an excellent business head and managed her affairs with wisdom and discretion. Although her son on attaining majority would under his grandfather's will succeed to a considerable fortune, her own income amounted to little over £700 a year. Out of this she had to defray the cost of living and to provide for the boy's education—which under modern conditions took some doing. She allowed him 10s. a week for pocket-money, but this sum, as we shall see, was hardly commensurate with his expenditure.

Although by the generosity of the Crown as little as possible was brought out at the trial as to Merrett's undesirable qualities, it is otherwise established that during the last months of her life he habitually deceived his mother. This course of deception appears to have begun at Palmerston Place, where Mrs. Merrett occupied a bedroom in one house and her son slept next door. Thus, when he had said good-night and gone ostensibly to bed, he was free to set out upon his own amusements. At Buckingham Terrace, where he occupied the front bedroom with a balcony, it was his practice, having put his shoes outside his door and locked it, to descend from the window by means of a rope, with which by day the window was protected upon the pretense that he walked in his sleep! The chief resort of his choice was a dancing-hall in Picardy Place, rejoicing in the dreadful designation of the Dunedin Palais de Danse, where as a regular patron he was known as "Donnie." The establishment has since been closed. With one of the instructresses, Miss Betty Christie, he spent much of his time, "booking out" that young lady at 30s. a night and 15s. an afternoon; presenting her with two gem rings, for which he paid respectively £2 and £2. 5s.; and taking her about on a motorcycle, which he bought, second-hand, on 6th March for £28. One does not need to have been bred a chartered accountant to perceive that Merrett had some further fund to draw upon than his official allowance of 10s. a week. What was the nature of the means employed by him to meet these "extras" we shall hear later.

That his mother knew nothing about all this is plain. He had matriculated at the University, she had paid his college and class fees, and he was supposed to be attending there daily. But though he left each morning with his notebooks his attendance was irregular, and after the beginning of February—a month before the removal to Buckingham Terrace—he ceased to go near the College at all. And his mother thought he was suffering from the effects of studying too hard! "Donald is doing well at the University," she wrote to her English banker, "and is quite settled down to the life here." Did he not keep for her satisfaction a careful account of his weekly expenditure, including his contributions to church collections? What more could the most exacting mother require?

## II

On the morning of Wednesday, 17th March, Mrs. Sutherland arrived at the flat about 9 a.m. Everything was as usual; Mrs. Merrett, in her customary good health and spirits, opened the door to her; mother and son had already breakfasted; and the maid went into the kitchen to take off her hat and coat. She next entered the sitting-room to clear the table. Mrs. Merrett was putting away the table silver in an open writing bureau, which stood against the wall near the door. The table was close to it, in the center of the room. By the time the maid had finished, Mrs. Merrett was taking her writing materials out of the bureau—she was accustomed to write at the table, the desk of the bureau being uncomfortably high. After washing the dishes the maid reentered the sitting-room to "do" the fire. Mrs. Merrett was then writing at the table with her back to the bureau, which was somewhat on her right. Merrett was sitting reading in a chair on the other side of the room, opposite his mother. (To appreciate the relative position of the parties the reader should bear in mind the smallness of the room—6 yards long by 5½ yards broad—which had been cut out of the original drawing-room, the rest of which formed the front bedroom and part of the hall. The distance between their respective chairs was 11 feet.) Seeing them both thus occupied the maid did not "do" the fire, but leaving the door open, got some coals from the cellar and then proceeded to tackle the kitchen fire. Just as she knelt down to the grate the sound of a pistol-shot rang through the house, and she stood up in astonishment. Next followed immediately a scream, and then a thud, as of someone falling heavily. She continued to stand still where she had risen. A few minutes later Merrett came into the kitchen and said to her: "Rita, my mother has shot herself!" He seemed very much upset. (Such is Mrs. Sutherland's account of the catastrophe, as sworn to by her in the witness-box. We shall presently find that the statements made earlier by her to the police vary.) As he approached the kitchen she heard some books fall, which she afterwards saw lying in the hall. The maid expressed her amazement, saying that Mrs. Merrett seemed "quite all right" when she spoke to her that morning. He replied "that he had been wasting his mother's money, and he thought she was worried over that." The two went into the sitting-room. Mrs. Merrett lay on her back on the floor between the table and the bureau; the chair on which she had sat was overturned, and she was bleeding profusely from a wound in the head. The maid noticed upon the top corner of the bureau, nearest the door, a pistol, which she had never seen before.

Now in these circumstances surely the first and natural thing to do was to summon a doctor. What they did was to telephone for the police. Merrett asked the maid to help him to lift his mother, who was unconscious, on to the sofa; but she wisely advised that nothing be touched till the arrival of the authorities. He then proposed that they should wait downstairs at the street door, which they did. Presently two policemen came with an ambulance, and Mrs. Merrett was taken to the Infirmary.

I wish to say nothing disrespectful of any members of a force for which I have in general a high admiration, but the choice of these two constables, Middlemiss and Izatt, who were first upon the scene was, to say the least, unfortunate. Doubtless they would have made a fine appearance in the chorus of *The Pirates*, but as investigators of a possible crime they were lamentably incompetent. Merrett told them, in reply to their questions, that he had been reading on the other side of the room from where his mother was writing; that on hearing the report of a firearm he turned round, and saw his mother falling on the floor; and that *"he went in to see Mrs. Sutherland in the kitchen,* and then they telephoned for the police." Asked why his mother should shoot herself? he replied: "Just money matters." Mrs. Sutherland, being asked what she knew of the matter, said *she was working in the kitchen at the time, when she heard a report like a shot, "and young Merrett came in and told her that his mother had shot herself."* The most striking ineptitude displayed by these constables was in regard to the position of the pistol, which Mrs. Sutherland swore was upon the top of the bureau, where Merrett himself afterwards said that he had placed it. The one who picked up the blood-stained weapon, wrapped it in a piece of paper, and put it in his pocket, was quite unable to say whether he lifted it from the floor or from the bureau. The other said that the pistol lay beside Mrs. Merrett's body, and that he *saw* his colleague lift it from the floor.

Having seen his mother safely in the Infirmary, where he gave as a reason for her rash act, succinctly, "money matters," Merrett called at the Dunedin and booked out Miss Christie for the day. He took her on his motorcycle to Queensferry, where he told her his mother had shot herself that morning with his own pistol. "He told me," says Miss Christie, "he had been sitting in the room at the time, and that *the maid was in the kitchen.*" They returned to the empty flat, from which Merrett telephoned to his friend Scott, a motor driver, with whom he wished to confer. To him he explained that his mother had shot herself. "He told me," says Scott, "he was in the room sitting by the fire when he heard the shot and saw his mother falling. *He said he had gone through to the kitchen and told the maid about it.*" These explicit statements of Merrett on the day of the occurrence fully establish, as will be noticed, the truth of Mrs. Sutherland's original account of her position when she heard the shot. But now comes one of the most inexplicable incidents in this strange case.

That same forenoon, to Mrs. Sutherland, left alone in the flat, entered Detective-Inspector Fleming of the C.I.D., accompanied by Detective-Sergeant Henderson. "She told me," says the former, "she had been in the kitchen about half-past nine and heard a shot, *and on going into the lobby she saw Mrs. Merrett fall off her chair and on to the floor, and a pistol falling out of her hand*"! The detective-officers were perfectly satisfied; here was a suicide committed in the very presence of two witnesses; there was nothing more to be done. Still, they had a look round the room, and on the open bureau they saw, laid out as if for inspection, two letters from the Clydesdale Bank to the injured lady, intimating that her bank account was a few pounds overdrawn. They also noticed on the table an unfinished letter, which Mrs. Merrett was writing at the time of the occurrence to her old friend Mrs. Anderson in Stirling. It was a friendly letter, telling of her difficulty in getting a maid, and that they were now comfortably established in the flat. *The letter was free from blood-stains*. It did not occur to these experts in crime that this letter was a valuable piece of evidence, the writing of the last word before the shot having a very material bearing on the question of the writer's suicide. They left it where it lay, and departed to report to headquarters. As the result of their report the Superintendent of the Royal Infirmary was instructed by the Chief Constable that the patient was "a prisoner charged with attempted suicide, and was requested to notify the police of the date and hour of her discharge, so that she might be taken into custody." Thus the matter was, officially, closed.

The discrepant accounts of the tragedy furnished by Mrs. Sutherland, first, to the two constables and, secondly, to the two detective-officers, struck even the official mind as

unsatisfactory; and four days after the event two other constables, Watt and Gibson, were sent to interview her in order
to clear up the point. They took from her a third statement, in
the course of which she said: "When working at the [kitchen]
grate I heard a shot and a sound as if someone had fallen. Then
the boy [Merrett] came to the kitchen door and informed me
that his mother had shot herself, and requested me to phone
the police." Asked why she had told Inspector Fleming that
she had actually *seen* Mrs. Merrett falling from her chair and
the pistol from her hand, she replied that she might have
said so, "as she was excited at the time." Incredible as it may
appear, these skilled seekers after truth never even asked her
whether in fact she had so seen; they left it at that.

### III

Meantime at the Infirmary Mrs. Merrett was confined in Ward
3, being that in which would-be suicides were kept secure
behind locked doors and barred windows. She was found to be
suffering from a pistol-shot in the right ear, and her wound was
treated as accords. An X-ray examination disclosed the presence of a small bullet embedded in the base of the skull; it was
impossible to operate. It appears to be the practice in such
cases as hers was assumed to be, that no one must speak to the
patient about the cause or nature of the injury; so throughout
the duration of her illness she was never told what was the
matter with her or why she was in the Infirmary! She became
the victim of a conspiracy of silence which, in the mysterious
circumstances of the case, was most regrettable. When she recovered consciousness on the night of her admission her first
question to the doctor in charge was: What was the cause of
the pain in her ear of which she complained? "Oh," said the
doctor soothingly, "you have had a little accident." Next day

she again asked him the reason of her suffering; "could she not see an ear specialist?" But no information was vouchsafed.

Of the nursing sister, that first night, she inquired: "What has happened? Why am I here? It is so extraordinary; I cannot understand it." The sister replied, officially, that she didn't know; but the woman in her being stronger than the nurse, she added: could not the patient tell her? Mrs. Merrett then said: "I was sitting writing at the time, when suddenly a bang went off in my head like a pistol." "Was there not a pistol there?" suggested the sister; whereupon Mrs. Merrett in great surprise exclaimed: "No; was there?" Asked further whether she was certain she was writing when this occurred? she answered: "Yes; quite sure. Donald can tell you. He was standing beside me, waiting to post the letter." This conversation, which was overheard, and later corroborated, by Nurse Innes, was forthwith reported by Sister Grant to the doctor. Dr. Holcombe then for the first time asked the patient how the "little accident" happened. "I was sitting down writing letters," said she, "and my son Donald was standing beside me. I said: '*Go away, Donald, and don't annoy me*'; and the next I heard was a kind of explosion, and I don't remember anything more." So significant did this statement seem to the doctor that he at once communicated it to the police.

Next day Inspector Fleming, who had charge of the case, called at the Infirmary and saw Dr. Holcombe, who told him that the lady was dangerously ill, but yet fully conscious—this with a view to her dying deposition being taken. It is well-nigh incredible that not only did Fleming not see and question the patient then and there, but although she continued conscious and conversable for another six days, nothing more was done in the matter, and no statement whatever—let alone dying deposition—was taken from her at all! Of the unfortunate infallibility of the police when once the official mind is made up about a case, I know no more glaring instance than this—

unless it be the persistence with which in the affair of Oscar Slater the Glasgow police clung convulsively to the false clue of the wrong brooch. That same day Dr. Holcombe first met Merrett, then on a visit of condolence to his mother, and asked him for an account of what had taken place. He replied that "his mother was sitting down writing letters, and she said to him: '*Go away, Donald, and don't annoy me*'; that he went over to the corner of the room, and the next he heard was a shot; and that he looked round and saw his mother falling to the ground, with a revolver falling from her hand." The coincidence of these accounts by the mother and the son, *with one vital exception*, is striking.

The reader may recall that on the afternoon of the occurrence Merrett and his friends Christie and Scott were together in the flat. Thence the three proceeded in a taxi to the Infirmary, where Merrett asked Sister Grant whether his mother was "still alive"? Informed of her condition, he asked the sister, "if his mother got better, *not to tell her what had happened, as he did not wish her to know anything about it*." So he, too, joined in the conspiracy of silence. At his interview with Dr. Holcombe at the Infirmary Merrett was warned by the doctor that his mother was very seriously ill, although she had "a fighting chance" for her life. "So it's still on the cards that she will recover?" was the comment of her affectionate son. Dr. Holcombe said that in view of the patient's grave condition her relatives should be informed, but Merrett said that they were on bad terms: it was no use sending for them, they wouldn't come. So no word was sent to her two sisters of her perilous state. It is remarkable that though Mrs. Merrett had several friends in Edinburgh, her son told none of them that she was lying dangerously ill in the Infirmary, and as a matter of fact the first they heard of the matter was the announcement of her death in the *Scotsman*.

Merrett, with a natural repugnance to living in the flat,

had taken a room in the County Hotel, Lothian Road. On one of his rare visits to the Infirmary, Sister Grant remarked that, should "anything happen" in the night, she supposed she could get him at Buckingham Terrace? He hesitated, and said he was "staying with friends." "What is the address?" she asked, and he named the hotel. "Shall I find you there any time I want you?" He stepped out to consult his girlfriend, whom he had left in the corridor. "Betty," said he, "what is the number of the Dunedin Palais?" and having learned it, he told the sister she would get him there at any time up to 1 a.m.

One friend of the poor lady had been advised of her situation: Mrs. Hill, who in response to a telegram from Mrs. Merrett, sent by Donald at her request, came at once from Brighton, arriving in Edinburgh on the morning of Friday, 19th March. From Merrett Mrs. Hill was amazed to learn that his mother had shot herself, *having heard from her banker that her account was overdrawn by £20;* that she had done so in his presence and with his own pistol; that he had been beside her, when she said: "Go further back. I cannot write; you overlean my shoulder"; that he did so, heard a shot, and saw his mother fall. He then took Mrs. Hill to the Infirmary and left her. That lady, having been duly warned by the sister to say nothing to Mrs. Merrett about the cause of her "accident" or the nature of her injury, was allowed to visit the patient. Mrs. Merrett was delighted to see her and thanked her for coming. Then she put again her unanswered question: "Why am I here? What has happened to me?" Mrs. Hill, mindful of the injunction to secrecy, replied: "You have had a fall." "No," said the patient, "I have not had a fall. I was writing a letter to Mrs. Anderson, and a pistol went off under my ear." The conversation continued: "Did you see a pistol?"—"No."—"Did you handle one?"—"No."—"Was there one there?"—"No." Not wishing to excite her, Mrs. Hill gave her a drink and changed the subject. Mrs. Merrett asked her to write to her sister; also to go to the flat for money for her own expenses. "You know my little purse?" said she; "there are £6 in it; take what you want to go on with."

Now Mrs. Hill, although she did not tell her friend, had to return to London that night, and wished to hear more of the matter from Merrett before she did so. He had promised to come back for her at lunch-time, but failed to appear; she waited some hours in vain and then returned to the hotel, whence she rang up the Infirmary at intervals without getting hold of him. Sister Grant referred her to his spiritual home: the Dunedin Palais de Danse, where she was equally unsuccessful. Mrs. Hill then telegraphed to her friend's sister, Mrs. Penn, who with her husband was on the Riviera. They at once set out for Scotland, and in London heard from Mrs. Hill on her return so much as she knew of the mystery of Mrs. Merrett's injury and illness.

The Penns reached Edinburgh on the morning of the 24th, exactly a week after the shooting. Mrs. Merrett welcomed her sister with joy. She asked Mrs. Penn to get her an ear specialist; the Infirmary people said she had had a fall, but she didn't believe it. "She said she was sitting at the table writing, when a sudden explosion went off in her head"—to which she added the arresting words: "as if Donald had shot me." Mrs. Penn replied that of course that was impossible. Mrs. Merrett then asked her to get a present for Sister Grant, who had been so good to her; to go to the flat for her fur coat; to live there meanwhile "and look after Donald," etc., all which Mrs. Penn promised to do.

Next day, the 25th, Mrs. Merrett was able to sign a check for £5 for Mrs. Hill's expenses, being supported in bed to that end—her left side was paralyzed as the result of her injury. Late that night she became delirious; on the 26th, incoherent; on 27th, unconscious, in which state she continued until she died early in the morning of Thursday, 1st April, a fortnight after the infliction of her wound. The cause of death was certified as basal meningitis, following a bullet wound in the cranium.

That day a post-mortem examination of the body was made by Professor Harvey Littlejohn, of Edinburgh University, in presence of Dr. Douglas Kerr, his assistant, and of Dr. Holcombe. They found in the outer part of the right ear a small perforating wound, and behind this a larger wound, which passed into the skull. On removing the skull cap the brain membranes were found to be inflamed; the brain was uninjured, but embedded in the bone of the base of the skull was a nickel-plated bullet. The report concludes:—

> The direction of the wound, judging by the external wounds and the position of the bullet where found, was horizontal and slightly from behind forwards, the bullet lying about an inch anterior to the external wound. . . . There was nothing to indicate the distance at which the discharge of the weapon took place, whether from a few inches or a greater distance. So far as the position of the wound is concerned, the case is consistent with suicide. There is some difficulty in attributing it to accident, although such a view cannot be wholly excluded.

On 3rd April Mrs. Merrett was buried in Piershill Cemetery, in a grave bought for her by her sister. But the mystery of her tragic fate was not, as we shall see, buried with her.

IV

In common with everyone who knew Mrs. Merrett's sterling character, high courage, and religious principles, Mrs. Penn from the first refused for a moment to believe that her sister had committed suicide. On Friday, 26th March, in the nurses' room at the Infirmary, Mr. Penn, his wife, Merrett, and Mr. Jenks (Mrs. Merrett's man of business, who had been wired for to London) being present, Mrs. Penn "asked Donald if he could explain matters," *i.e.* give his own opinion as to the circumstances in which his mother received her injury. "He [Merrett] said he had not shot his mother." Such is the lady's report of what, for all concerned, must have been a painful interview. Her husband's version of what passed on this occasion is more dramatic. "When she [Mrs. Penn] was sitting down she looked across at Donald, who was on one of the settees, and she said: 'Donald, didn't you do it?' and Donald said: 'No, auntie, I did not do it, *but if you like I will confess*'! I said to him at once: 'What a ridiculous thing, boy! You cannot do a thing like that.''' It was then proposed that they should adjourn to the flat for the purpose of letting Merrett reconstruct the position of matters when the shooting occurred. He repeated his story of "Don't lean over me, Donald; I cannot write while you are there"; and how he had then gone to the other side of the room, had heard a shot, and saw his mother falling off her chair. "Well," continues Mr. Penn, "we could not make any more out of that." "The suggestion was," says Mrs. Penn, "that the pistol was in the secretaire [bureau] drawer, and that it might have been taken out [by Mrs. Merrett] in some papers and gone off accidentally."

Mrs. Penn fulfilled her promise to her dying sister. She and her husband went to live in the flat, where they were joined by Merrett. There they all remained until the end of the tenancy in June. That her undertaking to "look after Donald" proved to be no sinecure we shall see hereafter. On 30th March Mr. Penn found on the sitting-room floor near the bow window, 6 or 8 feet in front of the spot where Mrs. Merrett had been sitting when shot, an empty cartridge case, and communicated the fact to the police. This stimulated Inspector Fleming to further investigation. He called at the flat, saw Merrett, and took from him a statement—the first time he was officially questioned. He said he bought the pistol because they thought of going abroad at the Easter holidays. "When in Palmerston Place she got on to me for spending too much money. She also got on to me for going out too much and neglecting my lessons." On the morning of the tragedy she got a letter from the Clydesdale Bank, intimating the overdrawal of her account.

> After breakfast I went into my room, which adjoins the dining-room, and mother got the dishes removed. When I returned to the dining-room mother was sitting at the table writing. When I saw an envelope my mother had addressed to Mrs. Anderson, 64 Murray Place, *Edinburgh*, I pointed out the mistake [Edinburgh for Stirling] and she said: "Go away, you worry me."

He repeats his former account of what happened, and continues:—

> About noon on Saturday, 13th March, I had the pistol and loaded it with six cartridges, one being in the breech and the safety catch on. I was going to the Braids *to shoot rabbits*. I wanted to take it on the Sunday morning, but she took it from me, and put it in the small drawer in the bureau. *I think* I told my mother to be careful, that it was loaded. I never again saw the pistol.

He said he had lifted the pistol off the floor and put it on to the corner of the bureau, after his mother fell and before he saw the servant.

In reply to further questions Merrett afterwards told the Inspector "he had purchased it [the weapon] from Hardy Brothers, in Princes Street, along with 50 cartridges. *He did not think his mother knew he had the pistol*. £5 was what he paid for it." This would have been a very grave admission indeed had he not already told Fleming about his mother taking the pistol away from him. Like Mrs. Sutherland, Merrett spake with two voices. Whichever be the true one, he certainly was wrong as to the price: he paid £1.17s. 6d. for it. The Inspector asked for the unfinished letter, which he had seen and so incompetently left upon the table at his first visit to the flat. Merrett said he had destroyed it, *"as there were some blood marks on the letter."* The Inspector, though not of an observant nature, was clear that there were none. He had seen no envelope upon the table. Merrett, however, had considerably preserved the unstained letters from the Bank, and of these, seeing that Merrett said "his mother had been worrying herself over money matters," Fleming took possession, as also of Mrs. Merrett's papers, bank-book, check-book, etc., which he found in the bureau and in Merrett's bedroom. Lying loose in a drawer in that bedroom he found 38 cartridges similar to those in the pistol.

Before leaving the flat the Inspector again interviewed Mrs. Sutherland—whom Mrs. Penn continued to employ—and took from her a fourth statement. Asked why she had varied her story to him, "she gave no excuse at all. She said she was upset on the morning of 17th March when I saw her, and did not remember what she said." But she stuck stoutly to her first and last version: that she *saw* nothing of what happened in the sitting-room.

Mr. and Mrs. Penn kept house for their nephew in the Buckingham Terrace flat until the termination of the tenancy. It was a strange household: the uncle and aunt perplexed by the enigma of the mother's death; the son, who alone knew the answer; and the servant, who had claimed to know and afterwards denied that she did. Merrett had now ostensibly resumed his studies, but, as we have seen, the college doors remained undarkened by him, and his only instructors were those professional ones who taught the disciples of the Palais de Danse. The balcony scene was often repeated by night and the rope proved as serviceable as ever. These amusements were agreeably varied by a visit to London, on which Merrett was accompanied by a male friend and by two young ladies. His aunt defrayed the cost of the excursion, being informed by him that its object was to consult a famous detective concerning the mystery of his mother's death. Be that as it may, the party was broken up at the suggestion of the police, one of the damsels being under sixteen, and their protectors arrived at Buckingham Terrace a week later in an exhausted state, having, as they alleged, walked back from London! What Mr. Sherlock Holmes thought of the case, if he were in fact consulted, is not recorded.

It must, therefore, have been with great relief that in June Mr. and Mrs. Penn shook the dust of Edinburgh from their feet, leaving their nephew to the care and guidance of the Public Trustee, on whom, in terms of Mrs. Merrett's will, devolved the invidious task of "looking after Donald." Edinburgh University would have nothing more to do with so unsatisfactory an alumnus; so it was thought best that he should go to a private tutor, in order to be prepared for Oxford. But before this was done the Public Trustee, in view of the peculiarities of conduct presented by his ward, thought it well to have him medically examined. The examination was made accordingly by two eminent Edinburgh specialists, who reported, *inter alia*:—

> The lad is exceptionally developed physically for his age [seventeen] and looks at least over twenty years. He talks intelligently and confidently, and is clear and lucid in his statements on general topics. He is sound in every bodily organ, and mentally he is perfectly sane.

They advised his removal from Edinburgh and prescribed an open-air life in the country, where he might be prepared for his University career. Such a retreat was found for him in the

vicarage of Hughenden, near High Wycombe, in Buckingham-
shire, where we will leave him for the present.

V

When the Public Trustee in the discharge of his duties investigated the financial affairs of the dead lady, he got a considerable surprise. Mrs. Merrett's income was something over £700
a year. She was an admirable businesswoman and most particular in preserving a record of her expenditure. She kept a private account book, in which she entered all payments into and
drawings from her bank account, together with the resultant
balances. Nay more; when she drew a check, she noted on the
counterfoil the balance as affected thereby, as also the increase
arising from any payment into the account, so that her pecuniary position at any time could be seen at once. Her principal
account was with the Midland Bank at Boscombe; but when
she came to Edinburgh in the beginning of 1926 she opened another account with the Clydesdale Bank, George Street, upon
which it was arranged she should draw only to the extent of
£30 at one time, this account being supplied by checks drawn
by her upon the Midland Bank account, as and when required.

Upon investigation the state of these accounts presented
certain singular features. In less than six weeks—between 2nd
February and 17th March, the date of the tragedy—checks
payable to and endorsed by "J. D. Merrett," amounting in all to
£205 odd, had been cashed by him. After his mother's removal
to the Infirmary he continued to present and cash checks to
the value of £156 odd. All these checks were in his own handwriting and purported to be signed "Bertha Merrett." Thus in a
period of under eight weeks this painfully prudent lady, whose
annual income was £700, had drawn over £360! And the
checks amounting to £156 were all presented by and paid to

her son while she lay helpless in the Infirmary—the last two, after she had lost consciousness! There were other strange things, remarkable in a lady so particular in money matters. Until she was in the Infirmary these checks were taken from the beginnings and ends of her check-books and the counterfoils relative thereto were torn out. After her imprisonment in Ward 3, however, they were drawn consecutively. One checkbook was missing and was never found; the Clydesdale Bank book had also vanished, but was subsequently recovered—from the boiler-room of the Palais de Danse!

In view of these facts the authorities began to realize that they had not quite solved the mystery by confining Mrs. Merrett as a would-be criminal and closing her mouth. It occurred to them that in prejudging her case and declining to listen to her account of what had happened, they had perhaps been somewhat over-confident in their own wisdom. The circumstances in which this large amount of money had disappeared—no mention of these sums being found in Mrs. Merrett's private account book—and divers jugglings with check- and bankbooks of which she could have had no knowledge, plainly called for further inquiry. So Professor Littlejohn was instructed to carry out certain experiments with the actual weapon and cartridges; and Mr. Gurrin, the eminent handwriting expert, was furnished with many documents unquestionably written and signed as well by Mrs. Merrett as by her son, including the striking series of checks above mentioned.

The result of these experiments and examinations as reported was that on 29th November a warrant was granted for the arrest of Merrett, who was accordingly apprehended by the local police and handed over to two detective-officers from Edinburgh. On 9th December he was by the Sheriff committed to prison until liberated in due course of law. The indictment was served on 14th January 1927, the trial being appointed to take place before the High Court on 1st February.

# VI

As I have elsewhere furnished a complete account of the case, which I was privileged to attend and of which I edited the report in the Notable British Trials series (Edinburgh: 1929), all that I propose to do here is to give the reader an impression of these interesting and important proceedings. The Lord Justice-Clerk (Lord Alness) presided; the Lord Advocate (the Right Hon. William Watson, K.C., later Lord Thankerton), assisted by the Right Hon. Lord Kinross, Advocate-Depute, appeared for the Crown; Mr. Craigie Aitchison, K.C. (later Lord Justice-Clerk), Mr. (later Lord) Macgregor Mitchell, K.C., and Mr. Clyde, advocate, conducted the defense. The charges upon which the pannel (prisoner) was indicted were as follows:—"(1) On 17th March 1926, in the flat at 31 Buckingham Terrace, Edinburgh, then occupied by Bertha Merrett, your mother, you did shoot the said Bertha Merrett in the head with a loaded pistol, whereby she was so severely injured that she died on 1st April 1926 in the Royal Infirmary, Edinburgh, and you did murder her." And (2) that on certain specified dates he uttered as genuine to tellers of the Clydesdale Bank 29 checks, payable to "J. D. Merrett" and bearing to be signed "Bertha Merrett," such signatures being forged, and thereby induced the tellers to pay him sums amounting to £457. 13s. 6d.

The accused was so fortunate as to have several points in his favor: his youth (18); over and above the legal presumption of innocence, the immense antecedent improbability of the first charge; the fact that his defense was in the capable and experienced hands of such eminent counsel; and that his position enabled him to secure the services of an expert so distinguished as Sir Bernard Spilsbury, who made in the accused's behalf his first appearance as a witness before a Scottish court of justice. There was also the lamentable delay—ten and a half months—in bringing the prosecution; for although Mr. Aitchison complained of this as highly prejudicial to his client's interests, I submit, with all respect, that it was not less so in regard to those of the Crown. Finally, at the eleventh hour, a certain Dr. Rosa volunteered his evidence for the defense. He said that Mrs. Sutherland had consulted him professionally on the evening of 17th March, and to him had given a new version of her story, namely, "that *as she was leaving the room her mistress shot herself.*" She had noticed Mrs. Merrett removing her false teeth immediately before, and thought it strange. There is no other evidence as to this incident, which Mrs. Sutherland in the witness-box characterized as "a downright lie."

The first witness called for the Crown was Mrs. Sutherland. She swore to her original version: that she had seen nothing of what happened, being in the kitchen—from which it is impossible to see into the sitting-room—when she heard the shot, the scream, and the fall. And it is to be remembered that the accused himself corroborates the witness upon this matter, seeing that on the day of the tragedy he informed his friends Christie and Scott that he went to the kitchen and told the maid that his mother had shot herself. He further corroborates her as regards the position of the pistol on the top of the bureau, *pace* the two active and intelligent police officers who deponed that it was upon the floor. Her explanation to the Court of her conflicting statements was this: "I was mixed up with what I heard and what Donald said. That may have been the cause of my saying what I did say." Which, looking to her excitement, to the shock of the event upon a young woman unaccustomed to weigh her words and perhaps, like her class, not indisposed to share in the limelight, is natural enough. Mr. Aitchison elicited from her the fact that Mrs. Merrett had once remarked she had had a hard life; but this, from what we know of that lady's history, is not surprising and does not take us far upon the road to suicide.

With the thorough, efficient, and satisfactory handling of

the case in its earlier stages by the police the reader is already acquainted, and it is needless to recapitulate their evidence. Other witnesses proved the purchase by the accused of the pistol and ammunition for £1. 17s. 6d. and 7s. 6d. on 13th February; of a second-hand A.J.S. motorcycle for £28 on 6th March; and his ordering on 22nd March from Rossleigh an H.R.D. motor racing cycle with side-car, the price of which was £139, payable by installments. On that date, as we know, his mother lay dying in the Infirmary.

The reception, treatment, and condition of Mrs. Merrett —physical as well as mental—in that beneficent institution were described by the doctors and nurses by whom she was attended. Dr. Bell, who examined her injury, on her admission as "a police case," in the out-patient department, stated that he looked specifically for any sign of blackening round the wound and found none: neither was there any appearance or smell of singeing. Dr. Holcombe, who dressed the wound in the surgical theater, found no blackening; Nurse Innes, who did so in the ward that evening, saw none. The absence of blackening had an important bearing upon the distance from which the shot was fired, and Mr. Aitchison cross-examined with a view to showing that it might have disappeared as the result of washing the wound. He strongly objected to the admission of the statements made by Mrs. Merrett as above described, and this on several grounds, one being that they were not sworn by her in the form of a dying deposition. The Court, after debate, admitted the statements. In cross-examination, Mr. Aitchison brought out that none of the witnesses had taken notes of the conversations at the time, and were now repeating these from recollection, ten months after they occurred. As regards Mrs. Merrett's mental condition when she made the statements, doctor and nurses were at one, namely, that until the night of the 25th the patient was perfectly normal, in full possession of her faculties, and clear and very positive about what had happened before she lost consciousness on the morning of the 17th. Mrs. Hill, an excellent witness, was unshaken in cross-examination as to her friend's mental state when she spoke to her, ten days before any symptom of delirium developed. Mrs. Penn, who was naturally nervous in the box, was more amenable to cross-examination; but to counsel's objection that she had made no written note of the conversation at the time, she replied with much cogency: "Her words were burnt into my mind."

I have been taxed ere now by sentimental reviewers with hardness and lack of sympathy in my treatment of crime. In the present case one jurywoman, at an adjournment of the Court, was overheard to say to another: "I'm *so* sorry for that poor boy!" Yet throughout the seven days of the trial no one, so far as I am aware, expressed any sorrow for the "poor boy's" mother. Despite my alleged callosity of heart I should like to do so now. Lying for a fortnight helpless and in pain, as much a prisoner in the Infirmary as if confined in jail; neglected by the son to whom her whole life had been devoted; encompassed by an atmosphere of mystery, her questions unanswered, her friends forbidden to discuss with her the reason of her sufferings; tormented, as surely she must have been, by the dread suspicion to which once only she gave expression: "Did Donald not do it? He is such a naughty boy!" and dying—even on the medical hypothesis offered by the defense—without knowing what was wrong with her, why she was so treated, or that she was paralyzed on the left side as the result of a bullet wound in the head. Well might the hapless woman have exclaimed, with Webster's doomed Duchess:—

> Any way, for heaven-sake,
> So I were out of your whispering.

To a less extent, but with equal sincerity, I find it in my insensitive bosom to feel for Mrs. Penn. That lady was of a different type from her sister: highly strung, emotional; it was not to be expected that, in such painful circumstances, she should do herself justice in the witness-box. Convinced that her sister had not committed suicide, she grasped at the theory of accident sooner than envisage the one horrible alternative. For three months she loyally discharged the thankless duty of "looking after Donald," at what cost to her feelings may readily be imagined. Yet she was treated by his legal representatives as a hostile witness; it was put to her that there was insanity in the family, and the suggestion was made that as her own son stood to gain financially by her nephew's removal, she would not be inconsolable should the verdict go against him. The Lord Justice-Clerk observed that counsel's comments upon Mrs. Penn's attitude and evidence seemed to him a little less than just, and in that opinion I respectfully concur.

Mr. Penn was fairer game. Aggrieved, irritable, and very deaf, he could only be interrogated through an ear-phone. "What are you?" asked Mr. Aitchison. "I am a poor devil artist," replied the witness. With regard to the alleged admission by the accused in the nurse's room at the Infirmary, when witness stated that he was not using his ear-phone, counsel made a dramatic point. He asked witness to lay aside his instrument; and then, stepping back to the rail of the dock, Mr. Aitchison said in ordinary tones: "I will confess if you like." Witness heard nothing. Next, coming nearer, he repeated the words; still witness could not hear them. Finally, again, standing close to the witness; who triumphantly announced: "You said, 'I will confess if you like'"! The inference was obvious.

## VII

The position of Professor Littlejohn also invites sympathy. For such an eminent expert and so proud a man to have to admit that he had made what on reconsideration he deemed a mistake, was peculiarly trying. Having first reported that the injury was "consistent with suicide," but that the possibility of accident could not wholly be excluded, he had now to support his subsequent conclusion that suicide was "in the highest degree improbable," and that everything—the direction of the bullet, the position of the wound, and the distance at which in his view the discharge had taken place, "all pointed to the weapon having been fired by another party." Elaborate experiments carried out by himself, and in conjunction with Professor Glaister, of Glasgow, with the actual pistol and cartridges had satisfied him of that. He stated that before the symptoms of meningitis set in late on 25th March, he saw at the post-mortem no reason why the patient's mental condition should earlier have been affected. The brain itself was uninjured. The experiments showed that at anything up to 3 inches there resulted from the shot blackening around the wound and "tattooing" from particles of powder embedded in the skin. At 9 inches the shot showed nothing beyond the hole produced by the bullet. In Mrs. Merrett's case, the patient had survived for fourteen days and the wound had been repeatedly dressed. He made particular inquiry from Dr. Holcombe and Dr. Bell, who had attended her in the Infirmary: they saw no signs of either, though Dr. Bell looked specially for blackening and found none. In witness's opinion blackening, if existing, must have been observed by the doctors on 17th March. Cross-examined, Professor Littlejohn said that from the facts now known to him suicide was inconceivable; but agreed that if there were a doubt as to the weapon having been discharged within 3 inches, neither suicide nor accident could be excluded. In his view the discharge was at a distance of over 3 inches. Professor Glaister and witness found it impossible to remove by washing or swabbing the blackness caused by the cartridges used in this case. Witness knew by experience many cases of severe head injury where the person remembered everything up to the infliction of the injury. Reliance could be placed on statements made by a patient within 24 hours of an acute delirium, provided the doctors and nurses saw no marked change in the mental condition. Reexamined, his opinion was strengthened by the fact that Mrs. Merrett had made previously similar statements.

Professor Glaister, of Glasgow University, supported the conclusions arrived at by his Edinburgh colleague, based upon the experiments jointly conducted by them. He relied not only on the absence of blackening but on the direction of the wound, which he deemed inconsistent with suicide.

To rebut this weighty evidence the defense called no less an authority than Sir Bernard Spilsbury, who held that neither the site nor the direction of the wound was inconsistent with suicide. The bleeding from and rubbing of the wound might well have removed any blackening. Taking all the facts of the case, he found nothing to exclude either suicide or accident as a possible explanation. Any statements made by a patient within 24 hours of delirium must be accepted with great caution. Cross-examined, witness admitted that the position of the wound was unusual in suicide. As regards removal of blackening, much depended upon the amount of rubbing and the condition of the skin. In this case, the discharge was certainly not in contact with the skin. By the Court, if no blackening were present, one must conclude that the muzzle of the pistol was at least 3 inches from the head.

Shooting experts were examined on both sides. For the Crown, Alan Macnaughton, gunmaker, Edinburgh, described the character of the pistol. It could only be used for self-defense; it was useless for rabbit shooting or for target practice, owing to the shortness of the barrel. Cross-examined, the smokeless powder in the cartridges produced caused less discoloration than ordinary gunpowder. For the defense, Robert

Churchill, gunmaker, London, stated the results of experiments conducted by him both in London and Edinburgh along with Sir Bernard Spilsbury. He concurred with that witness as to the ease with which blackening could be removed by bleeding, washing, etc. He cited a case of a woman who shot herself behind the right ear, and demonstrated the several manners in which it was possible for Mrs. Merrett accidentally to have shot herself. Cross-examined, witness admitted that it was uncommon for a woman to commit suicide with a pistol, especially if unused to firearms.

In this conflict of skilled opinion, inconclusive to the lay mind, much depended on the testimony of Mrs. Merrett herself in the Infirmary, and it was desirable in the accused's interest that the value of her evidence should be so far as possible discounted. To this end the defense produced that distinguished alienist Dr. George Robertson, Professor of Mental Diseases in the University of Edinburgh and head of Morningside Asylum, whose mastery of his art was such that he could have proved Solomon senile and Solon certifiable. He had not had the advantage of hearing the evidence or of reading the post-mortem reports; but having read about the case in the newspapers, was familiar with the medical facts. In his judgment the patient first suffered from shock, and afterwards from an inflammation surrounding the brain. Full doses of morphia were given daily throughout the illness. From his experience such an injury as that sustained by Mrs. Merrett would produce certain mental changes, resulting in what was termed altered consciousness or dissociation. In her case all the conditions accompanying altered consciousness were present. These changes might not be apparent to an ordinary observer. He gave two examples of this condition: one of a man who hanged himself, and on being timeously cut down, had no recollection of having attempted suicide; the other of a cyclist rendered unconscious by a collision, who on recovery blamed the doctor

545

attending him as having caused the accident. In view of Mrs. Merrett's condition, therefore, witness said her statements should be received with the very greatest hesitation. Cross-examined, it did not necessarily follow that a person suffering from hemiplegia was mentally affected. Witness admitted that if what Mrs. Merrett said were otherwise corroborated, it was of value as evidence. By the Court, on the facts before him witness was unable either to affirm or to deny that Mrs. Merrett's state was one of altered consciousness. It will be remembered that Mrs. Merrett's last words before the occurrence were: "Go away, Donald, and don't annoy me"; that these were corroborated *verbatim* by her son; and that he said he then crossed the room and immediately thereafter heard the sound of the discharge. So even if she *did* suffer from altered consciousness, it could only have been a matter of seconds.

## VIII

The evidence relating to the second charge—that of uttering forged checks—occupied a great part of the proceedings. It is unnecessary to consider this at length, because upon that branch of the case the jury returned a unanimous verdict of Guilty. I shall therefore only glance at it as bearing on the other question at issue. Mr. Gerald Francis Gurrin, the well-known London handwriting specialist, and Mr. William Morrison Smith, a local expert, severally selected from the mass of documents submitted to them *the same 29 checks,* as bearing the forged signature "Bertha Merrett." In the witness-box, each swore that they found thereon *a double signature,* one superimposed upon the other. The method employed by the forger was this: between the check to be forged and a specimen of the genuine signature was placed a sheet of carbon paper; the signature was then traced with a pencil, so that it appeared in violet outline upon the blank check; it was afterwards gone over with ink, and the result was sufficiently good to deceive a casual inspection. But examined microscopically the double outline was unmistakable, as was the difference in color between the ink and the outline. Mr. Gurrin was able to establish that three model signatures, varying in details, had been employed: one for the first or trial forgery; a second for 17 forgeries; and a third for 11. This branch of the case was in the strong hands of Mr. Macgregor Mitchell, K.C., who with great ingenuity, perseverance, and skill cross-examined the specialists upon many minute points; but in the main he failed to shake their testimony. He called no expert evidence to controvert their findings; and the best he could do was to put into the box the bank officials who had cashed the checks, and who still maintained that they saw nothing wrong with them.

How the accused manipulated the two bank accounts, keeping that of the Clydesdale fed by forged checks on the Midland; how he intercepted and suppressed one bank-book, which was found in his bedroom, and left the other in the basement of the Dunedin; how he purloined blank checks and even an entire check-book, making his mother believe that it was lost—all these matters were proved beyond question and also his application of the proceeds of his labors to the amelioration of his lot, as before narrated. By the end of the day, when his mother died, he had stolen £457. 13s. 6d. of her money; depleted both her bank accounts; and reduced the balance at her credit to £4. He had indeed made the most of his time.

A curious chance precipitated the tragedy. On Friday, 12th March, the factor for the flat called on Mrs. Merrett and asked her to pay the balance of her rent, which was not due till the end of the tenancy. She paid him by a check for £25, drawn on the Clydesdale Bank. Now Merrett, who had hitherto been careful to keep the Clydesdale account on the right side and had himself drawn 15 guineas the day before, knew nothing of this payment by his mother, which overdrew her account. On Saturday, the 13th, the Bank wrote to her, pointing out that she was £22 overdrawn, and suggesting that she should put matters in order by a Midland check. It seems highly probable that Mrs. Merrett never saw that letter, which was deliverable at Buckingham Terrace by the first post on Monday, 15th. Had she received it she would have made instant inquiries at the Bank, as her private account book and counterfoils showed no such debit. But on Tuesday, 16th, this debit was corrected by a £30 Midland check, payable to and presented by Merrett, who paid in £25 and took £5 in cash. *This check was proved to be forged.*

On the 15th he had cashed another false check for £22. 10s. 6d.; and on the 16th the Bank again wrote to Mrs. Merrett, advising her of a fresh overdraft of £6. 11s. 3d. This letter would be delivered at the flat on the morning of the tragedy. Did she receive and read it? The accused stated that *both letters were delivered on the morning of the 17th*. How had that posted on the 13th been held up for three days? Mrs. Sutherland, when she cleared away the dishes that fatal morning, noticed on the bureau an opened letter with a printed heading, addressed to Mrs. Merrett. When Inspector Fleming arrived on the scene at 10 a.m. he saw laid out upon the bureau, and read, the *two* letters from the Bank. If, as would appear, Mrs. Merrett knew nothing of the first letter, was she likely to take her own life for £6? But if, on its receipt, the whole matter of Merrett's nefarious operations was somehow brought to light, then she may, in grief and horror at her boy's "naughtiness," possibly have committed suicide.

It is obvious that we have not got the whole truth. Something certainly occurred in that room that morning which would explain the subsequent event. What really happened was known to one person only: the accused, who did not avail himself of his statutory right to give evidence on oath in the witness-box. Mr. Aitchison, in his powerful and impressive address to the jury, thanked God that there were those who would go to their death with sealed lips rather than speak a single word that would reflect upon the sacred name of mother. It is presumable that his client is to be numbered among such filial martyrs. At any rate he held his peace.

## IX

The Lord Advocate's speech for the prosecution was in the best tradition of the Crown Office: fairness, moderation, and as the learned Judge observed of it, even generosity, were the marks of the address. His Lordship's task was not lightened by the fact that his chief witness had told two stories, that his leading medical expert had changed his mind, that in its initial stages the case had been hopelessly bungled by the police, and that well-nigh a year had passed since the events with which he had to deal took place. He began by inviting upon both charges a verdict of Guilty against the accused; and his handling of the proof as to the second charge left little room for doubt that to that extent he had proved his case. With regard to this charge he explained to the jury that by Scots law it was not necessary to prove that the accused was the actual fabricator of the false checks; the crime was not the forging of the signatures, but the uttering or presentation of these checks to the Bank. The whole actings of the accused in connection with these false writings unquestionably inferred guilty knowledge.

With respect to the major charge of murder his Lordship's path, in view of the obstacles to which I have referred, was less plain and easy. He dealt first with the evidence of Mrs. Sutherland, with what Mrs. Merrett said in the Infirmary, and with the statements made by the accused. He argued that there was no proof, except for Merrett's word, that his mother knew anything whatever about the pistol. The account to which Mrs. Sutherland had sworn in the witness-box was that which she gave to the two constables immediately after the occurrence; her subsequent variation was due to reaction from the shock she had sustained. Her original and final statement was corroborated by the accused himself, who on the very day that his mother was shot informed his friends Christie and Scott that he had "gone through to the kitchen and told the maid." As to the Infirmary evidence, the doctors and nurses, the friends and relatives who saw and spoke to Mrs. Merrett, were all fully convinced that she was then perfectly clear and normal. Professor Robertson admitted that if there were corroboration of what she said, it was of value as evidence; and so far as possible this *was* corroborated. Not until experiments had been made at the flat in the week following the tragedy did the accused say that the pistol was in the bureau drawer, and suggest that there had been an accident; till then his story to his friends and to the police was suicide.

Having reviewed the evidence relating to the position of the pistol when found and the disappearance of the unfinished letter to Mrs. Anderson, counsel turned to a consideration of the expert evidence. If Mrs. Merrett knew nothing about the pistol that evidence was of no value, and the alternative of suicide or accident was excluded. Was it conceivable that this lady, sitting quietly in her room, writing a letter to her friend that had nothing to do with money matters, should suddenly take the pistol out of the bureau, and shoot herself in the presence of her only child? After going through the medical evidence on the question of the distance of the discharge, he argued that if there had been any sign of blackening it must have been seen by the Infirmary doctors and the nurse, who looked for it and found none. Therefore this was not a near discharge. Mrs. Merrett had no motive to commit suicide: the circumstances were all against it. She had seen the second letter about the overdraft; and she sits down placidly to write to her friend. The position of the accused that morning was this: he had stolen his mother's money, and the risk of detection and all that it involved was drawing near. His Lordship submitted that what happened was that the accused stood beside his mother with the pistol in his hand, and whether the fear of detection or the impulse of the moment was too much for him or not, he was exactly in a position to inflict the wound found in Mrs. Merrett's head. In conclusion his Lordship maintained that looking to the facts proved in evidence it was clear beyond all reasonable doubt that the accused was guilty of the first, as well as of the second charge, and he asked a verdict accordingly.

I have said that the accused was fortunate in his counsel, and the singular ability with which they had handled their respective branches of the case was conspicuous. It now fell to Mr. Aitchison to make the speech for the defense. An incomparable jury pleader, he was ever at his best and most impressive in defending a prisoner upon a criminal charge— irrespective of the guilt or innocence of his client. Here it will be apparent even to the lay mind that he had his work cut out for him. I wrote of his address at the time:—

> Yet, notwithstanding the perils and dangers by which he was beset, his address was a triumph of forensic oratory. Not a point was missed, everything favorable to the accused was displayed in the strongest light, the thinness of the ice in parts was deftly negotiated; and he was not more felicitous in what he actually said than in what, in his wisdom, he refrained from saying.

It was the most dexterous speech I ever heard at the criminal bar, and I am not likely to hear a better. In contrast to the classic example: that of John Inglis in 1857—which I had not the advantage of hearing and only know from reading—

delivered in the same Court in behalf of the beautiful Miss Madeleine Smith, its appeal was more to the heads than to the hearts of the jury, as in the circumstances was to be expected. Counsel took his stand on that maxim of our law known as the presumption of innocence, whereby the accused must be deemed innocent unless and until the Crown established his guilt. Suspicion, conjecture, and probability were not proof. This was a stale prosecution, ten months after the events they were investigating, and every circumstance that might have exonerated the accused was obliterated. He demurred to the Lord Advocate's suggestion that they must make up their minds as to which of the three possible and conflicting theories was the true one. The single question they had to answer was this: Had the Crown proved that the accused murdered his mother? They were invited to find a verdict against him solely because he was present in the room when his mother received the wound of which she died. Counsel would deal first with the evidence of Mrs. Sutherland, next with the alleged statements of Mrs. Merrett, and then with the medico-legal aspects of the case; and upon the whole matter he would invite their verdict.

Having considered what he termed Mrs. Sutherland's "revised version," counsel said he did not care which version they accepted, because either was favorable to the accused. Did the Crown suggest that Merrett deliberately shot his mother at a time when there was a maid in the house, when the dining-room door was open, in a room into which the maid could see, and which at any moment she might enter? If impulse were suggested, that was a very dangerous theory for the Crown; was it not equally probable that the mother might in a moment of impulse take her own life? He attached the utmost importance to the fall of books in the lobby, heard by the maid, which showed that the accused was engaged in his work up to the very moment of the tragedy. The alternative suggestion was that this was a device on the part of the accused; if that were so, then he must be a consummate actor. After dealing with the maid's statements to Inspector Fleming and to Dr. Rosa, that she had seen her mistress shoot herself, he said he never heard a more extravagant or monstrous proposition than to ask a verdict of guilty of murder where the only witness said she actually saw the woman shoot herself. Yet what the Lord Advocate said in effect was: "Fling over an experienced officer of the police like Inspector Fleming, fling over Detective-Sergeant Henderson, fling over Dr. Rosa, and accept the revised version which Mrs. Sutherland now gives us." It was proved by the two constables that the pistol was found on the floor beside the body; yet Mrs. Sutherland said it was lying on the bureau.

With regard to the statements of Mrs. Merrett, why should an accused person be at the mercy of the recollection of witnesses as to what was said ten and a half months after the words were spoken? She had sustained a severe head injury, she was suffering from shock, she was in great pain, she was getting large doses of morphia, and she was paralyzed on the left side. And yet in the face of these facts the Crown doctors said her statements could be accepted as those of a perfectly normal woman. But Professor Robertson—and there was no more eminent authority—told them that there might be a condition of altered consciousness. The Infirmary authorities informed the police authorities of what the patient was reported to have said, and a superior officer was sent to investigate, was told that this lady was critically ill, and that her life was in danger. Yet no dying deposition was taken from her.

> I want in this case to speak with moderation, but I am bound to say that the failure to take a dying deposition in the circumstances which were brought to the knowledge of the Criminal Investigation Department was in my judgment not only gross neglect on the part of

the responsible authority, but almost criminal neglect of an obvious and imperative duty.

If such had been taken, the accused would never have been put on trial.

After criticizing the evidence as to the alleged statement in the Infirmary, counsel turned to that regarding the conduct of the accused, and denied that the boy was dancing while his mother was dying. He was a stranger in Edinburgh, he had no friends. Why should he not go to the Dunedin, where he had made the acquaintance of Miss Christie? The flat was empty; he had no guardian, no relatives in Edinburgh; where was he to go? When Mrs. Hill suggested that a third party might have fired the shot, the accused repudiated her suggestion. When he became aware that his mother was to be charged with attempted suicide, though that would have exonerated him, he said it was not suicide but accident. Having dealt very severely with Mr. and Mrs. Penn, counsel passed to the evidence relating to the second charge, namely, of uttering. For the reasons before given I do not propose to spend time on this, though Mr. Aitchison did all that was humanly and legally possible to clear his client. The last part of his address concerned the medico-legal evidence, the balance of which he maintained was in favor of the accused. In a moving peroration he besought the jury, though there might be things they would like to have had explained of which there was no explanation, not to jump to conclusions.

I claim from you with a clear conscience a verdict of Not Guilty upon both these charges. Give him by your verdict a reputation up to which he will have to live for the rest of his life; and I will only say this to you—and it is my final word—send him out from this Court-room this afternoon a free man with a clean bill, and so far as I can judge he will never dishonor your verdict.

The clear, logical, and carefully constructed charge of the Lord Justice-Clerk I lack space adequately to consider. Unless, said he, the Crown had excluded accident or suicide as a reasonable hypothesis, the accused was entitled to a verdict. Mrs. Sutherland's statement to Inspector Fleming was detailed and circumstantial: that she went into the lobby, saw Mrs. Merrett fall, and saw the pistol falling from her hand. Was any temporary confusion adequate to explain that triple mis-statement of fact, as she now described it? She denied her similar statement to Dr. Rosa. It was for the jury to say whether these statements, if made and if true, were not in themselves destructive of the Crown case.[1] The police account of the circumstances in which Mrs. Merrett was found: what they saw and what they did: was loose and hazy; and their subsequent actings were unsatisfactory, inconclusive, and perfunctory. As to the statements made by Mrs. Merrett in the Infirmary, his Lordship greatly regretted that they had not before them a sworn, authentic, and complete statement made by her to a responsible officer by way of dying deposition. They had instead to depend upon the recollection of seven persons. Having examined the several statements, his Lordship asked the jury to put to themselves the following questions:—

---

1. In *The Principles of Judicial Proof*, by John Henry Wigmore, Professor of the Law of Evidence in Northwestern University, Chicago, p. 426 (Second Edition, Boston: 1931), occurs this passage: "ERRORS OF RECOLLECTION, NOT DISTINGUISHABLE FROM ERRORS OF PERCEPTION. One of the most baffling features in the study of testimony is that constantly, where some error is obvious, we find it impossible to *distinguish errors of recollection from those of perception*. The ordinary example of this is found in inconsistent assertions of a witness, where it is apparent that one or the other statement is erroneous, but the source of the error cannot be determined." The learned author cites as a striking example of this difficulty the discrepant versions of Mrs. Sutherland, as printed in my edition of the trial, pp. 62, 204, 206.

First, were the statements imputed to Mrs. Merrett made by her at all? Second, could they be sure of their complete accuracy as reproduced more than ten months after the event? Third, if made and accurately reported, could they be implicitly relied upon, having regard to her mental condition as conceived by Professor Robertson? And lastly, accepting them as accurate, and accepting the view that her mental state was such as to render the statements intelligible and reliable, how far did they advance the Crown case, which was one of murder?

No one who heard these statements made at the time thought they attributed or involved the guilt of the accused. Were the jury not being invited to draw an inference of guilt from these statements which no one at the time drew? It was accepted on all hands that the case was one of suicide.

Turning to the medical evidence, his Lordship pointed out that Professor Littlejohn based his second report on the absence of blackening around the wound. The chief objection suggested to the theory of suicide was from the direction of the wound; but that was met by the simple explanation of a sudden and instinctive aversion of the head by the person who was about to fire. Assuming that blackening had been present, might it have been rubbed off? Upon this point Professor Littlejohn differed profoundly from Sir Bernard Spilsbury. As to the distance from which the shot was fired there was a direct conflict of skilled evidence. That of Professors Littlejohn and Glaister on the one hand, and that of Sir Bernard and Mr. Churchill on the other, were not susceptible to reconciliation on those vital points. Professor Littlejohn was asked: "If experts differ, what are we to do?" and his reply was: "I don't know!" Yet the jury had to decide with regard to that matter.

Having examined the conduct of the accused, his Lordship observed that they were not there as a Court of Morals. It was proved that the accused was attached to his mother, that he was so upset at the time of the incident that he could look no longer at her body, he left the pistol lying about, he wired for Mrs. Hill, he visited the Infirmary, and he kissed his mother. Was it the kiss of Judas? Did Mrs. Penn harbor for three months her sister's assassin? These were questions which they must consider. Was the Crown claiming a verdict of murder against the accused upon evidence which they deemed insufficient even to warrant his arrest? Mr. Gurrin reported upon the forgeries on 4th November; the accused was arrested on 3rd December. Was *that* the new factor which induced the Crown to act? Motive to commit a crime could not atone for the absence of evidence to prove the commission of that crime. Was the motive now suggested at all commensurate to the alleged crime? Was it a safe inference that the accused would kill his mother sooner than that she should discover his perfidy?

His Lordship then briefly but firmly disposed of the second charge and his finished analysis of the evidence left no reasonable doubt as to the question at issue. "If you think the checks were forged," said the Justice-Clerk in conclusion; "that they were presented by the accused, and that he knew they were forged, then it will be your duty to convict him upon the second charge."

The jury retired at 4:35 and returned at 5:30. Their verdict was as follows:—On the first charge, murder, Not Proven, by a majority; on the second charge, uttering, Guilty, unanimously. The vote, as I afterwards learned, was on the murder charge 5 for Guilty and 10 for Not Proven. It will be seen that despite the powerful and eloquent appeal of Mr. Aitchison and the strong lead given them from the Bench, not one of the fifteen members of the jury was prepared to find the accused Not Guilty. The Lord Justice-Clerk then pronounced sentence of 12 months' imprisonment, and the Court rose. "An unsatisfactory ending to a rather unsatisfactory case," was the judicious comment of the *Scotsman* in a leading article thereon, which it dismisses as an unsolved mystery.

## X

The convict served his time not in some grim, black cell beneath the frowning, bastard battlements of the old Calton Jail, but under the modern conditions obtaining in His Majesty's new prison of Saughton, a sort of penal garden city, affording in its humane and hygienic régime the advantages of a rest-cure in a criminous nursing home, and combining agreeably punishment with amusement.

Mr. Aitchison's estimate of his client's future good conduct proved in the event more generous than just, for in the following year the name of John Donald Merrett was once more prominent in the popular Press. It appears from the newspaper reports[2] that on the expiration of his sentence he was offered by a friend of his late mother a temporary asylum. This Good Samaritan was a lady named Bonner, who lived in Bexhill. She had a charming and attractive daughter, Vera, aged seventeen and a ward in Chancery. The guest repaid the goodwill and hospitality of his hostess by eloping with the girl, and the young couple were, according to the bridegroom's statement, married at Glasgow in March 1928, just two years after Mrs. Merrett's death. In June of that year the happy pair emerged from their hymeneal shade into the limelight of publicity in the dock at Newcastle, where they had been living for a space in the suburbs, and at the time of their arrest were reduced by force of circumstances to take up residence in a tent at Kenton, on the outskirts of the city. The charge upon which they were arraigned was that of obtaining goods worth over £200 by false

---

2. *Daily Record, Daily Mail, Weekly Record,* etc., 15th, 16th June 1928.

pretenses. The bridegroom gave their names as Mr. and Mrs. John Chesney, late of Bexhill, Surrey. He produced no certificate of marriage. Unfortunately known to the police, he proved to be our old acquaintance Merrett. Although living under canvas, he had given to sundry local tradesfolk the substantial, and in a double sense imposing, address of the Grand Hotel.

Merrett, who was now 19, would on attaining majority become possessed of a sum of £8000 under the will of his grandfather. Meanwhile his guardian, the Public Trustee, was allowing him £2 a week. The reason for the smallness of the allowance was said to be that the costs of the defense at the trial in Edinburgh, which were defrayed by that official, had created a heavy overdraft on the income of the trust. Be that as it may, Merrett, as a family man, found the amount inadequate to his requirements and decided to put his considerable banking experience to some use. To this end he called upon the National Provincial Bank at Gateshead, stating that his name was M'Cormick and that he was in receipt of £300 a year from the Public Trustee. He forthwith opened an account, paying in the sum of £1 and obtaining a book of twelve checks. Among the first-fruits of this transaction was a large order to a local firm of drapers and outfitters, the purchases being paid for by a check signed "J. M'Cormick." Mr. M'Cormick ordered the goods to be sent to him at the Grand Hotel. Earlier in the day someone had telephoned to that hostelry, requesting that a room be reserved. Subsequently Mr. M'Cormick called, and inspected the bedroom, of which he approved; but being asked for a deposit as a guarantee of good faith, he indignantly departed, taking with him the parcels duly delivered at the hotel by the drapers. On another occasion a young lady and gentleman drew up their car at the shop of a local jeweler. After examining a number of rings, a valuable single-stone diamond one was chosen and the male customer presented his check in payment of the price. But the salesman uncharitably declined to part with the ring until the check was cashed. "I have a green Austin car outside," said Mr. M'Cormick, and mentioned that he wished the ring to wear at a dance, to which he was going that night. In the end, the jeweler, seduced by the customer's agreeable manners and also, perhaps, by the attractions of his fair companion, suffered the ring to be removed. Next day the check, being presented to the Bank, was dishonored.

It were tedious to follow further the fortunes of the enchanted check-book; but it is interesting to note that one of the articles secured by its nefarious aid was a motorcycle, bought on the "pay-out-of-income" system, with which, in his Edinburgh days, the purchaser was familiar. The couple were arrested on the eve of their departure for Dundee, whose merchants were fortunate to escape the patronage of Mr. M'Cormick. As the result of the prosecution the young lady was discharged, on the grounds that she had never given an order for any of the goods and was merely in Merrett's company and under his control. One hopes that she returned to her own folk. Merrett, *alias* Chesney, *alias* M'Cormick, having pleaded guilty, was sent to prison for nine months with hard labor. It was intimated that the Public Trustee was prepared to make restitution of the stolen goods and to pay the costs of the prosecution. We have not heard from his ward again; but you never can tell: we may do so yet. Doubtless both would welcome the termination of the guardianship.

# TITLES IN SERIES

HINDOO HOLIDAY
MY DOG TULIP
MY FATHER AND MYSELF
WE THINK THE WORLD OF YOU
J. R. Ackerley

THE LIVING THOUGHTS OF KIERKEGAARD
W. H. Auden, editor

PRISON MEMOIRS OF AN ANARCHIST
Alexander Berkman

HERSELF SURPRISED (First Trilogy, Volume 1)
TO BE A PILGRIM (First Trilogy, Volume 2)
THE HORSE'S MOUTH (First Trilogy, Volume 3)
Joyce Cary

PEASANTS AND OTHER STORIES
Anton Chekhov

THE PURE AND THE IMPURE
Collette

THE WINNERS
Julio Cortázar

MEMOIRS
Lorenzo Da Ponte

A HIGH WIND IN JAMAICA
THE FOX IN THE ATTIC
THE WOODEN SHEPHERDESS
Richard Hughes

THE OTHER HOUSE
Henry James

BOREDOM
CONTEMPT
Alberto Moravia